Governing Ourselves?

# Governing Ourselves?

## The Politics of Canadian Communities

Mary Louise McAllister

**UBC**Press · Vancouver · Toronto

15 14 13 12 11 10 09 08 07 06 05 04     5 4 3 2 1

Printed in Canada on acid-free paper.


National Library of Canada Cataloguing in Publication

McAllister, Mary Louise, 1957-
    Governing ourselves? : the politics of Canadian communities / Mary Louise McAllister.

Includes bibliographical references and index.
ISBN 0-7748-1062-9

    1. Municipal government – Canada. I. Title.

JS1708.M324 2004      320.8'5'0971      C2004-901750-0


Canadä
UBC Press gratefully acknowledges the financial support for our publishing program of the Government of Canada through the Book Publishing Industry Development Program (BPIDP), and of the Canada Council for the Arts, and the British Columbia Arts Council.

Printed and bound in Canada by Friesens
Text design: Artegraphica Design Co. Ltd.
Copy editor: Andy Carroll
Proofreader: James Leahy
Indexer: Noeline Bridge

UBC Press
The University of British Columbia
2029 West Mall
Vancouver, BC V6T 1Z2
604-822-5959 / Fax: 604-822-6083
www.ubcpress.ca

For
Mom and Dad,
Rob,
Cathy, and Christina

# Contents

# Tables, Figures, and Boxes

## Tables

## Figures

## Boxes

# Preface

The perspective taken in this book is somewhat at odds with the conventional textbook portrayal of Canadian local politics. Emphasis here is *not* placed primarily on the largest cities with the densest population concentrations. Rather, these cities share equal time with small and mid-sized places scattered across the country. Attention is given to physical factors that, while frequently overlooked in political studies, are relevant to any study of influence and power between, and within, communities. This work also examines the fluid and interdependent relationships between many governments, organizations, and interests as well as their cultural, communications, and physical contexts. The aim is to highlight the ways in which such interactions might affect local decision-making processes.

This text does not confine itself solely to the study of how governments alone operate and make political decisions; rather, it addresses how politics is influenced by the broader system of *governance,* including both formal and informal players. The following chapters consider a variety of political factors and actors that shape local communities. Different conceptual lenses are employed – from the conventional, institutionally focused analyses to broader, holistic perspectives.

By tackling the project in this way, we can discuss the many ways in which power and influence are brought to bear on political decision making as well as consider who benefits. The book is divided into five parts, each dealing with a different conceptual lens or perspective through which one might examine the question of local governance.

Part 1, "Local Democracy, a Contested Notion," considers the ideological underpinnings of local institutions and changing notions about what constitutes local democracy. It also discusses the varying ways in which different political actors use the term *local democracy* to advance their own particular perspectives about how a democratic society should operate. Finally, this section explores the relative ability of different societal groups to actively participate in local governance.

Part 2, "Shifting Responsibilities: Intergovernmental Relations," outlines the historic and contemporary relationships between the different orders of government in Canada's federal system. Most notably, it details the attempts of local governments to achieve sufficient influence and resources from the provincial and federal governments in order to respond to growing citizen demands and pressures.

Part 3, "The Politics of Space, Place, and Ecosystems," recognizes that local governance is about more than institutional arrangements. It suggests that we need to pay close attention to the relationship between societal and political forces and the biophysical environment. Questions of location, land-use development, spatial relationships, urban planning, and environmental degradation are all important factors in local politics and decision making.

Part 4, "The Business of Local Administration and Policy," explains the basic machinery of government, local public administration, and policy. It explores the important influence that the private sector has had on the principles, structures, and priorities of local governments.

Part 5, "Surfing into the Twenty-First Century: Local Political Communications," highlights the crucial role that communications plays, and has always played, in local politics. This is discussed both in terms of the content of the message and in terms of the medium by which it is conveyed. Today, information technology brings these issues to the forefront of political discussions. The integration of mass media, the emergence of communications networks, and the burgeoning application of new information technologies are all introducing new challenges to decision makers and citizens, and they raise interesting questions about governance, democracy, and the future of civil society.

Some governments and analysts have reacted to the world's growing intricacy, complexity, and limited resources by providing their own formulaic responses that rely on market mechanisms, narrow conceptions of a rational or efficient government, or streamlined forms of political representation. Other actors and observers, however, are acutely aware that environmental, social, and political challenges do not go away when they are ignored; rather, understanding and dealing with complexity require a more holistic approach – one that recognizes that political, social, economic, and natural systems are inextricably intertwined. The complex web of local politics interacts at many different levels with human and biophysical systems. "Systems" perspectives recognize that a multiplicity of actors interrelate in myriad ways to shape the political environment.

The goal of this book is twofold. As an analytical study, *Governing Ourselves?* examines, from various perspectives, the role different factors have played in shaping the patterns of local political influence and decision making. As a descriptive work, it attempts to foster an understanding of local politics in Canada in a contemporary setting, illustrated with examples from different communities.

# Acknowledgments

Several years ago in June, after attending a conference located in historic St. John's, Newfoundland, a group of colleagues decided to take a boat tour off the Atlantic coast. The idea for this book set sail among the icebergs and puffins. There, in the bracing Atlantic breezes, Peter Milroy, Director of UBC Press, offered sound ideas and practical advice about how to tackle what became a very large endeavour. My father, Ed Black, contributed his considerable knowledge and expertise to this project. His careful editing of the manuscript led to many lively discussions about ideology, theory, structure, and content. On the rare occasions when he did not feel well informed about a particular subject area, his well-known Socratic method of engaging debate inevitably led me to question my assumptions, dig deeper for evidence, or at least come up with a good rejoinder. Perhaps more than anyone else, Jim Lightbody has taught me a great deal about local government. Jim's "boot camp" approach to manuscript review was simultaneously energizing and entertaining – particularly in those areas where we were not necessarily in agreement! I am very grateful for, and impressed by, his scholarly rigour, patience, and willingness to help me produce a much better piece of work than would otherwise have been the case.

A number of citizens and city staff of the case study communities I studied contributed a significant amount of time educating me about their cities. From Prince George, British Columbia, I would particularly like to acknowledge Bill Kennedy, Paul George, Judy Dix, Ruth and Jack Rushant, Ron East, and Tom Steadman, who have shown me, and so many others, what the term *civic responsibility* means in practice. Their positive contributions to their various communities extend far beyond Prince George. On the other side of the country, in Saint John, New Brunswick, Susan Greer, in the position of the city's information officer, has served as a wonderful ambassador. Susan reinforced my positive impression of Saint John with her enthusiasm about the city and her readiness to provide invaluable background material. Ed Farren also kindly offered some very helpful insights into Saint John. In Sherbrooke, Quebec, Margarita Bezina uncovered many worthwhile and important pieces of information about the area. I would also like to thank Pierre Daganais and Charlotte Gosselin, who made available some useful material about the city's history, culture, and operations. Lynne Woolstencroft contributed perceptive insights about local politics in Waterloo, Ontario, with specific reference to the role of a municipal mayor. Peter Woolstencroft also reviewed the manuscript and with his sharp eye caught some important things that I had overlooked. Teresa Soulliere from the City of Waterloo, who warmly welcomed me to the city when I first arrived, has been able to answer all my questions quickly and efficiently. A diversity of people, particularly those associated with the Compass Kitchener initiative, helped me to develop an appreciation of the vibrant community spirit that has long been a part of Kitchener's history. A number of other municipal employees from various cities – too numerous to mention – filled in many gaps. They reinforced my impression that a great many municipal employees throughout the country do not get as much public recognition and appreciation as they deserve. My collegial department of Environmental and Resource Studies at the University of Waterloo has provided me with a very supportive environment and community of friends. Numerous students over the years contributed in valuable ways, offering interesting pieces of information and challenging ideas and perspectives.

Anonymous peer review is an extremely valuable contribution to the academic world and to the authors who benefit from it. Throughout this process, I have been very grateful for the care, attention, and time the reviewers selflessly gave in order to improve this manuscript. I did my best to respond in kind to their suggestions.

Randy Schmidt of UBC Press has once again helped me through the long, involved process of manuscript preparation with a blend of helpful advice, expertise, humour, and good instincts. Randy is one of a team of first-rate professionals at the Press, many of whom have patiently responded to numerous questions. At the end of the long, weary process I was placed in the competent hands of project editor Camilla Jenkins, who steered the final project home with the very intelligent and able assistance of copy editor Andy Carroll. To put it simply, UBC Press is composed of a likeable group of people who know what they are doing.

I would like to mention many other people but the list would be much too long. All of the individuals acknowledged above hold diverse views of local governance and, no doubt, would disagree with some of the positions taken in this book. None of them is responsible for any errors or sins of commission or omission.

At the heart of any initiative, academic or otherwise, is the part played by one's own family. My Mom and Dad were always available to help and share their wise insights when asked and offer moral support when needed. Rob, who has seen me work through many academic projects over the past thirty years, and our two daughters, Cathy and Christina, have provided me with a much needed sense of perspective, reminding me that there is so much more to life than academia. Both Cathy and Christina, at various times, freely gave their time to this particular project, becoming involved in tasks that ranged from creating organizational charts to managing files. Most important, my family supported me through what turned out to be a much larger and more challenging project than I had anticipated when first chatting about the possibilities in the chilly sea air along the shores of Newfoundland.

Governing Ourselves?

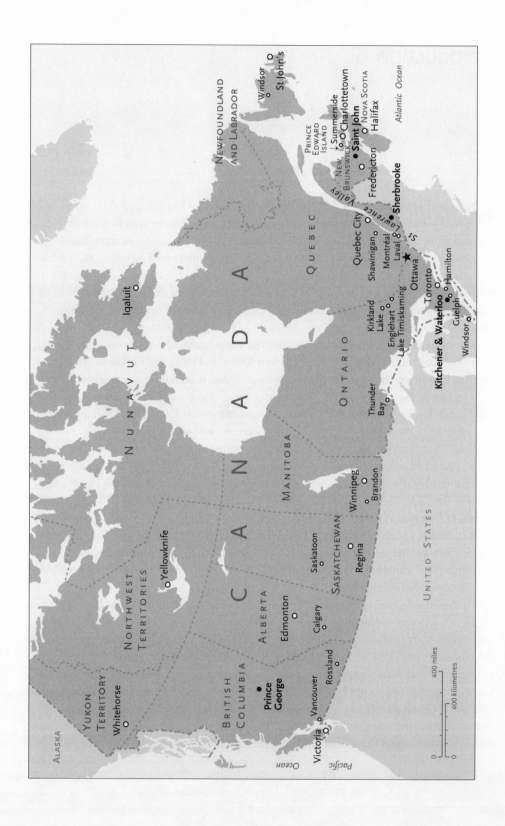

# Introduction

Popular rhetoric suggests that the twenty-first century has ushered in an era of homogeneity. Canada's distinctive local communities appear to be weighed down with baggage from the post-industrial world. Urbanization, globalization, amalgamation, media conglomeration, and technological convergence are terms coined to reflect the cumulative effect of diverse forces at work in communities across the country. Given such pressures, to what extent can people living in those communities make decisions about their own environments, either individually or collectively? To what extent can they govern themselves?

Many Canadian communities have adopted some standard responses to the imperatives of globalization. Indisputably, Canadian towns and cities are similar in many ways, and it is important to recognize those commonalities. It would be a serious error, however, to ignore the unique set of circumstances that shapes and influences the way in which each locality governs itself. Canada is an interwoven tapestry of diverse communities situated in their own social, political, economic, and physical landscapes.

Each Canadian community has a distinctive political culture. To be persuaded of this point, one need only pause to consider how local governance might differ in places such as Toronto, Ontario (one of the largest cities in North America), the wheat-based prairie town of Brandon, Manitoba, or the remote (primarily Inuit) community of Iqaluit, the capital of Nunavut. A closer observation would reveal how each of these communities has its own mix of social, cultural, and physical characteristics that offer specific challenges for governance. Across the country, communities and their governments provide a mosaic of responses – sometimes creative and sometimes mundane – to unpredictable global and domestic environments.

Each of the following chapters offers vignettes and illustrations about how some very different Canadian communities govern themselves and are governed. Examples from communities across Canada highlight these discussions, with particular attention paid to the medium-sized cities of Saint John, New Brunswick; Sherbrooke, Quebec; the twin cities of Kitchener and Waterloo, Ontario; and Prince George, British Columbia (see Table I.1). These municipalities were chosen to illustrate some of the differences and similarities between five Canadian cities in four regions, each of which possesses its own unique set of characteristics, including political culture, history, economy, physical location and characteristics, institutional structures, and communications patterns.

TABLE 1.1

**Examples of mid-sized cities**

| City or region | Population[a] | Land area (km²) |
| --- | --- | --- |
| Saint John | 69,661 (2001) | 316 |
| Sherbrooke (2002)[b] | 75,916 (2001)<br>140,000 post-amalgamation (2002) | 58<br>366 post-amalgamation |
| Region of Waterloo (includes Kitchener and Waterloo) | 438,515 (2001) | 1,369 |
| Kitchener | 190,399 (2001) | 137 |
| Waterloo | 86,543 (2001) | 64 |
| Prince George | 72,406 (2001) | 316 |

a  The population statistics often do not capture university and college students. The City of Waterloo, for example, has well over 100,000 residents if the population of its two universities is included.

b  This land mass is an approximation based on the former Sherbrooke metropolitan census area, much of which is now covered by the new City of Sherbrooke. As such, large portions of this city are now rural, encompassing many former cities with their own urban centres.

*Sources:* Statistics Canada, Community Profiles, http://www12.statcan.ca/english/Profil01/PlaceSearchForm1.cfm; Société de Développement Économique de Sherbrooke (SDES), http://www.sdes.ca/tourism/ .

Saint John is Canada's first incorporated city, and it is situated beside its historic port in eastern Canada. The traditional perceptions of local self-government go back to the Loyalist settlers who first demanded some local political autonomy (see Box I.1).

The newly amalgamated City of Sherbrooke, in the rolling hills of the eastern Quebec townships, comprises a majority of French-speaking residents and a significant minority of English speakers, who are represented by strong community associations. One can find evidence of both French- and English-Canadian cultures in the city's landscape, history, and municipal politics (see Box I.2).

Occasionally referred to as the "Twin Cities," Kitchener and Waterloo are situated in densely populated, heavily industrialized, southwestern Ontario. The business sector has been strongly influential in shaping all cities, but early in their history, these two munici-palities developed a reputation amongst others for entrepreneurialism, industriousness, and active private-sector involvement in civic affairs (see Box I.3).

Prince George is a rugged resource-based city located in the centre of British Co-lumbia. A pioneering spirit has shaped Prince George's political culture, with the long-time local residents accustomed to self-sufficiency and a tough physical environment (see Box I.4).

## I.1  Saint John, New Brunswick

Saint John is Canada's oldest incorporated city, although St. John's, Newfoundland, is thought to be the oldest city in Canada. It had been inhabited for thousands of years by indigenous peoples and eventually became a French colony in 1608. Early inhabitants of the area included the Micmac and then the Meliseet peoples. Today Saint John is the province's main metropolitan centre, and it is the only city in the province with a charter (this is characteristic of Canada's oldest cities). Because of its history, Saint John boasts many Canadian firsts, including the country's first political riot (1785), the first chartered bank, the first municipal water system (1837), the first penny newspaper (*Saint John News*), and the first Town Planning Act (1912). The historic port City of Saint John has often struggled with poverty and can be characterized as an industrial town with a history of economic difficulties. Journalist Charles Lynch described his hometown in the following terms:

> Once the grimy place that no amount of cosmetic paint could disguise or brighten, its only refuge in the vocabulary of tourism being the words "old" or "quaint." But once moribund industries came back to life and the city reached the point where finally, in the 1970s, it could stand back a pace and get a look at itself and decide to create some beauty to go with its commercial achievements. And so in the 1980s, Saint John became a city reborn, a better place for those who live there.[1]

This city has seen a number of successful urban revitalization initiatives in the core area, including the "oldest continuous market" in the country. The industrial presence is quite visible, with its refineries and pulp and paper mills. Recently, arts festivals and other economic development, as well as tourism – based on historic sites, parks, gardens, and the Fundy tides – have contributed to a more diversified cityscape.

Saint John was the provincial capital of New Brunswick for only a brief period in the late 1700s. Nevertheless, it has many attributes of a capital city, in terms of its political history, economy, culture, and location. Early in its history, Saint John became the commercial centre of New Brunswick.[2] It is the province's largest city, with a population of approximately 70,000 people (or 123,000 if one also considers the nearby parishes and towns in the census metropolitan area). It is a bilingual city in Canada's only bilingual province (a benefit of its English and Acadian heritage) with an increasingly skilled workforce, backed up by a good communications and transportation infrastructure. As an important centre in the province, Saint John appears to have a strong sense of local political culture, the seeds of which were planted long ago with the United Empire Loyalists who emigrated here in the thousands from the United States after the Revolutionary War.

---

1  Malcolm M. Somerville, introduction to *Saint John: A City of Achievements*, 2nd ed. (Saint John, NB: ImPresses, 2000).
2  Dan Soucoup, *Historic New Brunswick* (Lawrencetown Beach, NS: Pottersfield Press, 1887).

## I.2 Sherbrooke, Quebec

This mid-sized city celebrated its two-hundredth anniversary in 2002; its roots can be traced back to a small village named Hyatt Mills in 1802. Unlike other parts of the province, the majority of settlers in the area were primarily of British origin. Hyatt Mills was renamed Sherbrooke in 1918 after the governor general of Canada.

Historically, Sherbrooke has acted as the hub of the Eastern Townships of Quebec. With its motto being "More than just a City," it draws attention to the fact that residents and visitors can benefit from all the conveniences of diversified urban centres located in the middle of a natural resort.

Like any mid-size city, the old City of Sherbrooke has its share of industry and of strip malls lining some main streets. It also boasts some gracious old stone churches and halls built in the early part of the twentieth century. Walking paths and biking trails traverse the Rivière Magog and the Lac des Nations. The hilly terrain offers numerous vistas of old residential areas, parks, light industrial development, modern subdivisions, and parks. The new city has a number of French and English universities and colleges.[1]

Sherbrooke has seen many changes over the years. Debate over language rights has played an important part in defining the local political culture. This issue has not only affected the nature of federal-provincial Canadian politics, it has also had a profound effect on local politics. At the beginning of the twentieth century, for example, the interests of the English were given priority in business and other decisions governing the community. In Sherbrooke, it was noted that in 1912, "not only did the city council conduct its meetings in English but the city employees were also all English-speaking and spoke only their own language. The most important part of the course at the technical school in Shawinigan consisted of learning English, since this was the only way a French-Canadian worker could obtain a promotion in the town's large factories."[2] Over the course of the twentieth century, the domination of the English language over French was to be reversed. Today, Sherbrooke sees itself as a bilingual city, although French predominates.

In 2002, Sherbrooke's population swelled to approximately 140,000 when it was amalgamated with a number of other cities in the region as part of the provincial government's overall municipal restructuring initiative. In the process, the much smaller anglophone communities that were merged into the new city found themselves facing a new dynamic, as the majority of speakers in the restructured region spoke French as their first language.

---

1 Sherbrooke Historical Society in Cooperation with the University of Sherbrooke, *Sherbrooke 1802-2002: Two Centuries of History,* CD-ROM (Sherbrooke: Sherbrooke Historical Society, 2002).

2 Paul André Linteau, René Durocher, and Jean-Claude Robert, *Quebec: A History, 1867-1929,* trans. Robert Chodos (Toronto: James Lorimer, 1983), 53.

## I.3 Kitchener and Waterloo, Ontario

The two cities of Kitchener and Waterloo (KW) are generally undistinguished by their physical appearance from other municipalities in densely populated southwestern Ontario. The two cities, each with its own municipal government, have physically grown together. They share a main street that traverses two urban cores, both of which are in various stages of decline and renewal.

Kitchener and Waterloo are part of a two-tier system of government. The upper governing tier is the Regional Municipality of Waterloo. The Regional Municipality also has responsibilities for Cambridge, another mid-size city in the region, as well as the townships of North

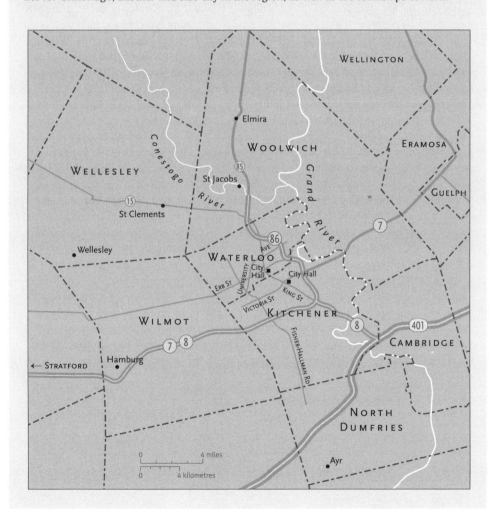

Dumfries, Wellesley, Wilmot, and Woolwich. The regional government coordinates joint services, while the city governments administer in distinctly different styles reflecting their unique political cultures, heritage, and requirements.

Both cities have a generous share of parks and wooded areas that encircle well-kept residential areas, and they have burgeoning suburbs on the edges. Waterloo received the gold award at the 2003 International Awards for Livable Communities. Congested streets, growing automobile traffic on the encircling expressways, and poor air quality, however, are unfortunate by-products of the cities' location and rapidly growing population. KW can also boast a unique cultural heritage that can be traced back to the early settlers of the towns, many of whom were hard-working Mennonites and industrious German immigrants.

A closer look, however, reveals some interesting distinctive characteristics of each city. Kitchener is the larger of the two, with a population of approximately 190,000 people. The older part of Kitchener, once called Berlin, reveals its manufacturing legacy as aging industrial buildings intermingle with residential areas in the centre of town. The business community has always played an active role in city politics, and a strong civic culture permeates the operations of the business community. Activism also constitutes part of the downtown culture, where public campaigns bring attention to politically marginalized citizens, such as the poor or homeless, or rallies encourage environmentally friendly transportation alternatives.

Kitchener's adjoining neighbour, Waterloo, has a population of 86,500, but over 100,000 if its student population is included. Waterloo has quite a different political and social culture. It is best known for being the location of the head office of large insurance corporations, for having two universities, Waterloo and Wilfrid Laurier, and for its technological economic base. Throughout the 1990s, Waterloo's local government administration decided to adopt a business mantle. Its emphasis has been on service delivery, economic and operational efficiency, and attracting investment. Historically, Waterloo has not had to support social services to the same degree as Kitchener, in part because many important social services and the most affordable housing are located in Kitchener. On the other hand, Waterloo does have to deal with housing and other challenges associated with a large, transient student population.

Although the political cultures of Kitchener and Waterloo seem quite different from each other in a number of ways, even more distinct are the neighbouring self-governing Mennonite communities. The German and Mennonite heritage remains a strong part of the social and physical composition of the Region of Waterloo. Peaceful Old Order Mennonites farm the nearby rural areas and shun many modern conveniences, along with the politics, lifestyles, and local governments of their urban neighbours.

I.3  Kitchener and Waterloo, Ontario

## I.4  Prince George, British Columbia

Prince George, a city of approximately 72,000, lies at the confluence of two great rivers, the Fraser and the Nechako, and at the intersection of two main provincial highways. The self-titled "Northern capital of British Columbia" is close to 55 degrees latitude, in the geographic centre of the province. To the vast bulk of the Canadian population, which has arranged itself along the Canada-US border, however, Prince George is viewed as a remote city located in the vast, undefined north.

From the top of high, sand-cut riverbanks, one can readily observe that pulp and paper has served as the economic staple for the life of this relatively young city. Pulp mills provide a backdrop, while other signs of industry and rail yards wind around its perimeter. In the "bowl," a depressed downtown reflects hurried early growth and lack of careful town planning. Modest residential areas composed of older frame and stucco houses give way to modern suburbs as streets climb up rolling hills covered with spruce, pine, and fir. Beyond is wilderness and scattered subdivisions, where bears and other wildlife share space with residential and commercial developments that line the two major intersecting highways.

As can be seen from Table I.1, Prince George has a large land mass relative to its population, allowing plenty of room for growth. (This stands out in contrast to the physically smaller city of Waterloo, for example, where residential development is pushing up against municipal boundaries.) Signs of recent economic prosperity in the "Spruce City" are evident in the juxtaposition of the new with the old; the 1990s saw the construction of numerous public buildings as the city experienced rapid growth and economic renewal. In less than two hundred years, this city has seen dramatic change from its inception as an isolated trading post to a sprawling city of contrasts. The city faces some challenges related to unemployment, social disparity, environmental concerns, and stresses to its traditional pulp and paper resource economy – specifically the ongoing Canada-US softwood lumber dispute. The first inhabitants of the region, the Carrier First Nations, are struggling to achieve political voice, economic necessities, and social stability in the city.

Prince George's locally elected, at-large city council is a fairly homogeneous, middle-class group that, over time, has worked actively with business and community leaders to bring development and services to the city. The local political culture is very lively, with a strong sense of self-sufficiency. Community leaders are also determined to obtain their fair share of provincial resources. As a northern city, Prince George strives to gain political recognition from the provincial government and to achieve equitable treatment with southern communities in terms of adequate services and resources. Its tenacity has paid off in many ways, one of the most notable being the successful campaign by many community leaders in Prince George and other northern towns to acquire its most recent, free-standing, post-secondary educational institution – the University of Northern British Columbia.

Part 1    Local Democracy, a Contested Notion

This book poses a question: Are we governing ourselves? It also raises a series of related questions, and one of the first to come to mind is "Who are we?" Are *we* all the citizens and residents of Canada and its communities? Are *we* elected officials, grassroots activists, members of multicultural associations, volunteers, public administrators, or business people? We might also ask ourselves – as individuals and members of a collectivity – whether we actually do govern ourselves or whether we have abandoned our responsibility for decision making by allowing other forces or actors determine our political environment. Does the mere act of voting constitute self-government, or is active citizen engagement required for a self-governing community?

If we do govern ourselves, how do we do it? What factors, tools, or avenues do we use to influence community decisions? Do we participate through the formal political process or informally through community associations? Perhaps we are non-voting individuals who participate unknowingly in local politics through personal choices that govern our daily lives.

The answers to these questions, and the relative degree of political influence we have individually and collectively, depend on the framework we use to make sense of our local political environment. Questions of political influence can be considered through different approaches that emphasize the relative importance of some factors over others. It is through an examination of these differing perspectives that we can identify the different actors and influences that shape local political power structures and communities. Much depends upon the relative weight given to determining variables (such as physical context, institutions, economics, and so on) as well as to their interrelationships.

Academic discussions invariably revolve around how local communities are shaped and by whom – or to put it in traditional political science terms, "who gets what, when, and how."[1] The ability of certain individuals or groups to influence local politics reflects how well these actors are positioned to take advantage of the key factors that affect local politics. These factors include ideology, political and cultural values, legal and political institutions, administrative and organizational structures, economics, geography, the biophysical and social environment, and communications.

The rapidly changing global environment and a diminishing sense of citizen effectiveness at the local level have many observers debating the fundamental values underpinning our governing institutions. One persistent belief is that local government can and should play an important role in promoting some form of democracy through local elections and public participation. The public is expected to influence political agendas through their local councillors, mayors, and those elected to other positions. In turn, those elected are supposed to represent the needs of neighbourhoods and local communities.

Political theorists debate the degree to which formal governing institutions can achieve this democratic ideal. Some suggest that democratic politics is most likely to occur outside the state (that is, outside the formal political institutions) where activists pressure for change in society-centred activities. A distinction is drawn between the study of *government,* which focuses on the formal structures of government, and the study of *governance,* which sees local politics as taking place beyond formal institutions and operating within society as a whole. From this focus on governance, it can be argued that democracy might best be pursued through the activities of grassroots citizen activities, volunteer organizations, social, cultural, and religious organizations, and pressure groups. Civil society, then, becomes the important centre of democratic activity. Directly or indirectly, citizens are influential participants in local governance.

George Francis offers the following distinction between *governance* and *government*: "Governance can be defined as the collective results from the exercise of authority and control through multiple governmental and other organizations, each following their own decision-making processes. The concept of governance extends beyond 'government' and the roles that government agencies play, to include corporate and other private sector, non-governmental organizations."[2]

Governments, communities, and others are now grappling with this concept of governance and how, and if, it should be applied or encouraged. The founding principles and practices of formal representative institutions leave local governments ill equipped to respond to many popular demands that spring from differing contemporary conceptions of a democratic society.

# 1
# Local Self-Government: Perspectives on Democracy

This book focuses on local government and local communities because this is the arena of politics that most directly affects our daily lives. Whatever chance we have of building and maintaining a sustainable, healthy society rests squarely on our ability to shape these communities. Questions about whether or not we govern ourselves are inevitably related to democratic ideas and the degree to which they can be realized in day-to-day practice.

That practice is necessarily limited by the constitutional fact that our physical communities – the cities, towns, and villages of Canada – are all situated in the midst of a larger territory. Because of that, our ambitions for self-control at the community level are always subject to the whims, fancies, and passing prejudices of larger governments – provincial and federal – as well as the compelling influence of other powerful forces, such as the global economy. Whatever a state's claims of sovereignty, all of its political authority must coexist with equally powerful cultural, geographic, economic, and environmental forces. That means our ability to govern ourselves is necessarily partial at all levels. Even in the ideal democratic state, citizens' powers of self-government will always be limited – divided first among the three physical political arenas, the local, provincial, and federal, and then among all their other political activities. Any healthy democratic society would necessarily be one in constant tension, as people endeavoured in these various spheres to promote their competing values, which might include individual rights, social equality, economic vitality, and biophysical sustainability.

Local government is but one organization that influences the way in which we govern ourselves. It shares the stage with a variety of other governmental actors and non-governmental and private-sector bodies that contribute to the "governance" of our communities. Local government is, however, a very important member of the cast of players, and as such, is worthy of closer consideration. How much local government contributes to, or detracts from, the quest for a democratic society is an important question.

One way to untangle this issue is to consider who holds power in a community. Governments, communities, businesses, and associations compete with each other, and within their own organizations, to set agendas and to see their perspectives predominate. Their agendas are not only limited by each other but by the different settings and sets of circumstances in which they find themselves. No one group has absolute influence.

Citizens of multiple communities interact with, and shape, their environments in diverse ways. That said, the distribution of political power and influence is unequal; some groups have many more access points than others, constraining the ability of the latter to effectively participate.

To many, democracy is most likely to be found where citizens are part of the governing process. In an ideal situation, this would occur when an informed public participates in political decisions. Henry Milner suggests that "Democracy is ... stronger in a community blessed with a substantial stock of civic literacy. Stronger in the sense that levels of political participation are higher; stronger, too, in the sense that policy decisions are more likely to take into account the full gamut of interests and perspectives in society ... High civic-literacy societies are more likely to attain long-term egalitarian economic outcomes."[1]

It has also been noted that a local government that exercises some degree of autonomy and operates within a community where citizens are able to experience a measure of self-determination can contribute to a more democratic society.[2] Political institutions play a crucial role in shaping our environment. If we accept this assumption, we might then ask how political institutions can be influenced in a way that will allow individuals living within communities to have choices about how they live out their lives. The prescription of this book is that this goal is best achieved if three conditions are realized:

1   The authority and resources of local government need to be enhanced if it is to cope reasonably effectively with the onslaught of global imperatives, provincial off-loading, and citizen demands.
2   Enhanced local institutional authority must be accompanied by a strengthening of the public accountability of that institution.
3   A strong, diverse network of active groups and individuals must be at work within civil society and operate with a degree of autonomy from the formal governing institutions.

The term *civil society* may be defined in at least two ways. One definition emphasizes liberal-democracy and speaks about political society composed of citizenship, rights, democratic representation, and law. The other definition presents civil society as an "intermediate associational realm situated between the state on the one side and the basic building blocks of society on the other ... inhabited by social organizations with some degree of autonomy and voluntary participation on the part of their numbers."[3] This book focuses on the second definition.

The difficulties in achieving the three conditions mentioned previously are not to be underestimated. There is certainly room for skepticism about the ability of formal local governing institutions to pursue or advance a broadly inclusive democratic society. Some suggest that our best hope for democracy rests with a form of governance focused around society, where grassroots organizations and social movements can articulate the needs of economically and socially disadvantaged groups. It is reasoned that these civil organizations can contribute to better governance by calling for more transparency and information availability in government practices and policies and by taking on a public advocacy role.[4]

Much can be said about the important political role played by social movements and activism in challenging the status quo, establishing communities of interest, and forcing governments to respond to important public concerns. A strengthened sense of civic and community responsibility alone, however, cannot replace good government. As Mohammad Qadeer warns, with respect to those who (for different reasons) wish to encourage community capacity building, "The current thrust toward minimal government and retrenching of public responsibilities cannot be rationalized on community self-help ... Let us not fool ourselves that citizens' welfare and health can be sustained by communities. Such communities are very scarce in post-industrial societies. There is no substitute for a good and caring government."[5]

It does not necessarily follow that giving enhanced powers to local government will ensure a more democratic society. But local government can better serve this role if it gains more authority and the accompanying resources, and if it also becomes more accountable to a diverse, politically educated, and engaged civil society.

The International Institute for Democracy and Electoral Assistance (IDEA) suggests that citizens look to local government "to solve their immediate social problems."[6] IDEA suggests that this is also the tier of authority that offers the best prospect for citizen engagement on community matters. Furthermore, the institute suggests, "a vigorous local democracy is the basis of a healthy national-level democracy," arguing that

- local governance is a basis of citizenship and community
- democracy involves ongoing deliberation – meaningful dialogue, debate, and discussion in an effort to solve problems that arise before the community
- citizen participation allows individuals to gain knowledge about community affairs that otherwise resides with the elected officials
- participatory democracy tends to enhance good relations among the citizens, building a community that is self-reliant and public-spirited.[7]

Local government in Canada does play a valuable role in providing a number of important services to a plurality of interests necessary to maintain the quality of life that Canadian society currently enjoys. This should not be discounted nor undervalued. Nevertheless, in many ways, the institution falls short of fulfilling its role as an agent of a healthy, democratic polity, as described above. It is circumscribed by financial and legal controls exercised by senior governments, the systemic dominance of private-sector interests (globally and locally), and ideological assumptions that are out of step with the varied needs of a large, urban, heterogeneous population.

## Local Governments: Agents of Democracy?

Democracy is a contested notion. Democratic theory has evolved as the values that dominate political discourse have shifted with respect to considerations such as human rights
and freedoms, property rights, and the public interest. Some classical notions of democracy were based on principles such as "liberty, equality, and fraternity," that were to be
achieved through representative government and regularly held universal elections. In the
1800s, *universal* generally referred to male, property-owning citizens.

Two nineteenth-century theorists, Alexis de Tocqueville and John Stuart Mill, argued
that the institution of local government was a necessary element of democracy. Although
their notion of democracy did not support the idea that the average person should participate in the actual process of governing, these theorists saw democratic value in local
government. They argued that it provided citizens with an ideal setting in which to learn
about civics, form a social bond, and advance common interests. These ideas are popular
today. Although definitions vary, it is generally recognized that democracy requires a well-
informed, politically aware citizenry. Publicly available information, as well as effective
channels of communications, serve as vital means by which to achieve such a citizenry.[8]

In the mid-1950s, a scholarly debate took place in Europe about whether a measure of
local self-government was a prerequisite for democracy. George Langrod, an advocate of
the more centralized system of government (such as can be found in France), argued that
the fundamental requirements of democracy include majority rule, equality, and uniform
standards. Democracy, in this view, requires a centralized government that would represent the interests of the whole or the majority. In fact, Langrod suggested, local government might be antithetical to democracy. He claimed that local government tends to
favour parochial, vested, private interests rather than those of the nation or the broader
public.[9]

Defending the British tradition, Keith Panter-Brick argued that the "egalitarian uniformity" described by Langrod should not be accepted as the "hallmark of democracy." Panter-
Brick claimed that local government was an important part of democracy and served a
role complementary to that of the central government. Affairs that require democratic
resolution, including measures to promote equality among different groups of citizens,
do not only happen at the national level. Local governments are an essential requirement
for democracy because they are expected to resolve conflicting demands by settling local
issues on the grounds of "what is fair and just." Moreover, Panter-Brick asserted that a
valuable public education could be gained in the course of resolving local conflicts in a
democratic manner.[10]

A citizen can learn much about both politics and democracy when the issues at stake
are close to home. But what exactly is meant by close to home? In the 1960s, Robert Dahl
drew parallels between local government and democracy by referring to the early Greek
city-state that he saw as both manageable in size and possessing a healthy form of self-
government. Dahl observed that by the 1800s, however, the notion that republics could

only prosper in smaller communities was replaced by the idea that democracy could be fostered through effective representation in the nation-state. Smaller units of government became viewed as subordinate to the nation-state. If local governments had too much power, the argument went, the resulting factionalism would disrupt the stability of the whole country. How then, Dahl asked, do members of the community participate in the democratic life of a state that has become too big for citizens to engage directly in discussions with government officials? Voting is obviously one means of political participation. Yet the larger the constituency, the more indirect the channels of communication become between the citizens and their elected leaders.

In his quest for the "ideal" size city to achieve the goals of democracy, Dahl presented his readers with a conundrum. Larger units of government could deal with larger problems, such as air and water pollution, racial injustice, or war. Yet the larger the unit, the more complex the issues, and the more the citizen was reduced to participating primarily through the vote. On the other hand, with small units of government, the opportunity to participate was much higher, but the issues involved were of limited scope and had less impact.[11] Dahl concluded that the optimum size of a city would range between 50,000 and 200,000 citizens. This figure, of course, was subject to much discussion at the time. Today, it would raise even more questions, given developments in communications and information technology and in the global economy that have altered people's concepts about space, time, and governance. Nevertheless, Dahl was looking for a "political unit of more truly human proportions in which a citizen can acquire confidence and mastery of the arts of politics – that is, of the arts required for shaping a good life in common with fellow citizens."[12] The views of Robert Dahl continue to hold meaning today for those who seek a measure of self-governance over their local environment as a vital component of a healthy democratic society.

Is this democratic notion of citizens collectively "shaping a good life" one that can actually be advanced through local government institutions? Over the years, a number of analysts, including Robert Dahl, set out to investigate just who governs. A number of researchers collectively referred to as the *community power school* came to the conclusion that political influence was at work in social and economic structures as well as in formal governing institutions.[13] In their debates, such theorists fell into several camps. One group argued that every community contained ruling elites (people in a position of economic or social privilege) who dominated political decision agendas. The second group argued that power in a community was more dispersed or pluralistic, where the balance of power shifted between groups of people over periods of time or on an issue-to-issue basis. In other words, each community contained "multiple centers of power, none of which is completely sovereign."[14]

While the elite versus pluralist debate raged on, still other analysts pointed out that the question of who ruled did not necessarily have to be a matter of one or the other. Rather, they suggested that a variety of different elites exercised power in different places and at different times. Moreover, communities will vary in their power structures. A political or economic elite will dominate some of them, while others will be more pluralistic depending on a variety of factors, including the political culture. In 1963, Nelson W. Polsby published *Community Power and Political Theory,* which examined the question of who rules in American communities: "who participates, who gains and loses, and who prevails in decision-making."[15] In his study, Polsby concluded, "Careful examination of the evidence at hand seems to indicate that elites are freest in their power to commit the resources of the community when decisions are relatively routine and innocuous; other kinds of decision-making – of a nonroutine, unbureaucratized, or innovative variety – seem to require special consent by citizens who fall outside the small decision-making group."[16]

Community power studies, such as those undertaken by Polsby and other researchers, made an important contribution to the understanding of the distribution of power and influence within a community, and hence, to the general literature on local democracy. The community power theorists emphasized that local political power resided not only in the hands of political elites or bureaucrats but in the social setting of neighbourhoods and other groups as well. The recognition that important questions of local politics extended beyond the formal institutions was an important contribution to the field.

Almost two decades after Polsby published his work, Clarence N. Stone added to this debate by discussing the role that elites played in shaping the systemic power that underlay community decision making. Stone suggests that systemic power – that which is "furthest removed from open competition" and "purposive activity" – is dominated by certain socio-economic elites.[17] In other words, these elites influence the context of local decision making – the "institutions, procedures, and norms" – rather than influencing the direct political conflicts. Stone suggests that an understanding of these underlying systemic forces can help explain why citizen groups can sometimes be successful on an issue-by-issue basis, or can mount successful election campaigns if they act as well-organized and focused groups. In terms of overall community decision making, though, the upper strata are strategically advantaged. These strata include those with wealth and control over major economic enterprises in a community, who can "mobilize and sustain resources" to achieve goals and who have social position, public esteem, and the lifestyle that goes along with them. Government officials, Stone argues, find themselves most rewarded for cooperating with those elites (or what he refers to as "upper-strata" interests) rather than lower-strata interests.[18] Obviously, business interests are important to governments because they are revenue generators rather than consumers. Business influences are "embedded" in the situational context of local decision making.[19] As government officials pursue their own interests, they are aware that they are operating within institutions that also need to thrive. As such, these officials are "guided by a set of strategic dependencies that grow out of a stratified socioeconomic system."[20] Systemic power is not overriding – it is one of a number of influential factors – but it does affect who has access to decision makers and what proposals garner policy attention.[21]

By the end of the twentieth century, *urban regime theory* was gaining ground in the academic literature. Building on work advanced by people such as Stone, regime theory considers how different types of governing coalitions emerge and evolve and eventually become dominant or transform.[22] Urban regime theory emphasizes how political coalitions, often dominated by business interests, become established and govern. It is used to help explain the behaviour of individual political and economic actors who build alliances to support the local system, and how and why concessions are made to low-income residents as a result of social movement pressures or political struggles.[23] Urban regime theory, with its focus on coalition building by actors pursuing their own self-interests (rational-choice theory), has been critiqued for paying insufficient attention to influences played by broader institutional, physical/spatial, and economic factors that go beyond the urban setting itself.[24] Recently, Christopher Leo and others have taken the urban regime analysis and have placed it within a broader global context (see Chapter 9).

Some theorists who are interested in the role that global capitalist forces play in shaping our communities might point to the relative weakness of local governments in the face of more powerful forces, including global economic imperatives as well as the desires and interests of economic elites that dominate politics at all levels.[25] From this perspective, local governments might be seen as little more than captive agents of private-sector forces efficiently organizing social processes for the benefit of propertied interests. Some may see these power relationships as very direct, while others see the connections as operating at a more systemic or structural level.

Many of those who reject the idea that local government acts as an agent of democracy suggest that if any form of democracy is to be pursued effectively, the quest will have to occur outside state-centred relationships, in a place where individuals, grassroots organizations, and other groups might find their own political space.[26] It is within society itself, not the limited and limiting municipal institutions, that scholars like Warren Magnusson see the most opportunity for local democracy: "It finds expression in self-education and consciousness raising, communication and direct action, affinity networks, information exchanges, cooperatives, institutions for public service and self-help and so on. Whether we are talking about feminists, native people, environmentalists, labour activists, or any number of others, we can sense the development of new institutions and practices that embody an ethic of democracy."[27] This argument is quite persuasive, particularly if one notes how societies have changed, in part as a response to the active political involvement of such groups.

Yet not all observers of the local scene are as ready to discount the democratic function of local government. Some have argued that this institution also has served as an important "agent of societal and governmental" change.[28] Neil Thomlinson suggests this when he considers local government from the context of one particular group – the gay community. He argues that local governments, unlike provincial and federal governments, are more responsive to the specific composition of their constituencies. If, for example, there is a sizable, well-defined minority community in a city, its concerns are more likely to find their way onto the municipal agenda than they would in the larger, more senior levels of government. Any distinctive community of interest might constitute a significant political voice at the local level, whereas its agenda could be lost among those of many other groups vying for space on provincial or federal discussion agendas. Local government recognizes the political interests of groups whose concerns might otherwise be ignored. Thomlinson also suggests that local government is important because it can most readily address the issues that affect the daily human needs of the community.[29]

What, then, can we conclude about influence, democracy, and local politics as articulated by some contemporary theorists? In an insightful essay, R. Scott Evans suggests that politics constitutes more than "statecraft"; it is a form of governing that is an extension of citizenship. It is at the local level, he argues, where "substantial issues are defined and contested" and where one finds definition of society's values, and decisions about what constitutes the collective good.[30] Evans offers a succinct summary: "The important local nature of democracy lies in the proximity and personal nature of politics. As such, local politics serves as a bridge between the private world of family, friends, and work, and the public arena wherein public agendas are formed and contested. It is here that the normative contours of legitimacy and democratic participation acquire content and meaning."[31]

The extent to which *we* govern ourselves has much to do with choice. The greater the number of meaningful choices people have over their environment, the more opportunities they have for self-government. However, the ability of the majority of people to exercise choice is contingent, to a degree, on a community's overall capacity to ensure that diverse societal groups are heard and recognized in public decision making. Otherwise, the rights of the powerful few come at the expense of others who, by reason of law, economics, political structures, or social constraints, are at a decided disadvantage.

## Conclusion

A number of theorists believe that local politics can be a useful channel through which people can advance democratic society. For some, an important part of this process may take place through the formal institutions of local government. For others, democracy is more likely to happen informally in society and through activism.

Analysts who look elsewhere for an understanding of political power and influence suggest that local government and politics may be irrelevant in discussions of democracy. Some of these people emphasize the relative inability of local governments or communities to achieve any degree of meaningful autonomy in the face of paternal senior governments or global economic imperatives.

Then there are those who prefer to adopt either a pluralist or systems approach and recognize that a democratic society may be achieved through various forms of political activity and organization.

Underpinning all these viewpoints are differing perspectives of power, influence, and democracy. Do we govern ourselves? Much depends on one's definition of democracy and beliefs about who has influence and how. As has been persuasively argued by others, local governments have been structured in many ways that limit or contain, rather than promote, democracy.[32]

That noted, municipal governments do play an important role in shaping the fabric of society. Increasingly, the needs and concerns of citizens are played out in local arenas as urban populations swell and municipal responsibilities grow. As such, local governments are worthy of closer consideration.

The quest for democracy might best be pursued if a number of political avenues are open to citizens wishing to influence the political process. If sufficient pressure and leverage are brought to bear, local institutions can be one of the more accessible vehicles for advancing diverse public concerns and views that differ from those expressed by the dominant elites. The historical record demonstrates, however, that the battle for local self-government is not easily won. As the next chapter shows, when there have been victories, the gains have not been equitably distributed within the local population.

**2**
# Local Democracy and Self-Government: The Historical Legacy

The degree to which there should be local self-governance has always been subject to dispute. The debate has often taken place between central and local authorities, each vying to maintain or increase its own level of authority and resources, or to avoid responsibility for unwanted burdens. This is a struggle that has continued since the early days of local government in Canada over 150 years ago. The institutions of Canadian local government were not designed to encourage a form of autonomous self-government, despite some rhetoric proclaiming otherwise. Rather, rooted in the traditions of a colonial past, these institutions were structured to ensure economic progress and an orderly system of government.

## Aboriginal Peoples

Local government in Canada, as generally understood, dates back to the arrival of immigrants from France. Prior to contact with Europeans, Aboriginal peoples in North America had their own forms of government that were integrated with social and economic arrangements. What ideas existed about land and government were based on kinship or territories inhabited by groups.[1]

Today, Aboriginal governments possess distinct sets of political arrangements and powers within the Canadian state. Many of these governing arrangements require different types of legislation and agreements than the more limiting forms of municipal government. This reality was highlighted by a 1997 Supreme Court of Canada decision known as *Delgamuukw v. The Province of British Columbia.* This decision, among other things, recognizes that First Nations are distinct societies with collective rights and that they hold aboriginal title to certain lands and resources, guaranteed under Section 35 of the 1982 Constitution Act. As Paul Tennant notes from a local-government perspective, this means that "within [British Columbia], the simple but utterly important constitutional reality is that every recognized local native Indian community (that is, First Nation) has both its identity and its rights confirmed and guaranteed. This constitutional status of First Nations, which is a status Municipalities can for the moment only dream of, was evident prior to Delgamuukw, but it is amplified by the ruling. First Nations and their rights are here to stay."[2]

First Nations governance has its own set of challenges that are distinct from those of non-Aboriginal communities. Nevertheless, despite the number of legal, cultural, and socio-economic differences that might distinguish a First Nations community from municipalities, Tennant asserts that 80 percent of the day-to-day concerns that preoccupy local municipal politicians would be the same as those that concern First Nations leaders.[3]

While the practical administrative concerns of governing a small group of people in a specific locality may be similar to those of small municipalities, the approach for arriving at a decision may differ depending on the traditions of the particular band concerned. Bish and Cassidy, for example, note that traditional Aboriginal communities often place much more emphasis on direct community participation in political decision making. While chiefs may provide leadership, that leadership is contingent on the approval of the community that actively participates in decision making. Most distinctive is the much heavier reliance on consensus-based decision making than in non-Aboriginal governments, and also the greater leadership role of community elders.[4] In Canadian municipalities, consensus-based processes are now making their way into some local governing processes, such as citizen advisory committees. This is a very recent development and was certainly not part of the governing practices of Europeans when they landed in North America a few centuries ago.

## The Loyalists and Home Rule

Upon arrival on Canadian shores, French and British authorities brought with them their own sets of imperialist traditions to govern early local settlements. In Quebec, prior to its transfer to the British in 1763, the French government had imposed a centralist and absolutist form of government. Quebec experienced only a few short-lived, isolated attempts to hold local elections. After the British assumed control of the Canadas, the Court of Quarter Sessions governed local communities of British North America (from the mid-1700s until around the mid-1800s).[5] The court appointed local property owners who, in turn, provided advice on matters of local concern. Crawford suggests that, outside of church matters, general members of the population had little, if any, role in local administration.[6]

General John Graves Simcoe presided over Upper Canada, which was established by the Constitutional Act of 1791. Local government meant little to this military man, who was once described in the following manner: "Almost incapable, by temper and experience, of recognizing any other form of administration, he sought to organize his Government as nearly as possible on a military basis. Self-government by the people at large he fervently and frankly abhorred. Aristocratic military and ecclesiastical rule he considered to be the only possible form of stable government ... He was sent out to administer a British colony in the interests and for the glory of the country which sent him."[7] Simcoe's views were not universally embraced by the local population.

At the end of the American Revolution, thousands of people loyal to the British Crown – the Loyalists – immigrated to Canada from the former American colonies. Some of the Loyalists brought with them the New England tradition of *home rule*, one form of direct democracy that included town hall meetings. The British authorities opposed any sign of independence and rejected several local attempts to achieve some autonomy, but they were unable to resist the settlers indefinitely; 1785 saw the establishment of Canada's first municipality, Saint John, New Brunswick (see Box 2.1).[8]

After the rebellions in Upper and Lower Canada, Britain charged Lord Durham with producing a report concerning the future government of the provinces. By this time, a number of municipalities had been incorporated. In his 1839 report on the affairs of British North America, Lord Durham promoted the formation of municipalities because he viewed them as an "essential part" of the 1840 union of Upper and Lower Canada.

A number of new municipalities were incorporated after the release of Durham's report. The report did have limitations stemming from Durham's biases against French-Canadian traditions in Lower Canada and his lack of first-hand knowledge of Upper Canada. Yet the report, which recommended the establishment of responsible or parliamentary government, has been referred to by a number of historians as "the charter of Canadian democracy and self-government."[9]

Others, however, have not viewed the Durham report and its recommendations in the same light. Rather than being a means by which the citizenry could be liberated, the report sometimes has been considered another type of colonialism; municipal institutions, among others, were to be used to bring administrative efficiency to the British colonies. Engin F. Isin refers to this new approach as "liberal colonialism." Colonialism served the British Empire's economic interests; civil unrest did not, nor did centralized government of local affairs. Liberal colonialism could be distinguished from traditional colonialism because it would allow a measure of local decision making in certain matters, but it was designed to ensure efficiency, order, and stability. Britain's interests would still be protected because the proposed system would ensure a continuing expansion of markets and the enlarging of the field of production, which consisted of land, labour, and capital.[10] Lord Sydenham, appointed governor general of British North America in 1839, was charged with establishing municipal institutions.

In Ontario, Robert Baldwin's Municipal Corporations Act (1849) provided for a comprehensive system of government that influenced today's structure of local governments. In this system, power was vested in municipal corporations, not individual citizens themselves, lending weight to Isin's argument that "the modern principles that 'people should manage their own affairs' was not reached out of some abstract affection for citizenship nor as a result of a popular, grassroots movement that agitated for local self-government."[11] Neither was it the outcome of some enlightened political philosophy. Rather, municipalities were established to make the colonies more efficient and effective.[12] In fact, as the following chapters discuss, local institutions were sometimes imposed upon a rather reluctant citizenry.

## 2.1 The Incorporation of Saint John

Of the 12,000 Loyalists who left New York for New Brunswick, most of them settled in the St. John Valley, leading to the rapid establishment of the City of Saint John, the town of Fredericton, and other villages. It has been argued by some that as a result of Loyalist pressure for self-government, Saint John became the first incorporated city in Canada in 1785. Other cities did not fare so well and continued to be governed by the Courts of Quarter Session. The next incorporation happened half a century later.

It is important to note that while some of the Loyalists may have brought with them notions about a form of local self-government, their concept of democracy was not universally applied. Rather, it was directed primarily at white, male property owners. A number of Loyalists, for example, brought black slaves with them from the United States (although slavery also existed in the area prior to the arrival of the Loyalists). The practice of slavery was not abolished until the early 1800s.

*Sources:* Dan Soucoup, *Historic New Brunswick* (Lawrencetown Beach, NS: Pottersfield Press, 1997), 61, 65, 76; Donald J.H. Higgins, *Local and Urban Politics in Canada* (Toronto: Gage Publishing, 1986), 41.

In the unsettled western provinces, municipal-style government did not arrive until the late 1880s because the population was scattered, small, and inhabited remote pockets of land. The Hudson's Bay Company and the Canadian Pacific Railway were dominant corporate forces that shaped early settlement and development patterns. The territories were given a different type of administrative structure to accommodate their unique cultural, political, and geographic needs.

Prevailing attitudes toward local self-government in the eighteenth and nineteenth centuries were not imbued with the democratic values often popularly promoted today. The political and economic elites tended to interpret democracy as a form of mob rule, in which the underprivileged classes would be incapable of making wise and economically sound choices. Many ordinary citizens, however, also viewed the institution of local government with suspicion. Farmers, in particular, often considered local government as a means by which the elite would raise taxes for their own projects. This perception was not far from the mark. Although some New England Loyalists did bring with them the idea of the town hall meeting, in general, progress toward municipal reform was slow. Where it did occur, local democracy, as commonly understood and practised in the nineteenth century, excluded many groups, such as women (unless they were unmarried property owners), those without substantial property, and members of some minority groups.

## Urban Reform: Efficiency versus Local Democracy

By the late 1800s, North America was caught up in rapid industrialization and factory automation. Huge influxes of migrants from the countryside flooded into the cities seeking work. Waves of immigrants arrived from other countries. The flourishing economy fuelled the notion that the application of technology, science, and business principles to human problems would lead to a good life for all. The North American embrace of the *urban reform movement* suggested that the role of local government was to be the efficient and professional provider of services. The urban reform movement was a middle-class reaction to corruption and inefficiency and unchecked local political patronage.

Throughout nineteenth-century North America, much city activity had been organized around individual economic interests. The job of local government was to protect those interests and to maintain social order and public safety. Services, such as sewers, fire protection, waste removal, and policing, were developed primarily to protect private property and were a response to emergencies caused by devastating epidemics, fires, and mob violence.

In the absence of much public welfare, poorer citizens often had to rely on the patronage of wealthy and powerful individuals who controlled city politics. The chaos and disorganization of civic affairs in large North American cities, particularly in the eastern part of the United States, created an environment whereby individuals with resources were able to set up what came to be known as powerful urban political machines. The local

system of government was used as a vehicle whereby corrupt political and business organizations could promote their interests through entrenched, hierarchical networks of
power (or machines) that operated throughout urban municipalities.

During the time in question, cities were divided into physical political territories called
*wards*. Each ward would elect an alderman to represent that area's interest on city council. The ward system exists today in many places in the United States and Canada and is
often seen as the way to foster a measure of local democracy, ensuring adequate representation of diverse communities from different parts of a city. Unfortunately, in the past
the ward system was sometimes associated with widespread municipal corruption.

By the end of the nineteenth century, middle-class citizens began to agitate for reform
in reaction to the corruption, unreliability of services, urban decay, and lack of efficiency
in city government. These reformers saw local politics as the source of the problem because they believed that it served the personal interests of self-serving, corrupt individuals who held their positions through a tightly controlled system of ward-based elections.
In the United States, the urban reformers lobbied for "at-large" city elections, the elimination of parties, and the introduction of business principles to increase administrative efficiency. One of the goals was to introduce the merit principle into the hiring of public
employees. Those who were to be employed by the city would have to demonstrate that
they had the relevant qualifications to perform efficiently. It was hoped that it would no
longer be enough to know someone who worked in government. In a number of cases,
application of this principle turned out to be more of an ideal than reality. Yet the initiative was a concerted attempt to introduce some agreed-upon principles and organization
into a chaotic system.

For their part, city councillors and appointed officials were expected to represent the
whole city's interest rather than particular wards. It was argued that this approach would
uphold democracy by ensuring that governments would serve the broader public interest.
It would remove the corrupt aspects of patronage from municipal politics by providing
social services in a more equitable fashion and by using merit as the impartial hiring standard. Under the at-large (or general vote) system of elections, Crawford noted that "much
of the 'log-rolling' or 'backscratching,' by which a representative undertakes to support
action to benefit another ward, in return for expressed or implied promises of support for
something for his own ward, is eliminated. Those elected at large can afford to take a
community rather than a sectional view, for they are compelled, by the nature of their
constituency, to support measures designed to benefit the greatest number rather than
one section."[13]

It could be argued that those cities that attempted to avoid the unsavoury aspects of
politics by eliminating the ward system and removing politics from the decision-making
process also ensured that many less-privileged citizens and minority groups were left
without representation. On the other hand, Crawford also observed that the practice of
"dividing the community into sections, with sectional representation, is detrimental to
the best community spirit and may serve to perpetuate and intensify objectionable racial

or class feelings."[14] He believed, however, that in big cities, the at-large system of politics made it difficult, if not impossible, for the citizens to get to know the candidates, and election costs could be very high.[15]

The effects of the American urban reform movement influenced the development of western cities both in the United States and Canada, where at-large elections and the institution of business principles informed many of the operating assumptions of local governments. The extent to which American machine-style urban politics and the subsequent reform movement influenced Canadian cities is a matter of some debate. Although analysts will acknowledge the influence of American developments on Canadian municipal government, they also note that there were many contributing indigenous factors.[16] The structure of Canada's western urban government, for example, was heavily influenced by Ontario's municipal system.[17] Canada's own urban reform movement was also a reaction to particular domestic social and economic developments. Nevertheless, Canada's urban centres did share some experiences with their American counterparts.

Patronage, for example, has played a large part in Canadian political history. Allegations of corruption – fact and fiction – have always been part of the culture of city politics. This was the case in the City of Toronto during the urban reform era at the turn of the twentieth century. A number of middle-class civic leaders preached their ideas of efficiency and morality in reaction to what they saw as Toronto's version of shady machine politics. Civic elections, newspaper coverage, and business deals all were subjected to the reformers' public scrutiny. From time to time, the reformers would make accusations about ballot box stuffing or point fingers at local aldermen who might be trading on their positions in city government for financial gain.[18] One particular section of the city, known as Ward 3, was the source of considerable angst on the part of the reformers. The ward was inhabited by many poor immigrants who had different cultural practices and belief systems than the dominant elites. These individuals were forced to live in substandard housing and unhealthy conditions. In the twenty-first century, many might argue that religious tolerance and encouragement of such diversity are a source of strength in a community and a hallmark of democracy. One hundred years ago, however, this perspective did not sit well with middle-class, predominantly Anglo-Saxon Protestant reformers.[19] At that time, successive aldermen governed their ward using a form of machine politics that curried favour with the predominantly poor inhabitants. In particular, the voters appreciated the fact that, unlike the reformers, their alderman did not try to impose his own brand of morality and religion on the ethnically diverse ward. On the other hand, Ward 3 saw little accomplished in terms of social and health improvements.[20]

Reformers attempted to impose control over inner-city wards by introducing an executive body or commission, the Board of Control. By 1904, it was decided that the Board would be elected at-large and would not be accountable to the city council. As Weaver notes, the more established Canadian cities were caught between the British tradition (where historically there had been a measure of what had been viewed as local democracy) and the American business-dominated reform movement.[21] By the early twentieth century, modern management top-down practices were replacing the older style of city politics, which was more fragmented and chaotic. The hold of corrupt members of political and economic elites on municipal politics was replaced by a different set of power dynamics. The new structures continued to favour the interests of the privileged and powerful, but the rules of the game had begun to change.

Along with the reform movement came some social assistance, housing, and improved health conditions for the poor. At the heart of this community economic development was a dynamic business community that saw the well-being of the city as synonymous with the well-being of their economic interests. Economic issues were not all that motivated the business people. As citizens who wished to contribute to their community, many business people were active volunteers in local politics and educational and public works, and many community objectives would not have been achieved without the initiatives of local business associations. Notions of community development, however, were linked to economic prosperity and liberal democracy. Largely unconsidered were all the interests and problems that fell outside of the priorities of the dominating elite. This was the case where business interests did not have a personal interest, or where their priorities may have conflicted with other public concerns. Examples of these conflicts are the adverse health impacts caused by the emissions of smokestacks, poisonous wastewaters, and garbage when industrial enterprises intermingled with residential housing in the early days of urban development. Nevertheless, there were some counterbalancing influences to the dominant business perspective. One was the role played by women who were members of the social elite, although this was not always well documented.

In her research on Kitchener-Waterloo, Susan Wismer observes that prior to the Second World War it was difficult to find much information at all "about the ways that race, class, (dis)ability, language of origin or sexual orientation have interacted with patterns of community in Kitchener-Waterloo" (see Box 2.2).[22] This situation is hardly surprising, given the dominant societal views of that time, which saw the well-being of the community as synonymous with a healthy economy and stable administration. Men dominated both areas of life. Yet the shaping of local community politics and culture cannot be attributed simply to the leadership of men and the business community they represented – far from it. Middle-class women, for example, were a leading force in the North American reform movement. Many women's associations mobilized to fight against inadequate health and safety standards, and against what they saw as pervasive immoral behaviour (prostitution, gambling, alcohol consumption, and political corruption). Women played an important, if unrecognized, role in the local politics of the day, shaping community standards and setting priorities. Yet the activities and concerns of women were seen as "private," apolitical matters associated with the well-being of the family. In contrast, the concerns of men were "public" matters considered worthy of recording, and thus making their way into historical accounts.

An influential component of local political activity, therefore, remained largely unacknowledged and was discounted in a manner that persisted throughout the next century.

## 2.2  Early Community Participation of Women in Berlin (Kitchener)

One of the earliest institutions in which community work took place was the Young Women's Christian Association (YWCA), which focused on the moral foundations of society. In Berlin, the YWCA was founded in 1905 by social reformers to provide safe and affordable housing (as well as some courses on the domestic arts) to young single women who worked in the factories and could not afford good alternative accommodations. The goal was to help young women help themselves. The low wages caused a problem for the founders of the YWCA (who ironically were often the wives of the industrialists who paid low wages) because they could not increase rents to cover the costs of running the facility. Jacob Kaufman (a factory owner) and his wife, Mary Kaufman (president of the first YWCA), frequently donated money to cover the cash shortages.

*Source:* Susan Wismer, "Sustaining Communities," in *The Dynamics of the Dispersed City,* ed. Pierre Filion, Trudi E. Bunting, and Kevin Curtis (Waterloo, ON: Department of Geography, University of Waterloo, 1996), 362-3.

Some assert that this situation prevails today. Linda Trimble suggests that, "In this way children are seen as 'private goods' and potholes, malls, and sports arenas are regarded as matters of public concern."[23] Private considerations, however, are public when concerns for the health and safety of one's family extend to the neighbourhood, educational opportunities, and social and health provisions – all essential considerations of local community politics. Susan Wismer notes that "the development of community in its fullest sense is fundamentally dependent on unpaid labour participation." Wismer suggests that women have contributed much more than half the community work.[24]

Yet the suspicion of society-oriented politics and a belief that the government should be a business-like enterprise have historically excluded other political perspectives and voices – a trend some argue persists today. In the early 1900s, while the concerns of the propertied class were well served, the business view of government did not reflect the needs of the factory workers, the poor, or other groups. The 1919 Winnipeg General Strike offers an excellent example of the unequal distribution of power during those times (see Box 2.3). As Doug Smith notes, local governments were captured by business owners, while the effectively disenfranchised workers took their protest to the street.[25]

Activists in the Winnipeg General Strike may have had a clear idea who they were fighting when it came to political and economic bosses. During the ensuing decades, however, the task of holding decision makers accountable for their actions became more challenging; those responsible were buried in the administrative folds of a bureaucracy hidden away in complex decision-making processes or another level of government. Intensive national government activity during the two world wars, subsequent reconstruction, and the centralized provision of health and social services reduced the political authority and power of local governments. Subsequently, local politics was increasingly devalued on Canadian political agendas. As a consequence, today's cities are ideologically, financially, and structurally unequipped to respond to many significant challenges confronting Canadian communities. Local politics – at least as represented through municipal institutions – left certain individuals and groups feeling shut out of the formal governing process. They sought other avenues of political expression.

## The Era of Activism: The 1960s and 1970s

The 1960s have been well documented as a time of optimism, youthful rebellion, and social protests. Student radicals were at the forefront of the political scene as they raised awareness of the rapid degradation of the environment, the inequality of women and minority groups, and the needs of the politically marginalized and socially disadvantaged. In Quebec, for example, the Quiet Revolution marked a surge of radicalism and the defeat of the oppressive Union Nationale provincial government. University intellectuals and students often aligned themselves in solidarity with the working class while protesting the economic domination of Quebec by English-speaking interests. In March 1969, radicals

## 2.3  The 1919 Winnipeg General Strike

For six weeks in the spring of 1919, tens of thousands of workers in Winnipeg went on strike – whether or not they belonged to a union – and frightened business leaders hired a police force to crush the strike action. After weeks of peaceful gatherings and speeches in city parks and squares, the strikers held a parade down Main Street. The parade was to oppose police raids, in which the workers' leaders had been arrested and thrown in the penitentiary. Doug Smith notes that the protest action resulted in the death of a striking worker, mass arrests, and the patrolling of the streets by armed soldiers. "Bloody Saturday," as it came to be known, put an end to the Winnipeg General Strike. Smith explains the reasons for the upheaval:

> The General Strike pitted one Winnipeg, South Winnipeg, against the other – the working-class Winnipeg that was growing up on both sides of the Canadian Pacific railyards. There, newly arrived immigrants were crammed into poorly built rooming houses on tiny lots. Bosses ruled by divine right. The city's raw and rough industries turned those immigrants into class-conscious workers, and in the face of discrimination and exploitation, they began to organize themselves. They adopted the values of the labour movement, principally sacrifice and solidarity, and they extended those values from their individual workplaces to their industries to the world of politics.[1]

---

1  Doug Smith, "A Strike with an Elusive Meaning," in *Compass Points: Navigating the 20th Century,* ed. Robert Chodos (Toronto: Between the Lines, Compass Foundation, 1999): 70-2.

held a large demonstration demanding that the predominantly anglophone McGill University in Montreal make French the dominant language. Protests of this kind inspired Montreal Mayor Jean Drapeau to institute an anti-demonstration bylaw.[26]

This era also signalled the beginning of an urban activism (often associated with Saul Alinsky and his *Rules for Radicals*) that gained impetus in the large inner cities of the United States. Canada's urban areas also experienced tremendous social, political, and economic ferment. A huge wave of property redevelopment in city centres accompanied a population boom and burgeoning suburban growth. Before the massive property redevelopments, inner-city areas were not vacant; they often consisted of old ethnic neighbourhoods, recently arrived immigrants and new Canadians, as well as many poorer people. Spirited civic debates about the future of urban centres were stimulated by the political activism of the 1960s, which continued its momentum throughout the 1970s. One of the best known of these debates revolved around the efforts of Toronto's Stop Spadina, Save Our City Coordinating Committee (SSSOCCC). Referred to as one of the "benchmarks in the contemporary reform era," the SSSOCCC was formed in 1969 to stop an expressway from being built through urban Toronto neighbourhoods.[27] The group was successful. Vancouver also had its own expressway protest action. As Gutstein relates, "The 'great freeway debate' of late 1967 led to the withdrawal of the plan and the formulation of new political parties to challenge the NPA's vision of the time."[28] The NPA (the Non-Partisan Association) is a business-led association that has often dominated city politics by running its own slate of candidates for local office.

Smaller cities were not immune to the activist politics of the time; particularly in those places with universities. Sherbrooke, Quebec, for example, saw a rise in activism in the 1970s following the Quiet Revolution of the 1960s (see Box 2.4). The success of the protest movements in Canadian cities highlighted the growing ability of citizen groups to effect change (or stop it) if political conditions were favourable. Christopher Leo suggests that in the 1970s, the "series of citizen uprisings against urban expressway schemes proved partly responsible for the fact that most Canadian inner-city neighborhoods remain largely unscathed by multilane highways."[29] He goes on to state, however, that their success was also due to the lack of available federal funds for expressways. He notes that such efforts have been "sporadic and have been preceded and followed by periods of dormancy."[30]

It was becoming clear that citizens expected to be able to participate politically beyond the ballot box when decisions directly affected their interests. The notion of community or neighbourhood associations was popular with certain groups. Established in a number of places throughout Canada, these associations had little, if any, formal political authority. While these organizations were sometimes given official status, they lacked financial resources, voting powers, and information about internal decision-making processes, and they did not fit well within the decision-making hierarchy of local governments. They did not have much direct political influence as part of the institutional structures.[31] Outside the operations of the municipal institutions, however, another story was developing – particularly in the larger cities.

## 2.4 Activism in 1970s Sherbrooke

According to La Société d'histoire de Sherbrooke, francophone groups did not have the established history of anglophone groups in terms of organizing for social change. Francophone society had tended to work through the Church, acting at the parish level. By the 1970s, however, major community groups emerged in Sherbrooke: one was known as the Association communautaire de Centre-Sud (ACCENTS), based in Catholic community action. Another was the Association cooperative d'économie familiale, concerned with consumer protection. A more radical organization, assisted by the university's social work department, was the Union des citoyens de Sherbrooke. As with many other citizen-organized disputes going on across the country, one of the Union's initiatives was to fight the demolition of the Saint François neighbourhood, which was to be replaced by an urban redevelopment project. The citizen group was known as the Comité de citoyens du Saint-François.

*Source:* La Société d'histoire de Sherbrooke/Sherbrooke Historic Society in collaboration with Le Départment Histoire et Sciences politiques, Université de Sherbrooke, "Community Groups," *Sherbrooke: Deux siècles d'histoire/Two centuries of history (1802-2002)*, CD-ROM.

Many pressure groups, such as Toronto's SSSOCCC or Sherbrooke's less well-known Comité de citoyens du Saint-François, lobbied against city government decisions that would allow developers to demolish established, treasured, urban neighbourhoods. Throughout Canada, political debate coalesced around two competing groups of interests: pro-development advocates versus populist activists fighting to protect the interests of city residents, the working class, and the inner-city poor. While local groups won some high-profile disputes, many more neighbourhoods were lost. City governments were dominated by pro-development ideology and practice.

As the inner-city debates carried on, the sprawling development that was taking place on the outskirts of urban centres also stirred political controversy. Rapidly growing suburbs fuelled the demand for extensive and expensive infrastructure and services, which led to other political debates about the proper allocation of resources between the core and the peripheries. Critics of suburban development ranged from those who wished to prevent the adverse impacts of unbridled development on rural and natural areas to those wishing to protect the vitality of the city centres. Large commercial projects on city peripheries contributed to the erosion of city centres. Shopping centres, big box stores, and, ultimately, mega-shopping "power" centres gobbled up land, resources, and retail dollars. In the early 1980s, the opening of the mammoth West Edmonton Mall offered one of the most prominent examples of the times. Christopher Leo claimed it to be the "prime cause" of inner-city Edmonton's stress.[32] Billing itself as the world's largest entertainment and shopping mall, the complex contained over 800 stores, a water park, an amusement park, a full-sized hockey rink, and a hotel.[33]

Assertions of property rights, the need for revenues, and a rising demand for housing continued to generate outward pressures for growth. Local governments were facing a host of growing and competing demands, many of which were related to land use, but others began to coalesce around social and health issues. At the same time, councils were hampered by diminished provincial grants and limited authority. Local governments' ability to maintain the provision of a number of generally available services was eroding. Governments began to rely more heavily on user-pay practices – fees, licences, and permits – to make up for revenue shortfalls.

## Local Politics at the Turn of the Millennium

Over the course of the twentieth century, local government saw many changes in form and substance. The franchise had been broadened to include all adult Canadian citizens with few restrictions. Many "universal" services were provided for the benefit of citizens. The ability of citizens to participate effectively in local politics, however, was still constrained by economic, legal, and social forces. Local social agencies and neighbourhood groups had limited resources with which to advance their causes, and local governments were also squeezed for resources and looked to the private sector for alternative ways to deliver services. The radical era of the 1960s and 1970s largely gave way to a private-sector-driven ideology in the 1980s and 1990s. Global corporate forces played no small part in local decision making.

Many governments, proclaiming that they were once again "open for business," zealously pursued a business-based agenda that left little room for a meaningful institutional response to the public's rising demands. Cracks in the health care systems and social services, growing child poverty, and emerging environmental problems left many city residents skeptical about governments' ability to respond to public needs.

Diverse communities of interests demanded that they be able to participate more actively in major policy decisions. A not-in-my-backyard (NIMBY) phenomenon gained momentum, along with concerns about the rising scarcity of land and broadening environmental problems. Citizens were prepared to mobilize and adopt pressure techniques in order to influence government decision making that affected their neighbourhoods. Ratepayers insisted on the right to be consulted when a locally unacceptable land use (LULU), such as a waste site or a halfway house, might be located in their neighbourhood. Single-issue groups formed to fight highway development, road widening, or other local initiatives. Different groups representing minority interests lobbied for recognition of their rights to participate in local decisions. Established non-government environmental or social organizations, growing in status and power, often gave their support and resources to local causes. By the 1990s, public participation had become a central theme in politics internationally, nationally, and locally. Speaking of the times, B. Guy Peters stated "This is clearly an age in which government finds it difficult to legitimate its actions without active public involvement."[34]

These developments have not been without consequence. Governments find it difficult to get new policy decisions agreed to and implemented if it looks as though they might cause public protest. Change is also difficult to effect because one group or another might protest local decisions and pursue avenues of appeal through provincial governing bodies. Despite the efforts of some members of the public, however, the turn of the millennium has been a time that does not readily reward political engagement. John Ralston Saul argues that a corporatist, managerial, technocracy has limited the avenues for public participation: "Corporatist society has structured itself so as to eliminate citizen participation in public affairs, except through the isolated act of voting and through voluntary activities. These voluntary activities involve sacrificing time which has been put aside, formally, for other activities. Thus sports, meals, holidays, to say nothing of work, are actually structured into our financial and social reward system. Citizen participation is not. In fact, almost everything we do – except our participation as citizens – is formally structured into our social system."[35]

Some might argue that while this is true, the ability to get one's voice heard through both formal and informal channels has increased in recent years, as has public access to numerous, interactive, communications channels. One study has also suggested that it appears employers and corporations may be giving workers more support for volunteer work.[36] Yet who actually is able to, and does, participate in publicly recognized ways? Those who have the time and resources inevitably become most active in local affairs. Volunteers in civic affairs often consist of the same group of people who serve on a variety of citizen committees. Saul notes that today's society is not structured in a way that would encourage widespread citizen political engagements whether locally, nationally, or globally. The following three Ontario examples suggest that citizen engagement in local government issues can often be a challenging and, sometimes, personally costly exercise.

## Mega-City Toronto: Citizens for Local Democracy

At the end of the twentieth century, some provinces were overseeing the amalgamation of local governments, including ones that took place in Canada's two largest cities: Toronto and Montreal. In the case of Toronto, after tremendous public upheaval and protests, the provincial government imposed the amalgamation of six local governments to create "mega-city Toronto." Composed of 2.4 million people at the time, the new City of Toronto was incorporated on 1 January 1998. A group named Citizens for Local Democracy (C4LD), a number of whose members were veterans of 1970s activism, had unsuccessfully fought a grassroots crusade to prevent the proposed merger. The debate revealed two fundamentally different perspectives about how the institution of local government should be defined and what roles it should perform.

The governing provincial party had adopted an administrative perspective of local government, viewing it essentially as a "creature of the state." Advocates of local democracy held a diametrically opposed view. In his address to C4LD, John Ralston Saul observed, "There is a pattern, a disturbing pattern, a disturbing attitude towards democracy, which has been repeated and repeated by this government. Their attitude is you win a majority and then you can do whatever you want for four years ... A general election is reduced to a manipulative blank check referendum in a Napoleonic tradition ... The truth is, that yes representative democracy is tough, but it's also real and getting a majority is just the first step in the democratic process.[37]

Saul articulated a perspective that is becoming increasingly popular with the public. That is, the democratic process involves more than publicly held elections. It includes open, transparent government, the active engagement of citizens in formal and informal political processes, and a measure of grassroots control over the decisions that most directly affect them. A closer examination of the activities of the C4LD offers an illustration of this view. Before amalgamation, the City of Toronto was known as the Municipality of Metropolitan Toronto, a two-tiered government comprising six municipalities and an upper-tier regional government. The amalgamation was first proposed on 16 December 1996 as Bill 103 by a government that had received the bulk of its electoral support from outside the boundaries of the city and had made no mention of amalgamation in its electoral campaign. The bill received support by groups such as the Toronto Board of Trade and the Homebuilders Association.[38]

As Julie-Anne Boudreau describes in her detailed account, a number of groups were ready to fight against the amalgamation and other "anti-democratic" initiatives. Protesters included social activist groups such as the Metro Network for Social Justice and the Ontario Coalition Against Poverty which was already mobilized in its protest of welfare cutbacks. Toronto was already home top progressive middle-class activists who had a long history behind them in fighting for the preservation of their downtown neighbourhoods and community services.[39] These groups and citizens formed the core of the new social movement entitled Citizens for Local Democracy, led by John Sewell, one-time mayor and long-time Toronto activist. Operating without a formal organization, this loose association of concerned citizens, groups, mayors and councillors, artists, and authors constituted the protest group. A steering committee of fifteen people provided some direction.[40] C4LD coalesced around the issue of amalgamation, but the concern went far deeper, as its members reacted to what they saw as an illegitimate and concerted agenda on the part of the provincial government to undermine local democracy. Moreover, the activists were alarmed at the imposition of a number of "disentanglement" initiatives that would dismantle primary services and undermine the social, cultural, and economic fabric of Toronto while doing little to untangle provincial-local responsibilities. They launched media campaigns and a Web page on the Internet, wrote protest songs, and held well-attended protests and meetings.

The mayors of the affected cities held referendums on amalgamation. Seventy-eight percent of respondents voted against the initiative. The turnout of 31 percent was consistent with voting patterns at municipal elections.[41] From the beginning, the provincial government proclaimed the referendums not legally binding and announced that it would disregard the vote. It did, and it pointed out a number of voting irregularities. One citizen's group (Toronto Citizen's Legal Challenge) and five of the six municipalities launched a legal action arguing that amalgamation without the consent of the affected municipalities was constitutionally illegitimate. The argument was based on the conventional practice of "reasonable autonomy" for local governments, and it was bolstered by references to the federal Charter of Rights and Freedoms. Although it was critical of the approach taken by the government, the Ontario court ruled that the provincial government was within its constitutional rights to amalgamate the cities.[42]

If the success of the C4LD movement is to be measured in terms of stopping the provincial Harris government from amalgamating Toronto or imposing its sweeping "common-sense revolution" agenda, then it failed. On the other hand, the C4LD initiative revitalized the debate over local democracy, stimulating many people to take part once more in civic politics. C4LD and the efforts of other related coalitions trailed off after the amalgamation fight, but some initiatives and connections were maintained and have continued on various social and political fronts.

Julie-Anne Boudreau noted that this C4LD was an important "insurgent form of political action" but not one that would maintain momentum in many of the participants' lives. Importantly, it failed to win active participation from youthful groups that did not identify with municipal institutions or with groups that did not share the same progressive or urban middle-class values. Many other participants in the movement, however, viewed municipal institutions as important means by which to challenge the other levels of government. Boudreau observes that "this focus on the constitutional and institutional framework worried other C4LDers because it prioritizes formal challenges of participation in the state such as electoral reforms and rules of procedures over political activity in civil society."[43] In her conclusion, Boudreau writes, "Democracy, as I use it here, is not only a question of accountability and adequate representation, but rather a day-to-day practice of public debate located in every corner of society. Politics takes place in both the 'formal' and the 'informal' realms of politics, but also in everyday life, in the tiny actions that shape the city ... The city is a key site of politics. However, it also takes place within a broader structural and conjunctural context that defines new institutional arrangements and a new political terrain."[44]

The C4LD issue illustrates the tension between those who believe that a stronger, more autonomous local government is the route to a more democratic society, and those who feel that it is more effective to focus on a broader society-centred notion of governance. This dynamic not only plays out in the metropolitan centres of the country; the debate about the most appropriate forum for democracy can happen in remote regions and smaller towns, as the next two cases suggest.

## NIMBY: Toronto's Waste and the Adams Mine

Activism in rural regions of Canada emerged in much the same fashion as it did in large urban centres. While the issues may vary, the fundamental concern about lack of local control and the types of strategies employed to achieve influence are very similar.

In the 1990s, northern grassroots groups formed a movement to oppose the economically and politically powerful metropolitan City of Toronto and their own elected council on proposals to deal with urban waste. In 2000, Toronto was confronted with the reality that it was running out of room at its Keele St. Waste Management site. It decided to ship its residential waste to the abandoned Adams Mine in northern Ontario. The area was suffering economically from a series of mine closures and needed alternative sources of revenue. Proponents of the project saw this waste proposal as an opportunity to bring much-needed revenue to the North.[45]

The majority of the councillors at the nearby communities of Kirkland Lake and Englehart supported the project (except for the mayor of Kirkland Lake). Many citizens of the region (extending to the Quebec side of Lake Timiskaming), however, vehemently fought the proposal through large rallies in the North, energetic campaigns, and a journey south to occupy Toronto City Hall when the debate to approve the proposal took place. They were concerned about possible aquifer contamination throughout the region if polluted groundwater seeped out of fractured rock in the mine. Other communities were worried about the transporting of waste by rail from Toronto to the North.

"Not in my backyard" (NIMBY) is a common phenomenon that frequently occurs when it comes to determining where to dispose of waste. In this case, the scope of the project, the revenues involved, public reaction, and political fallout were all of sizable proportions. Diverse groups banded together. The Adams Mine Intervention Coalition was formed to fight the proposal and included environmental organizations, members of northern communities, and local First Nations (Timiskaming First Nation). Support came from sympathetic politicians, including some from Toronto City Council, as well as from environmental organizations and citizens from outside the region. According to one report, "one of the most divisive municipal debates in recent memory took place" as Toronto City Council debated the proposal for four days.[46] The extended debate was accompanied by procedural delaying tactics by some councillors, and by angry protests from citizens. On 11 October 2000, the city council voted by a margin of 32-24 to send the trash to the abandoned Adams Mine, but only with amendments intended to absolve council of liability. One of the most important amendments was that the RCN private-sector consortium, not the City of Toronto, would be financially responsible for any unforeseen legal changes during the twenty years of the contract, including regulatory changes that might raise the costs of operations. Because of the economic and political risks involved, the deal fell through, and Toronto decided to truck the waste south to Michigan. (That raised a new set of issues for potentially affected communities.)[47]

Some declare that this particular failed deal signalled a victory for the coalition of groups and citizens that opposed the Adams Mine proposal, demonstrating that a coordinated activist approach can change the course of events. This could have been the case, but one editorialist offers an alternative analysis. He suggests that the final result may have had more to do with economic considerations, and that the business plan had never made sense when there were other lower-priced alternatives.[48]

The Adams Mine debate raises important political questions about the roles of elected councillors in a representative democracy and those of citizens who wish to participate actively in decisions that vitally affect them. Who should decide the issues? Northern citizens, operating outside of their elected councils, proved themselves capable of mobilizing to effect change when they were able to draw on a broad base of support. Their efforts stimulated a lengthy debate in Toronto City Council that led to a careful examination of the proposed deal and the subsequent amendments. Will such citizen participation be seen as a legitimate representation of the public interest, even though it is unclear what segment of the population they represent? On the other hand, should a few municipal councillors be entrusted to make an important decision for thousands of northerners when they might not have been elected by a majority of the population?

From the perspective of this chapter, it is interesting to note that many citizens did not view the initial adoption of the waste plan by the northern municipal councils as a democratic decision. At one rally, a member of the provincial legislature, David Ramsay, claimed, "This is not just a war over garbage. This is a fight for democracy."[49] In this version of democracy, conventional decisional approaches of local governments are no longer considered legitimate actions. As in the mega-city debates, the issue was raised whether local governments can be viewed as legitimate representatives of citizens.

## Centre Wellington and the Cost of Citizen Protest

In the latter half of the 1990s, the Ontario provincial government imposed a series of amalgamations on various cities. At the same time, local governments found themselves short of revenues to fulfill existing and new responsibilities. Municipalities scrambled to find ways to make up the financial shortfall. On 25 February 2000, the newly amalgamated town of Centre Wellington (population 24,000) announced that it could establish a racetrack and accompanying slot machines as one way of generating much-needed revenue. Many citizens were opposed to the idea and formed the Centre Wellington Citizens Coalition (CWCC) to fight the move, and they gathered over 2,000 signatures on a petition to reject the proposal.

The CWCC's Web site describes the following sequence of events. The town held a public meeting on 29 March to discuss the subject. The next day, the council voted by a slim margin (with the mayor casting the deciding vote) to make the required zoning change and amendments to the city plan to allow for the construction of the facility. In Ontario, citizens have the right to appeal municipal planning decisions to the Ontario Municipal Board (OMB), an appointed tribunal that, among other things, has the authority to hear appeals on municipal planning decisions. The CWCC did so, and 100 people, acting on behalf of the CWCC, made an application to the Superior Court saying that the public consultation process was flawed and did not give citizens adequate time to make representations. The Court determined that the process was less than ideal, but that the municipality had acted in good faith. The CWCC took the issue to the Court of Appeal, which ultimately dismissed the case. The OMB also dismissed the appeals against the racetrack.

Meanwhile, another municipal election was held. Two of the three incumbents who supported the racetrack lost the election, while the third won by a narrow margin. The mayor also won but was not supported by the citizens of the former village of Elora. The council decided to sue the citizens (who took the case to court) in order to recover the municipality's costs, estimated at over $86,000.[50] Political scientist Alan Cairns says, "The proposal to sue 111 members of the Centre Wellington Citizens' Coalition for over $85,000 is an unacceptable affront to democratic principles. The same process that supports the election of the Mayor and Councillors also supports the democratic right of dissent from their decisions, including resort to the courts. To punish individuals financially for acting as public spirited citizens is an abuse of power."[51]

The implication that citizens can be sued by their own city council when they try to appeal a government's decision poses some fundamental challenges for local democracy. Such actions can certainly serve to chill possible participation of civic-minded individuals if they believe that they may be financially penalized for their efforts.

## Global Forces and Local Governance

In this integrated economic world, some analysts are skeptical that local governments are or, for that matter, ever were capable of promoting a democratic environment. Janine Brodie, for example, has dismissed the notion that they ever played a democratic role. She argues that this view is not grounded in reality and says that there is no "obvious linkage between the local and the democratic."[52] Moreover, she asserts that the oppositional perspective that is sometimes presented – local forces resisting the global pressures – denies the reality that the "local" actually forms part of the global neo-liberal phenomenon sweeping the world, and does not sit apart from it. Brodie uses Robertson's term *glocal* to characterize the new phenomenon.[53]

Anti-globalization forces may point to grassroots examples that could influence local politics and governments throughout the world. Brazil saw the city of Porto Alegre host the World Social Forum in 2002 as an alternative to the World Economic Forum. Activist Naomi Klein reports that Porto Alegre represents part of a growing decentralist movement in Brazil. Many cities, such as Porto Alegre, have adopted a citizen-based "participatory budget." Klein reports that "through a network of neighbourhood and issue councils, residents vote directly on which roads will be paved; which health-care centres will be built. In Porto Alegre ... rather than scaling back on public services for the poor, the city has increased them substantially. And, rather than spiraling cynicism and voters dropping out, democratic participation increases every year."[54]

As Klein notes, the system is far from perfect. It also may not represent any significant change in the dominant patterns of decision making as they are shaped by global economic forces. Nevertheless, this example, as well as others closer to home, do suggest that local politics and activism can influence how resources are distributed and to whom. Certainly for those residents in the city who benefited from the institution of the people's budget, developments of this kind would imply a connection between democracy and the local government. The Porto Alegre project captured the imagination of a group of Toronto citizens, who initiated a call for 10 percent of Toronto's budget to be allocated on the basis of a community participatory initiative by 2010.[55]

What about the formal local institutions themselves? Brodie asserts that the local level of government does not represent a form of decentralized power and, therefore, cannot serve to enhance democracy. Instead, she notes that local governments are now being subjected to an "offloading" of responsibilities by senior governments, pressure to privatize government services (giving over formerly publicly decided responsibilities to the private sector), and significant fiscal constraints. She suggests, for example, that Alberta's revised 1995 Municipal Government Act, which is touted to have decentralized authority to the local level, is rather more an act of deconcentration. The initiative is not one that is "empowering, democratic or responsive to local needs and demands"; rather, the process of privatization and fiscal restraint only serves to increase inequalities at the local level.[56]

Caroline Andrew concurs that economic globalization has strengthened the influence of the private sector and that the concept of "local must be understood as being fully part of the global."[57] She notes, however, that there are times when civil society can have an influence on municipal government. She uses examples concerning the way in which the increased role of women in local government has influenced local changes. She also points to cases where recognition of multiculturalism has led to policy changes at the local level. These kinds of examples, she suggests, tell us that the results are not necessarily pre-determined: "Progressive local action is not easy or obvious, but it is not precluded by the working out of globalization."[58] As the earlier case examples illustrated, local activism exerted in the name of democracy takes place in the largest of urban centres, as well as those located in more physically isolated parts of the country.

These kinds of debates, that question local government's ability to act as a democratic representative of its citizenry, raise the issue of how the public can actually contribute to local decision-making processes. As the next chapter discusses, the means by which the public can participate ranges from the relatively passive exercise of becoming informed about local issues to active involvement in helping to shape and implement public policy.


## Conclusion

Early local government in Canada was not founded on broadly held philosophical beliefs in the democratic value of self-government. Rather, colonial rulers established some local institutions to achieve effectiveness, efficiency, and order to advance British economic in-terests. To the extent that local governments were given authority, it was vested in the municipal corporation, and not in an association of self-governing citizens.[59] Local gov-ernments were never meant to be autonomous governing units but vehicles of the state whose purpose was to provide economic and political stability.

In the nineteenth century, both the role of local government and people's rights to participate were narrowly defined. Aboriginal peoples, women, minority groups, and the poor were usually legally shut out of formal local political processes; it was a system that favoured those who brought economic and political clout to the decision-making arena. The progression of time saw the continued domination in city politics of business and propertied interests, as illustrated by our discussion of Kitchener's political development.

A North American reform movement emerged as a reaction to corruption and mis-management throughout the established American and Canadian cities, but the agendas of these reformers still favoured middle-class and business interests. The reformers man-aged to establish orderly approaches to the delivery of services and helped to introduce well-run, efficient government processes. At the same time, they contributed to the nar-rowing of the political scope of local governments by attempting to ensure that govern-ments operated as business-like enterprises.

The activism of the 1960s and 1970s, present in large cities such as Toronto and smaller cities such as Sherbrooke, made it clear that local politics and democracy, at least to some people, was about more than voting at election time. A society-centred view of democracy was beginning to take shape as critics questioned the ability of formal local government institutions to advance democratic goals. This underlying theme was very much present during the mega-city Toronto and Adams Mine disputes. In fact, as the case of Centre Wellington suggests, local councils sometimes may take decisions that could work to suppress participatory democracy.

Now, at the beginning of the twenty-first century, adult citizens meeting certain requirements (such as residency) can participate in formal political processes, including voting and running for office. A closer look, in Chapter 3, at some of those formal processes will explain how citizens can effect change. It also considers the various ways in which members of the public can be constrained from participating in local political institutions.

# 3
# Avenues of Participation in Local Governance

> Democracy refers to a form of government in which citizens enjoy an equal ability to participate meaningfully in the decisions that closely affect their common lives as individuals in communities.[1]

Popular conceptions of democracy, such as the one above, now encompass a broader understanding of public engagement in political affairs than was the case earlier in Canada's history. Individual citizens can participate in local governance in a number of ways. The best known is by voting for city council members, mayors, and representatives in other local governing bodies. Elected representatives are ultimately responsible for the decisions made by local governments, although, in practice, a number of actors influence the process. Many would argue that voting is one of the most important political responsibilities of an individual citizen. Citizens may also participate by voting on a referendum or plebiscite, running for office, individually communicating with a member of council, attending an open house offered by the city, or making a petition to council. Beyond this, individuals can volunteer their time on a number of local boards, committees, and commissions. Citizens can also belong to business organizations, professional associations, or community and neighbourhood organizations that, in turn, will liaise with government.

As noted in the previous chapter, if citizens feel that formal institutions do not represent their interests, they will work outside or around the local government. For example, members of the public can become active politically through indirect or informal means, such as through the media by writing a letter to the editor, setting up citizen Web sites, or participating in public rallies that are geared to gain widespread attention.[2] Citizens might also participate as members of pressure groups or social movements. This activity can take the form of a short-lived, single-issue initiative, such as when citizens try to stop the expansion of an expressway, the demolition of older houses, or perhaps the establishment of a halfway house. Longer-term, more institutionalized groups may act as watchdogs on behalf of socially and politically marginalized groups, downtown business interests, or the natural environment. Recognizing that vocal members of the population wish to participate actively in local decision making, some local governments are devising new consensus-based consultative processes to gauge and respond to public concerns.

## Public Participation in Local Government

The formal route to influencing local political agendas is through the electoral process. Electoral systems vary considerably across the country. The structure of those systems plays a significant role in determining who gets elected and what groups of interests are going to be the most influential on local agendas.

## Voting Eligibility

The right to elect one's government freely is considered a hallmark of democracy. Yet the ability to actually participate in the voting process is restricted by a number of factors, although much less now than in the early days of municipal government, when only property owners could vote. At various times in Canada's history, women and members of ethnic minority groups were not given the vote. In Quebec, women did not receive the right to vote provincially until 1940. This restriction also applied municipally except for widows and adult unmarried women who owned property. In the case of married women who owned property, however, their husbands voted on their behalf.[3] In Saint John, New Brunswick, on the other hand, women were allowed to vote in 1921 if they owned property, but it was not until 1946 that women without property could vote municipally. Today, the right to vote in city elections has broadened considerably. Although the rules vary somewhat, in general, a voter is required to be a Canadian citizen 18 years of age of older, who has lived in the city or province for a particular period (generally from several months to a year).

## Plebiscites and Referendums

Plebiscites or referendums are a form of direct democracy not common in Canadian federal and provincial governments but used more frequently in municipal governments in some parts of Canada.[4] The laws vary considerably across the country, and many are undergoing changes. In various jurisdictions, such as Quebec and British Columbia, municipalities have been obliged to hold a binding referendum when a council wishes to pass a borrowing bylaw. In Prince George, BC, for example, the most recent referendum question put to voters was in 1993. The city wanted to borrow money for the construction of a multi-use "Multiplex" arena and a new swimming pool complex. As the topic concerned a borrowing bylaw, it was considered a binding referendum. The citizens voted in favour of the development, funding was approved, and Prince George built the multipurpose complex.

In New Brunswick, referendums have been used when borrowing exceeded 2 percent of assessed municipal evaluations. In other provinces, sometimes only public notification is required.[5] Plebiscites, some binding and some only consultative, have been held on a variety of topics, often dealing with well-known contentious public issues, such as education, Sunday shopping, fluorides in water, proposed municipal amalgamations, or the building of large municipal facilities. In some jurisdictions, citizens can petition to hold a referendum. An argument could be advanced that these types of voting processes are the most democratic form of decision making. With referendums, an individual has the opportunity to directly vote on a particular issue that has been placed on the public agenda.

One must ask, however, how and why that particular issue got on the voter's agenda in the first place. A number of questions come to mind. Is the issue truly one that concerns most of the population or simply one of interest to a number of influential actors, such as the media, a powerful lobby group, or the governing elite? Who gets to choose which issue is important enough to merit a referendum? What other issues are being overlooked or downplayed in the process? Who crafts the wording of the question? Direct democracy can be anything but direct, and it is an instrument that can be easily manipulated by small groups of people with political, information, or economic resources. Louise Quesnel notes that the use of the referendum does not foster the emergence of the common interest. Rather, it is an instrument "suitable in a system of adversarial democracy when attempts at consensus have failed, when opposing views are irreconcilable and when only the mathematics of vote-counting will lead out of the impasse."[6]

One small community of less than 4,000 people, Rossland, BC, decided that the referendums should be used more frequently in order to hold local council more accountable for their decisions. André Carrel, who was the chief administrative officer of Rossland at the time, was instrumental in designing a referendum bylaw that the community subsequently adopted (see Box 3.1). In a book on the topic, Carrel addressed a number of the questions raised about the possible adverse implications for democracy of such a bylaw. He acknowledges that putting bylaws to citizen vote raises a possibility of a "tyranny of the masses." He also observes, however, that "if there is a legitimate concern that citizen empowerment would lead to the suppression of a minority, that concern is not alleviated by empowering a governing elite elected by the feared majority."[7] Louise Quesnel cautions that in the United States, where referendums are used much more frequently, experience has shown a "danger of individualistic and self-interested mobilization for referendum votes on the part of longtime residents and property-owners, at the expense of newer residents and to the detriment of innovation in urban planning.[8]

Finally, concerns might be raised about the possible adverse implications of referendums for representative democracy. Average citizens may not have the time, interest, or level of civic education required to make informed decisions about all the important political decisions that come their way. Political representatives are elected to become informed and knowledgeable about the broader concerns of the community and to understand the implications of their decisions. They have ready access to information and a large administrative support structure to assist them in understanding the context of their decisions. Direct democracy, as such, does not address these considerations. Advocates of referendums, however, might retort that the decisions made by the elected elite do not necessarily respond to the needs and concerns of the broader constituency either. Jack Masson, in his observation of Alberta municipal politics, points out that the representative electoral system, with its lack of a party system, falls far short of linking the electorate with public policy.[9] He suggests that there is a need for some other procedure that would allow the voter to exercise some choice. He concludes that the use of the plebiscite should be expanded rather than restricted because it is "a mechanism that allows the citizenry to have a direct input into the policy-making process and to make grassroots democracy work in the larger municipality as well as the smaller one."[10]

## 3.1 Referendums and Rossland's Constitution Bylaw

The small town of Rossland, British Columbia, adopted a municipal Constitution Bylaw based on a 1990 discussion paper written by its chief administrative officer, André Carrel. The bylaw calls for a referendum provision to be included before the fourth and final reading of any bylaw. This provision allows for a petition to be presented to council, if it is supported by 20 percent of registered voters, that calls for a referendum. The results of that referendum would bind the councillors to the outcome. In November 1990, the Constitution Bylaw received 65 percent voter support in a referendum. While the municipal government did not have the actual provincial legal authority to adopt a "municipal constitution," it decided to do so anyway and run the possible risk of court challenges should any arise.

The first test of the bylaw came when council wanted to give itself a raise. A petition was presented, a referendum was held, and the public rejected the raise. Another small BC community, Pitt Meadows, attempted the same process, but this time the issue was over a major land-development deal. The threat of lawsuits hung in the air while legal opinions advised that the referendum bylaw was illegal. Ultimately Pitt Meadows abandoned attempts to adopt a Rossland-type referendum process. As for Rossland, Carrel reports that during the first decade that the referendum bylaw had been in place, referendums overturned five and supported eight council decisions.

---

*Source:* André Carrel, *Citizens' Hall: Making Local Democracy Work* (Toronto: Between the Lines, 2001).

The debate about the value of the plebiscite, in terms of increased self-governance, is far from resolved. There appears to be more support for the mechanism in the western provinces, in both the literature and in governments, where plebiscites are used more frequently. Ultimately, whether this form of direct democracy contributes to a more democratic local environment will depend on how plebiscites are wielded, how the debate is framed, who decides the questions, and what the political context is. A plebiscite, for example, might be a very useful mechanism to help council gauge public opinion when they are determining whether to invest millions of dollars in a large sports facility. It may be difficult to use such a process to make more complicated decisions that are not easily reduced to a simple, closed question. Long-term land-use planning is a case in point. In these situations, some other public consultative mechanisms would be more appropriate.

## The Electoral Process: Electoral Systems and Boundaries

In general, local candidates for council are elected for a three- or four-year term on the basis of a ward system, an at-large system, or some combination of the two. The *ward* system operates with one or two councillors (formerly known as aldermen) elected from a specific territory within a city. *At-large* elections present all voters with the same set of councillor candidates who, if successful, are elected to city council to represent the views of all citizens in the city (see Box 3.2).

The type of electoral system does have an effect on the composition of council and its representativeness. For one thing, city-wide campaigning can be expensive. Moreover, as Jim Lightbody has explained, "For city politicians, elections at large generally favour the interests and political resources of business, certain of the professions, and upper-class civic reformers; smaller, block, wards benefit local community leaders, some single-issue pressure groups, neighbourhood ratepayers' associations, and political activists with a left-progressive bent. Heterogeneous 'strip' wards are modest compromises with the overall business advantages of at-large elections ... Vancouver remains the single major Canadian city still conducting civic contests city wide."[11] In the 2002 election, voters in Vancouver were asked to elect one mayor, up to ten councillors, up to nine school trustees, and up to seven park commissioners.[12] As Higgins once noted, it is difficult for the voter presented with so many choices to get to know and understand the positions of all the candidates. This situation also gives the incumbents an advantage over candidates running for the first time because their names will be familiar to the voters.[13]

On the other hand, the ward system has its share of problems, including many for which it was known historically. Ward-based politicians may be interested only in advancing the interests of their own area at the expense of the broader community, and such a system could also lead to divisive political debates. Difficulties might also arise in determining the appropriate ward boundaries. A mixed system with some at-large councillors and ward councillors tries to arrive at a compromise between the ward and the at-large system. A number of different systems are in place throughout Canada.

## 3.2 Electoral Systems for Choosing a Council, 2003

*Prince George, BC:* An at-large system is used to choose a mayor and eight councillors.

*Kitchener and Waterloo, ON:* The two cities are in the Region of Waterloo. The City of Waterloo has five ward councillors to represent the five wards in the city. Kitchener has a total of six councillors and six wards. Elections also take place for the upper-tier Region of Waterloo council.

*Sherbrooke, QC:* Since the 1 January 2002 amalgamation, the city council is composed of one mayor and nineteen city councillors representing different electoral districts in six boroughs.

*Saint John, NB:* An at-large system is used to choose a mayor and ten councillors. A deputy mayor is appointed by Common Council, determined by the number of votes received in the municipal election.

## Party Politics in Local Government

One of the distinguishing features of Canadian municipal governments, as opposed to the provincial or federal governments, is that they are not based on a party system of representation. Crawford once suggested that this might be a result of "over concentrating" on American experience. He noted that other countries, such as England, introduced a party system because of administrative complexity and the need for program continuity. It was suggested that these objectives were considered more easily carried out through a party-based organizational system rather than by a group of independent councillors.[14]

From the perspective of strengthening democracy, Masson has argued that it would be easier to hold a governing party accountable for its actions at election time, rather than an assortment of individual candidates who stand for a mixture of issues. Masson also notes that parties could increase the diversity of representation and "appeal to diverse socio-economic components." He also suggests that a party system would generate a higher level of political participation. Individual candidates do not have to pay for their own campaigns; parties have more resources. Moreover, the electorate may become more interested in an election where a clear platform is presented (for example, one that emphasizes development versus one that focuses on the protection of green spaces or the concerns of low-income groups).[15]

A quasi-party system has emerged in some of the larger Canadian cities. In part, this reflects the difficulty citizens have in trying to develop a close personal interaction with the various candidates, due to the size of the electoral boundaries and the large population base of big urban centres. In these situations, it is easier for a citizen to know which candidates to support if the latter agree on a common platform. Some advocates of a party system suggest that a civic party system introduces an element of competition and choice to local elections that would otherwise be dominated by one group of decision makers, particularly in an at-large electoral system.

In many cities, municipal political organizations are active at election time. Urban business interests frequently get together to support a set of pro-development politicians. That move often stimulates the rise of anti-development civic parties that are usually populist in orientation and include community protest groups and social activists. Anti-development activists have traditionally supported provincial and federal New Democratic parties. While other federal and provincial parties have not played an overt role in civic elections, many of their active members will often participate locally as well, although not under their party banner.

The general lack of formal local political parties might be attributed to the anti-politics and anti-corruption campaigns that characterized politics in the early part of the twentieth century. As discussed earlier, many civic-minded citizens considered party politics at the local level quite undesirable. Moreover, given the common administrative view that local governments should be viewed merely as efficient service providers, "politics" had no place in the municipal corporation, and parties should be left to the senior levels of government.

This was certainly the case in Vancouver when the Non-Partisan Association (NPA) was formed in 1937 in the first at-large city election. Gutstein says that "it was a corporate model of civic government, with council, as the board of directors, representing the ratepayers. The function of council was to provide services in a financially sound, efficient manner. The main activity for the 'party' was to find the best candidates for civic office – usually successful businessmen."[16] Although it had dubbed itself a non-partisan organization, the NPA successfully dominated local elections for thirty years. In 1968, new parties emerged to challenge NPA dominance and called for a more livable city. In 1972, the moderate TEAM (The Electors Action Movement) finally managed to displace the NPA. That election may have represented a time in which voters had become disenchanted with the development agenda; it must be noted that in subsequent elections TEAM lost its momentum and support, and the NPA regained its popularity with voters and once again reasserted its dominance on council (see Box 3.3).[17]

In the November 2002 elections, the Coalition of Progressive Electors (COPE), with its long history of promoting a social platform, won a majority of the seats, including that of mayor. This was the strongest showing in COPE's history. Some have attributed the win to public concerns about drug and social problems on Vancouver's East side and to a reaction to the provincial Liberal government's business-driven agenda.[18]

Montreal also experienced the emergence of a civic party system where development versus anti-development sentiments helped shape the debates. Mayor Drapeau's long-dominant Civic Party, which was linked with huge development projects, found itself facing its own set of challenges in the early 1970s. The Montreal Citizens' Movement made up of a coalition of citizens and groups, was concerned about the Civic Party's lack of attention to quality of life and housing issues. In their analysis of local governments, Graham, Phillips, and Maslove caution, however, that one should not too readily classify Montreal's party system along the lines of pro- and anti-development forces. The fracturing and merging of parties since the 1970s, as well as shifting internal dynamics, suggests that class, geographical, and language cleavages contribute to a complex political system that is not readily reducible to one civic issue.[19]

Other large cities, such as Calgary and Edmonton, have had their historic share of quasi-party activity, although they do not have party systems. Masson suggests that the lack of a formal party system in Alberta was attributable to a militant labour movement during the early reform movement era that turned the citizenry against a party system. After the Winnipeg General Strike in 1919, for example, organized labour called for a general strike in Edmonton. As both Masson and Lightbody observe, however, the actions of the labour movement mobilized conservative business interests to form quasi-parties in Edmonton. This initiative was "spawned by the business community both as a device to promote civic and business boosterism and as a response to labour's efforts."[20] Throughout

## 3.3 Civic Party Politics in Vancouver

In Vancouver, the development of a city party system has had an interesting history, which includes the development of an association that claimed it was non-partisan (the Vancouver Civic Non-Partisan Association, or NPA). The NPA was formed in the late 1930s as an alternative to party politics in local government. According to its literature, the NPA is opposed to party politics on the elected boards of the city and claims that a diversity of candidates is encouraged to participate.[1]

The NPA, however, is very much viewed as a party by another group of citizens, who formed the Coalition of Progressive Electors (COPE) in 1968. COPE claims that the NPA represented "a very specific set of pro-development interests." COPE sees itself as offering a clear alternative, claiming to be a progressive party that has an interest in protecting neighbourhoods and promoting low-income housing. To that end, COPE believes that it represents "economic groups at the opposite end of the spectrum from the NPA. COPE has drawn its membership, finances and support from labour, small business, professional groups, the middle class and community groups."[2]

In addition to the NPA and COPE, other recent Vancouver civic parties have included the Vancouver Organized Independent Civic Electors (VOICE), the Green Party Political Association of BC (Green Party), and the Labour Welfare Party.

---

1 Vancouver Civic Non-Partisan Association, "NPA Election 1999," http://www.npa.bc.ca/ (accessed 9 March 2004).
2 Coalition of Progressive Electors, "History," http://www.cope.bc.ca/index.cfm/fuseaction/page.mainsub/pageID/ C2E5FBCE-D262-4C44-AA8B59139BECC8E4/index.htm (the About Us link from the home page, http://www.cope.bc.ca/).

the twentieth century, quasi-parties would appear from time to time in Edmonton and Calgary. Masson refers to such organizations as *alphabet parties* because of the use of acronyms, such as Edmonton's CGA – the Civic Government Association.[21] According to Lightbody, the CGA, once known as the Citizen's Committee, was predominantly comprised of business interests. Its members presented the CGA, and its successors, as non-parties – an approach that worked well at election time. The organization's influence was reinforced by the city's business approach to administration, the at-large system of government (which was later replaced with a ward system), and the absence of a well-coordinated opposition.[22]

Urban parties may appear, on the surface, to share characteristics similar to those of a parliamentary party. The structures of local governments, however, are not constituted in a way that would facilitate party politics like those found in parliamentary governments, where majority-based cabinets usually confront an official opposition. In parliamentary systems, the party that wins the most seats forms the government, and the party that comes in second forms the official opposition. Parliamentary parties also choose their leaders at a party convention, and personal advancement depends a great deal on the favourable disposition of the majority leader, who chooses the cabinet ministers.

This is not generally the case in civic politics, particularly those without any form of party system. Mayors, for example, are not leaders of a party; the population elects them at large. Councillors are accountable to the voters, not to the mayor. In Manitoba, during the early 1970s, the provincial NDP government did try to introduce a measure of partisan politics into Winnipeg city politics by restructuring the local government. The 1971 Winnipeg civic election saw thirty-one NDP candidates running for membership in the newly constituted fifty-one-seat council, but only seven were elected.[23] Higgins has noted that neither civic culture nor the local government structure is well suited to the open participation in local affairs of a national or provincial party, although members of these parties may become involved behind the scenes during civic elections.[24]

## The Role of Mayor

In Canada, the mayor, elected to office by popular vote, is a member of the governing council as well as the head of the municipal corporation. Not all local governments have mayors. The title varies according to the local structure in place. For example, regional governments are steered by a *chairperson*, Aboriginal band councils may be governed by *chiefs* (with the guidance of the community), and *reeve* has been a commonly used term in a village or township. The responsibilities in each of these positions vary somewhat, although the general responsibilities of the mayor remain essentially the same throughout the country. The primary functions are to preside over council and maintain order; act as ceremonial leader of the community; sign all bylaws and ensure they are carried out; effectively communicate information to the council, the administration, citizens and other parties, and other governments; and ensure the effective management of the corporation.

The ability of a Canadian mayor to exercise authority and take decisions is limited compared to the *strong mayor* approach of some American cities. Nevertheless, the mayor may develop considerable informal power and ability to shape political agendas. In some exceptional cases, the assumed power has been considerable, as was observed during the tenure of Mayor Jean Drapeau of Montreal, who led the city from 1954 to 1957 and 1960 to 1986. Timothy Thomas recounts how Drapeau's vision of a world-class city was to be achieved through grand construction projects such as the metro, Expo '67, and the Olympic Games. His government directed funds away from a number of services to citizens and constrained democratic participation: "In the late 1960s and early 1970s most members of city council were Drapeau's handpicked candidates, a fact which ranks him among the most powerful of urban political figures and which contributed to his ability to treat Montreal as little more than a site for his personal dreams of glory ... One example is the Civic Party's short-lived initial decision to avoid holding meetings (by law only required four times a year)."[25]

While Drapeau's autocratic administration was atypical and offers an extreme example of the influence a mayor might exert, it does serve to underline the role that a mayor can play in shaping political agendas. Certainly, where a party system is in place in the larger cities, the mayor can prove to be very powerful. Drapeau, for example, chose from his own supporters an executive committee of council composed of the mayor and six councillors. This executive operated as a tremendously influential body. It had the power to present many of the motions to council and to set agendas, and it exercised considerable discretion over finances, budgets, zoning, taxation, and administration. Much of the city government's power was concentrated in the hands of a small group of people.[26]

Other mayors have much less power and influence over council, particularly where there is no quasi-party system. Nevertheless, all can lay claim to one of a mayor's most powerful tools – access to information. The ability to network is a very important attribute in anyone wishing to influence political agendas, and mayors have access to extensive formal and information-communications networks. The mayor has ready access to other influential political actors, including the premier of the province, provincial officials (assuming the relations are cordial), and many of the leaders of private and public organizations. An able mayor also has valuable access to financial and administrative information about the municipal corporation, and to communications with members of the community. Lynne Woolstencroft, mayor of Waterloo at the time of writing, suggests that the role of mayor is more influential than a formal description might suggest (see Box 3.4).

A deputy mayor also will be appointed to fill in for the mayor. Traditions of appointment vary. In a number of cases, the deputy is chosen on the basis of votes received in a general election.

## The Role of the Council

The elected municipal council, as a whole, possesses the legal powers delegated to it by the province. These councils may range in size from a few individuals to over fifty in large

## 3.4   The Role of Mayor, City of Waterloo, Ontario

Lynne Woolstencroft, former mayor of the City of Waterloo, Ontario, describes her experience of the mayoralty, October 2001.

When starting to knock on doors, I remember vividly people's surprise as they realized there was an election coming up and that a mayoral candidate would knock door-to-door. I had grand dreams about how to shape the city. They took the opportunity to talk about stolen lawn ornaments; gutter and roadway problems; wild animal infestations; and sidewalk repairs. *Nothing* that had preoccupied the council or the media came up that first night on the campaign trail.

In the first week of my mayoralty, once again the juxtaposition of expectations surprised me; a stream of mid- and senior-management staff who request time to discuss administrative challenges and staffing issues were balanced against the number of ordinary citizens with a torrent of advice, complaints, criticisms, and observations. Councillors needed personal time with the new mayor. The media wanted sage commentary. And *every* thought and remark seemed to measure the impact of the city's activities on the property tax rate.

I still want to think and talk about how the city will look and feel twenty years from now; others appear to think more about immediate issues, especially taxes.

The Municipal Act limits the power of the mayor to chairing meetings. In practice, the mayor can be much more. Why? Because the mayor is at city hall more often than any other politician; and, in our ward system, is the only city-wide politician, and is, therefore, aware of issues before others. Why else? Because daily and weekly, the mayor is invited to myriad activities and events and, as a result, is the most visible member of council. Personifying the city, the mayor can establish priorities, expedite or impede the progress of matters. Through visibility, accessibility, and personal drive, a mayor can influence the public agenda.

metropolitan areas. Councils can pass bylaws and resolutions within the limits laid down by provincial legislation. Such powers might include authorizing the funding for a new municipal project or other hard or soft services; authorizing changes to property bylaws (within the confines of the Official Plan) as well as bylaws dealing with a number of municipal matters, such as the restriction of smoking in public places; or regulating public use of parks or development of city transportation policies. Council also must approve administrative appointments to the offices of the clerk, treasurer, and manager or chief administrative officer, and it must pass bylaws governing terms of appointments. Councillors also regularly participate in a number of standing committees that have been delegated some responsibilities (see Chapter 10).[27] Councillors meet with other groups and with members of their constituencies; they bring issues of local concern to the attention of the appropriate governing body; they serve as sources of information, either through the media or by responding directly to the inquiries of citizens (at home and at city hall); and they make and attend presentations, attend the opening of new public facilities, schools, and parks, as well as attending numerous other public functions. It can be a very time-consuming job. It does, however, allow an individual to have a direct influence on public affairs.

David Siegel offers an example of council influence. He suggests that, in the case of small towns in particular, all the council members who know each other socially may meet informally before public council meetings to discuss the issues and decide the important questions. Public meetings are then held to ratify the decisions made in secret. Low public interest in civic politics also can result in limited media coverage of the city beat. Siegel notes, "In this environment, the council takes on the flavour of an old boys' club. It consists almost entirely of white, middle-class males ... With no serious opposition or even careful observers, a homogeneous group of councillors can sometimes forget that the municipal council is not their private club."[28]

It is debatable whether this is a trait primarily of small local governments. Ample evidence suggests that the politics of large political machines exhibit similar tendencies in North American cities, as well in more senior levels of government. Nevertheless, Siegel makes a valid point about the homogeneity of city councils (and about the lack of representation of diverse members of the community).

## Special-Purpose Bodies

Beyond running for mayor or council, an individual can serve in a number of other locally elected positions. These local agencies, boards, and commissions may include school or library boards, public utilities, and police commissions, among others. These special-purpose bodies are at arm's length from the municipal government and have their own budgets, mandates, and elected officials. From the point of view of efficient delivery of services, it can be argued that these boards are able to focus on the task at hand without worrying about competing political agendas interfering with their mandates, and that they are more flexible and responsive. Concerns about the lack of accountability, the fragmentation of responsibilities, and the weakening of the overall effectiveness of municipal government have stimulated a fair bit of debate about the effectiveness of these special-purpose boards and about their adverse impact on local democratic processes. As discussed in more depth in Chapter 10, however, it can also be argued that these bodies open up additional avenues for citizen involvement in public decision making.[29]

## Choosing Representatives: A Democratic Process?

One of the hallmarks of a democratic society is that citizens can choose their leaders or run for office themselves. Yet how representative is the process, if the most likely contenders for office often possess similar views, come from the same socio-economic background, and share ideological perspectives and visions for their cities?

It is certainly true that more members of minority groups and women are now running for office than was ever the case in the past. In fact, from the last two decades of the twentieth century onward, increasing numbers of women have held elected office, particularly at the municipal level in the larger urban centres. It has been suggested that this is due, in part, to the fact that women candidates face fewer obstacles at the local level, compared with provincial and federal politics.[30] Linda Trimble has also suggested that "women become involved in city government because of its profound influence on their lives; that is, women choose city politics because it is powerful in ways that matter to them."[31] In 2002, for example, both the City of Waterloo and the City of Saint John had women serving as mayor. Yet in our mid-sized, case-study cities (and elsewhere around the country) women are still significantly underrepresented on council (see Table 3.1). This is also the case with visible minority groups, an imbalance particularly noticeable in the larger cities.

TABLE 3.1

**Women on council in case-study cities, 2003**

| City or region | Total councillors and mayor | Female councillors |
|---|---|---|
| Saint John | 11 | 1 (mayor) |
| Sherbrooke (including councillors from all boroughs) | 24 | 5 |
| Kitchener | 7 | 1 |
| Waterloo | 6 | 1 (mayor) |
| Prince George | 9 | 1 |

*Sources:* All above information was drawn from city Web sites on 6 Jan. 2003. City of Waterloo, http://www.city.waterloo.on.ca/; City of Kitchener, http://www.city.kitchener.on.ca/; Ville de Sherbrooke, http://ville.sherbrooke.qc.ca/; City of Saint John, http://www.city.saint-john.nb.ca/; and City of Prince George, http://www.city.pg.bc.ca/.

Barriers to participation in elected office are still very real, and many of them are related to economic or social status. Even with the improvements, ethnic minorities continue to be underrepresented in cities today. Many immigrants – despite Canada's vaunted multicultural policy – face considerable challenges that include finding adequate housing and schooling, learning English as a second language, dealing with social discrimination, and obtaining adequate employment. In her analysis of the 1993 Vancouver municipal election, where only two of ten councillors were visible minorities, Abu-Laban notes that these groups are consistently statistically underrepresented and argues that stereotyping and discriminatory practices still appear to be contributing factors.[32]

Many women also face barriers to participation, particularly poorer single mothers. Finding time to participate in political life must come after taking care of basic necessities. One cannot assume necessarily that municipal political life generates many issues that are of direct interest to citizens concerned primarily with daily survival. Such people will have very different priorities from those that preoccupy a city council. For example, the issue of downtown parking and its relationship to downtown revitalization has been known to occupy council time in a number of municipalities across Canada. Resolving this issue may be seen as very important to a city's prosperity and economic development. It is not, however, much of a priority for a single parent who is more concerned about access to daycare for her children or homecare for an aging parent. With its narrow legal mandate and heavy reliance on property revenues, municipalities traditionally have not been as preoccupied with providing such soft services; to a large extent, these historically have been the responsibility of provincial governments. It is not surprising, then, that it is well-established members of the middle class, and often those in the business community, who are most likely (although certainly not exclusively) to run for office. They are the individuals who are most likely to identify with many of the issues dealt with by local governments.

Questions of effective representation are also influenced by the issue of who has the time and resources to run for office and who has the connections to raise funding and establish a team of supporters to run a campaign. In an attempt to generate a more equitable opportunity for people wishing to run for office, some provinces place legal limits on the amount that can be spent on a campaign. These limits are often based on the number of people on the electoral list.

For example, the Quebec Election Act allows an individual running for mayor to spend a base amount of $5,400 and then $0.42 for every person for the first 1,000-20,000 on the electors list, $0.72 for the next 20,001-100,000 registered, and finally $0.54 for any above 100,000. The amount allowed for councillors begins at $2,700, to be increased by $0.42 for every additional individual listed on the electors list above 1,001.[33] Ontario also sets limits on the amount of money that a candidate can spend on a municipal campaign.

In contrast, the provinces of British Columbia and New Brunswick do not specify any limits on municipal campaign election expenses. This omission can lead to questions about conflicts of interest. For example, the November 2002 Prince George municipal election was dominated by discussions about a possible connection between campaign donations and the council agreeing to rezone and sell municipal lands. The land was to be sold to relocate a gambling casino. According to the local paper, four members of council who voted in favour of selling the land to the casino owner had received campaign contributions from the owner in the previous election. Three councillors opposed to the sale had received no contributions from the businessman.[34] The casino owner was also purported to be a friend of the city's mayor, who favoured the sale. It is unclear from the available evidence whether or not any persuasive connections can be drawn between these events. The issue does highlight, however, how campaign contributions can raise questions about conflict of interest issues, as well as concerns about the openness of the electoral process. Political scientist Norman Ruff was reported as agreeing that one must be careful when drawing conclusions from campaign contributions. He was also quoted as saying, "The safest cliché to fall back on is that contributions make for good listeners."[35]

James Lightbody has discussed other ways in which the expense of running in city elections considerably narrows the pool of candidates for office. People who can afford to contribute financially in a substantial way to an election campaign come from a narrow segment of the population. They are less likely to be interested in supporting a candidate who does not reflect at least some of their own needs and desires. This limits the diversity of individuals running for local government and reduces the scope of civic debate. Lightbody writes that in the 1983 mayoralty campaign in Edmonton, Laurence Decore, the senior advisor to the successful candidate, had suggested that the candidate be wary of soliciting funds from developers. The response was that "there are basically no other sources."[36]

Obviously, there are times when a popular candidate does win office and is not well connected with the established elites. Campaign limits have been set, and a reasonable amount can be raised through numerous small donations. In this way, the advantage of the economic or social elites can be circumscribed. But as Clarence Stone has noted, this kind of win does not necessarily mean that the wealthy no longer have a systematic advantage: "Once the highly visible election campaign is over, officials display a marked preference for involving upper-strata interests in planning and formulating policy proposals ... In a similar vein, there are indications that mayors *elected* with strong lower-strata support nevertheless feel constrained to form policy alliances with business interests."[37]

After Vancouver's 2002 election, for example, the new council, dominated by a party whose platform was based on social issues, was reported as having decided to reduce business property taxes and shift some of the burden to residential homeowners. "Saying they wanted to send a positive message to the business community, Vancouver's left-leaning city councillors narrowly voted Thursday in favour of shifting a small portion of business taxes to city homeowners."[38]

Although measures to control election campaign costs or to limit the salaries of local councillors cannot deal with those systemic issues, efforts can be made to encourage those running for office to view it as a public service rather than a lucrative career. The

TABLE 3.2

**Remuneration for mayor and councillors in case-study cities, 2002**

| City | Population[a] | Wards | Councillors and mayor | Remuneration per annum[b] |
|---|---|---|---|---|
| Prince George | 72,406 | At-large system | 8 + mayor | Mayor: $76,281<br>Councillors: $19,638 |
| Waterloo | 86,543 | 5 wards | 5 + mayor | Mayor: $53,895.78<br>Councillors: $18,945.02 |
| Kitchener | 190,399 | 6 wards | 6 + mayor | Mayor: $67,448<br>Councillors:<br>$36,000-$38,000<br>(including fringe benefits) |
| Sherbrooke | 140,000 | 1 city and 6 boroughs | 23 + mayor (includes borough presidents and councillors) | Mayor: $121,000<br>Councillors: $25,650[c] |
| Saint John | 69,661 | At-large system | 9 + mayor + deputy mayor | Mayor: $57,000<br>Deputy mayor: $22,000<br>Councillors: $19,000 |

a The population statistics often do not capture university and college students. The figures are from 2001 except for Sherbrooke, which shows the 2002 post-amalgamation population.

b These amounts will also vary somewhat with the addition of various benefits.

c Sherbrooke's borough presidents can receive remuneration from $6,156 to $15,390 depending on the number of districts within a borough. Borough councillors, as opposed to city councillors, receive $10,260.

*Sources:* Statistics Canada, Community Profiles, http://www12.statcan.ca/english/Profil01/PlaceSearchForm1.cfm, and information provided by city staff and Web sites.

job of councillor, for example, has historically been viewed as one that is primarily voluntary. Early local government was not large, cities and towns were small, and a number of elected councillors represented a relatively small population. The position did not require a lot of time. Today, councillors are often responsible for increasingly large constituencies (see Table 3.2). More recently, with amalgamations producing ever-larger cites and towns, the roles and responsibilities of the councillor can sometimes require more time than what is normally viewed as a part-time job. Councils of even mid-sized cities, such as the ones in our case studies, are now in charge of large multimillion-dollar municipal corporations and much larger cities. In cities this size and larger, mayors often treat the job as a full-time position, even if it is not always designated as such. They are paid much more than councillors, whose positions are typically viewed as part-time employment.

It should be kept in mind that the salaries of municipal officials are often supplemented in various ways. For example, it has been common practice in many places for one-third of a councillor's salary to be tax free. Other benefits are also often attached to the position. In the Region of Waterloo, the city mayors also sit on the regional council and are compensated for serving in that function as well. Municipal salaries vary considerably across the country.

The issue of councillor salary can readily engage the public's (or the local media's) attention. In 2001, the City of Kitchener's council had given themselves a raise of 60 percent to reflect an increased workload from the provincially imposed reduction of the number of wards (from eleven to seven) and to bring their salaries in line with other municipalities. Although the overall salary was not out of line when compared to a number of other councils throughout the country, the increase became an issue in the local media. As a result, 20,000 people reportedly signed a citizen petition protesting the change. It was also pointed out that in the Region of Waterloo, the local government is a two-tier structure, and many important governing functions are handled by the Region. Council then reduced the increase, in keeping with the suggestion of their own committee, which had been appointed to make recommendations on the subject.[39]

It could be argued that by paying people well it is possible to attract more of a diversity of candidates for the position of councillor. The alternative view suggests that the position should be taken on in the general public interest rather than as a job that would advance the office holder's own personal interests.

## Expanding Civic Engagement

Voter turnout at municipal elections is lower than at the federal or provincial level. Over the past decade, it has tended to average around 35 percent, although the figure will vary depending on the issues of the day. Some elections have registered turnouts as low as 23 percent, while others sometimes reach 55 percent and higher, particularly if there has been a referendum.[40] When an issue does arise that leads citizens to question the decisions of the elected local representatives, many people may feel that councillors do not represent their interests because they did not vote for them. Low voter turnout, then, has an impact on the perceived legitimacy of a governing council. In recent years, local governments have been considering ways of broadening public participation in local affairs.

As discussed previously, traditional participation in local government is often understood in terms of citizens either running for office or exercising their franchise through the representative processes at election time. The electoral system in itself, however, cannot adequately reflect the variety of interests of modern, often heterogeneous, communities. For local governments to act as effective democratic institutions, then, they need to engage a wider diversity of the public in community decision-making processes. The incorporation of a diversity of perspectives and views helps to produce more widely accepted public decisions and to legitimate the local decision-making processes.[41] Citizens may be encouraged to participate in a variety of initiatives, ranging from signing petitions to joining neighbourhood associations; to engage in information exchange with the local government; to participate in consultative exercises or advisory committees; to serve on arm's-length bodies that have received municipal funding; or even to take part in collaborative decision making.

## Citizen Petitions

Beyond voting or running for office, citizens do have some alternatives if they wish to protest something that directly affects their neighbourhood or immediate environment. A parent might take a petition to neighbours requesting a stop sign at a dangerous traffic area near a public school. A retiree might rally her neighbours to protest the widening of a road and the destruction of valued old trees. An unanticipated increase in municipal taxes may cause a ratepayer to protest what he views as an illegitimate decision because the decision-making process was not transparent enough. The proposed establishment of a halfway house in a residential area can become a political matter when residents protest, fearing the possible impact on property values, public safety, the local culture, or the comfortable status quo.

Once the petition is signed, the city is contacted. Staff from the appropriate department, such as planning or city works or others, might be asked to attend a neighbourhood meeting and discuss options. The relevant city department might resolve the matter. Citizens might also present their petitions directly to the council as a whole or to a delegated council committee. This opportunity to present local concerns to council has often been seen as an important part of local democracy (see Box 3.5). Each of our case-study cities, for example, has a broadly advertised procedure about how a citizen might petition council.

As cities become larger, however, there are fewer opportunities for citizens to directly address elected representatives. Citizens may begin to work through other organizations in order to have their interests recognized.

## Neighbourhood Organizations

Local government advisory groups or neighbourhood committees constitute part of a long-standing tradition in Canada. Neighbourhood associations are often active in addressing issues related to recreational activities, the provision of services, community policing (such as Neighbourhood Watch), and quite frequently an association newsletter. A neighbourhood committee has been defined by Pendergrast and Farrow as an organization of citizens with the following characteristics:

- It is recognized as representing a defined neighbourhood or local community of interest.
- It is formally given specific advisory and/or consultative responsibilities by the municipal council.
- It may have a responsibility for taking specified actions on behalf of council.
- It may be recognized as a forum for consultation regarding the interests of the area's inhabitants.[42]

### 3.5 Citizen Petitions and Addressing Council: Case-Study Cities

The City of Waterloo's Web site states that "City Council is the democratic institution and level of government closest to its citizens and provides the most accessible forum for citizens to communicate with their elected officials." That noted, detailed information is provided, telling citizens how they can petition council. Citizen delegations are requested to contact the Clerk's Office on the Thursday morning before a Monday council meeting so that the meeting's agenda might be set. Delegations are given ten minutes to address council, not including questions from council. Council may choose to extend that period.

The cities of Kitchener, Prince George, Saint John, and Sherbrooke use the same kinds of procedures with some minor variations, as in the amount of time one is allowed to address council. At the City of Sherbrooke's council meetings, if there is time available, citizens can also be heard at the beginning or the end of a meeting without being added to the agenda. At the borough level, part of the agenda is routinely set aside for a public question period.

*Sources:* City of Waterloo, "Council Meetings," http://www.city.waterloo.on.ca/CS/Clerks/Minutes/index.html and information from other city Web sites and city staff.

They identify three different models of neighbourhood committees:

- grassroots "bottom-up" neighbourhood committees (common in most communities)
- appointed or elected advisory committees, linked to a community council (such as was the case with Winnipeg's Resident Advisory Groups)
- citizens' boards or councils representing local communities of interest, established by a senior government or a municipal charter (used in New York City in the United States).[43]

In Canada, with the recent amalgamations, rapid growth of cities, and "downsizing" of local governments, interpersonal communication between citizens and their council members has been seriously diminished. Neighbourhood associations have received renewed attention as a possible means by which to engage or re-engage citizens at the local level of politics. As Graham and colleagues noted, Calgary has one of the most extensive and well-organized systems of community associations in Canada (see Box 3.6). The case-study cities also have neighbourhood and community associations.

In Sherbrooke, one distinctive association is known as the Townshippers. The volunteer association was founded in 1979 to represent the minority English-speaking community in Quebec's Eastern Townships. The area was historically one of the few founded by English-speaking rather than French-speaking European settlers. By the end of the twentieth century, their numbers had dwindled, with anglophones constituting only 7 percent of the population (44,000 people). Today, the Townshippers' Association supports community and cultural events and advocates actively on behalf of minority English-speakers in such areas as health, social services, education, employment, and cultural heritage. The latter is actively promoted through a Townshippers' Day, which celebrates the heritage of the area, French-community relations, and community involvement. One major lobbying effort of the association was to ensure that members of the boards of health care institutions would remain elected rather than appointed, as was intended by a new law adopted in December 2002. The association was also active in promoting the interests of the English minority in the recent amalgamations.[44]

## Advisory Committees and Consultative Initiatives
Throughout Canada, local governments appoint citizens to special committees to advise the government on issues of local concern. They may be of a semi-permanent nature, such that after an election, a city will advertise openings on a number of voluntary citizen advisory committees available to the public. The committees might deal with broad policy areas, such as parks and recreation, environment, arts, heritage, or social services. An advisory body may also be formed to deal with a specific project, such as cleaning up a polluted waterway, revitalizing a downtown area, or developing bicycle trails. For example, the City of Sherbrooke decided to develop a working group on pesticides to look at city use in parks and green spaces. The working group was structured to include a city

## 3.6 Calgary Community Associations

Calgary has a well-established system of community associations. The earliest, going back to 1920, focused on issues such as recreational services. While many community associations in other parts of the country did not go much beyond this, Calgary's system continued evolving until the 1940s, when forty-seven community associations formed an umbrella organization – the Federation of Calgary Communities (FCC). In 1961, the FCC was incorporated under the Alberta Society Act and coordinated the extensive initiatives of thirty-seven community associations in Calgary (85 percent of the 137 associations).

The FCC and city volunteers are involved in a huge range of activities, working in active partnership with private- and public-sector organizations in the provision of services. The FCC also represents the communities' interests on a variety of policy and planning committees, and it offers information and educational seminars. The FCC reports that "annually, community association volunteers donated over 22 million dollars in volunteer service. These dedicated volunteers come from a widespread base with over one-quarter of the city's population supporting their community association through paid membership."

*Source:* Federation of Calgary Communities, "FCC History," http://www.calgarycommunities.com.

councillor, a citizen with a demonstrated interest in environmental issues, staff from municipal and other government organizations, a representative of the pesticides industry, a member of the farmer's union, and a representative from the Coalition for Alternatives to Pesticides.[45]

Beyond that, some advisory groups are recruited to participate in one-time "visioning" exercises that make recommendations for the future of the city; these exercises have taken place in many cities throughout the country, including ones entitled "Compass Kitchener" and "Imagine Waterloo." Citizens have many such opportunities to participate in consultation exercises and committees established by local governments. One does, however, have to apply and to have some qualifications, if only a well-developed, and often publicly recognized, knowledge of a topic. These qualifications are reviewed by city council or staff, who then determine who would be a valuable addition to the committee.

The City of Sherbrooke engaged in such a consultative initiative at the level of the boroughs (a lower-tier administrative structure of the municipality of Sherbrooke). The boroughs, which were introduced in place of the former cities, were established to help deliver services and to ensure responsiveness to local needs. In the fall of 2002, the City of Sherbrooke introduced a public consultative initiative, held within each borough, in order to receive feedback about how to encourage citizen participation in the new city (see Box 3.7).

## Government Funding and Grants to Civil Society

Members of the public also participate in local governance through groups and non-profit organizations that receive funds from local government but operate at arm's length. This means that they are responsible for making decisions about their operations and organization, but they receive funding from local government (often from provincial and federal governments as well) and from private donations to provide local services. As with the advisory committees, the range of activities is broad, dealing with a variety of social and environmental aspects of the city. Women's groups and organizations have been very active at the local level and have received various types of government funding.

Toronto's Metropolitan Action Committee on Violence Against Women and Children (METRAC) is a case in point. The group was initiated in 1982 by a group of Toronto women who approached the former chair of Metropolitan Toronto to take action to stop assaults on women. A task force comprised of government bodies, community agencies, support services, and individuals recommended the establishment of METRAC, to be governed by its own board of directors. METRAC takes a broad interdisciplinary approach to problem solving, and it networks with many other related community-based organizations, all levels of government, and professional legal and health services. It attempts to educate and advise members of the public, as well as government decision makers at all levels.[46] In 1993, the City of Toronto introduced a grants program (providing almost up to a million dollars annually) entitled "Breaking the Cycle of Violence." Community groups

## 3.7  The Borough Summits in the City of Sherbrooke

One of the major concerns about the amalgamation of cities into one larger city was the loss
of autonomy. The mayor of the new City of Sherbrooke had pledged during the election campaign that he would respect the autonomy of the local communities and work to preserve
their cultures. He initiated a consultative process with the presidents of Sherbrooke's six
boroughs in order to hold the "Borough Summits." The goal was to make contact with the
citizens and other stakeholders who signed up to participate in the summits, to provide information about the new city and the role and responsibilities of the borough councils, to listen
to the "expectations and concerns of the participants" in order to deliver the best policy decisions, and to "mobilize people to work together for the greater good." The summits were
held in the fall of 2002, resulting in recommendations for improved areas of service and
recommendations of various ways to include citizen participation in the new city.

*Source:* Ville de Sherbrooke, Communications Division, *Info Sherbrookois,* Municipal Information Bulletin 15, 5 (October
2002): 2-3.

working on behalf of vulnerable groups or trying to prevent violence against women can receive grants from this program.[47] Other cities provide funding to similar programs, such as Ottawa's Women's Action Centre on Violence Against Women. Provincial and federal governments also provide funding for local groups. Quebec's "Egalité pour décider" grant program (initiated in 1999) has provided $1,000,000 for five years in annual funding to women's centres and groups across the province to encourage women's participation in local and regional government.[48]

Beyond the well-established programs that receive yearly funding, other local groups may receive specific project-based grants for such things as sports or cultural events or limited assistance for programs ranging from social assistance to multicultural activities, among others. The aim is to assist those organizations that are perceived to be of benefit to the city.

Non-profit organizations look to local governments to provide much-needed funds, particularly in an era of fiscal conservatism. The movement toward alternative service delivery (that is, having non-government organizations handle the task) is one approach to dealing with public dissatisfaction with government-delivered services. Some people are concerned, however, that these organizations lose their autonomy and independence because they have to conform to government specifications to receive grants.[49] A reliance on non-profit organizations to deliver services once provided by the state can lead to un-even service provision and an unstable funding base. In addition, one Canada West Foundation survey of non-profit, social service organizations in the four western provinces notes that government funding is often accompanied by strict reporting requirements and service-delivery rules. This situation limits innovation, flexibility, and community responsiveness – all qualities for which non-profits are valued.[50] Although the survey revealed that non-profits often had good relationships with government agencies, the dependence of non-profits on government raises some serious questions about the actual role of these quasi-independent organizations vis-à-vis their relative independence and ability to respond to the needs of civil society. These problems plague many aspects of local government partnerships and collaborative forms of decision making.

## Challenges of Collaborative Decision Making

Collaboration is defined as the process by which the diverse interests that exist in a community are brought together in a structured process of joint decision making. Often, third parties are involved in helping facilitate agreement ... Collaborative decision making is linked to efforts to prevent disputes, to involve everyone in decisions before conflicts arise, to manage ongoing differences, and to settle disputes that threaten the health and cohesion of a community.[51]

Citizens who feel disaffected by the political process because it does not address their sets of needs, or because they feel it to be corrupt or ineffective, are reinforced in these perceptions by the media, who act as watchdog of local council. Along with the growth of ready access to information through the media – broadcast, print, and Internet – public cynicism has helped stimulate some governments to look for new ways to shore up their legitimacy. One of the avenues that elected councillors have taken has been to include the public in collaborative decision-making processes.

Traditional methods of participation fall well within the umbrella of the decisional view of government, where the role of elected representatives is to be the final arbiter of the public interest and to take decisions.[52] Citizens may vote, but in the end, councils decide. Policy processes that include the public, however, are becoming a fairly widespread phenomenon. These processes generally take the form of discursive round-tables, where citizens come forward as individual volunteers, or are nominated by a community of interest, or are recruited by local governments. Peters observes,

> In this version of the participatory state, advocates argue that public decisions should be constructed through a dialogical process permitting ordinary citizens to exert a substantial influence over policy. The public interest thus will emerge through the creation of processes that enhance the rights of citizens to say what they want from government. Citizens should be able to bargain directly with other citizens who have different views about the appropriateness of public policies as well as able to bargain directly with government bureaus. This "discursive" view stands in clear contrast to the "decisional" approach more characteristic of traditional representative and bureaucratic government institutions.[53]

The past two decades have seen a wide array of consultative initiatives. These have included the use of a few selected members of interest groups or "experts" to provide advice to governments, advisory committees, civic forums or roundtables, and "virtual roundtables," in which the Internet is used to educate the public and solicit feedback. Peters suggests that those who favour a more participatory state and would include citizens in substantive public decision processes are making a clear break with the decisional model of representative, accountable government. In the participatory approach, the public interest is thus created through citizen-based forums that bargain with each other and with government representatives. In contrast, in "the decisional view the capacity to produce decisions, rather than the ability to create consensus is the characteristic mark of governance."[54]

Extensive consultation with citizens and interest groups also means that once those exercises have taken place, it is politically very difficult for governments not to adopt, or at least appear to take seriously, the recommendations of that public consultation. To do so, governments must find policy and administrative mechanisms to coordinate their own activities with other departments and governments in a way that constitutes an acceptable response to those diverse constituencies. This objective is not easily achieved. The more broadly inclusive the initiative, the more difficult it becomes to reach and implement timely policy decisions. Yet, it could also be argued that a process will be seen as illegitimate if it only includes select members of interest groups.[55]

These consensus-based processes often involve diverse communities of interest, including government representatives. Roundtables have been employed regularly by government decision makers in order to resolve contentious political issues over public resources. Much of the literature suggests that these roundtables, or public consultation processes, serve to make policy processes more accountable, transparent, and democratic. Roundtable processes are used by governments to remove the perception that decision making is controlled by a narrow elite and to enhance the legitimacy of the governing processes. In addition, it has been argued that such participation improves the decision-making process. Stephen Owen, former commissioner of the British Columbia Commission on Resources and Economy, has suggested that "representative government can be supplemented effectively with greater public participation by drawing on the best of both direct democracy and sectoral-interest negotiation.[56] As yet, Canadian institutional and governing processes are ill-equipped to deal with competing public pressure on decision-making processes that are still formally governed by hierarchical, decisional, representative structures. Roundtables and consensus-based processes will, and often do, flounder if they do not have effective administrative or political support.

## Conclusion

Citizens can participate in local politics in a variety of ways. The early formal barriers that prohibited certain groups of adult Canadian citizens from running for office or from voting have been largely removed. Mechanisms have been introduced to facilitate public participation. The use of referendums, with all its attendant challenges, is receiving growing attention by those who wish to encourage that form of public input. In western Canada, it is a well-known method used to consult the public, as in the case of Prince George, where citizens voted in favour of spending funds on a large recreational complex.

The larger urban centres have seen the introduction of quasi-parties in order to let the voters distinguish between candidates on the basis of electoral platforms. It is not always the parties dominated by private-sector interests that win – in Vancouver's 2002 election, councillors representing an association (COPE) concerned with grassroots housing and social issues swept into municipal office. In some provinces, campaign spending limits are in place, which can help to limit the advantages of wealthy or well-connected individuals over candidates of lesser means – at least at election time.

When an issue has become publicly salient, such as through the public media, council will often listen to public sentiment and respond to it, as was the case with the Kitchener councillors' salaries issue. Many governments, including those in all of our case-study cities, have introduced public consultation forums and roundtables, from time to time, to try to respond to demands for more citizen participation in decision-making processes.

Despite these developments, significant groups of society are still effectively disenfranchised. It is not easy for someone to participate in a local council unless the individual has other means of support with flexible working hours. Getting elected still requires help from people well connected to the political process and ready with financial backing. Women and minority groups are still noticeably underrepresented. As cities continue to grow or amalgamate – gaining physical size while diminishing in representational capacity – prospective candidates new to local politics face daunting odds, as the competition becomes stiffer. Finally, marginalized citizens have little incentive to try to participate when they already have a low sense of efficacy and little extra time for civic affairs. Local government, with its traditional preoccupations, will not hold much interest for those individuals who have different sets of concerns. Those who do wish to participate may find that their concerns are not high on the list of institutional priorities, particularly when it comes to issues that have not captured the local media's or broader public's attention.

Participation in local politics, however, can also take place outside the formal governing institutions. Such participation may be realized through cultural, volunteer, or leisure-oriented associations. Activism, social movements, and the mass media all provide avenues for influencing political agendas through alternative methods.

Citizens can, and do, participate in local politics in a host of ways. The ability to govern ourselves as a whole depends very much on how well formal and informal political processes capture and respond to the concerns of a diversity of societal interests. Local political systems do respond over time to changing public demands; they have managed to support a reasonable quality of life for many Canadians. That said, it must also be acknowledged that conventional participatory processes favour economically and socially advantaged individuals. The obvious corollary is that Canada has its share of disadvantaged groups and individuals. Given these constraints, it is apparent that local democracy is an ideal that is much more elusive for some than others. It is also important to recognize that even if they were so disposed, local governments themselves are constrained in their ability to govern by the legal and constitutional limits imposed on them by provincial governments. It is to this topic that we now turn.

Part 2    Shifting Responsibilities:
         Intergovernmental Relations

KITCHENER CITY HALL

Canada's governing institutions operate within a federal system of government. Formal authority is shared by two orders of government, the national or federal government, and the ten provincial and three territorial governments. Jurisdictional powers between the two orders of government are enumerated under Sections 91 and 92 of the Constitution Act. Local governments fall under the jurisdictional authority of provincial and territorial governments, which have the authority to pass legislation regarding municipal affairs. First Nations governments, sometimes referred to as a third order of government, have distinct sets of legal and institutional arrangements reflecting their unique role in Canada.

Municipalities have often found themselves constrained by the decisions of higher levels of governments. Today, the vast majority of Canadians live in large cities with municipal governments that often lack the resources and authority necessary to meet the multiple demands and needs of their citizens. For their part, active groups of citizens are pressuring for more responsive governments that are receptive to increased public involvement in decision making. Some provincial governments have responded by revising pieces of legislation with the putative goal of giving municipalities an ability to make some more decisions autonomously and to form partnerships. Provincial governments, however, retain strong overriding authority in many areas of local affairs. Moreover, federal-provincial wrangling – a feature of politics throughout Canadian history – has left little negotiating room for municipal governments that, to a great extent, must rely on lobbying to achieve concessions from the higher orders of government.

**4**
# The Evolution of Provincial-Local Relations and Municipal Government

Early on in British Canada, colonial authorities dictated the governing framework for local government. The goal was to ensure a stable polity and a reliable economy. Later, provincial governments assumed that role. Local business and governing elites helped to maintain that status quo, ensuring that the administrative affairs of municipal institutions would complement the goals of local economic development and growth. As local government spread westward across Canada, local political agendas contained little of interest to those who were socially or economically marginalized or those whose interests did not coincide with the growth-oriented agendas of the day. There were, however, a few exceptions to elite-dominated local politics. Rural agrarian populism, for example, revealed a lively sense of civic engagement by self-educated farmers who kept themselves informed about the important issues of the day and actively contributed to community political life. For the most part, however, it would be an unusual occurrence in nineteenth- and early twentieth-century politics for decision makers, and perhaps for citizens themselves, to spend much time pondering what was meant by local democratic self-government.

## Atlantic Provinces

Early inhabitants of Canada were by no means united in wanting municipal government. More government meant more taxes – an unwelcome prospect. Under the French regime, the Acadians of New Brunswick and Nova Scotia did not have any form of local government.[1] The rapid influx of Loyalists from the United States led to the 1785 incorporation by royal charter of Canada's oldest city, Saint John, New Brunswick. Loyalists have been widely credited with bringing with them the practice of the town hall meeting and introducing a notion of local self-government. As discussed in Chapter 2, however, this form of self-government would not be viewed as democratic in present-day terms, and it certainly was not universal. One analyst has suggested that Loyalists were more influential in establishing local government in what is now known as Ontario than they were in New Brunswick. H.J. Whalen has noted that, outside of Saint John, local government was slow in coming to other towns in the province.[2] By 1851, a municipal act was eventually passed that would allow for municipal incorporation, in part because of a growing provincial deficit dealing with local expenditures. The Legislative Assembly, however, still largely controlled municipalities.[3] By 1877, this all changed with a municipalities act that required the incorporation of towns throughout New Brunswick. In an ill-considered move to bring together rural and town government, city representatives were given a place and vote on county councils, but rural councillors had limited, if any, influence when it came to the cities. This situation caused problems in the rural areas because their needs were very different from those of the cities. For the most part, rural residents saw the move as a "hideous invention to extort direct taxes from the people."[4]

Nova Scotia's first municipal charter was granted to Halifax in 1841. Despite the opposition of a number of rural residents, the provincial government implemented the County Incorporation Act of 1879. It divided all of rural Nova Scotia into districts to be governed by a council and warden. Nine years later, the Towns Incorporation Act of 1888 was passed to deal with the growing urban municipalities.[5]

Like New Brunswick, Prince Edward Island was once part of Nova Scotia, becoming a separate province in 1769. The tiny island province had no great need for more decentralized forms of government, although it did see the incorporation of both the province's capital, Charlottetown, in 1855, and Summerside in 1877. The Towns Act was passed much later, in 1948, in order to provide consistent standards for town charters. The Village Services Act followed in 1950.[6]

Municipal government came late to Newfoundland and Labrador. Although St. John's, the provincial capital, is the first known European settlement in Canada, it was not until 1888 that it was incorporated as a city with 30,000 inhabitants (at a time when the provincial total was 203,000). As an incorporated city, St. John's was responsible for providing some services, such as water and sewerage, and for relieving the colonial government of the financial responsibility (and some self-incurred debts). The wealthy elite controlled the councils, as both voter and electoral candidates were subject to stiff property qualifications.[7] After some governing misadventures and a disastrous fire, the council was abolished and replaced by a commission appointed by colonial authorities. St. John's finally obtained city status in 1921.[8]

Outside of St. John's, rural inhabitants were suspicious of local government, quite reasonably viewing it as a means by which the wealthier members of the colonial elite could impose taxes. Citizens received little by way of local democracy and opportunity for self-rule. Municipal government evolved slowly. Provincially appointed trustees governed local improvement districts (areas with low population density). Democratic, responsible government was suspended in Newfoundland and Labrador during the Great Depression of the 1930s because the colony was on the verge of bankruptcy, and Britain reassumed governing authority through the establishment of a joint commission that was to be accountable to British authorities – not to the citizens. Outside of St. John's, no municipalities existed until 1938, when the Town of Windsor was incorporated. Responsible government was once again achieved in 1949, when the citizens of Newfoundland and Labrador voted to join the Canadian confederation.[9] That year also saw the passing of a Local Government

Act, soon to be followed in 1952 with the Community Councils Act. By the mid-1950s, the province had 53 municipal units.[10]

## Central Canada: Quebec and Ontario

Until the British assumed control in 1763, a mostly French-speaking rural population inhabited Quebec (a former French colony). The Roman Catholic Church dominated political and social life. After the 1763 Treaty of Paris, a proclamation established new political and administrative structures. As noted in Part 1 of this book, one of the few regions of Quebec whose first European settlers did not come from France was the Eastern Townships. Loyalists, New Englanders, Irish, Scottish, and English immigrants comprised a majority of the population.

With the exception of Montreal and Quebec City, Quebec remained a rural province for much of the next two centuries. By the nineteenth century, Quebec was still predominantly francophone, although British immigration brought a significant increase in its English-speaking population. In the Eastern Townships, 58 percent of the region's population were English speaking in 1861 (90,000 people; a number that had diminished to 44,000 by the end of the twentieth century).[11]

Montreal became Canada's centre of finance, and the headquarters for many industries. Dickinson and Young note that by exploiting the advantages of their British and continental networks, anglophones were able to control much of the province's economic resources.[12] French Canadians were often relegated to less lucrative occupations, being employed as manual labourers, tradesmen, or workers in the resources sector, or being self-employed in small businesses. Many continued to work as farmers in rural areas.[13]

Up to the time that Montreal was incorporated with its own charter, magistrates governed through issuing local ordinances.[14] The new city charter was proclaimed in 1833, and with it came municipal elections. During a time of political turbulence and armed rebellion, however, the charter expired and the city reverted to magisterial rule. The city was granted a new charter in 1840 under the governor general of the United Province of Canada, and during this period English speakers dominated the economic and political centres of the city. That said, the position of mayor usually alternated between French and English speakers, a tradition that was also practised for many years in the City of Sherbrooke. Nevertheless, Quebec municipal government was primarily an English institution and was modelled after those structures rather than those of the French regime.[15]

By the twentieth century, anglophone municipalities were well established in some urban enclaves. Company towns throughout Quebec were also divided along linguistic lines, with anglophone managers living apart from the largely French-speaking workforce in their own separate sections of town. Farming was losing its predominance, and other industrial activities proliferated in the primary and secondary sectors, leading to a more urbanized society.[16]

In Montreal, during the early part of the century, suburbs were springing up all around, some of which the city annexed during the early 1920s. Anglophones began to leave the city to create English-speaking suburban municipalities, such as Baie d'Urfé, Beaconsfield, and Mount Royal. At the same time, French-speaking people started leaving their rural occupations and moving into Montreal in large numbers, resulting in a linguistic shift towards French in the city.[17] This linguistic segregation based on territorial boundaries persisted throughout the twentieth century, setting the stage for what was to become a source of contention decades later when the government of Quebec moved to amalgamate Montreal and many other areas, including the City of Sherbrooke, by January 2002.

Originally, local governments, by default, were responsible for delivering services that the more senior governments later took over. In the early days of Canada's history, right through the first few decades of the twentieth century, for example, it was customary for cities to provide whatever public social assistance was available in those times. The cost of these services was thought to be a cause of Montreal's financial downfall in 1940.[18] The city declared bankruptcy and the provincial government put it under trusteeship for four years.[19]

Smaller cities, such as Sherbrooke in the Eastern Townships, also rapidly urbanized in the early part of the century. Sherbrooke capitalized on the military industrial requirements of the First World War, offering low-price electricity to businesses willing to locate in the city. Numerous textile and other industries became established in the area. With economic expansion came population growth, forcing the municipality to improve its social and health services. During the Depression, the city developed a well-organized aid network, employing workers to improve the municipal infrastructure and parks. Garden plots, firewood, and charitable assistance were made available to individuals who found themselves unemployed. The Second World War revived the economy, industry, and the labour movement, which was no longer prepared to accept very low wages for workers.[20] After the war, the development of the welfare state saw the funding and delivery of many social and health services become the primary responsibility of the more senior, rather than local, governments.

The province of Ontario had its own distinct legacy that informed provincial-local relations. As in eastern Canada, many United Empire Loyalists emigrated to Ontario, a number from New York (hence Toronto's former name of York). After the division of Quebec into the provinces of Upper and Lower Canada in 1791, pressure from the Loyalists led to some local elections that resulted in a few limited responsibilities being delegated to elected town officials.[21] Hamilton was incorporated in 1833, and Toronto was incorporated in 1834, one year after Montreal (see Box 4.1). At that time, Toronto was less than one-third the size of Montreal, but it quickly grew to economic and political prominence in the heavily settled area of southern Ontario.

Toronto's first mayor was William Lyon Mackenzie, and the city's early exercises in "self-government" were not very impressive by today's standards, as can be noted in the following story told by John Mitchell: "Among his duties, the mayor sat as a magistrate in

SHIFTING RESPONSIBILITIES

## 4.1  The Incorporation of York (Toronto)

Prior to its incorporation, Toronto (then known as York) was an unorganized hamlet without taxes to pay for municipal services. The conditions of the times were reported to be "unbearable." The local aristocracy pushed for incorporation, and the first city council, with twenty members, was elected in 1834. From then on the city burgeoned, as John Mitchell relayed in his lively account of the times:

> For Muddy Little York, the horn of progress had sounded. Industry, Intelligence, and Integrity had climbed aboard the coach. Crack went the whip of higher taxes, the horses of industry sprang into their collars and the City of Toronto was on its way to glory. Steam engines were then being installed to supply industrial power. The population increased from 4,000 in 1832 to 15,000 in 1842. After a long struggle and many trials, Toronto had established itself as the commercial and industrial centre of the province.

*Source:* John Mitchell, *The Settlement of York County* (Toronto: Municipal Corporation of the County of York, 1952), 79.

the police court, and the last person to stand in the public stocks at Toronto was a woman sent there by Magistrate Mackenzie for throwing her shoe at his face in open court. The members of Toronto's first council borrowed money from the bank on their personal endorsements, promising to repay it out of a higher tax levy. The proceeds were used to lay plank sidewalks. The irate property holders seized their first opportunity to vote Mackenzie and his followers out of office."[22]

The colourful politician and journalist Mackenzie was also a member of the Legislative Assembly for York and leader of the Upper Canada Rebellion in 1837, which resulted in his exile in the United States. The rebellions in Upper and Lower Canada ultimately led to the establishment of the Durham commission, and its report called for responsible government in the reunited Canadas (see Chapter 2). By 1840, it was clear that the colonial system of districts governed by justices of the peace and Courts of Quarter Sessions was rapidly becoming outdated.

## The Baldwin Act, 1849

After the reuniting of the Canadas, two new acts were introduced in Ontario: the District Councils Act (1846) and the Municipal Corporations Act (1849). The Municipal Corporations Act – also known as the Baldwin Act after its founder Robert Baldwin – established the foundations for the system of local government that was to prevail throughout the next 150 years. Robert Baldwin, born in York, Ontario, came into politics as a reformer like his father before him. He was a keen advocate of responsible government and an influential member of the Legislative Assembly. He vociferously promoted French-English cooperation. Baldwin and Louis-Hippolyte La Fontaine formed a coalition government on two occasions in the 1840s. The second coalition government, from 1847 to 1851, saw the establishment of the Municipal Corporation Act. From this initiative came instructions for setting up councils and rules for elections, financial responsibilities, local administration, and public accountability.[23]

One innovation that generated endless academic debate as to its utility more than a hundred years later was the introduction of a two-tier system of government. An upper-tier county level of municipal government was made responsible for all local governance except in those areas where a lower tier of incorporated cities and separate towns possessed their own elected councils. The innovations of the Baldwin Act not only set the blueprint for local government in Ontario, but they were influential elsewhere in Canada. This was particularly the case with western provinces that had yet to develop their own municipal institutions.

## Western Provinces

The early settlement patterns of western Canada were greatly influenced by the fur-trade empire of the Hudson's Bay Company and the transcontinental Canadian Pacific Railway

(CPR). The Hudson's Bay Company was interested in promoting the fur trade, not permanent settlement. As such, municipal government was slow to arrive.

From 1914 to 1950, urban growth was dominated by five cities: Winnipeg (in Manitoba), Regina and Saskatoon (in Saskatchewan), and Calgary and Edmonton (in Alberta). Artibise notes that city politics was largely controlled by small, commercial elites. These elites encountered little by way of opposition, and citizen participation was a notion that would not attract much attention until after the 1950s.[24] The common practice and preoccupation was civic "boosterism" of one's own city, which fostered rivalry among urban centres. Boosterism, a notion by no means confined to the Canadian west, equated civic duty with economic growth and material prosperity. There was little room in this ideological mindset for alternative views, concerns of the working poor, or labour unions. Plainly put, in this view, the role of local government was to foster urban growth.[25] This approach prevailed throughout the Depression, and Artibise observes that while essential services and relief were curtailed, boards of trade continued to receive tax concessions.[26] This business approach left an indelible mark on the future direction of Canadian local government.

The province of Manitoba was created in 1870 from Rupert's Land, formerly owned by the Hudson's Bay Company. The County Assessment Act and the Prairie Assessment Act were passed in 1871 at the first meeting of the provincial legislature. The goal of this new legislation was to raise money from residents for small local improvements.

Winnipeg soon became the major provincial centre. Located at the junction of the Red and Assiniboine rivers, the former fur-trading post was transformed in 1812 into the first permanent settlement in the area by a group of Scottish immigrants. In 1873, Winnipeg became a newly incorporated city (population 1,869). Its city charter was modelled after Ontario's municipal structures, and James D. Anderson suggests that this was the case because it was the "nearest established system" and, in part, because many influential settlers in Winnipeg came from Ontario. He notes that many of these Ontario-born individuals would become members of the local political and economic elite, sitting on local councils and western boards of trade.[27] When the city was first established, Winnipeg's mayor was elected at large, and three aldermen were elected from each of four wards. As for the rest of the province, after trying various other schemes, the provincial government in 1886 took over functions previously performed by judicial boards, and it created a system of basic units of government to divide the province into a number of smaller municipalities.[28]

In 1902, a general province-wide act governed the establishment of cities, towns, villages, and rural municipalities, while the much larger city of Winnipeg retained its own charter. As with other Canadian cities during this era, the arrival of the Canadian Pacific Railway in 1885 was the key to Winnipeg's economic prosperity, as it brought both immigrants and easy access to markets. Winnipeg became the "Gateway to the West" as a financial and administrative centre. High wheat prices fostered rapid growth. The economy, however, stagnated from the First World War on through the Depression and into the 1940s.[29]

The city grew steadily after that, confronting the province with the question of how best to deal with urban growth.

In the territory that later became the provinces of Saskatchewan and Alberta, the North-West Territorial Council passed the Municipal Ordinance (1883). The first municipality created under the new ordinance was the town of Regina, Saskatchewan, formerly known as Pile o' Bones. A few other municipalities were incorporated, while the remaining small, scattered population was provided with limited government through local improvement districts. Saskatchewan grew more rapidly after the late 1800s, when immigrants began arriving in good numbers. By the time it became a province in 1905, Saskatchewan contained 4 cities, 43 towns, 97 villages, 2 rural municipalities, and 359 local improvement districts. New legislation in 1908 and 1909 consolidated the system of municipal government, and for much of the twentieth century, the legislation remained relatively unchanged.[30] Over time, Regina and Saskatoon expanded through annexation. In 1944, the Large School Units Act was introduced to establish 29 large school units covering a remarkable 2,331 school districts.[31]

An adequate understanding of Saskatchewan's politics demands full recognition of the province's critical dependence on wheat production. Its fortunes often rise and fall with changes in the physical, political, and economic climate – factors outside of its control. These factors, among others, led to the development of a local culture that was ripe for the introduction of grain producer cooperatives. As Dunn and Laycock point out, "A healthy distrust of all central Canadian political and economic institutions, as well as a fervent desire to use economic diversification as the basis of indigenous projects of economic self-determination, were thus established as the consequences of a political economy in which power was intentionally retained and extended by the 'imperial centre' in the cities and elites of the St. Lawrence Valley."[32]

Saskatchewan's populist culture, desire for local self-government, and practical necessity led to some creative local initiatives. For example, in the early 1930s and 1940s, it was difficult for rural Saskatchewan to attract and retain physicians. As a solution, many communities established a program whereby the municipalities paid physicians regular salaries for their services. The scheme worked well for both doctors and patients. By 1944, one-third of Saskatchewan's municipalities had doctors on their payrolls, providing a measure of security and predictability for all concerned.[33] Some urban areas also set up municipally run hospitals and medical care cooperatives (community clinics). These early precursors of Canada's medicare system were populist responses to a world that appeared indifferent to local rural needs. As Seymour Martin Lipset has observed, "Repeated challenges and crises force the western farmers to create many more community institutions (especially cooperatives and economic pressure groups) than are necessary in a more stable area. These groups in turn provided a structural basis for immediate action in critical situations."[34]

Also worthy of note are Lipset's observations about the healthy civic culture of the farmers that he encountered: "The farmers are interested in their society and its relation

SHIFTING RESPONSIBILITIES

to the rest of the world. Winter after winter, when the wheat crop is in, thousands of meetings are held throughout the province by political parties, churches, farmers' educational associations, and cooperatives. There are informal gatherings, also, in which farmers discuss economic and political problems."[35] The lively local political culture and citizen participation experienced in early-twentieth-century rural Saskatchewan communities stands in marked contrast to the usual depictions of early Canadian local politics, particularly those involving rapidly developing urban areas of the country.

In Alberta, Calgary was the first incorporated town in 1884, followed by Lethbridge in 1888 and Edmonton in 1892. Outside the towns, the province was sparsely populated, as was the case in the other western provinces. The early periods of Alberta's history, along with that of the other prairie provinces, were characterized by poverty and unpredictable natural occurrences. Few could afford much in the way of government services. Problems were dealt with on an incremental basis. For example, Alberta's 1887 Statute Labour Ordinance was passed to allow for the building of roads. As in early eastern Canada, residents paid for the service either by cash or in-kind labour (by working on the road crews).[36] Labour and fire districts were to follow, eventually evolving into local improvement districts, which were later to become known as municipal districts.

When Alberta became a province in 1905, it had two cities, fifteen towns, and thirty villages.[37] Many farmers, like their counterparts in the east, resisted incorporation because of the inevitable taxes that would accompany the move. Nevertheless, in 1912 the Rural Municipality Act was passed, expanding the size of districts, creating both rural municipalities and organized government districts. As Eric Hanson notes, under the new act the minister of municipal affairs could direct reorganizations of local improvement districts. By 1912, Alberta had fifty-five rural municipalities and ninety local improvement districts. The rural municipalities had stronger taxing powers and revenues than the districts, and during the Depression, a number of the municipal districts collapsed because they could not collect taxes.[38] Masson notes that the long-ruling provincial Social Credit government (1935-1971) supported the principle of autonomous local governments, although there was a major reorganization in the 1930s and 1940s of the rural governments, and larger school and municipal districts were created.[39] Following this, the 1950 County Act was passed to create an all-purpose local government unit within a geographic area in an attempt to resolve political and administrative conflicts among different municipal, school, and hospital authorities. Despite those efforts, hospital districts remained independent.[40]

British Columbia has its own distinct history. Barry M. Gough observes that within a period of forty years, the dominating influence shifted from First Nations territory and fur-trade realm to colony and finally to province in 1871.[41] The 1858 gold rush had brought prospectors north from California. A desire to assert control over the territory from American interests led the British to establish the Colony of British Columbia in 1858, ending the domination of the Hudson's Bay Company. With respect to Aboriginal peoples, Robin Fisher noted that the transition could be termed as a shift from the "colonies of exploitation" to "colonies of settlement."[42] During the fur-trade era, the Aboriginal peoples were important to European trade interests. Later, settlers' desire to acquire land traditionally used and occupied by Aboriginal peoples led to conflict and the dominance of European culture, economy, and politics. An imperial representative solely responsible to London governed the British colony. Any form of self-government was withheld because the region's population and society were thought to be "too wild," "crude," and unsettled to risk "the grand principle of free institutions."[43] The year after British Columbia entered confederation as a province, its legislature passed the Municipal Consolidation Act (1872). The new act laid out the rules of incorporation upon petition from residents.

The small logging community of Vancouver (formerly known as Granville) was chosen to replace Port Moody as the new site of the western terminus of the CPR in 1886 – the same year that it was incorporated and received its city charter. Vancouver quickly outstripped its more established, and much larger, rival cities of New Westminster and Victoria. The BC system of government was an adaptation of the Ontario Baldwin model, comprising cities and municipal districts.[44]

## Northern Territories

The 1867 British North America Act assigned constitutional authority over the territories to the federal government, not the provinces. In 1870, the federal government acquired the northern territories from the Hudson's Bay Company. At that time, the federal government did not bring Aboriginal peoples into the treaty process. Until after the Second World War, the indigenous peoples were left to their traditional lifestyles.

The Klondike gold discoveries brought in a flood of prospectors and other wealth seekers, leading to the permanent establishment of some mining towns. Soon after Yukon became a separate territory in 1898, legislation passed in 1901 allowing for the incorporation of towns by local petition. While the famous gold-mining town of Dawson City was incorporated in 1901, that status was withdrawn three years later after suspicions were aired about the nature of the petition for incorporation.[45] Despite being the largest city during the gold boom, Dawson lost economic pre-eminence to Whitehorse (established in 1898) because the latter was located near the Alaska Highway and, therefore, was more accessible.[46] Whitehorse became the territorial capital in 1953. Local government was slow to arrive in the vast territory, inhabited as it was by a small, scattered population.

The Northwest Territories, although still a large area of land, has had its size reduced a number of times since the area was first ceded to the Crown in 1870. Manitoba, Yukon, Alberta, Saskatchewan, Quebec, Ontario, and, most recently, Nunavut, have taken control of land that was once undifferentiated northern territory. The years 1939 and 1940 saw the establishment of the Yellowknife Administration District and the first municipal government in the MacKenzie district, respectively. In 1953, Yellowknife became a municipal district with its own elected mayor.

## Conclusion

The early development of self-government in Canada followed an inconsistent pattern, due to a number of push-pull factors. Sometimes colonial, federal, and provincial authorities, not wishing to lose control, resisted local pressures for self-government. This was most notably the case when American Loyalists arrived in Canada, bringing with them their own set of ideas about local decision making through town hall meetings and municipal government. Their activities, among other things, led to the establishment of Saint John, New Brunswick. On other occasions, particularly in the rural areas of Canada, farmers resisted municipal incorporation, viewing it as an additional tax grab that they could ill afford. It is worth observing at this point, however, that municipal incorporation need not be seen as the sole route to self-governance. In the west, the actual practice of self-government was just another word for self-reliance. In the harsh, isolated rural environment, people and communities were forced to take care of themselves; they pooled their resources to provide salaries for doctors and to create cooperative enterprises. Political institutions were something else altogether.

Nevertheless, as the transcontinental railway pushed its way west, settlements grew and municipal incorporation soon followed. After the Second World War, many provincial governments decided to tackle the proliferation of local government institutions and school boards. A period of consolidation set the stage for the rapidly growing financial and legislative control of provincial governments over municipal affairs. Local self-government would continue to be an elusive goal.

# 5
# Municipal Restructuring

Local governments have often been referred to as creatures of the province. In Canada, constitutional powers are divided between the federal and provincial governments, where the latter have jurisdiction over local institutions.[1] If a narrow interpretation of the formal written constitution were applied, municipalities would have no right of self-government. Provincial governments have often used this narrow interpretation to define the responsibilities and boundaries of local governments. When this approach is taken, the fact that local governments are important political, social, and economic institutions with customs and practices that have evolved to meet changing community needs is, at best, a secondary consideration.

An alternative view suggests that the Constitution, with its division of powers, was written under governing conditions that do not reflect the contemporary challenges of modern society. In the nineteenth century, many Canadians lived in rural areas or much smaller communities or cities, they lacked formal education, and they had comparatively limited knowledge about the world beyond their doorstep. Today's interconnected communities, with their radically changed socio-cultural, economic, and biophysical landscapes, bear little resemblance to those of earlier times. As such, a more flexible, adaptive approach is required when interpreting the Constitution. This perspective underscores the importance of conventions and traditions – the unwritten procedures that have developed over time to respond to changing societal requirements. It also recognizes the important roles that local governments have played throughout history, roles that cannot be readily discounted either in analyses or in prescriptions. Given the contemporary position of local government, some argue that it should be formally recognized as a vital part of the Canadian political system. This would not be an unprecedented change in North America. Some American states, for example, have adopted laws giving local governments constitutional recognition.

Federally, the formal constitutional situation of Canadian local governments is similar to that in the United States. The American federal constitution does not mention local governments; they are primarily created through state constitutions or state legislation and can be abolished or altered by the states.[2] A number of American states, however, have entrenched the rights and powers of local governments in their constitutions. As a result, local governments are somewhat less subject to the whims of unfriendly legislatures.[3] Over half the American states have a "home rule" constitutional provision that allows local governments to write their own *charters* or *local constitutions*. They are given broad areas of discretion, while operating within certain limits set by the states.[4]

In Canada, provincial legislation specifies the functions to be performed by local governments, although recently some provinces have been developing legislation with the stated intention of giving municipalities more flexibility. Critics argue that these new laws introduced by Alberta, Ontario, and British Columbia include long lists of restricted areas of activity, download provincial responsibilities, and limit fiscal capacity of municipalities, serving only to further constrain and weaken local governments.[5]

The last half of the twentieth century saw a notable decline in the authority of local governments, matched by a growth of provincial control over local policy.[6] One of the most prominent examples is education policy, an area that once primarily was the responsibility of local school boards governed by elected trustees. Canada's numerous school boards were subject to provincially imposed amalgamations in the 1960s and 1970s, and again in the 1990s, accompanied by a strengthening of provincial control.[7] The implications for governance are far reaching, as education both reflects and shapes community values. Schools teach cultural and social values, as well as civics. The issue of how much local discretion should be built into the provincial educational system raises a number of questions. Should provinces control this area of activity in order to ensure that schools meet certain province-wide standards no matter where the student lives? Should local communities have more control over the allocation of funds in order to reflect local priorities? How are minority group interests best protected? What about the needs of the majority of the school children? The centralization or decentralization of authority is an important variable in determining the answer to these questions.

Beginning in the 1940s, provincial governments determined that the municipal structures that had worked well for a primarily rural population were not well suited to manage urban development and overlapping jurisdictional responsibilities. Provincial departments responsible for municipal affairs were given enhanced responsibilities. Province-wide reforms were introduced to impose some uniform standards and coordination on the municipalities. The first task was to rationalize the proliferating numbers of school boards and municipalities. Although a number of amendments, annexations, and amalgamations took place throughout the rest of the twentieth century, the next major wave of municipal reform occurred in the 1990s. While their approaches were by no means uniform, it was clear that a number of governments were taking their cue from each other as they continued to engage in institutional tinkering and restructuring. The one issue that animated them all seemed to be a quest to promote fiscal restraint, local economic development, financial accountability, and government downsizing.

## School Board Reform

The mid-twentieth century saw the provinces starting to consolidate their school systems and to strengthen provincial control over education. School board restructuring in the western provinces began in the 1940s, followed by additional reforms in the ensuing decades. Saskatchewan, for example, passed the Large School Units Act in 1944 consolidating over 2,000 school districts into 60 larger ones.[8] In other provinces, education restructuring took place a few decades later. Donald Higgins reports that Ontario's 1,010 school boards, for instance, were reorganized in 1969 into 125 boards.[9] Higgins has speculated that it was the restructuring of the school board system that stimulated Ontario to embark on a broader municipal restructuring initiative at that time.[10]

A number of provinces, including Newfoundland and Labrador, Quebec, and Ontario, also confronted another, perhaps touchier issue – denominational schools. Under the British North America Act, the provinces had been given the right to make provincial laws with respect to education, as long as they did not affect the rights of denominational schools existing at the time of Confederation. Newfoundland and Labrador's system was primarily composed of denominational schools run by churches, a situation that led to increasing administrative problems. In 1969, the school system was reorganized. While the Roman Catholic, Pentecostal, and Seventh Day Adventists continued to manage their own schools, all the other denominational schools were consolidated into one system.[11] In a 1995 provincial referendum, voters approved amending the Constitution to allow for consolidating the schools under ten interdenominational boards.[12] On 2 September 1997, another referendum was called, posing the following question: "Do you support a single school system where all children, regardless of their religious affiliation, attend the same schools where opportunities for religious education and observances are provided?" Of the 53.5 percent who voted, 72.7 percent were in favour of a single system.[13] A single schools act was subsequently put in place.

In 1964, the government of Quebec proposed the creation of 55 regional school boards (from a previous total of 1,788). The initiative immediately encountered resistance on a number of grounds, not the least of which was a dispute around the proposal to remove confessional distinctions (all Quebec school authorities were either Protestant or Roman Catholic). The proposed "deconfessionalization" was subsequently withdrawn, although some structural changes were made over time. The year 1971 saw the establishment of 63 regional school boards. In the 1990s, the provincial school boards were finally restructured along linguistic lines.[14]

Things took a different twist in Ontario. There, in 1984, Premier Davis announced that the extensive Roman Catholic school system would be raised to full equality with the "public" or non-denominational system.[15] The educational funding issue was again revisited in 2001. The provincial Progressive Conservative government announced that it would give citizens a tax break that would, in effect, provide public funds to denominational and other private schools. The tax credit plan was cancelled, however, when a new Liberal government was elected in the fall of 2003. Similar debates about public and private school funding have taken place across the country.

SHIFTING RESPONSIBILITIES

## Modern Restructuring

### Newfoundland and Labrador

Municipal restructuring in Newfoundland and Labrador was part of an overall push by the provincial government to hasten industrial development and modernize the province. In the late 1960s and early 1970s, the federal and Newfoundland and Labrador governments initiated a rural resettlement program. The province invested heavily in infrastructure, such as roads, schools, hospitals, and energy, and resettled people into new communities from more isolated, economically poor fishing villages.[16] In 1979, a new Municipalities Act was passed, enabling the creation of regional governments.

At the end of the 1980s, a newly elected provincial government consolidated a number of municipalities, occasioning complaints about the lack of public consultation. After several studies, the capital, City of St. John's, became part of a metropolitan area that included a number of other small adjacent communities.[17]

The modernization efforts did lead to a more educated citizenry, but a number of the industrial projects failed. This left many villages and towns without the marginal living that inshore fishing used to provide and bereft of the cultural and social ties that bound the small communities.[18] The era was characterized by a number of economic problems, including the shutdown of the massive cod fisheries due to the collapse of the cod stocks. Whole communities were left without alternative means of employment. Once again, the province explored new models of local government, in part, to help stimulate regional development.

Various municipal restructuring initiatives were introduced in the 1990s. Thirty-three municipalities were amalgamated into thirteen.[19] Subsequently, in 1999, the provincial government developed a Strategic Social Plan that considered which services would be best delivered locally. Six regional steering committees were formed, with representatives from federal, provincial, and local governments. The planning process included public consultation, and a social audit was to be used to evaluate the government's success in implementing the plan.[20] Furthermore, a regionalization policy for government agencies was designed to distribute employment opportunities throughout the province. Other provincial initiatives stressed the importance of provincial-municipal partnerships and working with the Newfoundland and Labrador Federation of Municipalities.[21] A new legislative framework was to "ensure a strong and renewed foundation for local government" as part of an overall plan for increasing "municipal autonomy and empowerment." A new Municipalities Act took effect on 1 January 2000 and was soon followed by the introduction of a new planning act.[22]

Despite the various studies and recommendations made by various committees, Peter Boswell concludes that the actual developments in structural municipal reform have been quite modest. Local governments were given some additional powers and autonomy, but widespread reform did not take place.[23] That said, he observes that for Newfoundland, a "multiplicity of small municipal units" may be what is needed to ensure both efficiency and democratic representation.[24]

## New Brunswick

The government of New Brunswick decided to overhaul its local government system in 1966. A royal commission on taxation and municipal finance (the Byrne Commission) determined that services were managed inequitably throughout the province in ways that were particularly disadvantageous to the rural areas. Acting on the recommendations of the Byrne Commission, the province reallocated responsibilities. Local municipal service tasks were reduced to the provision of hard (infrastructural) services, police and fire protection, and garbage collection, while the province assumed responsibility for all social and health services and some support services. In rural areas, the old county system was replaced. Many villages were incorporated. The remaining less-populated areas became unincorporated local service districts in which the province assumed responsibility for services. The work of other royal commissions led to a series of amalgamations in the larger urban areas of Saint John, Fredericton, and Moncton.[25]

The disbanding of local government in rural areas resulted in enhanced services for those areas but left residents without local representation. For their part, urban taxpayers were unhappy about subsidizing the province's rural areas. Restructuring was again under investigation.[26] By the end of the twentieth century, the municipal system was still operating within the structures reorganized in the 1960s, although a number of reviews had been undertaken – specifically one dealing with revamping the Municipalities Act. In 1997, the provincial government announced that some municipal restructuring would take place in Greater Saint John (see Box 5.1).

In 2000, the minister of the newly restructured Department of Environment and Local Government announced the formation of a round table on local government. The round table was composed of members of municipal associations and individuals from unincorporated areas and commissions. The goals included resolving some service and taxation issues for unincorporated areas, considering ways to foster more effective regional planning and service delivery, and examining issues related to local finance. One objective that has since become somewhat of a mantra in local government reform was to look at local finance and find ways to enhance "financial stability and autonomy of local governments."[27] In its report, the round table emphasized the importance of "regional coordination in the areas of land use planning, infrastructure development and the protection of the natural environment." It also recommended that the "development and evaluation of funding mechanisms for local governments in New Brunswick be based on the principles established by the Round Table, including: fiscal autonomy, stability, predictability, simplicity, accountability, neutrality, and equity."[28] The New Brunswick government's response to the roundtable was to develop a plan that would, among other things, give local service districts an ability to acquire local representation and other local service powers and to improve the regional planning and decision-making processes. The government chose

## 5.1  Municipal Restructuring in Greater Saint John

In 1998, the number of municipalities in the Greater Saint John area was reduced from nine to four, although the government acknowledged that there were strong arguments for full amalgamation of all the communities. Ultimately the region consisted of the City of Saint John plus three new municipalities drawn from the suburban areas. A regional economic development agency was established for the Greater Saint John area to serve Saint John, Grand Bay-Westfield, Quispamsis, and Rothesay. Enterprise Saint John was formed in the same year to provide leadership and cooperation for all aspects of economic development. One of the reasons for the decision was to establish a mechanism to ensure that the surrounding communities supported the City of Saint John financially for the services it provided to the residents of the entire region.

*Sources:* New Brunswick Department of Municipalities, Culture and Housing, "Government Responds to Commissioners Report," news release, 22 April 1997; Enterprise Saint John, New Brunswick, "Welcome to Enterprise Saint John," http://www.enterprisesj.com/index02.html.

not to introduce a completely new act at that time because the work of the roundtable and other committees suggested that "recommendations that might emanate from these processes could eventually require significant changes to the legislative framework for local government." Instead, the provincial government introduced some amendments to the Municipal Act in April 2003. These amendments concentrated on clarifying rules around public access to municipal information, improving public accountability, and strengthening bylaw enforcement.[29]

## Nova Scotia

The most notable effort to restructure the Nova Scotia municipal system of government was the 1974 Graham Royal Commission on Education, Public Services, and Provincial-Municipal Relations. The commission recommended sweeping changes but faced considerable public opposition. Moreover, it did not make recommendations for implementation. The government decided to use it only as a policy guide, and some of the ideas of the commission were implemented in an incremental fashion in the ensuing years. Other structural changes included a few annexations in the metropolitan Halifax area in 1961 and 1969, and much later the consolidation of the school board system. Higgins argues that contrary to appearance, numerous changes were made with respect to provincial-municipal financial affairs and responsibilities, although there were no major changes to the overall structure of municipal government throughout much of the twentieth century.[30]

In 1991, the minister of Municipal Affairs established the Task Force on Local Government, which made a number of recommendations for reform concerning the reallocation of provincial/municipal responsibilities and the rationalization of municipal boundaries to reflect changed settlement patterns. These recommendations were followed by a 1995 Service Exchange agreement.[31] Also at that time, Nova Scotia also instituted a series of amalgamations, including the Cape Breton Regional Municipality Act (amalgamating six towns, one city, and a rural municipality), the Halifax Regional Municipality Act (amalgamating two cities, one town, and one rural municipality), and the Queens Regional Municipality Act (amalgamating one town and one rural municipality). As of 2001, there were fifty-five municipalities in total.[32] The new Halifax Regional Municipality covers a large coastal area stretching about 100 kilometres, encompassing the original urban City of Halifax and many rural areas. Andrew Sancton suggests that the new municipalities, in many ways, were modelled on a Manitoban initiative, referred to as Unicity Winnipeg. Unlike Unicity, however, the new community committees in Halifax have been given some real authority over zoning decision making.[33]

On 1 April 1999 the new Municipal Government Act came into effect, collecting together and modernizing several pieces of local government legislation. Incorporated into the new act were a number of other pieces of legislation, including the Municipal Act, the Towns Act and the regional municipality acts, the Municipal Affairs Act, the Municipal Boundaries and Representation Act, the Deed Transfer Tax Act, and the tax-collection provisions of the Assessment Act. A revised Planning Act was also included. The new legislation also covered villages that were formerly governed under the Village Service Act.[34]

In the autumn of 1998, a joint Municipal-Provincial Roles and Responsibilities Review was initiated by the Union of Nova Scotia Municipalities and the province. The goal was to undertake a "comprehensive examination of municipal and provincial service responsibilities and their delivery and funding mechanisms."[35] The review was stimulated, in part, by a difficult financial situation where municipalities were looking for continued grants and funding from a provincial government that was facing rising costs itself. Efforts were made to develop a new vision for provincial-municipal interactions and an improved working relationship. Attention was also given to separating and defining (or disentangling) provincial and local responsibilities in order to define provincial-local relationships more clearly. Three issues were of immediate concern – social services funding, bridges, and education – with a later addition of "equalization."[36]

As a result of the review, the provincial government proposed that there be a major shift in the way in which services were delivered and financed. The most controversial proposal was that while the province would take over responsibility for some services, municipalities would assume responsibility for the province's municipal equalization program.[37] After much discussion and negotiation between affected governments and parties, the provincial government withdrew the proposed initiative.

## Prince Edward Island

Prince Edward Island is the only Atlantic province that did not see much in the way of restructuring during the twentieth century. Structural reform was not a high priority. Successive premiers in the province defended and maintained the ideal of PEI as an agricultural community and sought chiefly to combat the decline in farm income with policies, programs, and rhetoric. By the mid-1950s, the provincial government turned its attention to industrial development based on enterprises such as fish and food processing plants. Farm community values, however, have always played a very strong part in Island culture and are not easily set aside.

The 1980s saw the provincial government introduce schemes to protect the traditional rural lifestyle with initiatives such as the Small Farm Program.[38] Despite the continuing strong attachment to the belief that PEI is essentially an agricultural community, tourism has become the second most important industry to the Island and is heavily promoted by government, while small-scale farming continues to decline. Since the 1970s, as David Milne points out, a number of community and activist groups, with the assistance of the media, have come to play a busy grassroots role in local and provincial politics in the highly politicized community of PEI.[39]

Municipal reform took place in the 1990s when some commissions identified the need for a restructuring of local government administration. In a province itself no bigger than a number of municipalities throughout Canada, there are many small towns governing relatively few people living at close proximity to each other. Charlottetown underwent an amalgamation with some outlying areas in 1995. As of 2001, its population was estimated at 32,245, followed by the next largest city, Summerside, with an approximate population of 14,654. The rest of the cities, towns, and villages range from a few hundred people to a few communities with populations of 5,000 to 6,000.[40]

## Quebec

Compared with the rest of Canada, municipal restructurings in Quebec throughout the twentieth century were relatively modest. When municipalities went through a province-wide set of amalgamations at the end of 2001, it was the first major change in a system that had evolved from parishes and villages. As Louise Quesnel points out, Quebec had an "exceptionally high" number of small municipalities, with only 125 of the 1,414 possessing a population of more than 10,000. While the vast majority of the population lived in urban centres, rural municipalities had disproportionate representation in the overall municipal system.[41] The Quebec government generally allowed the process of amalgamation to be a voluntary one, except in a few cases that proved politically costly to the provincial party in power.[42]

The number of municipalities was slightly reduced in the 1970s. In the late 1990s, the provincial government began to impose a system of municipal restructuring on rural municipalities that was soon followed by an overhaul of the municipal system and the province-wide amalgamations that came into force in 2002.

### Montreal Region

Quebec and Ontario are the two most populated and urbanized provinces in the country. Montreal is the second-largest city in Canada, after Toronto, and the province has six of the country's twenty-five metropolitan regions. As the City of Montreal grew, many incorporated municipalities sprang up outside the city on Montreal Island. In 1969 the Montreal Metropolitan Corporation was created and was subsequently replaced by the Montreal Urban Community (MUC).

The MUC was an upper-tier level of government (with twenty-nine municipalities as members) incorporated in 1970 to coordinate economic development, evaluate property values, provide transit, and take responsibility for environmental issues, food security, police, and emergency services. The formation of the MUC was stimulated by a number of factors. Andrew Sancton suggests that the main reason for the MUC was to get the suburbs to help pay the high costs involved in maintaining Montreal's police force.[43] The new second-tier government also assisted Montreal in getting revenues for its subway system and other services. This initiative also helped its ambitious mayor, Jean Drapeau, achieve his own often-grandiose goals of building mega-projects. Montreal possessed the majority of seats on the MUC Council, as well as seven of twelve seats on the MUC Council's executive committee. As a counterbalance to Montreal's dominance, any motion had to be supported by at least 50 percent of the suburban mayors to pass.[44]

In 1965, thirteen Quebec municipalities to the north of Montreal were amalgamated into the city of Laval, the province's second-largest municipality. Regional government was instituted in the Hull-Outaouais area with 32 municipalities forming the Outaouais Regional Community (ORC) and in the Quebec City area with 28 municipalities forming the Quebec Urban Community (QUC). "Voluntary" amalgamation of lower-tier municipalities was encouraged, but the province also established some deadlines for introducing some consolidations. Ultimately, the QUC was consolidated into thirteen municipalities by 1978 and the ORC into eight by 1975. The MUC did not include any consolidation among lower municipalities, even though that was the intention of the provincial government at the time. Then, as now, suburban anglophones were concerned about losing power and control to the predominantly francophone Montreal.[45]

The government created regional county municipality (RCM) urban communities in the 1980s. These RCMs were set up originally to develop the territory, coordinate regional services, and respond to regional needs. In addition to the RCMs, urban communities were given their own set of local responsibilities. The Kativik Regional Government was established to govern territory north of the 55th parallel.[46]

In 1996, the Ministry of Municipal Affairs initiated an amalgamation process for the smaller municipalities. If these municipalities failed to participate, the province would reduce municipal funding. The Association of Rural and Regional Municipalities, among others, resisted the amalgamation program, leading to delays in implementation. Nevertheless, 103 small municipalities were merged into 49 new ones.[47]

By 2001, the Quebec government was fully engaged in extensive amalgamation processes across the whole province. The restructuring was based on a tiered approach (see Box 5.2). In the most populated areas, government mergers created five new large cities: Montreal, Quebec, Longueuil, Gatineau-Hull, and Lévis. Montreal, with its population of 1.8 million, became Canada's second-largest municipality, after Toronto, and Quebec City its ninth largest with a population of 504,000.[48] This reorganization was a dramatic shift for Quebec, which used to be known for its many local governments, a voluntary approach to amalgamation, and a high level of representation with large councils.[49] As in Ontario, the forced amalgamations were not popular with many municipalities. A number of municipalities, particularly those that were predominantly anglophone, were concerned about the future of their communities. Baie d'Urfé, along with some other communities, attempted to legally block the decision but were unsuccessful.[50]

In spring 2003, the opposition party, the Liberal Party of Quebec, swept into power. One of their election promises was to revisit the question of amalgamated cities. The new minister who had responsibility for municipal affairs tabled a bill in the Quebec National Assembly entitled An Act Respecting the Consultation of Citizens with Respect to the Territorial Reorganization of Certain Municipalities, and it called for the consultation of

## 5.2  Amalgamation in Sherbrooke, Quebec

Sherbrooke was part of a province-wide reorganization of the municipal system. By 1 January 2002, the towns of Ascot, Bromptonville, Deauville, Fleurimont, Lennoxville, Rock Forest, Saint-Élie d'Orford, and Sherbrooke were merged to form one larger city of Sherbrooke. At the time, the new amalgamated city had a population of 140,000, making it the seventh-largest city in Quebec. The new two-tier governmental structure includes an upper-tier municipal council and a lower tier of six borough councils. Under this system, the electorate directly elects the mayor while the residents of the boroughs elect the nineteen municipal councillors. Both the municipal councils and the borough councils hold regular meetings.

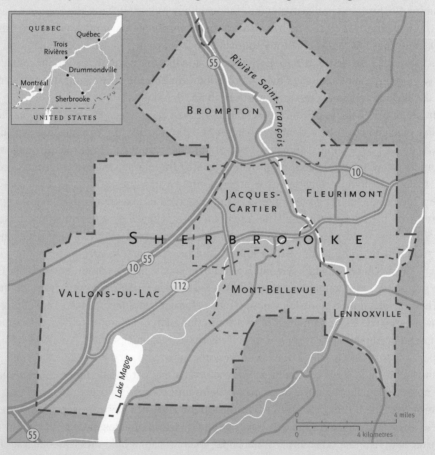

*Source:* City of Sherbrooke Transition Committee, "Towards a New City," *Chronicle* 1 (10 October 2001) and *Chronicle* 2 (11 October 2001).

SHIFTING RESPONSIBILITIES

citizens of merged cities. After public consultation, a process would be set in place that would allow citizens of the newly amalgamated cities to vote on a referendum about whether or not they wished to "de-merge."[51]

## Ontario

### Regional Government in Ontario

In the 1960s, Ontario introduced significant structural changes to both the municipal system generally and to the school boards. Regional economic development and planning problems were to be overcome by reducing, if not eliminating, political fragmentation. The solution came in the form of a two-tier regional government based on the old rural county form of government. According to Higgins, Ottawa-Carleton led the way in 1968, becoming the first regional government, followed by nine others (and the Regional District of Muskoka) in the ensuing five years. Together, the regional governments and Metropolitan Toronto accounted for two-thirds of the province's population. The Regional Municipality of Waterloo was one of the new restructured governments (see Box 5.3). Consolidation of some municipalities was the inevitable result of the introduction of regional governments.[52]

By the mid-1990s, the province was once more going through a massive reorganization. A newly elected Progressive Conservative government decided to introduce municipal reform as a way to reduce the number of politicians and introduce its idea of efficiency into the municipal system. Williams and Downey refer to this era as an "unprecedented departure" from any previous reform initiative. In previous restructuring efforts, reform took place after close consultation with those most directly affected, and after careful study and review.[53] In contrast, the Conservative Mike Harris government devised its own system of reorganization that, in effect, forced a number of municipalities to come up with their own restructuring plans or have a provincial restructuring commission do it for them.[54] The result was that almost half of Ontario's municipalities disappeared through consolidations, and a number of regional governments become single-tier municipalities.

This was certainly a radical departure from past years. In 1960, Premier Leslie Frost had addressed the Association of Ontario Mayors and Reeves and proclaimed the virtues of local government:

> Local government is predicated on the theory that people in a community are not only likely to, but do know more about their requirements than anybody else. Is it to be presumed that provincial administration or provincial Ministers, now, or in the future, are possessed of some mystic quality which enables them to know what people in the community want better than do the people themselves? ... We are living under a democratic system. Basically that means government according to the wishes of those governed. Can this be achieved if local government is subject to the interference of another government above? I think not.[55]

## 5.3 Regional Municipality of Waterloo

The Regional Municipality of Waterloo was created in 1973 to manage the needs of a rapidly growing area. This move followed a commissioned report by Stewart Fyfe and Ron Farrow, who presented two possible models for reform. One was a reorganized city council system, and the second was a regional government comprising seven local municipalities. The latter option was chosen.[1]

By 2003, the region included over 450,000 people (the fifth-largest urban area in Ontario, and eleventh in Canada). The region encompasses the seven lower-tier municipalities, including the cities of Cambridge, Kitchener, and Waterloo, and the townships of North Dumfries, Wellesley, Wilmot, and Woolwich. The regional chair and council are directly elected to represent the region. The seven mayors also sit on the regional council. Two councillors are elected from the City of Cambridge, two from the City of Waterloo, and four represent the City of Kitchener.

In recent years, the region has also become responsible for the delivery of many municipal services, including (among other things) all borrowing of money for capital expenditures; approval of area municipal official plans, amendments, and development; overall planning for the region; public health; public transit; regional roads; regional licensing; social housing; social services; waste management; water supply and wastewater operations, and the Waterloo Regional Airport.[2]

---

1  Stewart Fyfe and Ron M. Farrow, *Waterloo Area Local Government Review: Report of Findings and Recommendations* (Toronto: Ontario Department of Municipal Affairs, 1970).
2  Regional Municipality of Waterloo, "Home page," http://www.region.waterloo.on.ca.

To advocates of self-government, the vision of the provincial government forty years later, after radical surgery on the local system of representation, appears to be imbued with more of a myopic rather than "mystic quality." Between July 1996 and January 2001, the number of municipalities was cut from 815 to 447. The number of elected councillors was also almost cut in half, from 4,586 to 2,804.[56]

## Metropolitan Toronto

Toronto has experienced seismic municipal changes over the past fifty years. The first major municipal restructuring took place on 1 January 1954 and attracted considerable international and domestic attention with its urban adaptation of the rural county two-tier system. The reorganization was a response to growing transportation, water supply, and sewage-treatment problems, and the lack of coordination and integration of services. Moreover, some suburban areas did not have the resources to finance the growing service demands.[57] Other social welfare and economic issues associated with the rapid population growth contributed to the calls for reorganization.

Under the new two-tier metropolitan government, the City of Toronto and the twelve surrounding suburban municipalities retained their own municipal governments, providing services for their own cities. A new Metro Council (composed of representatives from the lower-tier councils) was assigned a number of regional responsibilities, such as capital borrowing, major roads, and property assessment. Other responsibilities were shared. In the case of sewerage and water, for example, Metro was in charge of regional water distribution and sewage disposal, while the lower tiers were put in charge of water supply and sewage collection.[58] In 1957, the council was also given responsibility for police services.

In the early years, the new organization was seen as quite successful in that it was able to meet many of its service requirements. The City of Toronto, however, was unhappy with the arrangement in which a strong metropolitan government diluted the decision-making authority of the largest city.[59] Another reorganization in 1967 consolidated the thirteen Metro municipalities into six and retained the metropolitan structure. In the ensuing years, the power of Metropolitan Toronto would be strengthened in such areas as financial assistance and housing policy. Plunkett and Brownstone suggest that this model weakened citizen access, noting that important decision-making responsibilities moved to the upper-tier regional level of government. The decisions there were made by indirectly elected councillors drawn from the lower-tier governments. They state, "little if any consideration was given to achieving a new spirit in city politics."[60]

In 1988, the composition of the Metropolitan Toronto council was changed to include thirty-four directly elected members with only the six mayors representing the lower-tier municipalities. The twenty-eight directly elected councillors chose the chairman of the council.

In 1995, a newly elected provincial government placed municipal reform high on its agenda. Other rapidly growing municipalities now surrounded Metropolitan Toronto. Two inquiries into the future of the Greater Toronto Area (GTA) made recommendations that emphasized the need to coordinate services in the region. Nevertheless, the provincial government focused instead on consolidating Metropolitan Toronto, setting aside the overall question of how the GTA should best be governed. In 1997, provincial legislation (Bill 103) eliminated the lower-tier governments of Metro Toronto, creating a single-tier "mega-city" in their place. The new city was established 1 January 1998. This decision was imposed in the face of considerable opposition by the affected local governments and citizens, who thought that the mega-city would be administratively unwieldy, as well as a threat to local democracy.[61] Amalgamation was one of the tools used by the Ontario government to achieve its agenda of eliminating what it saw as inefficiency and over-governance (i.e., too many politicians and local governments).

The opposition was expressed both in a court challenge and through the result of an independently initiated municipal plebiscite. The result indicated quite clearly, but futilely, that the citizens of Toronto, for the most part, did not want their "local" government to become responsible for a collective population greater than that of several of Canada's other provinces put together.

Ontario Municipal Act
In addition to a number of other comprehensive pieces of election legislation introduced since 1996, in October 2001 the provincial government also tabled a bill for a new Municipal Act (which went into effect 1 January 2003). Up to this point, municipal legislation had still been based primarily on the old Baldwin Act introduced in the 1800s. The stated intention of the new legislation was to give local governments more flexibility by expanding their powers in several spheres of jurisdiction, to strengthen public accountability, to provide municipalities with greater financial flexibility, to permit them more authority in some local service areas (roads, waste management, and public utilities), to strengthen community safety powers, and to encourage public-private partnerships.

In a discussion paper, the Ontario government suggested that the goal was to give municipalities "natural persons' powers" similar to Alberta's legislation passed in 1995. This meant the municipalities could conduct their business without always having to refer to explicit permissive legislation: "They could enter into agreements, purchase land and equipment, hire employees, and delegate responsibilities to committees, staff members of other bodies, such as boards of management."[62] In contrast to the previous "creature of the state" approach to local government, the new act was presented as one that would recognize municipalities as governments operating in their own jurisdictions. Under the new act, the province would consult with municipalities before making changes that would affect them in a new consultative process that was to be negotiated with municipal organizations such as the Association of Municipalities of Ontario.

Critics of the new act argued that the powers of municipal government had not been enhanced – quite the contrary. They claimed that the accountability sections and other parts of the legislation further reduced the power of municipalities. The most intrusive part of the bill, they argued, were Sections 299 through 303, which "state the minister can, by regulation, require any municipality or any municipal board, committee, or agency, to meet objectives and standards about 'efficiency and effectiveness' determined by the minister."[63] In addition many legislative controls remained in place. Coupled with recent provincial offloading and the limited financial means of municipalities, critics suggested that, contrary to the stated intentions, local governments in Ontario would end up with reduced, rather than enhanced, powers to govern themselves.[64]

The arguments of the critics would be difficult to dispute. In addition to the limitations implied by the legislation itself, there was little in the history of the current government's actions to demonstrate a desire to share authority with lower levels of government or with citizens. This, despite considerable rhetoric to the contrary. The people of Ontario had witnessed six years of a provincial government introducing and passing sweeping, comprehensive pieces of legislation in a number of areas that were of such a scope and magnitude that there was little room for democratic parliamentary or public debate. All this was accompanied by the issuing of top-down decrees and funding cutbacks. This was not a promising foundation on which to build a stronger, more independent system of local self-government.

## Manitoba
Manitoba's settlement pattern clustered the urban population around the capital region while sprinkling many much smaller municipalities throughout the rest of the province. The provincial capital of Winnipeg has received the greatest attention in the area of local government restructuring.

### Unicity Winnipeg
Throughout the twentieth century, the Winnipeg area grew rapidly to contain half of the province's population. By the late 1950s, the region encompassed twelve separate munici-palities and some intermunicipal special-purpose bodies. Area-wide planning was difficult to achieve, and decision making was fragmented. In the late 1950s, the Greater Winnipeg Investigating Commission recommended a two-tier structure based on the Metro Toronto system. When the structure was ultimately put in place, a number of political compromises had been made, leading to many difficulties. For example, under the new structure, all ten metro councillors were directly elected rather than chosen as representatives by members of the lower elected tier of government. This situation increased the conflict between the upper and lower tiers. Restructuring was once again considered.

By 1969, the provincial New Democratic Party (NDP) was elected to replace the Pro-gressive Conservative government. The NDP soon introduced a unique approach to mu-nicipal government – one that rivalled Metro Toronto's 1954 adoption of the two-tier county system of government. In 1970, a government white paper proposed "politicizing local government" and introduced a participatory model of decision making that actively engaged citizens. According to Lightbody, the initiative was consistent with some of the core values of the NDP. He states, "In Manitoba, the NDP, unlike preceding governments, was essentially an urban social democratic party and had traditionally represented the less advantaged core of the city. Because of this base the amendment of Winnipeg's local government was seen to be policy priority despite the provincial government's concerns with other major policy initiatives."[65]

The white paper suggested a model that would consolidate twelve area municipalities into one and decentralize power through the introduction of twelve community commit-tees of council. These committees were to represent the wards and resident advisory groups (RAGs) attached to those committees, forming a neighbourhood government. The paper also proposed a parliamentary form of government at the municipal level, where the council of fifty (representing each of fifty wards) would form into blocs of rep-resentatives. The largest bloc of elected councillors would choose the mayor from among themselves.

This "Unicity" reform initiative was based on a set of values distinct from other reform initiatives across the country. Brownstone and Plunkett note that municipal reforms such as Ontario's establishment of the municipality of Metropolitan Toronto were based on values of efficiency and service delivery. For Winnipeg, however, the ideological goals differed: "Thus a key goal was to reduce citizen alienation through electoral distribution and political decentralization ... A related goal was a structure that would politicize city issues, and make possible the adaptation of a form of responsible parliamentary govern-ment at the city level. It was believed that this would, in turn, provide a forum for debate, help focus discussion on the issues much more clearly, stimulate the development of al-ternatives to proposed policies, and raise public awareness."[66]

Paul Thomas also notes that, as with other cities, property and land development in-terests were seen by the Unicity creators as having undue influence on city hall. The insti-tutional reforms were seen as a way of placing citizens, non-profits, advocacy groups, and others on a more equal political basis.[67]

The inevitable political trade-offs, however, came into play. When Unicity Winnipeg was introduced in 1971, political wrangling had diluted many of the innovative aspects of the proposal. Over time, the attempt to formalize public participation through neighbour-hood government fizzled, due to the complexity of the structures and the lack of both re-sources and legal authority to implement change. The RAGs, as solely advisory bodies to relatively impotent community committees in the new governing structure, gave citizens little reason to participate.[68] The new model also lacked the political commitment needed to make it work as originally envisioned.[69]

The initiative did achieve some important objectives. As James Lightbody observes, an equalized property tax rate across the restructured municipality provided funding for city-wide objectives and responsibilities. These, he says, "were clearly intended to eliminate the property tax havens in several Winnipeg suburbs."[70] Twenty-five years later, Sancton attributes Winnipeg's equitable distribution of tax burden and delivery of services to the

Unicity model and says, "Unlike some Canadian cities, and most American ones, Winnipeg simply does not have wealthy suburban enclaves with low taxes and high service levels."[71]

A formal review of Unicity in 1976 concluded that the consolidation had helped to unify municipal services and administration in the region, and that it had introduced a mechanism allowing formal citizen participation. The review highlighted a number of deficiencies, many of which could be attributed to the modifications made to the original design. Criticisms included lack of accountability, confusion over responsibilities, complicated processes, parochialism on the part of councillors representing their own areas, and lack of city-wide coordinated decision making.[72] Additional structural changes only served to move the city farther away from the original design. The number of community committees and resident advisory groups were cut in half, their powers reduced, and their geographic area doubled in size. The number of wards was reduced to twenty-nine. The mayor continued to be directly elected but was removed as chair of the executive policy committee and as a member of the Board of Commissioners and was confined to serving as chair of the council and to performing ceremonial duties, further reducing the power of the position. These moves effectively ended the attempt to achieve a new parliamentary style of government at the municipal level.

In 1986, Unicity Winnipeg underwent another review. An executive committee was established, composed of councillors and chaired by the mayor. By 1992, the city council had been reduced to 15 seats, with the inner city given only three seats, weakening its political position while strengthening that of the suburban areas. Community committees were reduced to five and RAGs were abolished.[73] Also, the rural community of Headingly was separated from the city. As Tindal and Tindal state, "The bold experiment in citizen participation launched in 1972 was all but gone twenty years later!"[74]

Andrew Sancton suggests that Unicity designers made the mistake of believing that the creation of a new structure in itself would achieve their goals in terms of both the core and suburban areas.[75] Sancton remains skeptical that even significant structural changes of the kind brought about in the Unicity body can make significant differences in the way in which society operates. He suggests instead that "structural change is no panacea and that negative unintended consequences are inevitable. It is better, therefore, to get on with the business of governing and building our communities rather than constantly squabbling about structures."[76]

Winnipeg, however, does not appear to share the same sentiments. From 1993 to 2001, the city was once more engaged in restructuring initiatives that included public consultation. *Plan Winnipeg – Toward 2010* and its successor *Plan Winnipeg 2020 Vision* were accompanied by the city government's organization-wide plan, *The City of Winnipeg's Action Plan – Serving Citizens 2000-2002*. These initiatives, like many others elsewhere, reflected the contemporary government's approach to engage the public in a "visioning" exercise – an approach quite different from the one first attempted through the institutional restructuring more than thirty years before.[77]

Although structural changes in and of themselves may not be a panacea for various governing ills, they can make a difference in how services are delivered, as suggested by the example of Unicity Winnipeg. It is important, however, to also pay attention to Sancton's wise caution that institutional tinkering will have little impact on the status quo if there is an absence of political will to effect meaningful change. More comparative research is required to understand the policy results of different structures. Not enough is known about the impact of different governing structures on policies, distribution of policies, or access of people to government.

## Intergovernmental Coordination in Manitoba

By the turn of the twenty-first century, Manitoba's population of approximately 1,150,000 was so unevenly distributed that it posed continuing problems of resource distribution and intergovernmental coordination. The capital region included sixteen municipalities that, together with the City of Winnipeg, occupied 1.4 percent of the land base. The area had 60 percent of the province's population, labour force, and industry, with over 87 percent of those people living in the city of Winnipeg itself.[78]

The Manitoba government established the Capital Region Review Panel to examine land-use planning and decision-making structures among the growing capital region municipalities. In 2001, the provincial government released the document "Planning Manitoba's Capital Region: NEXT STEPS" in its response to the Review Panel's report, which had identified a number of legislative and policy weaknesses. The NEXT STEPS document identified ten steps to address issues related to the Capital Region. Among them was the decision to appoint a regional planning advisory committee (RPAC) "to assist in stimulating public discussion and to provide advice on regional planning policies."[79] The RPAC, chaired by Paul Thomas, released its final report on 24 October 2003. The recommendations of the RPAC focused on strengthening regional ties through a partnership of governments, revenue sharing, tax sharing, joint action on economic development, and improved mechanisms for conflict resolution. In addition, the committee made proposals for the establishment of an improved planning and land-use policy for the region.[80] The report would be considered by the provincial government when developing its policy plan for the region. Coordination and cooperation were not only required between the core City of Winnipeg and the surrounding cities but also between the Capital Region and the communities situated farther afield.[81] As far as the latter were concerned, farming and mining communities had a long history of struggle, and the situation continued to worsen as prolonged drought conditions affected grain crops and economic conditions robbed the province of adequate revenues.

The province of Manitoba engaged in a number of community development "partnership programs," through which the Department of Intergovernmental Affairs provided matching grants, team-building seminars, facilitators, and government liaison.[82] Richard Rounds suggests that governance in rural Manitoba has been accommodated by partnerships and special service agreements in extra-municipal areas rather than through the adoption of a two-tier county or regional system such as is used in Ontario, Quebec, or British Columbia.[83]

With reference to Winnipeg (and other municipalities), Peter Diamant suggests that "the future depends on strong municipal governments that have the powers to co-ordinate regional services and the sensitivity and mechanisms to respond to local concerns. It will take a new attitude at the provincial level to go beyond political restructuring and to provide the autonomy and access necessary to create those strong municipalities.[84]

In June 2002 the Manitoba minister of Intergovernmental Affairs introduced a new City of Winnipeg Charter Act – one that recognized the local government's right to take action with respect to areas of local concern. The stated goal of the act was to give the city greater flexibility, broader powers, and authority to manage its own affairs. The new act, in recognizing increased autonomy on the part of the city also emphasized the accountability of the city to the citizens, giving the latter an enhanced ability to participate in city issues.[85]

## Saskatchewan

Over the years, Saskatchewan's municipal institutions have changed very little. The province's pattern for amalgamation is through voluntary mergers. The two large cities, Regina and Saskatoon, expanded by annexation rather than by provincially mandated amalgamations in the early 1970s. In 1990, two rural municipalities, Greenfield and Mervin, similarly amalgamated voluntarily.[86]

By the year 2000, the issue of revising the 1984 Urban Municipalities Act became a topic of discussion. The Saskatchewan Urban Municipalities Association declared in its newsletter that the act was too "outdated and paternalistic." Instead it called for a general act that specified only areas in which municipalities were prohibited from acting, rather than one that listed only permitted areas in which they might act.[87]

In 2001, the mayors of Saskatchewan's thirteen cities presented the province with a proposal for a new Cities Act that would give them more autonomy and flexibility, a goal shared by many other municipalities across the country. As of 2002, Saskatchewan's population exceeded 1 million people, and although the province is commonly thought of as having a rural population, the vast majority (76 percent) of the people lived in relatively small urban areas. In addition to its cities, Saskatchewan was composed of 145 towns, 358 villages, 25 northern municipalities, and 297 rural municipalities. Its largest city, Saskatoon, had a population just over 190,000 at the turn of the millennium, while its capital city, Regina, contained a little over 180,000 people.[88] Given these and other developments, the Department of Municipal Affairs and Housing acknowledged that the municipal act needed to be modernized and that municipal governments were becoming more autonomous. The government instituted some initiatives to examine how more independence could be achieved.[89]

The Cities Act was passed on 1 January 2003. The act included a "statement of municipal purpose" outlining municipal powers as similar in nature to a business corporation.

The act stated that the cities are subject to provincial legislation and restrictions, but as local governments, they are also recognized as an accountable and responsible level of government. The act attempts to incorporate some of the ideas behind "natural persons" powers and "areas of jurisdiction," concepts recently employed by other provinces, such as Alberta.[90]

## Alberta

In its early years, Alberta was a rural farming province. Municipal reform focused on the amalgamation of rural communities, leading to the enlargement of existing municipal districts. The County Act passed in 1950 transformed the rural municipal system into thirty-one single-tier governments. Masson suggests that there had been too many school districts to support, and consolidation did produce a greater equalization of taxes. The initiative, however, did mean that children had to be bussed to school. Moreover, there was a sense that the loss of the rural boards reduced local control and undermined community identity.[91] This pattern of consolidation took place throughout the country with similar results.

The discovery of oil at Leduc in 1947 stimulated the rapid expansion of Calgary and Edmonton, transforming them into large urban centres. Rather than restructuring the two urban areas, as was the strategy in other provinces, the Alberta government relied on financial assistance packages from the oil revenues, and processes of annexation, to deal with population growth. A royal commission in 1954-55 investigated different models for urban government, including the two-tier Metropolitan Toronto model, and ultimately recommended large-scale amalgamation. Although the provincial government did not implement the recommendation of what became known as the McNally Report, the cities of Edmonton and Calgary did grow through annexations and amalgamations.

### Alberta Municipal Government Act

In 1994, the Alberta Municipal Government Act was introduced after several years of consultations with municipalities and the Alberta Urban Municipalities Association (AUMA). Rather than stating specifically what municipalities might be permitted to do, it assigned general spheres of responsibility to the municipalities. A new Municipal Government Board replaced three other provincial agencies, reducing provincial oversight of municipal activities. Structures were put in place to encourage intergovernmental cooperation and dispute resolution.[92] Local governments were also given more taxation room; that is, they were permitted more autonomy to make greater use of fees in some areas. The province retained authority in areas where a municipal taxation regime might not be operating well or where there was a clear provincial interest.[93]

This new act generated considerable interest among municipalities throughout the country. However, there proved to be two primary stumbling blocks in terms of furthering local self-governance in the province: one was in fulfilling the spirit of the agreement, and the other was financial. The AUMA was concerned that amendments to the Municipal

Government Act were taking place without adequate consultation or time for reflection on the part of the members of the association. In a discussion paper, AUMA reaffirmed the original intention of the act to provide open, publicly accountable government. The association asserted that that new amendments and the process of approving the amendments were eroding the spirit of the municipal act. Some municipalities, however, disagreed, pointing out that amendments were necessary because the act had introduced a number of changes that required some revision. Nevertheless, the AUMA noted the many ad hoc changes to the act and requested a halt to the "piecemeal" changes to the legislation.[94]

Also of concern was the provincial reduction in funding, relative to the mounting responsibilities for the delivery of services that local governments were expected to provide. For example, the AUMA has suggested that if the provincial government were truly interested in self-reliant municipalities, it should reduce the amount of money the province takes out of the municipalities in the way of provincial property taxes for education. Revenue from property taxes, the organization asserts, should remain with the local governments.[95] AUMA also has suggested that the finances of municipalities should be "de-linked" from those of the province, and that a financial and legal system that gives municipalities some autonomy, predictability, and flexibility should be developed. By 2003, however, AUMA proclaimed itself pleased with proposed amendments to the Alberta Municipal Government Act, believing that it would "give municipalities firm authority to collect levies that offset various infrastructure costs."[96]

Without revenues to fulfill their service responsibilities, local governments gained little, if anything, in terms of increased autonomy over local affairs. In fact, according to the AUMA, while Albertan municipalities were receiving cutbacks from the provincial government between 1996 and 2000, provincial government revenues rose 26 percent and municipal revenues rose only 11 percent.[97] Even given these financial constraints, municipal governments were still required to provide services in a matter that satisfied provincial standards and legislation. The putative goals of the 1995 Municipal Government Act appeared unfulfilled seven years later. Other municipalities across the country have found themselves in similar positions.

## British Columbia

Beginning in 1965, rapid growth related to resource development led to a reorganization of the municipal system in British Columbia. Boards of directors, composed of mayors and other elected representatives (from the municipalities) and elected directors from the districts, governed the regional districts (see Box 5.4).

These districts were created to deal with growing municipalities, particularly in the rapidly expanding metropolitan areas of Victoria and Vancouver, and to cope with problems of service fragmentation. Intermunicipal special-purpose bodies were replaced with regional districts, which led to a different system of representation and service delivery in areas of economic development, water supply, sewage disposal, and solid waste management.[98]

## 5.4  Amalgamation in Prince George, British Columbia

Before 1915, a government agent administered the three small communities of Prince George, Fort George, and South Fort George. Subsequently, Prince George was incorporated as a city in 1915, and in 1953 the smaller town of Centre Fort George was amalgamated into the City of Prince George. In order to control the rate and nature of development, the city became involved in real estate developing and in selling "fully serviced" subdivisions. In 1975, large tracts of land of outlying areas and South Fort George were amalgamated into Prince George. The amalgamation linked vast areas of undeveloped wilderness together in anticipation of future growth.

Prince George (along with three other municipalities and rural communities) falls within the regional district of Fraser-Fort George.

*Source:* Bev Christensen, *Prince George: Rivers, Railways, and Timber* (Burlington, ON: Windsor Publications, 1989), 42-44.

Hodge and Robinson note that regional districts are not regional governments as might be found in Ontario; they are "parallel" governments and provide cooperative services by agreement among participating municipal councils. They were intended to be functional rather than political units.[99]

A lack of coordination of local services, and problems related to the funding of hospitals, led to additional restructuring. Up to that point, cities and towns had previously been responsible for funding the capital costs of hospitals. This meant, for example, that Prince George taxpayers paid for the higher costs entailed in a regional rather than just a city hospital because it was located in their city. This inequitable situation was addressed in 1967 with the introduction of regional hospital districts. In sum, in the period 1965-70, the whole province was divided into a series of regional districts. Regional districts were once again revisited during the 1980s, leading to additional restructuring as well as improved provincial-local intergovernmental processes of collaboration. Each region is composed of several regional districts, of which there are approximately twenty-five in total.[100]

Considerable municipal restructuring has taken place over the years in British Columbia. These primarily functional shifts have taken the form of boundary extensions, incorporations, or restructuring of districts or other forms of government. This has particularly been the case in the rapidly growing Lower Mainland, lower Vancouver Island, the Fraser Valley, and the Okanagan.

### Greater Vancouver Regional District

Vancouver is the third-largest city in Canada with 546,000 people (in 2001) in a densely populated region of approximately 2,000,000. While numerous studies have been devoted to the transportation problems caused by rapid population growth, the province had not moved to amalgamate all the municipalities in the Greater Vancouver Regional District (GVRD) by 2003. Under the GVRD, a system of cooperation evolved to coordinate the delivery of some services, such as water, but other services, like policing and snow removal remained local responsibilities. Intermunicipal agreements among the loose association of municipalities developed over time.

Amalgamation has been a comparatively rare phenomenon in British Columbia, although it does happen. In 1995, for example, some communities merged to form the larger City of Abbotsford. In British Columbia, amalgamations are approved by the electorate through the municipal voting process.[101]

### British Columbia Local Government Act

In 1996, the provincial government in cooperation with the Union of British Columbia Municipalities began the process of revising the Municipal Act. In September 1998, the Local Government Statutes Amendment Act (Bill 31, 1998) came into effect "recognizing local government as an independent, responsible and accountable order of government." Moreover, it gave local governments broad corporate powers in a number of areas, such as agreements with public- or private-sector partners, the acquisition or management of land, increased discretion with respect to the allocation of revenues, and more flexibility in decision making.[102]

## Community Charter Council Act

On 23 August 2001, the newly elected Liberal government's Bill 12-2001 the Community Charter Council Act received third reading. Among the principles, the Charter stated that local governments were to be recognized as an order of government and that the provincial government was to "respect municipal authority in areas of municipal decision-making."[103] The preamble of the charter begins on a promising note:

> WHEREAS the Provincial government believes that
> (a) municipalities should have greater autonomy,
> (b) municipalities should have a wider range of tools to reduce reliance on property tax revenues, and
> (c) the Provincial government should not reduce its costs by transferring responsibilities to municipalities.[104]

The government then established the Community Charter Council, which in turn prepared a report that was to provide a foundation for the future of local government in British Columbia. The final outcome was the Community Charter Act, which received royal assent on 29 March 2003. The Act stated that municipalities and their councils are provincially recognized to be democratically elected, "autonomous, responsible and accountable," and that they required the ability to draw on financial sources adequate to provide services to communities.

## Northern Territories: Devolution

Local government in the territories requires different responses from senior governments than in other parts of the country. For example, Aboriginal communities have distinct governing arrangements from non-Aboriginal localities, and they are a significant component of the territorial population and culture.

After 1960, some devolution of authority from the federal to the territorial government took place. While pressure on senior governments for increased self-governing authority and more revenue sharing has been intensifying in all parts of Canada, arguments for devolution of powers in the territories were bolstered by a number of factors, some cultural, others practical. Pressure for further devolution of authority from the territorial governments down to local communities accompanied the negotiation of treaties and self-government for Aboriginal peoples. There are also practical considerations, such as the challenges of attempting to govern isolated and remote communities by a centralized authority. Given the sparse population spread over large territories, communities are not easily governed at a distance.

## Yukon

In Yukon, 1998 saw the introduction of a new municipal act covering a broad range of responsibilities. The territorial government stated that the new act would allow citizens to have more control over local matters and would provide for rural communities to organize local governments and develop partnerships with each other in order to deliver services.[105]

By 2002, the Yukon Territory population was approximately 30,000 (living in a territory covering 483,450 square kilometres). While the majority of inhabitants were of European descent, one-fifth was Aboriginal.[106] Economically, the territory has been heavily dependent on mining for its wage economy, although tourism is becoming increasingly important. Hunting and trapping remain an important aspect of the Aboriginal population's traditional economy. The population is organized into one city (the capital, Whitehorse, with a population of 22,000), seven towns and six local advisory areas. In the capital, government employment and a diversity of businesses are important sources of income for this community that houses 70 percent of the population.[107] The other communities are spread out over a vast area, with Dawson City as the second-largest community (almost 2,000 people) and Watson Lake following close behind. Most of the communities contain a few hundred people. Like the other northern territories, the geographical dispersion of the population makes it inevitable that some form of decentralization and self-government will happen by default, if not by design.

In spring 2002, however, the Yukon government introduced two structural changes affecting local government. The first was the introduction of a new Department of Community Services under the territorial government's "Renewal of Government," and the second was an Accountability Plan. The Community Services department has adopted the business approach to structural change with the goal of being "service-oriented and customer focused" toward its citizens.[108] Neither the department nor the plan directly dealt with the topic of decentralizing authority to local government. The Accountability Plan discussed developing and strengthening the capacity of Yukon communities, and it would encourage "meaningful" participation by citizens in local government, pursue service-delivery partnerships with communities, and "facilitate direct consultation" between the territorial government and communities.[109]

Nevertheless, the territory is involved in the process of devolution with the federal government, and First Nations peoples are actively involved in self-government processes. Communities are spread far apart geographically. These factors may well influence some future devolution of authority to the municipal level of government.

## Northwest Territories

In 2002, over 41,400 people populated the Northwest Territories (NWT). The territory, situated in the western Arctic, was subdivided into two territories in 1999 with the eastern half becoming Nunavut. The remaining landmass in the Northwest Territories covers 1,172,918 square kilometres. Half of the population of the territory is Aboriginal. Yellowknife, the territorial capital, is the only city. In addition, the territory contains one village, three settlements, four towns, ten hamlets, four charter communities, and ten designated authorities.[110] In 1967, the territorial council was relocated from Ottawa to Yellowknife, which became the first city in the Northwest Territories in 1967. By 2001, the city contained 16,541 people.[111]

In 1997, the territorial government introduced a number of legislative changes dealing with local government in the territory. In the ensuing three years, the Ministry of Municipal and Community Affairs and the NWT Association of Municipalities comprehensively reviewed municipal legislation. Changes to the existing legislation were to provide the foundation for local government in the newly divided territories of the Northwest Territories and Nunavut.[112] The outcome of the review was a report entitled *Empowerment through Community Government Legislation,* and it covered the Communities Charter Act, the Cities, Towns, Villages Act, the Hamlets Act, and the Settlements Act. Other, smaller Aboriginal communities are not covered by these acts, but they do provide local services through band councils.[113] The report recognized the changing role of municipalities, and that those roles went beyond the provision of infrastructure into other areas, such as economic development and community wellness, as has been noted in the rest of the country. The Government of the Northwest Territories also stated that it wanted to encourage community empowerment, while at the same time noting that it had limited resources to distribute to communities.[114]

One of the challenges facing the Northwest Territories (as well as other governments in Canada) was determining how to develop good municipal relationships with First Nations peoples, who had very different governing arrangements. Aboriginal peoples in the north were continuing to develop their own self-governing arrangements while dealing with the unsettled state of many treaty negotiations. The position taken was that municipal legislative review should continue (because many communities required some form of local government), but at the same time, the review should recognize that self-government arrangements would remain paramount.

The territorial government initiated a Building Communities strategy to encourage self-reliant communities and to assist with community governance.[115] The approach is distinct from southern municipalities because much of the initiative is geared toward helping Aboriginal peoples achieve a form of self-governance and to provide local services.

## Nunavut

After more than twenty years of negotiation among the Inuit of the eastern and central Arctic, the federal and territorial governments, and other stakeholders, Canada's newest territory, Nunavut, officially came into being 1 April 1999.[116] Nunavut, formerly the eastern part of the Northwest Territories, comprises one-fifth of the landmass of the entire country and has approximately 28,000 residents living in 26 communities. The capital of Nunavut is Iqaluit – a community of slightly over 4,000 people.[117] In 1993, the Nunavut Land Claims Agreement was signed, whereby the Inuit received a $1.1 billion settlement to be paid by the federal government, 356,000 square kilometres of land, constituting 18 percent of Nunavut, as well as 38,000 square kilometres of subsurface mineral rights. The Inuit also received the right to self-government and self-determination.

The citizens of Nunavut chose to adapt a conventional government structure (like those elsewhere in Canada) to suit its needs and represent all residents, rather than adopting specifically Inuit governance structures. That said, these governing institutions reflect many more of the ideals of local self-government than do their southern counterparts. Municipal governments play a much bigger role in program and service provision.[118] For example, the territorial justice system relies more heavily on community-based policing approaches and healing circles. The Government of Nunavut also emphasized the importance of decentralization by developing a plan that would distribute regional government department offices throughout a number of communities in each of Nunavut's three regions: Qikiqtaaluk (Baffin), Kivalliq (Keewatin), and Kitikmeot.[119]

The territory possesses some unique geographical and demographic characteristics of the territory coupled with traditional cultures (85 percent are Inuit). These factors have led to an institutional design comprised of a combination of conventional governmental structures, and laws that have been modified to reflect some of the goals and belief systems of the indigenous peoples. The governing principles of the Territory of Nunavut emphasize the importance of healthy communities and local authority where possible. The responsibility of the Department of Community Government and Transportation is to work in partnerships supporting the development, provision, and maintenance of programs and services that affect the communities in all areas of municipal responsibility and transportation, thus enhancing community quality of life and social and economic opportunities. The legislative acts for which it has responsibility reflect many of the same priorities of more densely populated areas of the country, including the Cities, Towns, and Villages Act, the Planning Act, Property Assessment and Taxation Act, and Settlements Act.[120]

## Conclusion

Geographic imperatives, specific regional cultural characteristics, different settlement patterns, shifting ideological approaches, and changing fortunes all contributed to a wide array of provincial innovations when it came to dealing with local government. Nevertheless, it is possible to detect some commonalities across the country. The abilities of local governments to assert authority vis-à-vis the provinces have always been constrained by lack of independent constitutional status and the fact that they fall under provincial legislative authority. Mid-twentieth-century consolidations of school boards and restructuring of municipal systems further reinforced the authority of the provincial governments. The introduction in the 1960s of two-tier regional government in Ontario and Quebec and the system of districts in British Columbia were attempts to deal with regional growth and to coordinate services while maintaining a level of political autonomy at the local level. The Metropolitan Toronto exercise at first appeared to achieve that goal, but it never truly satisfied all the influential political actors. The goal behind Unicity Winnipeg was to introduce a more democratic system of representation, and amalgamation led to a more equitable distribution of resources. The goal of achieving a radically restructured government that supported a more democratic, representative government, however, fell far short of the mark.

By the 1990s, municipal governments were experiencing further erosion in their abilities to respond to local demands. Provincial grants were reduced while the more senior governments imposed new responsibilities upon the local entities, which had no legislative power to resist. *Alternative service delivery* (ASD) and *public-private-sector partnerships* became the buzzwords of the day. If they wished to have increased revenues, local governments would have to work closely with private-sector interests as well as with the province. The extent to which municipal governments could respond to the demands of their citizens was constrained by the more powerful dictates of provincial and commercial interests.

An examination of amalgamation in our case-study cities shows different responses to the pressures of growth. Both the City of Sherbrooke and the City of Saint John became part of an amalgamation process. In the case of both cities, it was noted that the core areas had been providing services for the region and the outlying suburban communities. Amalgamation could serve to redistribute the tax burden much more equitably. In Kitchener-Waterloo, amalgamation was an issue that popped up at irregular intervals through the twentieth century. Although amalgamation did not take place, the upper-tier regional government was given a number of additional responsibilities, greatly strengthening its abilities to provide regional services in such areas as transportation, social housing, and policing. Prince George had been amalgamated in the 1970s by a council that anticipated future growth. The early amalgamation included vast areas of undeveloped land, leaving plenty of room for urban development.

By the late 1990s, municipal associations across Canada were intensifying their pressure on provincial governments to decentralize more areas of decision making and control over revenues. Some provinces had responded by introducing legislation that purportedly gave local governments more flexibility and authority to act in certain broad areas without having to check whether provincial legislation permitted them to do so. Given the strained financial position of these local governments, however, it would be very difficult to capitalize on any areas where there was increased flexibility.

Why have so many provincial attempts at reforming the structures of local governments run into such difficulty? Conventional answers run the gamut from local community antagonism to inadequate leadership to lack of financial resources. All these explanations ignore that structures by themselves are seldom, if ever, either the basic cause, or the probable solution, of the problems they are designed to fix. The challenges go far deeper. They are rooted in differing ideological and ethical perspectives about what constitutes good government; in battles for control, influence, and resources; in inadequate knowledge of critical data and situations; in secrecy; and in information systems grossly inadequate to the tasks of modern, democratic governance. Institutional tinkering has rarely been demonstrated to be a panacea to the systemic problems that characterize modern societies. Yet few decision makers are willing, or perhaps able, to grapple with modern dilemmas in ways that harmonize with modern complex human and biophysical systems. Furthermore, solutions are not readily distilled in a way that sounds good during an election campaign or a sixty-second media clip. For all too many politicians, institutional reform is the most visible and readily identifiable step that a government can take to effect change.

That stated, some institutional changes are necessary as society evolves over time and as demographic and settlement patterns shift. It has been noted that at the time of the first census in 1871, only 18 percent of Canadians lived in a community that had more than 1,000 residents. By 2001, that figure had grown to 80 percent.[121] During the rapid population growth of the twentieth century, intergovernmental relations became increasingly contentious as governments wrangled for resources and control. Provincial off-loading, amalgamations and disentanglement, and the concerns of the mega-cities, mid-sized cities, and rural and Aboriginal communities became topics of great debate, cast against the background of global-local, federal-local, provincial-local, and intermunicipal relations. At the beginning of the twenty-first century, local governments are still very much creatures of the state. The goal of self-government continues to be elusive, despite some initial steps.

Donald Higgins once defined the term "local self-government" as the devolution or distribution of "significant decision-making power to localities," where local governments have a measure of autonomy or discretion over local matters. André Carrel reports that in 1998, the Federation of Canadian Municipalities adopted a renewed Worldwide Declaration of Local Self-Government. The principles begin with an assertion that the principle of local self-government should be included in a country's constitution. The declaration also calls for local authorities to have increased discretion, authority, decision-making responsibility, adequate resources to carry out their responsibilities, legal protection, and autonomy.[122] As the next chapter discusses, recent provincial legislative and policy responses indicate that progress towards this goal will continue to be an uphill battle.

# 6
# Contemporary Intergovernmental Relations

Many different actors and institutions influence the transactions and relations between governments. Provincial-municipal relations are governed by acts and regulations administered through provincial departments or ministries. Although the federal government does not have a department directly responsible for municipal affairs, it influences the local environment in myriad ways. Municipal associations and other professional associations lobby actively on behalf of their constituents, attempting to influence provincial, federal, and sometimes, international decisions.

The 1980s and 1990s saw a growth in tension between local and upper-level governments as a result of provincial off-loading, decreased funding and grants, and sweeping top-down initiatives. New provincial regulatory standards were to be implemented by local governments, service responsibilities were realigned, and in several areas, provinces amalgamated local governments. Sometimes these decisions were made and carried out very quickly. In the mid-1990s, for example, the rapid manner in which Ontario's legislation regarding local affairs was passed without careful parliamentary scrutiny helped stimulate lively debate about whether or not these changes would eventually provide a more efficient, let alone equitable, system.

Today, local government in Canada is composed of many urban centres where most of the population lives. A significant diversity of smaller, rural, and remote communities are scattered throughout the country's vast territory. Some members of these communities feel that provincial policies and standards are too often designed with urban centres in mind, and leave them with limited ability to influence provincial agendas. Ironically, the large city centres also feel powerless, lacking revenues enjoyed by cities of comparable size in the United States and Europe. They sometimes argue that suburban and smaller communities may have too much political influence relative to their size. Small and large local governments, however, do have a shared goal; many, if not most of them, are intensively lobbying provincial governments, pushing for both more autonomy and adequate resources. The following overview of some of the basic intergovernmental structures and organizations will help set the context for these contemporary debates.

## Provincial-Municipal Relations

Each province has a municipal act setting out general provincial policy and laws for local governments. A municipal act will usually state the rules of incorporation, the procedures for financing and running an election or other forms of voting, the kinds of bylaws that might be passed by municipalities, the rules governing taxation, debt management and auditing, licensing and regulation, acquisition and disposal of property, the management of various local services, community planning, and so forth.[1]

Primary responsibility for provincial-local relations has fallen under the mandate of specific provincial departments carrying a wide range of responsibilities and titles, such as the Department of Municipal Affairs and Housing, Department of Intergovernmental Affairs, Department of Environment and Local Government, or in British Columbia, the Ministry of Community, Aboriginal, and Women's Services (created in 2001). The responsibilities of these departments or ministries include developing policy and legislation for governing the overall municipal system; providing advice and services to communities; administering financial assistance programs, emergency planning, and assistance; and developing regulations and ensuring compliance. Provinces also decide municipal boundaries and responsibilities. Most other provincial departments also have roles in municipal affairs, given that their operations affect the daily life of citizens.

Traditionally, land-use policy has been the area in which local governments have had the greatest authority and autonomy, although subdivision planning and other policies are also subject to approval by the province (see Chapter 7). The stakes over land use have become higher and higher as the implications of land-use decisions spill over municipal boundaries. Planning plays a lead role in shaping local communities – the way in which physical spaces are planned goes far beyond the separation of incompatible land uses. It is an activity that determines the culture, politics, and living spaces of societies.

The powers of local governments are also limited by specific acts relating to policing, education, health, planning, environment, property assessment, social services, and so on. This is by no means a new phenomenon. Almost fifty years ago, Crawford noted that "continuous lip service has been paid to the importance of maintaining strong and autonomous local government at the same time that local government was being weakened and its autonomy whittled away by provincial action."[2]

## Federal-Municipal Relations

Because municipalities fall under the constitutional jurisdiction of provinces, the federal government's role is not as obvious and direct as that of the provinces. In recent years, the public visibility of the federal government in communities has diminished because many of its physical manifestations, such as government wharves, local post offices, customs offices, and other federal government buildings have disappeared from the local landscape. Nevertheless, the federal government does play a very important role in municipal politics, and many of its decisions about program funding, taxation, and regulations deeply affect communities. Recent programs that transfer federal funds to municipalities have included the Infrastructure Canada Program, Green Municipal Enabling Fund, Green

Municipal Investment Fund, and National Homelessness Initiative. Other expenditures do not go directly to municipalities but nevertheless assist in services that directly affect communities, including settlement and language programs for recent immigrants, funds for a National Crime Prevention Program, and the federal government's Technology Partnerships Program.[3]

As urban centres continue their rapid growth, municipal issues spill over into areas of national jurisdictional concern. Examples include immigration policy, air and water quality issues, international trade agreements, and transportation and communications. An ongoing softwood lumber dispute between Canada and the United States, for example, has had a serious impact on local communities. This is particularly the case for resource-based communities, such as Prince George, that rely on the softwood lumber industry to sustain the local economy. The mayor of Prince George participated in a Federation of Canadian Municipality's taskforce to Washington to solicit support from US mayors to protect communities from further damage caused by the dispute. The dispute, which resulted in US-imposed countervailing and anti-dumping duties directed at Canadian softwood exports, threw thousands of citizens out of work.[4]

One of the earliest and best-known examples of federal activities in municipal affairs was the housing policy and the Canada Mortgage and Housing Corporation (CMHC). This corporation came into operation in 1946 to develop much-needed housing stock and administer the National Housing Act. Housing construction has often been used to stimulate the economy, and this was the case in post-war Canada. The primary goal of the corporation was to increase the availability of low-cost housing through various types of financial assistance and incentives. CMHC expanded gradually into other areas of urban renewal and neighbourhood improvement plans. Into the 1980s, CMHC played a huge role in assisting in the building of new homes. Higgins points out that "between a third and half of all housing built each year in Canada since 1946" was financed through the National Housing Act.[5]

Yet the initiative did not come without social or environmental costs. Christopher Leo notes that the activities of the CMHC, in combination with provincial and municipal regulatory and planning activity, contributed considerably to suburban development and a planning regime that encouraged low-density planning and the use of the automobile at the expense of public transit.[6]

By the mid-1980s, the era of fiscal restraint and privatization had taken its toll on such government corporations. CMHC's role was significantly reduced to focus primarily on low-income families, non-profit housing, and housing rehabilitation. The federal government began to disengage in many areas, leaving the field open for the provincial governments to deliver programs and the private sector and municipalities to develop new housing stock.[7] It did maintain its role in the area, working through tri-level cooperation that resulted in a large affordable-housing federal program in the early 2000s.[8]

Despite such initiatives, the federal government has been constrained in terms of direct intervention in areas viewed as provincial jurisdiction. For example, in 1971, the federal government created the Ministry of State for Urban Affairs (MSUA). In an attempt to deflect criticism from provincial governments about incursions into their jurisdictional territory, the MSUA was supposedly to design national urban policies rather than specific urban programs. The MSUA was underfunded and was also seen as cutting into the jurisdiction of other federal departments (such as CMHC) in addition to that of the provincial governments. It was terminated in 1979.[9]

Since that time, the federal government primarily has been involved in specific national institutions that have affected communities. A number of tri-level initiatives have been developed in areas such as transportation and information-communications infrastructure, affordable housing, community health, and environmental concerns. All these areas involved a number of high-profile tri-level discussions and initiatives in the early 2000s.

In 2001, Prime Minister Chrétien established the Caucus Task Force on Urban Issues to see how the federal government, within its area of jurisdiction, could work collaboratively to improve quality of life in urban centres. As the federal minister of Intergovernmental Affairs noted, the federal government must stay away from municipal affairs because that is the constitutional mandate of the provinces. He asserted, however, that this situation did not preclude the federal government from addressing rural and urban issues "from a broader sense."[10]

As urban centres grow in size and importance, some analysts have called for a more active federal role. Thomas Axworthy has suggested that, in this respect, Canada compares unfavourably to the United States and Europe where the senior governments have played a more active part in sustaining their cities.[11] In one comparative study of six western American and six western Canadian cities, it was discovered that the Canadian cities were highly dependent on property taxes: the Canada West Foundation study noted that

the six western cities, on average, have 88.7% of their tax revenue coming from property taxes compared to 52.0% for the six U.S. cities. Unlike most of the U.S. cities, however, property tax revenues in western Canada are not capped. Most of the U.S. cities have access to a general retail sales tax. Western Canadian cities do not. The most significant difference between western Canadian cities and their U.S. counterparts is that most of the American cities included in this study have their own local general sales tax – only Boise, Idaho does not have a general sales tax.[12]

Axworthy suggests that one way of helping to "shore up" Canadian cities would be through dedicating monies collected through the federal gasoline tax for infrastructure needs – an approach that has been used in the United States. The use of dedicated taxes is not favoured by the federal government, which prefers to have more flexibility.[13] Enid Slack argues that "there is a role for the federal government arising from economic competitiveness, federal policies that have a financial impact on cities, and international commitments. Where there is a fiscal gap [when municipalities have inadequate revenues to meet their expenditure needs] however, it is probably more appropriate for provincial governments to provide assistance or change the expenditure and/or revenue-raising abilities of cities."[14]

It is important for any student of local governance to be aware of the role played by national government, and not only because of the way its policy decisions may affect communities. Christopher Leo warns that any potential progressive role that might be taken by a senior government on behalf of local governments is threatened by global market regimes, which have reduced the capacity of national governments to act in a supportive manner or "to intervene in market operations."[15] These constraining forces must be recognized in any intergovernmental analysis.

That said, in the 2 February 2004 Throne Speech, the government of Canada (headed by the new Liberal prime minister, Paul Martin) announced a "New Deal for Communities." To that end, the federal government would work with other governments either to share a portion of the gas tax revenues with municipalities or to find some other fiscal measures to provide long-term stable funding for communities. In terms of immediate action, the government pledged that it would relieve all municipalities from paying their portion of the federal Goods and Services Tax, a concession that was estimated to provide municipalities with $7 billion over a decade. According to the Speech from the Throne, "The new deal means that city hall has a real seat at the table of national change."[16]

## The Role of the Courts: The Case of Pesticides in Hudson, Quebec

Court rulings often have had an impact on how municipal authority and jurisdiction might be interpreted. One decision that has some important implications for municipal autonomy is a Supreme Court of Canada case about a bylaw of the city of Hudson, Quebec, which banned the cosmetic use of pesticides within municipal boundaries. On 28 June 2001, the Supreme Court of Canada upheld the municipality's right to pass such bylaws as long as it did not conflict with legislation at the provincial or federal levels.

This issue pitted the Canadian Environmental Law Association (also representing nine other environmental groups) against two companies that used pesticides. The companies were appealing the right of the city to pass a bylaw that controlled the use and application of pesticides. Many of the interveners represented organizations with national scope or anti-pesticide groups in other communities.[17] Among other things, the case illustrates how local environmental groups can now network with outside non-governmental organizations in a way that makes them influential forces when dealing with other powerful actors. In this case, the environmental groups were supporting a local government's decision. This is certainly not always the situation, as the earlier discussion of the proposed waste site in Adams Mine would indicate (see Chapter 2).

There are other interesting aspects to the case. Jerry DeMarco notes that most provincial municipal acts (including Quebec's) allow for the passing of bylaws that promote

SHIFTING RESPONSIBILITIES

general welfare or the environment. This decision cited international law, emphasizing the *precautionary principle,* upholding the right of local governments to take preventative action to stop environmental harm. DeMarco also stressed the importance of this decision for local autonomy, quoting the following sections of the Supreme Court ruling:

[para 3] The case arises in an era in which matters of governance are often examined through the lens of the principle of subsidiarity. This is the proposition that *law making and implementation are often best achieved* at a level of government that is not only effective, but also *closest to the citizens affected* and thus most responsive to their needs, to local distinctiveness, and to population diversity ... The so-called "Brundtland Commission" recommended that "local governments [should be] empowered to exceed, but not to lower, national norms." [para 49] A tradition of *strong local government* has become an important part of the Canadian democratic experience. This level of government usually appears more attuned to the immediate needs and concerns of the citizens.[18]

During the course of Canadian history, the Supreme Court has made decisions that have, by turns, served to centralize and at other times to decentralize authority. It has ruled on issues as diverse as school board authority, amalgamation, and the ability of municipalities to pass bylaws. Decisions like the one in the case of Hudson, Quebec, underline the important roles that courts play in determining the relative degree of autonomy that a municipality might exert.

## Municipal Associations: Influence and Lobbying

Many of the previous sections might lead the reader to believe that municipalities have little or no influence in intergovernmental affairs. While at times this might appear to be the case, municipalities do have some impact on the behaviour of senior governments. They can be very effective lobbyists, both individually and as members of associations. Most municipalities are members of province-wide associations that represent the broader interests of municipalities when negotiating with the provinces. These negotiations often focus on obtaining more resources, revenues, assistance, or political authority from the provinces. These municipal associations represent an important vehicle through which local communities lobby provincial governments. In Saskatchewan, for example, municipal associations include the Saskatchewan Urban Municipalities Association, the Saskatchewan Association of Rural Municipalities, the Provincial Association of Resort Communities of Saskatchewan, the Saskatchewan Association of Northern Communities, Urban Municipal Administrators' Association of Saskatchewan, and Rural Municipal Administrators' Association of Saskatchewan.[19]

## Federation of Canadian Municipalities

Municipalities also organize themselves at the national level, as is the case with the Federation of Canadian Municipalities (FCM), and internationally. Professional associations deal with specific areas of municipal interest (such as in the areas of planning or policing). The federation was formed in 1937 under the name Canadian Federation of Mayors and Municipalities (CFMM) in an initiative to get unemployment relief from the federal government during the Depression. The CFMM's roots were planted in earlier national meetings of municipalities, one of which was a fight for more control over the activities of local utilities. In the 1980s the organization became known as the Federation of Canadian Municipalities. Since its formation, it has acted as a vociferous lobbyist of municipal interests ranging from property tax issues, grants, housing, service provision, and so on. One of the most successful of the FCM's programs was the lobbying that led to the establishment of a $6 billion tri-level shared-cost government infrastructure program.[20]

FCM membership ranges from small rural communities to the largest urban centres, and also includes all the provincial and territorial associations. The organization represents municipalities in all areas of federal jurisdiction. In recent years, it has been tackling international and global issues related to international trade negotiations, such as the North American Free Trade Agreement (NAFTA). Questions have been raised about whether NAFTA might restrict the ability of municipalities to set bylaws related to such areas as the natural environment, land zoning, and other land-use matters. This issue is particularly relevant with respect to the public-private partnerships that present a way for cash-strapped municipalities to provide services. FCM has been concerned that, under NAFTA, a private-sector company might be able to challenge a government at a tribunal if the government's decisions adversely affected investments.[21] In such cases, the FCM acts as liaison for the municipalities by lobbying the federal government about their concerns.

The FCM has not been without controversy. It has had difficulty in portraying itself as the representative of all the municipalities. Higgins noted that in the 1970s, "Neither the small municipalities nor the big urban members saw their interests as being well served by the organization, and the big urban members in particular threatened to create their own national voice."[22] More recently the "big city" mayors have formed their own group to ensure that their interests are recognized. It is difficult for a national organization to represent all the municipalities when their interests differ and when the provinces hold constitutional jurisdiction over local government.[23]

Despite such difficulties, the wide-ranging work of the FCM has extended to virtually all policy areas that might affect municipalities, including international affairs, with respect to the impacts of climate change negotiations on municipalities, municipal-aboriginal relations, environmental issues, housing, infrastructure, urban strategies, and taxation. Its membership contains over 1,000 municipalities representing over 80 percent of the Canadian population. It also has 113 corporate partners that provide services to municipalities and all the provincial and territorial municipal associations.[24] It is an important voice for local governments, and it draws much-needed public attention to the struggles of municipalities to achieve a measure of autonomy and the financial resources to carry out their functions.

It should be noted that although the FCM is a very important national lobbying voice for municipalities, the provincial associations are also very powerful and work actively to represent the interests of municipalities. Such organizations play an important representative role, particularly when one considers complex contemporary issues related to disentanglement, revenue sharing, amalgamation, and other intergovernmental affairs.

## Disentanglement

As local governments evolved, their main responsibilities were to provide *hard services,* such as municipal roads, sewers, water, and intra-city public transit. The money was to come from property taxes. They also had an important responsibility in governing public education through local school boards. The provincial government retained responsibility for *soft services,* such as social and health services. While it seemed to be a clear-cut fiscal approach in principle, in practice property taxes fell far short of providing the necessary revenues for local provision of services. Over the years, local governments increasingly relied on grants from senior governments to subsidize the rapidly growing costs of providing infrastructure. In addition, in the past few decades it has become apparent that local government responsibilities for soft services have been rapidly growing. Local governments are now often confronted with social issues that the other levels of government have not adequately addressed. Clearly, more money is needed for social housing, multicultural programs, provision of English or French language assistance to new Canadians and landed immigrants, complex environmental issues, halfway houses, shelters, community health, home care, and welfare. Yet funding proportionate to need has not been forthcoming from the provinces.

Recent provincial government attempts at disentanglement appear to have increased complexity rather than simplifying service delivery. Enid Slack notes that in Ontario, the local-services realignment transferred responsibility for both hard services (waste, sewerage, roads, and transit) as well as soft services (social housing, some areas of public health, and other services) to the local governments. At the same time, the province assumed educational funding responsibilities and cut educational property taxes by half.

The provincial rationale for downloading such programs as social housing was based on the assumption that local governments are closest to the people and thus best understand the needs of the community.[25] Slack says that this realignment goes against "advice given by every committee, task force, and panel commissioned in this province over the last decade to sort out responsibilities between the provincial government and municipalities."[26] Essentially, all these committees recommended that only the provincial government should fund all social services. She stated three main reasons why this should be the case:

- Social services should be funded through income, not property taxes.
- Provincial restrictions on the way local governments can borrow funds deprive local governments of the flexibility to respond with social services when needed.
- The provision of social services requires uniform standards and treatment.

If local governments are required to provide those services, they must cover the cost but they lack flexibility in the way these services are delivered.[27] Only one other province besides Ontario – Manitoba – required municipalities to fund social services, a requirement strongly opposed by the municipal association.[28]

Graham and colleagues, however, provide a different perspective than the one argued by Slack and others. They suggest "the ideas that cities are primarily deliverers of hard services and that there should be a separation of responsibilities for physical and human services into watertight compartments remain strong themes in municipal political discourse. But this mantra is fundamentally flawed."[29] They note that the main responsibilities of local government can be found in "building citizenship and social harmony." They also stress the importance of voluntary organizations in sustaining communities, and the requirement to "deliver human services in urban centres in a manner that is sensitive to the needs of their diverse populations."[30] Local governments then, despite traditional perspectives, could potentially play an important part in the social and health needs of a community. These needs will vary from place to place. The goal should be to respond to this reality with appropriate public policy, legislation, and funding.

Without increased funding and political will, such changes are unlikely to come to pass in the near future. Throughout the 1990s, the approach taken by many provincial governments was firmly rooted in fiscally conservative ideology, as proponents argued that the post-war growth of the welfare state had led to a bloated political and bureaucratic system of governance. Accordingly, their answer was to increase economic productivity through debt reduction, scaling back political representation, and amalgamating localities to achieve "less government" – at least in the case of municipalities. The concept of revenue sharing was not something that fit well with the governing ideology.

### Intergovernmental Transfers and Revenue Sharing

In the 1970s, provinces introduced a degree of certainty and consistency into provincial-local funding arrangements by establishing a number of revenue-sharing programs. By the 1990s, many of these programs had suffered serious cutbacks, leaving municipalities more dependent on property taxes, user fees, and other forms of revenues. Provincial transfers consist of both conditional grants (to be spent on a specific service) and unconditional grants (to be spent on any expenditure or tax reduction). Slack notes that "provincial transfers to municipal governments have declined significantly from 21.8 percent of municipal revenues in 1988 to 14.4 percent in 1998."[31]

By the turn of the twenty-first century, municipal associations across the country began to lobby more intensively for a redistribution of funds from provincial and federal coffers to the local levels of government. Saskatchewan provides one such example. In Saskatchewan in the late 1970s to mid-1980s, a revenue-sharing grant program of unconditional operating grants was established. It consisted of a basic grant, a per capita grant, and a foundation (equalization) grant for each community. According to the Saskatchewan Urban Municipalities Association (SUMA), these grants were to grow as the provincial government tax base grew. During the 1990s, however, funding for this program dropped by 60 percent. The program was also frozen at 1997-98 levels and had not been increased by 2001.[32] In addition to these grants were a series of unconditional capital grant programs. Capital grants that had been provided for urban highways and municipal infrastructure had also been significantly reduced.[33] SUMA introduced a committee by the name of Opportunities for Alternative Revenue Sources. One of the main proposals of the committee was to see the municipalities receive the revenues from a province-wide municipal fuel tax, and the monies would be used to provide infrastructure.[34] The fuel tax is something that other municipalities across the country have argued for in recent years as a way of redistributing revenues. All of our case-study cities, from the period of 1988 to 2002, had experienced a decline in provincial grants.

The options for addressing the fiscal gap include either increased transfer of funds or allowing the local governments to tax other sources in such areas as income, sales, fuel, or hotel occupancy.[35] Enid Slack has suggested that "revenue sharing, when it allows local governments to levy their own tax rates, provides the most autonomy and accountability at the local level. Particularly for large metropolitan regions, having appropriate revenue sources will allow them to be financially independent of other orders of government. Intergovernmental transfers may still be needed, however, to address issues of externalities and equity."[36]

## Amalgamation

As noted earlier, some provincial governments introduced a series of amalgamations changing two-tier governments into one level of government. Many affected citizens and councils strenuously resisted these moves. Three notable cases include Halifax (1996), Toronto (1998), and Montreal (2002). In each case, the new cities comprised a large proportion of the province's population. In the case of Montreal, opposition to amalgamation took on its own flavour, as the issue revolved around concerns about language and culture.

Linguistic majorities in former municipalities became linguistic minorities in the larger amalgamated cities. James Lightbody, however, points to a number of problems associated with multiple fragmented governments:

- avoidance of dealing with externalities or spillovers (that is, the effects of decisions taken by one local government having an impact on another local government)
- inability to develop the coordinated provision of services
- unequal distribution of costs; this is often the case when suburban municipalities surround a core, older city and take advantage of the services it has to offer without absorbing any of the costs associated with the provision of services, including social and health programs
- problems of jurisdictional responsibility and accountability.[37]

Lightbody has noted that the problem of spillover and the offloading of costs to core cities on the part of the outlying areas are not confined to large census metropolitan areas. He suggests that this was also the case in very small metropolitan areas, such as St. John's, Newfoundland, with seventeen units of government for about 162,000 people in the mid-1990s. St. John's, itself, carries many of the costs for the smaller surrounding bedroom communities.[38] Today the population has grown to over 173,000.[39]

The same argument was used by the mayor of the newly amalgamated City of Sherbrooke when announcing the 2003 budget. He noted that taxpayers in the former suburbs would see a 5 percent increase in their taxes in order to achieve equity between the taxpayers in the core area of the former City of Sherbrooke and the former suburbs. There are, however, some additional infrastructural costs that also go along with an amalgamation process.[40]

Lightbody contends that two-tier metropolitan systems of government (what he calls "Jurassic" era governments) were inevitably bound to offer limited answers to problems of effective governance. First, he argues that an upper tier of government rarely, if ever, can be effectively delineated. Governments rapidly outgrow their boundaries, and the demarcation of those boundaries is always problematic, rarely being comprehensive enough for land-use planning purposes. As such, "effective metropolitan planning will always reside with the most authoritative and territorially comprehensive unit, the provincial government."[41]

Moreover a regional form of government is not an effective structure through which to address the growing popular demands of citizens for direct involvement in decision-making processes. Accountability is fuzzy because it is hard for the citizen to know which of the two is responsible for what service. Finally, if the upper tier of government were to be comprehensive enough to deal with large planning issues, elected representatives inevitably would be responsible for very large constituencies and could not readily be held accountable to their electors in any meaningful sense, and certainly would not be responsive to the needs of minority interests.[42] Lightbody concludes,

There no longer really is a significant proactive role for historically defined cities in the governing of entire Canadian CMA [census metropolitan area] regions. To advocate otherwise is to prolong the inevitable weaning from the bi-level diversion, a compromise that stays off serious re-examination of what local government really should be in the 1990s. It also prevents the serious provincial initiatives now needed, and it delays focused attention on the do-able. The provinces have the taxation base to redress inequities and to innovate and integrate program areas. They have the geographic scope to manage, to coordinate and to delegate as appropriate. And, they possess the ideological legitimacy that partisan elections can provide. The two-tier metro format obscures all of these things."[43]

Anti-amalgamation analysts base their concerns about the potential effects of amalgamation on local democratic representation, efficiency, economic effectiveness, and innovation, as well as on the possible undermining of a community's culture, traditions, and practices. In their examination of the numerous amalgamations that took place in Ontario in the late 1990s, Downey and Williams argue that the province's restructuring mandate was assigned to municipalities with little evidence of negotiation, despite government rhetoric to the contrary. They note that municipally held referendums that overwhelmingly rejected the amalgamations were dismissed as illegitimate. The opposition of city councils was ignored. "The Harris government proceeded to implement its own agenda on the assumption that its majority in the legislative assembly gave it a justification to remake the entire municipal system."[44] Municipalities had no choice but to implement the structural changes.

The Ontario government's imposition of sweeping reform on municipalities and its dismissal of hundreds of community institutions with the often-heard mantra of "less government" and "more efficiency" did not persuade critics. The critics were often bemused by the apparent assertion that the centralization of power and the imposition of sweeping pieces of legislation somehow constituted "less government." Beyond their concerns about the process taken by the provincial government, a number of critics opposed to amalgamation are concerned about the long-term implications for the democratic role played by municipalities. As Downey and Williams observe, "The ratio of elected officials to electors may have been very high in some sparsely populated or small-scale municipalities, and there may now be techniques available to keep voters more closely in touch with their representatives that were not available in the 1840s when the municipal system was devised, but the representative capacity of the municipal system has been severely hampered by the elimination of significant numbers of elected officials."[45]

Another critic of amalgamation, Andrew Sancton, asks whether or not the initiative would bring about the much-proclaimed cost savings for taxpayers. Sancton contends that, over the years, there has been no persuasive research demonstrating that amalgamation reduces costs; in fact, the reverse might be the case. For example, services may be consolidated, and overlapping responsibilities reduced, but there are other costs that have to be figured into the equation. Amalgamation can lead to the raising of citizen expectations throughout the new large cities. Citizens in all parts of the new city will expect the same level of services, and municipal employees will expect the same level of pay and benefits. Sancton also draws on the public-choice argument that suggests consolidation eliminates competition among municipalities to keep taxes low, while adopting innovative new approaches to deliver services. Sancton acknowledges that consolidation can lead to the more equitable distribution of resources, thereby promoting equity and fairness. However, he suggests that the main argument in favour of it – that it will produce cost savings – remains unconvincing.[46] On the other hand, in a comparative study between Calgary and Edmonton, Lightbody offers evidence suggesting that Calgary, as the more unitary of the two cities, can offer more cost-efficient services.[47]

Finally, some raise the concern about the impact that amalgamation might have on local community, cultures, and traditions. The consolidation of communities built on old traditions and shared histories can undermine the citizens' identification with their villages, towns, and cities, and can erode their sense of place. It is this sense of place that gives people feelings of belonging, efficacy, and responsibility toward their community. Citizens provide a valuable social, economic, and political service in maintaining the fabric of the communities. As volunteers, they help maintain services far beyond the capacity of paid local employees. Lynne Woolstencroft, elected mayor of Waterloo in 2000, wonders if one of the most important implications of amalgamation has been virtually ignored. "In the late 1990s, when the City of Waterloo did a very rough inventory of volunteers, council was told that the financial value was $8 million per year. The City of Waterloo prides itself on partnerships with volunteers. When amalgamations occur, the volunteer base erodes visibly."[48] The costs of amalgamation are more than simply those directly associated with services provided by the municipal government itself. Amalgamations affect the volunteer base and an individual's sense of civic attachment.

When working one's way through the complexities of the amalgamation debates and the question of whether it is more equitable, efficient, and democratic to merge cities or to keep them distinct entities, it is important to recognize that amalgamation can be put into place for very different reasons, and it can achieve different results. A single amalgamated city, for example, carefully conceived to be democratically responsive (such as was originally intended with Unicity Winnipeg) can produce a more equitable and effective level of services across a large area. In a fragmented political system, wealthier suburban enclaves can profit at the expense of core areas while limiting the opportunities to develop a more sustainable, livable city. Equitable treatment is an important aspect of modern democracies.

On the other hand, the recent amalgamation exercise in Ontario was driven solely by quests for efficiency. The trade-off between efficiency and representation was notable in the forced reduction of municipal councillors without the introduction of other compensating mechanisms. Amalgamation does not need to be accompanied by the elimination of local representation. In Sherbrooke, Quebec, for example, when the cities were

SHIFTING RESPONSIBILITIES

amalgamated, attempts were made to retain the culture and sense of community in the former municipalities through the institution of boroughs. Members of council are now elected to represent individual boroughs within the City of Sherbrooke, and the boroughs themselves have regular council meetings. As discussed in Chapter 3, after the amalgamations, a series of round tables were held in Sherbrooke in order to confer with citizens about how services could best be delivered and how citizens could become engaged in community initiatives. This is a markedly different approach from what was experienced in various parts of Ontario after the sweeping amalgamations of the 1990s, where one of the stated goals was to reduce the number of politicians.

## Post-Amalgamation and Intergovernmental Relations

In the coming years, the amalgamation exercises may lead to some interesting results in terms of intergovernmental relations. The new larger cities that constitute a good proportion of a province's population will have more combined resources and political influence. Their abilities to set agendas and to resist provincial dictates may be much stronger than was the case in the past. As Stéphane Dion, then president of the Privy Council and minister of intergovernmental affairs, noted in a speech at the 2001 annual meeting of the Federation of Canadian Municipalities,

> the size of some of our major cities is increasingly outstripping that of many provinces, a phenomenon that is accentuated by recent or future amalgamations. The municipality of Toronto alone has more inhabitants than do six of our provinces. It will be the same for the future City of Montreal, enlarged by amalgamations. The mayors of these large cities are becoming increasingly important figures, both nationally and internationally. Within the provinces themselves, large cities have taken on a tremendous weight: 55 percent of Manitobans live in Winnipeg, 37 percent of Nova Scotians live in Halifax, and 28 percent of Albertans live in Calgary. As well, 25 percent of Quebecers will live in the future City of Montreal.[49]

As a result of the amalgamations and off-loading of government responsibilities, the FCM initiated a campaign to promote the idea of greater self-sufficiency and autonomy for local government. Five of Canada's largest cities began to meet regularly to lobby for special recognition of their unique needs and roles in the provincial economies. These mega-cities argue that they are now of such a size that they can more efficiently and effectively govern their own affairs and need their own special pieces of legislation that are distinct from the laws that govern much smaller communities (see Chapter 7). Activists in these larger cities recognize that the only hope for achieving a measure of self-government is by developing a unified strategy among all municipalities. John Sewell observes,

The only way forward is for Toronto to link its demands with those of other municipalities towards which the provincial government does not bear so much hostility. One demand all municipalities can agree on is the demand for more autonomy – all want the ability to make their own decisions without provincial interference just as they were able to do until 1995. They also want to be protected from provincial decisions to force its financial responsibilities on them. What they require is a statement – perhaps a law – that the province will respect local autonomy and will not change financial arrangements without substantial notice, without full independent impact studies, without prior discussion and without full discussion in Queen's Park committees and the legislature.[50]

More autonomy to make decisions would certainly be a shared common concern between urban and rural or remote regions of Canada, but for such autonomy to have meaning it must be accompanied by adequate financial and legal resources. However, the distribution of resources and decision-making powers within the province between the metropolitan and rural regions (that is, how the pie should be divided) is not an area where consensus will be readily achieved. This is particularly the case where there is no shared sense of political culture, as the following discussion illustrates.

## Northern Communities: "Beyond Hope and Proud of It"

"Beyond Hope and Proud of It" is a slogan that was found on T-shirts sold by the public library in Prince George, BC, in 1996. It is a slogan fraught with meaning for the citizens who live in the interior and northern areas of British Columbia. These residents, like others who live in rural and remote areas, are increasingly intolerant of the dismissive way in which their communities have been viewed by the metropolitan centres of the country.

In British Columbia, Hope is a community at the head of the lower Fraser Valley. From Hope, Highway 97 stretches northward along the Fraser River, dotted with small or resource-based communities such as Spuzzum, Lillooet, 100 Mile House, Williams Lake, Quesnel, and Prince George. These communities, and others like them, are geographically located "beyond Hope" and are often referred to as such by people living in the populated southern areas of the province. Many have chosen to live in these northern communities, however, for reasons much to do with quality of life and lifestyle.

Factors such as the northern reliance on resource development and external capital, and the political, geographical, and social isolation, render these communities particularly vulnerable to outside forces. Communities in the provincial north throughout Canada share a number of concerns. Residents of remote communities often feel that while the resources sector is still the primary engine of the economy, this fact is not sufficiently recognized in the redistribution of provincial revenues.

Northern communities are also concerned that because they do not possess a great deal of voting power, northerners lack political clout with provincial decision makers when policy decisions are made that affect the well-being of northern communities. Moreover, there is a frequently stated belief that the "urban" south lacks an understanding of the role that natural resources play in maintaining the national standard of living. One House of Commons report notes, "rural communities provide much employment and economic benefit to all Canadians. Canada's international success and image is based primarily on natural resources. However, rural Canadians are now 'a voice in the wilderness,' as they often go unheard. Government must recognize the important contribution from this sector. This recognition should be heard and be celebrated by those of influence, the politicians."[51]

Supporting these arguments, economists Baxter and Ramolo in their 2002 study noted that in British Columbia, over the previous decade, the regions outside the metropolitan areas generated 71 percent of the province's wealth in exports. The findings are even more dramatic in terms of per capita wealth. Baxter states that "relative to the provincial annual average of $8,659 per capita in international export earnings, non-metropolitan areas produce a $6,261 per capita surplus while metropolitan areas have a $4,146 per capita deficit."[52] Baxter and Ramolo share some interesting observations on the recent "charter city debates" (see Chapter 7) and the demands of the big cities for more autonomy and financial resources commensurate with their size. They consider what would happen if metropolitan areas were truly independent city-states, putting them in a trading position with the non-metropolitan areas. Their data suggest that the latter regions would have three times as much per capita to spend than the metropolitan regions. Obviously, these speculations do not include the provision of services and a number of other important resources that the metropolitan areas have to offer. Nevertheless, decision makers will have to ensure that the non-metropolitan parts of the province have the resources and infrastructure they require if these areas are to continue to provide the export-based wealth deemed vital to the provincial economy.[53]

Rural and remote communities have grounds for concern because the resource industries are becoming increasingly automated and internationalized, and they provide fewer guarantees of employment, particularly for individuals without university education. Furthermore, although there are many educated northern citizens, as a demographic group they possess a lower level of post-secondary education than those in the southern urban centres. Many low-skill jobs in the resource sectors have been replaced by automation, and unemployment rates have been consistently higher in northern parts of the country.

How well a community survives will depend on its location, economic basis, the health, energy, and adaptability of its citizens, its ability to face challenges posed by the new information economy, and the nature of its relationship with the provincial government. In particular, those communities that will be successful are ones that can adapt to changing world economic and political institutions and can influence decision-making agendas that affect their welfare.

Northern local governments have to grapple with many new challenges as they attempt to wrestle with decreased grants from downsizing senior governments and with the new responsibilities that are accompanying the provincial off-loading. That said, it could also be argued that as the capacity of provincial governments decreases, northern governments may also find themselves in a position to exercise more discretion and flexibility to deal with northern issues.

Often neglected are some of the centre-periphery differences that revolve around the nature of political accountability in the decision-making process. Smaller municipalities, for example, can have the same number of political representatives as a much larger city. In 2002, for example, Smithers, British Columbia, had five councillors, a deputy mayor, and a mayor representing approximately 6,000 people. Camrose, Alberta, had eight councillors and a mayor, and a population of just over 15,000. On the other hand, Waterloo had five councillors plus a mayor representing over 86,000 (without including all the university and college students), while the City of Toronto had forty-four members of council plus a mayor representing approximately 2.5 million people. It is obviously much easier in a small town to approach your elected representative on the street, or to raise some issues of local concern in council chambers. That said, a good ratio of representation per population in itself does not necessarily add up to a more democratic environment, and there are other, possibly more effective, ways in which citizens can participate in the political system. A small community, for example, might have a sizable municipal council, but that is no guarantee that it will be responsive to the concerns of the citizenry or the diverse groups that might live within the town.

Other issues about the distinctiveness of northern government revolve around questions of autonomy. The House of Commons report has noted that northern communities require a measure of autonomy in order to develop policies that will help them thrive or just survive: "Although small and rural communities frequently fall under the supposedly protective arm of governments and major resource companies, a community will be better off if it assumes responsibility for its own affairs and makes its own commitment to a viable future. Self-assertive communities develop the means to survive and prosper over the longer term using their own value judgments."[54]

Provincial policies that impose blanket regulations without regard to the effectiveness of that policy for different communities constitute a major portion of northern communities' frustrations. Environment, transportation, or health policies designed with the large metropolitan areas in mind may be counterproductive if they are unilaterally imposed on small communities spread over a wide geographic area (see Box 6.1). The health, and even the survival, of these communities depends in large measure on their ability to exercise measures of both economic and political independence from the more senior levels of government.

## 6.1 One Size Fits All? The Waste Management Decision in Prince George

In response to growing environmental concerns, the British Columbia government developed a number of regulations in 1989 requiring 50 percent of municipal waste to be diverted from landfill sites, as well as improved environmental standards for managing landfill sites. A policy to reduce, reuse, and recycle makes good environmental sense. Yet when applied to northern British Columbia, the environmental and financial costs of the policy will be different from those found in such areas as the Greater Vancouver Regional District. In order to implement the policies and meet the new environmental landfill standards by 2003, northern communities spread throughout a regional district the size of Switzerland decided that they would have to combine their resources. Numerous small landfills throughout the region were closed and replaced with transfer stations that would transport the wastes to a central location. A central composting station was also constructed, and a centralized recycling system was set up in Prince George.

A number of environmental costs are associated with transporting the wastes to the landfill site and the recyclables down to markets. Provincially imposed policies of this kind are often designed with dense urban centres in mind. As such, they do not give smaller, more remote communities the flexibility to develop policies that would best achieve an effective environmental solution.

Source: Regional District of Fraser-Fort George. *Executive Summary: Regional Solid Waste Management Plan Stage III,* 18 March 2001, http://www.rdffg.bc.ca/departments/envserv/Env0101.html.

## Centralization or Decentralization: A Zero-Sum Proposition?

Before we close this particular discussion on intergovernmental relations, it might be worth considering one more perspective – one articulated in 1973 by Stewart Fyfe, then special commissioner of a report on local government in the Waterloo Region, and Ron Farrow. Fyfe and Farrow argued for recognition of the important, complementary roles served by all levels of government (see Box 6.2). Recognizing this interdependent relationship is even more relevant in today's complex world. Attempting to simplify the respective roles of government and staking out territory will do little to resolve the global challenges facing local communities. Structural debates should not take place out of the context of this reality.

It may well be argued that the global corporate environment has outstripped Canadian senior governments in terms of the impact it has had in limiting choices available to local communities. Lightbody offers the following reality check: "the new localism thrust in recent democratic social theory, and its refocusing on 'traditional' community size, may be on the verge of being totally overwhelmed by the economic linkages of the global community."[55] Governments require new decision-making frameworks to respond to the evolving needs of their constituencies, to deliver services in an effective, responsive manner, and to sustain healthy communities. Each order of government will require the resources and authority in their own spheres of jurisdiction.

## Conclusion

Institutional actors influence local autonomy in a variety of ways. The formal role of the provincial and federal governments and the courts is specified in the written constitution, carried out through legislation, implemented through regulations and policies, and delivered through government bodies. Municipal associations such as the Federation of Canadian Municipalities are becoming increasingly vocal in terms of vying for resources as environmental, social, and economic pressures mount and the problems are unloaded on municipalities. Recent amalgamation and restructuring initiatives have led to debates about the implications for the economy, natural environment, society, and local democracy. Despite recent significant changes in municipal structures, with amalgamation in some areas and revised municipal and planning acts throughout the country, little has changed in terms of the fundamental relationships between municipalities and other levels of government. Without the requisite financial resources, local governments are not well positioned to respond to the responsibilities placed on them, nor do they have the constitutional or legal basis on which to exercise much political leverage vis-à-vis other political and economic actors.

In such a situation, some worry that amalgamations and the growth of mega-cities will serve only to further weaken the democratic basis of local governments (such as

## 6.2 Reconciling Provincial-Local Responsibilities

In their review of local government structure more than thirty years ago, Fyfe and Farrow noted that "the most important consideration is that there is far too much at stake for all levels of government in evolving rational public policy to allow local government to isolate itself from the others in the hope of gaining ... a very illusory autonomy ... Ultimately they are all responsible to the same electorate, although in different ways, and for different things. It would be more relevant to talk in terms of enlightened responsible government, with all three levels having complementary roles to play in meeting the needs of the public, both in general and in terms of particular communities and needs."[1] These ideas continue to have resonance today.

---

1  Stewart Fyfe and Ron. M. Farrow, *Waterloo Area Local Government Review: Report of Findings and Recommendations* (Toronto: Ontario Department of Municipal Affairs, 1970), 6.

existed) by reducing accessibility to municipal council and staff. Others argue that amalgamation can strengthen municipalities that had previously suffered from a fragmented political base. Amalgamation would allow them to combine resources, give them additional political and economic power, and enable them to develop a unified strategic approach for dealing with external and international forces.[56]

The last three chapters have highlighted the historic, constitutional, and structural restraints placed on local governments. As a result, the reader may come away with the impression that the activities of local governments are of very little importance. That is not the case. Local governments are influential in a number of ways, with respect to their areas of jurisdiction. How governments and citizens choose to deal with these challenges will have an impact on the abilities of communities to foster healthy and sustainable environments.

One of the most important areas of local government responsibility is that of community planning. This responsibility will become ever more important in the future as decision makers attempt to design cities that meet competing demands while land and resources become increasingly scarce. As the title of Part 3 suggests, it is through community planning and its implementation that decision makers shape the natural, built, and social-economic environment of a community. Those who can influence this important process are individuals who play a significant role in local decision making.

# Part 3     The Politics of Space, Place, and Ecosystems

Patterns of governance are shaped by forces operating in human and biophysical systems. The connection between physical geography and politics, for example, affects political dynamics between, and within, municipalities. Resource-rich towns and cities situated along favourable transportation and trading routes have benefited politically and economically from their locations, unlike other communities located off the beaten track. Within cities themselves, urban designers, planners, and decision makers inevitably have favoured particular groups of interests over others, frequently without acknowledging or even recognizing the political and social implications of their decisions. Urban planners and physical geographers are now beginning to pay closer attention to the related political aspects of their activities.

Canada's political history has been moulded by the imperatives of other states – first France and Britain, then the United States. Today, Canadian communities are deeply influenced by the collective impacts of the contemporary forces of globalization brought about by rapid developments in transportation and communication. Communities find themselves responding to a multitude of global events, including economic, health, and environmental concerns. In recent years, Canadian cities have found themselves buffeted by a whirlwind of events, ranging from internationally spread diseases, such as Sudden Acute Respiratory Syndrome (SARS) or West Nile Virus, to economic disputes such as the US-Canada softwood lumber issue, to the signing of international agreements such as the Kyoto Accord. All these types of events have a profound impact on the well-being of communities and have highlighted the limits of local government to control or limit the impacts of these events. All too frequently, local governments find themselves reacting to crises or the threat of crises, leaving them with limited buffers to govern in a proactive, precautionary manner.

Urban growth and rapid industrialization throughout the twentieth century have generated environmental problems unconsidered even a couple of generations ago. Concerns about air and water quality, land-use degradation, human health concerns, congested highways, and the bulldozing of valued wetlands, forests, and landscapes has generated a host of new preoccupations for local decision makers. Interconnected human and biophysical systems require policy responses that recognize ecosystem complexity, yet political jurisdictions were not devised to recognize natural boundaries posed by important watersheds and other physical characteristics. Recognition of these boundaries will require flexibility and adaptable systems of governance.

# 7
# Core and Peripheries to Networked Societies

The emergence of local communities, towns, and cities along major transportation routes reflects historical attempts to link together the country's vast geography into a distinct, if not autonomous, country. Immigration was encouraged to help populate and settle the remote territories and stimulate the development of a resource-based economy. Canada's advanced telecommunications system evolved, in part, to respond to the needs of its staples-based industries. Today, modern telecommunications networks are making it possible for citizens to communicate within and between communities, connecting rural, remote areas from the Northwest Territories to Toronto to other places around the world. All of these developments have implications for local politics.

Spatial and temporal factors have affected patterns of political influence and governance in a variety of ways. Trade routes – particularly waterways – shaped the original settlement of villages, towns, and cities, so much so that one observer declared "Canada is a canoe route."[1] These early development patterns helped determine which towns and cities would ultimately become centres of political and economic power and which ones would become resource suppliers to the centres. Such factors shaped how some localities would grow and thrive, others would decline and die, and still others would struggle along. Some cities would become known as an economic core or hub, and others would be relegated to the peripheries.

Climate, geology, physical location, and the resource base of towns and cities also influence local and regional political cultures. In 1938, Lewis Mumford emphasized the close connection between human communities and the physical landscape: "Rationally defined, the locus of human communities is the region. The region is the unit-area formed by common aboriginal conditions of geologic structure, soil, surface relief, drainage, climate, vegetation and animal life; reformed and partly re-defined through the settlement of man, the domestication and acclimatization of new species, the nucleation of communities in villages and cities, the re-working of the landscape, and the control over land, power, climate, and movement provided by the state of technics."[2]

In his depiction of rural Saskatchewan, George Hood offers a stark example of this as he describes travelling long expanses of unpaved roads and passing landscapes dotted with shuttered stores, rock piles, rusted cars, and abandoned farm machinery. These rural communities have always experienced isolation and hardship due to extreme weather conditions (ranging from droughts to floods) and marginal farm-based economies. The harsh physical conditions have had a powerful effect on local social and political culture. Hood observes that people in rural Saskatchewan have been "shaped by their closeness to the land and the elements." Community life could "be divided in two: farming and everything else. Significant public events are generally not scheduled during seeding or harvest."[3]

The way people decide to bridge physical distances or to erect barriers between their own and other communities also affects local politics. Developments in transportation and communications have contributed to the rise and fall of various localities. They also fostered rapid urbanization, alterations to the physical environment, and changes in the social composition, political interactions, and cultural identities of urban areas – particularly metropolitan regions. Most recently, the explosive growth of communications technology is radically changing the social and political significance of physical space and territory.

## Hinterland and Metropolis

European colonization in Canada was based on the exploitation of staples: fish, fur, timber, minerals, and agriculture. Explorers and traders were helped along significantly by First Nations peoples, who were intimately acquainted with the terrain and could navigate the way to resource riches. In the ensuing centuries, Canadians earned their well-used moniker from the bible, "Hewer of Wood and Drawer of Water." Hugh Mellon noted that "the nineteenth century had within it the golden days of wood, wind, and water when the ports of the Maritime Provinces were integrated within the global shipping patterns of the British Empire. With the passing of this economic order, iron, steel, and railroads came to prevail."[4] Saint John, New Brunswick, offers an excellent example of how a strategic location and plentiful natural resources can lead to a city's early strength and long-term advantage (see Box 7.1).

Champlain's 1608 trading post in New France eventually became the provincial capital, Quebec City, and it was not until the 1880s that Montreal gained economic advantage over Quebec City. An influential Montreal business and political elite encouraged the development of a transportation network that favoured the continued expansion of the city's manufacturing enterprises. Water power, canals, railways, and the growth of financial institutions soon ensured Montreal's pre-eminence as Canada's economic, financial, and industrial centre.[5] After Confederation, the development of the Canadian West, the St. Lawrence Valley, the Grand Trunk Railway, and the grain trade were uniting factors in Canada. As one popular quotation goes, "Canada is a nation created in defiance of geography and yet the geographic and economic factors have had a large place in shaping her history."[6] In a classic essay, H.A. Innis pointed out that Canada's economic history has been dominated by the discrepancy between the centre and the margin of western civilization.[7]

THE POLITICS OF SPACE, PLACE, AND ECOSYSTEMS

## 7.1 Saint John: A Strategic Position

Saint John, New Brunswick, is located at the mouth of the St. John River on the Bay of Fundy. The first permanent development on the site was a fort first built in the early 1630s during the French regime. It would develop into a sizable fur-trading centre. Eventually, the area was taken over by the British in 1758. Saint John also benefited from its position strategically when in 1783, the "vast majority of the twelve thousand Loyalists who left New York for New Brunswick settled throughout the St. John River valley, instantly creating the City of Saint John, the town of Fredericton, and villages along the river."[1] Saint John also gained early economic and political strength from its winter port; "as one of Canada's national ports, the entire Saint John harbour was integrated and organized into part of Canada's national transportation system"[2] by the early 1900s.

Today, the port is a source of new opportunities. Along with its traditional functions, the port facility is now being used for tourism and services generated from the cruise liner industry. Access to road, rail, air, and sea transportation and a high-tech infrastructure also give the city strategic advantages.

---

1  Dan Soucoup, *Historic New Brunswick,* (Lawrencetown Beach, NS: Pottersfield Press, 1997), 61.
2  Ibid., 191.

Much has been made of how the quest for certain commodities – fish, fur, timber, and wheat – shaped the development and settlement of Canada. This depiction (also known as the Laurentian thesis) is a matter of some debate. Some analysts suggest that the thesis overemphasizes the role that a single commodity at a particular time might play in establishing the trade and settlement patterns that progressed along the St. Lawrence Valley on through to the West. The Laurentian argument also tends to ignore the role of various actors or other agents of change. Linteau, Durocher, and Robert note that the Laurentian thesis on its own, with its concentration on relationships between different regions, fails to explain other internal development patterns and influences that took place throughout Canada.[8]

A related perspective that garnered historical prominence in political geographic studies considers the dynamics at work between a hinterland and a metropolis. According to this core-periphery perspective, remote, isolated, resource-based communities in the economic hinterland produce raw resources for external markets in a distant metropolis. Strategically located cities develop as economic hubs of trading activity. Those hubs diversify and grow as they import resources from a variety of staples-producing regions. The primary producing (*supply*) regions remain underdeveloped, their survival dependent on favourable external factors. These supply regions lead a precarious existence, relying on market demand for their particular product. If market demand declines, these regions lack alternative sources of economic wealth and employment. Urban planner Jane Jacobs has drawn an analogy between a healthy diversified economy and a natural ecology: "Economies that are producing diversely and amply for their own people and producers, as well as for others, are better off than specialized economies like those of supply, clearance and transplant regions. In a natural ecology, the more diversity there is, the more flexibility too, because of what ecologists call its greater numbers of 'homeostatic feedback loops,' meaning that it includes greater numbers of feedback controls for automatic self-correction."[9]

Core urban areas possess what peripheral areas often lack in large quantities – ready market access, assorted cultural activities and amenities, and innovative, diverse economies with linked enterprises that can produce goods and services for internal and external consumption. Higgins noted that "A city can ... be considered a place where production facilities are concentrated; those facilities being equipment, labour, buildings, and transportation infrastructure."[10] Toronto, Canada's largest city, gained its early advantage with its connections to New York City and southern markets after the Erie Canal opened in 1825. A railway terminus was established in the city. Through the railways, Toronto was linked to the West, giving it access to resources. As Warren Magnusson observes, it was also the centre of southern Ontario, "the most populous and prosperous region of the country."[11]

According to core-periphery perspectives, the requirements of the country's metropolitan centres influence many decisions of regional, provincial, or national importance, including those that affect "peripheral" communities. Dominant core areas in Canada are the Windsor-Quebec City corridor, which includes the two largest urban centres of Toronto and Montreal, southwestern British Columbia, and the Edmonton-Calgary corridor.[12] McCann and Simmons suggest that the phenomenon of "metropolitanism ... accounts for the growth of a dominant city (or dominant cities) that leads the national urban hierarchy, and so controls the geographical structure of core and periphery. Once achieved, this dominant status overshadows that of all other towns and cities."[13] Within the urban hierarchy, metropolitan communities dominate the others. This phenomenon is played out both at a global level, where cities such as New York and London may eclipse Toronto, and at regional levels,[14] where places like Prince George serve as a hub of activity for northern British Columbia (see Box 7.2).

Two other communities in northern British Columbia, Tumbler Ridge and Kemano, serve as illustrations of the difficulties faced when towns are located in remote areas and developed for the specific purpose of supplying one resource. Kemano, a community of 220, was built to provide a home for workers at the largest North American smelter, located at Kitimat. Alcan, the company that owned and operated much of the town, decided that it was too costly and shut down Kemano in the summer of 2000.[15] Tumbler Ridge, incorporated in 1981, was built to support a coal project that consisted of two major mines, and one of the mines closed in 2000. The town, although built for the coal projects, has operated independently from the company, with elected mayors and councillors. In October 2000, the province provided provisional funds to assist with municipal debt and to handle the transition after the mine closure. The isolated town continues to pursue opportunities for diversification rooted in natural gas, recreation-based tourism, and forestry.[16]

This story has been repeated throughout Canada's resource towns. In these places particularly, the ability of citizens to govern themselves is greatly influenced by the fortunes of the companies that built them. The political life of small, single-resource towns is no longer controlled by the company managers as in times past, although they are influential members of the communities if they still live in the town. These towns have their own elected mayors and councils. Nevertheless, the community is planned and governed, in many ways, in reaction to the activities and decisions of a company. Only comparatively recently have companies realized (sometimes as a result of legislation) that major decisions taken about industrial operations, employment, closure plans, and the like, must include representatives from the community itself. If the community is able to successfully diversify, the citizens and their elected representatives can make choices about the future directions of their community. The all-too-common scenario is that the major community employer and revenue generator operates in response to the needs and demands of the global marketplace rather than those of the affected communities.

Patterns of development and geographical location have been important determinants of local politics and the relative influence of a particular community vis-à-vis other centres of political power. A number of other geographical and spatial factors, including location, climate, resources, landscapes, and economic base also affect the local political environment.

## 7.2 Prince George: Centre and Periphery

Prince George offers an excellent example of how location and geography can affect the political orientation of a city. Given its strategic location, Prince George serves as the economic hub of the British Columbian north, expanding services used by smaller outlying communities. The city, however, suffers from its location, which is far removed from the provincial capital and from the metropolitan centre in the southwestern corner of the province. As a resource-based community, it is subject to both the vagaries of international market demand and a provincial government insufficiently responsive to its unique requirements. It did, however, receive some provincial support over the years to build up its infrastructure and to provide new regional facilities that would serve both Prince George and other northern communities.

The longevity of a city is intimately connected to its communication and transportation links. This was true as much in the early days of Canadian towns as it is at the beginning of the twenty-first century. Prince George traces its beginning to 1808, when the explorer Simon Fraser constructed Fort George – one of a series of fur-trading posts. In 1912, Premier Richard McBride gave approval to build the Pacific Great Eastern Railway, which would run from Vancouver to the Peace River. Bev Christensen reports that George Hammond, one of the promoters of the Fort George townsite, claimed at the time: "Just as in ancient times all roads led to Rome, so all present and future railroads in central British Columbia lead to Fort George." The Pacific Great Eastern Railway, however, was not completed until forty years later, earning it the name of Prince George Eventually and Past God's Endurance. It is now known as BC Rail Limited.[1]

On 15 March 1915, Prince George was incorporated but immediately suffered many blows due to the onset of the First World War and the collapse of the land boom and the railway construction in the central interior. The first two difficult decades were followed by the severe impact of the Depression of the 1930s. Christensen observes that the railway that had promised prosperity in good times carried in a number of "drifters" searching for food during the Depression.

The Second World War stimulated an economic boom in the lumber industry and a surge in population growth, housing development, and transportation infrastructure. In the 1960s, three pulp mills were constructed, forming a notable part of the Prince George physical and cultural landscape. The introduction of the pulp mills led to a housing construction boom. By 1981, Prince George was the second-largest city in the province, a distinction lost a little later because of rapid population growth in the lower mainland. After recovering from the damaging effects of a recession, the Prince George economy once again picked up the momentum that carried it through to the end of the century boasting of many new developments, including the main campus for a new university. Faced with a US-Canada softwood lumber dispute and other forces threatening its resource-based economy, however, Prince George has economic challenges to keep it busy well into the twenty-first century.

---

1 Bev Christensen, *Prince George: Rivers, Railways, and Timber* (Burlington, ON: Windsor Publications, 1989), 76-117.

## The Politics of Economic Development and Location

In recent years, a number of international political and economic developments, such as the introduction of the North American Free Trade Agreement on 1 January 1994, have been changing the competitive nature of city and regional planning. A community's serious economic competitors are not necessarily located in the next closest city but might be somewhere in the United States or offshore. Cities and regions throughout the country are seeking global investors, and the process of positioning themselves to attract global investors changes the dynamics between neighbouring cities, as well as a city's approaches to urban and regional planning.

In southwestern Ontario, four cities (Kitchener, Waterloo, Cambridge, and Guelph) in partnership with the private sector, have combined efforts to attract investment to the region and dubbed themselves "Canada's Technology Triangle." The Region of Waterloo, which contains Kitchener, Waterloo, and Cambridge (as well as the townships of North Dumfries, Wellesley, Wilmot, and Woolwich) is one of the fastest growing in Canada and the tenth largest in Canada, boasting a $15 billion economy.[17] In Sherbrooke, Quebec, the region has promoted economic development by capitalizing on its location that gives it access to US markets (see Box 7.3).

In part, many of the amalgamations that have taken place in recent years have been justified with the idea that the new larger cities will be more economically competitive in the global marketplace. The types of economic enterprises attracted to a region affect land use, intra-regional planning, and cooperation between communities. These developments lead to many other opportunities and challenges that are affected by regional economic strategies, including implications for the local cultures, biophysical environments, and political decision making.

One way in which governments have tried to manage urban growth and deal with the complexities of inter-jurisdictional negotiations is to amalgamate cities and regions into larger jurisdictions. As discussed in the past chapter, in a few cases, such amalgamations have resulted in very large cities, including mega-city Toronto. This has had its own spin-off effect. These large cities now command powerful budgets and are responsible for large populations. They are now lobbying for political influence commensurate with their size.

## Global and Charter Cities

Throughout the 1990s and into the early 2000s, a series of amalgamations took place throughout the country (see Chapter 4). Groups of prominent activists and citizens from a number of large urban centres, most notably Toronto, began serious discussion about reinstituting the idea of "charter cities" to recognize the importance of these regions both domestically and globally. As part of this discussion, Joe Berridge has pointed out that Toronto and area (also known as the Greater Toronto Area or the Golden Horseshoe)

## 7.3 Greater Sherbrooke Economic Development Corporation

In 1991, several neighbouring municipalities formed the Greater Sherbrooke Economic Development Corporation (SDÉRS). The goal of the organization was to coordinate the tourism, culture, and industrial development activities in the geographic region. As a cooperative partnership that shares technical and financial resources, these municipalities have worked together to attract investment projects to the region. Other goals include technological development, local development, and market development. The corporation also assists approximately 500 manufacturing firms in the region. SDÉRS's philosophy is that the whole region can benefit through the promotion of overall competitive advantage rather than through smaller operations.

The newly amalgamated City of Sherbrooke covers much the same territory that has been served by SDÉRS, and as such, the move complements the goals of the corporation.

*Source:* Greater Sherbrooke Economic Development Corporation (SDÉRS), *Industrial Department*, pamphlet, n.d.

is rich in cultural and educational institutions and is now probably the fourth or fifth most important financial centre on the continent: "Business in the Golden Horseshoe not only accounts for half of the province's economy – and almost one-third of the nation's – it is very heavily based on exports. Half of the United States' consumer market and more than half of its manufacturing firms are within one day's trucking distance ... The city is already home to more than half of the country's corporate head offices, all five major banks, and the Toronto Stock Exchange, which processes 89 percent of the nation's stock transactions."[18]

Ontario includes more than one-third of the Canadian population, and the vast bulk of that population is located within a 160 km radius of Toronto, and the City of Toronto itself is one of the largest cities in North America.[19] This city and the other large metropolitan areas could be seen as the major financial engines of the country, sources of employment, generators of environmental waste, centres of multiculturalism, and providers of specialized services to the rest of the country, including their own large populations and more. For better or worse, they have an enormous impact throughout Canada.

Yet Canada's largest cities are hampered in their ability to respond to the complex challenges of governing diverse societies, economies, and environments because of their lack of independent legal status from the provincial governments. As a result, the larger cities are now lobbying for special status.

Municipalities may be incorporated as legal entities under a special charter or a general municipal act. Originally, charters were designed to deal specially with urban areas. As Higgins notes, this process later fell into general disuse for many newer cities because every change to a charter required a special act of the provincial legislation. Moreover, it is difficult to deal with all municipalities in a similar or uniform manner if individual charters must be accommodated. General municipal acts became the norm.[20] Some cities do have their own charters, such as Montreal, Winnipeg, Saint John, and Halifax. Canada's largest city does not have a charter as such, but is governed under the City of Toronto Act. Although some cities do have their own charters or pieces of legislation, given the vast size of some of these urban engines of growth, many argue that they still need more authority and resources to effectively govern.

In 1999, a small group convened to ask questions about how Toronto, "a region of global citizens," could evolve toward self-government or at least could evolve in a way that would allow Toronto "to assume greater control of its own destiny."[21] The advocates for a special charter for Toronto argued that by making the large metropolises – the economic hubs of a province – stronger and more resilient, the rest of the province and the other regions and cities within it would also benefit. In a discussion about the future, Richard Gwyn suggested that, "Essentially, the argument is that Toronto needs some increased political and financial autonomy to enable it to be an international presence so that it can help Ontario and Canada."[22] Toronto, the argument goes, creates more wealth than the outlying regions, but its ability to develop wealth is constrained by its lack of political autonomy and because it doesn't have the political and financial resources commensurate with its role within the country.

## Implications for Other Regions

After the 1999 discussion about Toronto, meetings expanded beyond Toronto to other large "hub" cities, including Montreal, Calgary, Winnipeg, and Vancouver, also referred to as the C5.[23] The mayors of these cities have met to devise strategies to increase autonomy for cities of regional and national importance because they act as hubs of economic activity and innovation.

Hub cities and other large urban centres also are confronted with the problems posed by the political influence wielded within the provincial governments by municipalities surrounding the core areas. Those outlying regions can, and often do, have a strong voice in political issues affecting the centre cities without having to pay the cost of living with those decisions. The situation is magnified by the way in which provincial legislative seats are distributed, which can lead to an under-representation of the concerns of the large, densely populated cities. Whether you are speaking about Toronto, Montreal, or elsewhere, suburban areas can be "free riders" of services provided by the urban centres, such as museums, universities, arts centres, and the like. As a result, the suburbs have fewer responsibilities for providing services or dealing with social and health problems while benefiting from a cleaner living environment and higher standard of living.[24] Moreover, the problems, as well as the goals, objectives, and cultures of the suburban versus the urban regions differ and can often compete with each other, contributing to internal political fragmentation of the region.[25]

Granting cities more autonomy and local control could lead to two results. On the one hand, increased autonomy and decentralization of power could give each jurisdiction more flexibility to develop the resources and policies that could best capture opportunities to innovate and to respond to their own particular geographic, cultural, social, and economic conditions. On the other hand, some suggest that hub or core cities should be given increased legal and fiscal autonomy and resources commensurate with their large population size and economic activity. If this were to happen, there would be a subsequent reduction in the abilities of provincial governments to redistribute resources or to regulate the entire province in a way that would benefit all citizens. Smaller communities, as well as the rural and remote parts of the country, would be reduced in both political influence and resources. To some, this state of affairs might be seen as appropriate, given the huge difference in population size and economic importance. It does not, however, deal with serious rural economic problems or the issues of underdevelopment and underservicing of Canada's extensive resource-based regions. Consequently, the already struggling, less populated regions of the country could more rapidly decline as people and investment depart in search of more promising economic prospects. Given the neo-liberal trends associated with globalization, together with challenges to the welfare state, it is by no means a foregone conclusion that the less prosperous, undiversified regions of the country would necessarily benefit from providing the "global cities" with more power, autonomy, and resources.

THE POLITICS OF SPACE, PLACE, AND ECOSYSTEMS

## Barriers to Charter Cities

Notwithstanding the potential virtues or problems of establishing charter cities with increased self-government, there are numerous barriers to achieving this goal. Many have to do with Canada's federal-provincial configuration of power. Alan Broadbent has noted that the intergovernmental power struggles in many strategic areas of national importance – particularly those that take place between the national and Quebec governments – leave very little room for other players seeking more autonomy for themselves.[26] Moreover, as creatures of the province, local governments do not have the constitutional power to claim the right to assume jurisdiction over local matters. Aside from the constitutional constraints, the political culture of Canada would need adjustment. Politicians, analysts, or academics outside of the local government arenas have not generally thought about this level of government in Canada as important in its own right. Finally, federal and provincial governments concerned about their own priorities will not readily embrace a reduction of their own power or revenue bases.

Throughout Canada's history, core-periphery debates lie at the heart of regional politics. The decision about how power and resources should be distributed between communities often comes down to two basic arguments. One suggests that a strong economic urban centre is essential to the health of a region because it acts as an engine of growth for an entire region or province, thereby benefiting all from the multiplier effects of its activities. The alternative argument is that these engines of growth also consume vast quantities of natural, political, and economic resources, operate beyond their own environmental carrying capacity, and leave outlying areas impoverished. As a result, the rural and remote regions are left with few opportunities to diversify and, sometimes, suffer serious environmental degradation from intense primary industrial activities that have long supported the manufacturing and service core of the region.

## Information Technology and Regional Politics

What kind of impact will new technologies have on the comparative influence of communities located in areas typically viewed as the geographical and political peripheries of Canada? Some optimistically suggest that disparity between regions may diminish because information technology makes it possible to do business and operate from any location. Information technology enables companies, such as call centres, insurance services, cottage industries, or other information-based businesses to locate in areas with low overheads and low taxes. Remote towns and cities can also provide the comforts of a slower-paced lifestyle and the absence of traffic jams, while business can be carried on globally via the Internet. In his analysis, Roger Gibbins raised the following questions: "If there is no centre to the digital world, can there still be regions and regional marginalization? Can there be a periphery without a centre? In the global framework of the digital world, for example, how western Canadians connect to international markets will be more important than how they connect to the dated notion of a 'central Canada.'"[27]

The City of Grande Prairie, located in northern Alberta, undertook a strategy in 2000 based on the view that it can have that kind of competitive edge that Gibbins speaks about by developing a high-tech interconnected community. Decision makers in Grande Prairie saw new developments in information technology as a revolutionary tidal wave in terms of its implications for society, politics, and economics. To avoid being submerged by this wave, Grande Prairie developed the CyberCity Initiative: "Ultimately, the target of the CyberCity Initiative is to reach every residence, business, institution and office with an effective interactive electronic connection to the world, and to help every Grande Prairian acquire the know-how necessary to exploit it. To the degree that we succeed, it will deliver very significant benefits to Grande Prairie and the region, and substantially achieve our purposes."[28]

Technology may certainly generate economic benefits for remote communities, but it will not necessarily improve their position relative to other larger, more diversified, centres. Most of the population growth still happens in large city centres that contain the bulk of political power and resources. Businesses in the high-tech industry will want access to the largest pool of workers with specialized skills and knowledge. The synergy caused by diverse economic opportunities, cultural diversity, and a variety of private and public services provide businesses and other organizations with a critical mass of customers, consumers, and contributors. Regions located on the peripheries still rely heavily on provincial and federal governments to provide physical communication infrastructure and human and social services. Information technology will do little to change that reality.

As was mentioned, however, information technology may make it easier for those businesses located in rural and remote parts of the country to sell their products in the global marketplace. Yet if the products are tangible, such as those produced by resource industries, they still must be transported to market in a cost-competitive manner. Many of Canada's rural regional economies are supported by resource industries. As Gillespie and Hepworth have noted: "the uneven development of modern capitalism ensures that social inequality at national and international scales will increase, owing to cumulative processes of economic growth which favour people and places whose 'head start' in the 'information age' derives from past patterns of industrialization."[29]

It also might be argued that while businesses could locate in remote areas because physical place is no longer as important an economic consideration, the reverse is also true. Cities make it possible to conduct business from a centralized location. Traditional industries such as mining can now be run by smaller "fly-in, fly-out" work crews in highly automated operations with the head offices located in major centres such as Toronto or Vancouver. It is no longer necessary to build towns in remote areas to supply a readily available workforce. More important, perhaps, is that head offices and business leaders are located in the economic hub, where airports, a diversity of services, and other related businesses are all situated in a convenient metropolis.

Finally, many analysts point to the challenges posed by a society divided into the information rich and the information poor (see Chapter 12). Residents of towns and regions located on the peripheries do not have the same access to advanced levels of education and training, nor the opportunities to take optimum advantage of information technology, as do the inhabitants of larger urban cities.

## Conclusion

Physical geography and historical patterns of development and settlement help determine the political influence one community may have relative to another. This is the case whether considering metropolitan areas or resource-based towns.

All of our case-study cities, at various times, were positioned in a way that would allow them to take advantage of location and natural resources. Saint John, given its early advantage as an important port, quickly grew into an important commercial and political centre. Prince George and Sherbrooke also developed into economic and political hubs for their regions. Kitchener and Waterloo are well situated in densely populated southern Ontario and have taken advantage of their industrial heritage and spin-off benefits from local universities. They are part of one of the fastest-growing regions in Canada.

It is possible that changes in information and transportation infrastructure may lead to a reallocation of power between the economic hubs and smaller, more remote towns and cities. But technology in itself will not eliminate the problems faced by small, isolated places where, in comparison to the larger cities, the provision of services is costly, the population small, the physical terrain challenging, and the employment and economic opportunities limited. Some towns do survive and thrive after the mine has closed or the mill has shut down, but they must possess other characteristics or qualities besides technology.

The ability of local governments and citizens to make political decisions is very much affected by geographical position and access to, and control over, resources: physical, financial, human, political, or information. Small resource communities often find themselves dependent on external market forces and decisions made by a head office or provincial legislature located far away in an urban centre. It is very clear to them that power and influence concentrate in the centre. Yet the metropolitan centres will also argue that they lose power and influence to the suburban and rural votes because the outlying areas possess more voting power than is proportionate to the size of their population. The large cities have been lobbying for more resources, influence, control over their local affairs, and specific governing charters. All local governments may benefit from the lobbying efforts of these large cities, if some degree of overall decentralization of authority and resources occurs. The antithesis of this position is that any power and influence made available to local governments and their citizens will be concentrated in the large cities at the expense of the smaller locales. As it stands now, however, Canadian local governments are all feeling the limitations of too few resources, and of limited authority.

# 8
# The Politics of Urban Planning

Geography and physical factors do not just influence interregional politics. They also affect politics within cities, as different communities of interest battle to set local decision-making agendas. Land-use questions, in particular, have been the subject of many intense local political struggles.[1]

The primary means of raising revenue for local governments is the property tax. A major jurisdictional responsibility has been the provision of hard services – although recently their responsibilities increasingly have expanded into soft services and the promotion of "healthy communities." Questions of land and resource use have intensified with increasing competition over valuable urban spaces. As a result, local politics and planning have become arenas of great interest to speculators and developers, as well as to social and local heritage groups. All of these actors have had an interest in maintaining a landscape that reflects their own interests and values. During the course of the past century, land-use issues have typified city business to the extent that one individual claimed, "the real business of city government is property."[2]

The politics of urban planning also influences how we choose to organize our lives in a spatial and physical context. In earlier years, and even in some places today, planning has been viewed as a scientific, objective process that separates incompatible uses through subdivision and zoning.[3] But even the most professional planner makes choices among competing values. Decisions about the specific mix of land-use development, recreational areas, and protected woodlands are as much, if not more, a reflection of the political ideology, institutional structures, and constitution of influential elites as they are a scientific, neutral process.

The choices made by planners and other influential actors contributed to today's city form, with land designated for commercial areas, suburbs, light industrial areas, parks, and so on. As time passes, central cores undergo decline and gentrification and the suburbs evolve to become a diverse mix of local shopping "power" centres (clusters of large shopping box stores), industrial areas, and housing.

Cities, as demographically diverse entities, are also organized spatially along social-economic divisions. Large, multicultural cities are sometimes segregated by cultural or ethnic characteristics. This may be a matter of choice as is the case when people who share similar traditions and languages are drawn together in the same neighbourhood. Financial or social variables can also lead to other kinds of territorial segregation, whether it be urban ghettoes filled with tenements or luxurious gated communities equipped with high-tech security fences.

In sum, physical geography, as it interacts with historical developments and influential actors, affects local politics. This applies whether we are talking about the relative influence of communities in a broader region or province, or whether we focus on the internal dynamics of a city.

## Growing Cities

By the beginning of the twentieth century, planning reflected the "progressive" business mood of the day. The groomed "city beautiful" approach was based on notions of efficient, scientific planning and zoning. The notion was that through planning parks, boulevards, and civic centres, planting trees, and establishing good transportation routes, a beautiful and prosperous city would result.

All this was achieved in the name of the broader public interest. Whether there was any role here for city residents to help determine the shape and form of their cities was a question seldom, if ever, asked. The "scientific planning" approach fitted well with the business ethos that prevailed at that time of rapid industrialization and urban growth. It also emphasized the need to develop the aesthetic beauty of a city so people would be drawn to the community. Land developers, businesses, and homeowners whose views dominated municipal councils reinforced the value placed on private property. Local boosterism accelerated land development through policies that provided incentives for businesses and industry to locate in the city.[4]

Kitchener, Ontario, is a classic example. Although the city was built in a place that had no natural location advantage, the city leaders made good use of the industriousness of its inhabitants and its local culture. The city, previously named Berlin, became well known elsewhere in the country for its local civic pride, work ethic, and ability to promote its own interests. One newspaper editor from a nearby town wryly commented in 1912, "About the nearest approach to perpetual motion is the wagging of the Berliner's tongue in laudation of his town."[5] City councillors, business leaders, and the Board of Trade actively promoted their city's businesses as well as community services, social amenities, health, and education (Box 8.1).

Local governments have always relied heavily on property taxes for revenue. Land value, therefore, has been a very important consideration to decision makers who needed revenues to provide services.[6] The priorities of local governments, particularly in the early 1900s, were directed more toward economic development rather than other considerations, such as environmental conservation or social health. Nevertheless, even in those days a few early, radical planners recognized that planning should incorporate the goals of a healthy social, living, and natural environment. Thomas Adams, an influential planner of the early twentieth century, argued for a holistic planning approach with a strong

## 8.1 Kitchener: Berlin and Boosterism

Canada's economic history provides ample evidence of the role played by waterways, other strategic transportation routes, and plentiful natural resources in the development of local communities. But there are exceptions. Contrary to popular wisdom, cities with thriving economies are not always located in places that boast natural geographic advantages. Kitchener (originally named Berlin) is one of them. What it lacked in resources and location may have been compensated for by community industriousness, although Kitchener's position relative to other communities also helped it to grow and prosper.

King Street is now the busy central route on which both Kitchener and Waterloo have located their downtown cores. Two hundred years ago, it was a swampy trail traversing forests and sand hills. At the beginning of the 1800s, the first settlers of European origin in the area – Mennonites from Pennsylvania – travelled along this trail, soon to be followed by many others. By the mid-1820s, a large number of German immigrants arrived. In 1852, Berlin became the seat of Waterloo County (the upper tier of local government). Rail service came to Berlin in 1856, giving it a significant competitive edge over its twin city of Waterloo. By that time, Berlin, with its population of 1,000 people, contained thriving factories, newspapers, a brewery, and a tannery. In 1870, Berlin became an incorporated town. In need of power for its factories, a convention was organized at Berlin to bring hydroelectricity from Niagara Falls. From that came the Ontario Hydro Electric Power Commission. Prosperous Berlin became the City of Kitchener in 1916.

From a planning perspective, the city left much to be desired: railway tracks split the community, King Street was frequently congested, and factories intermingled with residential homes. This haphazard approach to development was soon to change, as Kitchener became Ontario's first municipality to establish a City Planning Commission in response to Ontario's Planning and Development Act of 1917. It commissioned its own official plan and hired Thomas Adams as a consultant. In 1923, Canada's first zoning bylaw was adopted for Kitchener and Waterloo.

By 1965, Kitchener had become the fastest-growing city in Canada. Now at the beginning of the twenty-first century, both Kitchener and Waterloo are wealthy cities by comparative economic standards. While much has changed in the area that was once swamp, forest, and sand hills, the tradition of civic pride based on industriousness and community appears to be very much alive.

---

*Sources:* John English and Kenneth McLaughlin, *Kitchener: An Illustrated History* (Waterloo, ON: Wilfrid Laurier University Press, 1983); Bill Moyer, *Kitchener Yesterday Revisited: An Illustrated History* (Burlington, ON: Windsor Publications, 1979), 83; Paul Tiessen, ed., *Berlin, Canada: A Self-Portrait of Kitchener, Ontario before World War One* (St. Jacobs, ON: Sand Hills Books, 1979), introduction; Gerald Hodge, *Planning Canadian Communities: An Introduction to the Principles, Practice, and Participants* (Toronto: ITP Nelson, 1998).

government presence to ensure the well-being of the entire community.[7] Within each neighbourhood, there would be ample gardens, parks, town centres, libraries, and shops. Some elements of these ideas can be found in cities today. However, other competing community goals and political realities made it difficult to adopt anything but some general principles.

The goal of conservation was not entirely ignored by the governing bodies of the day. A federal Commission of Conservation was established as an advisory body to the Government of Canada in 1909, and it included recognition of urban planning: "Prime Minister Laurier introduced in Parliament an Act to Establish a Commission for the Conservation of Natural Resources ... Committees were established for each of the major-resource areas – lands, forestry, fisheries, game and fur-bearing animals, public health, waters and water powers, and minerals ... Of special importance, however, was the Commission's committee on public health for it was this committee which forged a link between conservation and urban planning ... Thomas Adams was invited to join the Commission as Advisor on Town Planning in 1914."[8]

The roots of the Canadian city-planning profession can be traced to the commission's work. Dr. Charles Hodgetts (formerly a medical health officer) and Thomas Adams adopted land-use zoning and emphasized the importance of "city healthy" over the previous notion of "city beautiful." Adams moved to the United States in 1921 but left behind the "seeds of planning" and was credited with establishing planning as a professional activity in Canada.[9]

In 1935, the Research Committee of the League for Social Reconstruction produced a proposal for social planning in Canada and for the creation of a National Planning Commission. The League suggested that Canadian planning should be based on principles of socialism. It was concerned that capitalism was the cause of many urban ills, including "land speculation, insufficient housing, premature subdivision of land, inadequate parks and public buildings, shack towns and housing policies only for the well off."[10] While the committee work did not change the direction of professional planning, it heavily influenced the formation of the Co-operative Commonwealth Federation (now the New Democratic Party), and, in particular, oriented its members toward the importance of good housing standards for all.[11]

A few others at the time expressed alternative views about how to manage human interaction with the natural and built environments. American social philosopher Lewis Mumford suggested in 1938, "we can no longer leave soils and landscapes and agricultural possibilities out of our calculations in considering the future of either industries or cities ... There is no place left to move. We have reached the end of our journey, and in the main, we must retrace our steps, and, region by region, learn to do intelligently and cooperatively what we hitherto did in such disregard for the elementary decencies of life."[12]

Discussions about the appropriate role of planning had to compete with the more immediate concerns generated by the Depression and, later, by the Second World War. In the post-war period, though, housing developments became a top priority and the profession of community planning once again began to pick up steam. By the 1970s, planning had become a major consulting activity and big business. Critics soon raised questions about the path the planning profession was taking in Canada. It was accused of taking a back seat to the corporate sector, allowing private interests to structure the future direction of Canadian cities and their politics: "Without any historical perspective, it is very difficult to understand how planners came to have the political and administrative functions they now possess, and how they became so firmly allied with the exponents of growth, with policies like expressways and urban renewal which citizens have often resisted so fiercely, and with the property industry and land developers.[13]

The 1960s and the 1970s were a time of intense social activism (see Chapter 3). During this era, critics questioned municipal decision-making processes that promoted large real estate development projects over the objections of neighbourhood groups. Other citizens found support within a broader social movement sweeping North America – a movement that focused on human rights, environmental degradation, and poverty. Citizen groups and university students protested the disintegration of urban neighbourhoods, the "block-busting" techniques of various developers, and the lack of attention towards alleviating the housing and health problems of the urban working class. In Canada, John Sewell, one-time Toronto mayor and long-time political activist, championed the populist cause of citizens who were trying to protect their inner-city neighbourhoods from demolition to make way for large new development projects. This struggle took place between the large property development interests (primarily supported by majority views on local councils) on the one hand, and, on the other, activists leading a populist movement supported by a few mavericks sitting on city councils. The effort was documented through journals such as *City Magazine,* the James Lorimer publications, and books with such provocative titles as *Up against City Hall.*[14]

Concerns about the close connections between property developers and local governments continued long after the 1970s. Jim Lightbody, for example, reports some of the more overt examples of interference by developers in city politics in the late 1980s: "In Edmonton where in 1986, during the final votes on detailed amendments to a complex concessions package for the Eaton Centre development, the developer from the public gallery was so boisterously gesticulating yeas and nays to his advocates on council that Mayor Purves inadvertently tried to summon 'alderman' Ghermezian to order. In a similar case in Toronto in 1987, developers' lawyer Patrick Devine stood up, reached over, and tapped Alderman Betty Disero on the shoulder 'to vote in favour of a 13-story luxury condominium project he was representing.'"[15]

Local land-use debates and discussions about the appropriate relationship between developers and elected councillors continue to shape many local political agendas, and at the same time, local activist agendas are diversifying and gathering support from broad-based community movements.[16] These populist groups often call for the decentralization of economic and political decision making in order to foster healthy, sustainable localities.

THE POLITICS OF SPACE, PLACE, AND ECOSYSTEMS

## Planning Processes Today

Many people associate urban planning with the process of zoning, whereby incompatible land uses are separated into different areas of the city. Light industrial areas are separated from residential areas, which are in turn distinct from the downtown business district. This approach has worked well when one considers the adverse health, social, or economic implications of situating a factory within a residential area – not an uncommon situation in the nineteenth century. On the other hand, the application of this method of zoning has contributed to urban sprawl, to the segregation of different groups of society, and to economic and environmental costs.

Attempts to counter these adverse impacts saw the emergence of new planning approaches, such as the new urbanism or neo-traditional suburban development. These new areas were designed to reduce public reliance on cars and to increase community interaction. The deliberate designing of "mixed" residential neighbourhoods led to the placement of schools, stores, and public transportation within walking distance. Local parks and public meeting places were designed to introduce a sense of community into these new areas. The attractive designs with verandas and gingerbread roofs are evocative of a peaceful, small-town environment of a bygone era that, in reality, few Canadians ever experienced in its idealistic form. While some may criticize this new design as once again catering to the upwardly mobile professional classes, others have noted that sometimes this approach is also used for social housing.[17]

Urban renewal and infilling empty or decayed core areas with new high-density residential developments also became a subject of planning interest as the costs of putting services into new suburban areas soared, downtowns decayed, traffic congestion increased, and environmental issues moved up a notch or two on public agendas. It was hoped that old city core redevelopment would help solve a number of social, economic, and environmental problems. Sometimes the economic success of redevelopment fostered gentrification of a downtown area, displacing existing tenants with wealthier individuals who could afford high-priced condominiums built out of old warehouses. Social housing units constructed for the displaced residents were frequently placed in less desirable areas of town, where lack of transportation, poor environmental quality, and cramped living accommodations made it difficult for the area residents to integrate successfully into the workforce or the broader society.

In the suburbs, despite some efforts to alter existing planning patterns, these developments have continued apace, gobbling up desirable farmland and natural areas. Developers and homeowners continue to pursue their mutually reinforcing goals of supply and demand. The *smart growth* strategy is one recent type of initiative employed by governments in hopes of satisfying both environmental and development interests. The stated objective is to balance development with principles of a more sustainable, livable urban environment. Much like the term *sustainable development*, however, there are inherent contradictions in the concept that make it difficult to implement. Provincial and local legislation and the official community plan continue to be the governmental means to control these developments and regulate activities.

## The Community Plan

An *official plan* (also known as the *community plan*) is generally required of municipalities by provincial governments and must operate within the legislative guidelines set out by the provincial planning act. All development is expected to conform to the community plan, which is commonly reviewed every five years and revised every decade. The plan is a reflection of the vision that the community holds for its future evolution. While many actors are usually involved in the process of designing the community plan, planners do play an important role in implementing that vision. Christopher Leo suggests that public goals of a community plan today must incorporate a number of considerations: "Concretely, an official plan may include economic and population growth targets and projections as to what kinds of growth are likely to take place, as well as discussions of the implications of that growth for infrastructure development, the transit system, parks, other city services, the environment, adjacent agricultural and resource areas and so forth. The plan tries to bring these elements together in a coherent way so as to maximize the well-being of residents, promote economic growth, make wise use of resources, and protect the environment from unnecessary harm."[18]

For a number of decades, the public has been consulted to a greater or lesser degree in the design phase of these plans. It is only relatively recently, however, that attempts have been made in some cities to include members of the public in more of the planning process. Most communities also have advisory planning bodies or planning commissions that can include members of the public. Once adopted, the revised official plan can result in myriad "non-conforming uses" in the municipality. To deal with individual cases that do not conform to the official plan, most governments have some sort of adjustment mechanism, often composed of a committee of council, or of councillors and members of the public, to resolve the anomalies and consider applications for minor variances from the zoning by-law.

The development sector dominates local planning processes – so much so that, in the United States, American analysts refer to it as an "urban growth machine."[19] Private-sector actors in this machine would include landowners, real estate developers, mortgage bankers, realtors, construction companies and contractors, cement and sand and gravel companies, and building suppliers. Local government may also be viewed as part of this machine because of its role in determining zoning codes, building permits, land-use regulations, and investments in roads, sewers, and other necessary infrastucture.[20]

In Canada, the federal and provincial governments play a different role than in the United States, but much of the analogy holds true in this country as well. Eben Fodor suggests that local governments can affect land development profits in a number of ways:

- increasing the intensity of land use (rezoning or annexing land, for example)

THE POLITICS OF SPACE, PLACE, AND ECOSYSTEMS

- reducing the cost of development (reducing regulations, fees, and delays)
- diverting public resources to support local land development (new roads, sewers, and other facilities)
- stimulating the demand for new development (economic development programs, tax incentives, and other subsidies).[21]

Christopher Leo notes that it is not uncommon for local governments to proceed with a planned initiative, primarily on the developers' terms, in exchange for economic benefits.[22] New subdivisions, for example, are often proposed by a private-sector developer who submits a subdivision plan to the city. Elected officials, planners, and other members of city government consider whether these new subdivisions conform to the official plan and whether there will be sufficient revenues to cover any costs that the city might incur. Councillors are keenly aware of the much-needed revenues that developers might bring to the community. Fodor suggests that a major problem with this kind of process is that the direct "benefits flow to the few while the costs (congestion, quality of life, higher taxes) are spread among the many."[23] In Canada, a number of provincial governments have been considering approaches that would give local governments the flexibility to further develop public-private-sector partnerships.

Concerned citizens may remind local elected councillors that possible economic benefits must be weighed against the possible social or environmental costs involved. Such costs are difficult to calculate and have led to the introduction of new types of assessments or indicators to include values that are non-economic in nature. The best known of these are quality of life indicators that help decision makers, citizens, and others develop a reporting system against which to assess the direction in which the community is heading. In 1999, for example, the Federation of Canadian Municipalities (FCM) released a report that offered a framework to monitor quality of life in Canadian communities. This framework included indicators related to demographic characteristics, community affordability, employment, housing, stress, health, safety, and public participation.[24]

Cities equipped with limited resources are struggling today to provide a healthy quality of life. Their ability to incorporate such quality indicators in planning processes, however, is inevitably constrained by the need for revenues. Nevertheless, tools that help assess the broader needs of a community will enable decision makers to decide whether they are moving closer or further away from their goals for a healthy community. Such tools could also make it possible for a wider constituency to participate in decision making – an important component of civics.

## Organizing Socio-Political Territory

Not unlike the earlier radical planners, increasing numbers of city planners now acknowledge the relationship between homelessness, poverty, cultural enrichment, public participation, healthy environments, and healthy economies. In doing so, planners recognize that their profession is subject to competing public demands and interests. In their discussion of what planners do, Jamieson, Cosijn, and Friesen suggest that "planners work to shape city form by interpreting social purpose and regulating individual ambitions to fit a conception of the public interest. This mission is made difficult by the fact that planners must sort through the competing individual and collective priorities of thousands of citizens."[25]

As this statement implies, planning is essentially a political process. However, this recognition raises a troubling problem. Planners are public employees who are appointed, not elected. Is it the role of planners to "sort through" the priorities of citizens, or should that task be the responsibility of democratically elected officials? The preceding passage highlights one of the realities of government decision-making processes on a daily basis – planners and other non-elected government employees make political decisions that necessarily are filtered through their own sets of experiences and value systems. One of the ways of representing a broader public interest is through public participation processes, but who decides who has a legitimate right to participate, how, and when? The practice of shaping city form is obviously not a scientific process but one that must necessarily choose among different sets of values. Increased public participation through advisory groups raises the troubling problem that those members of the public who choose to participate may not be broadly representative of the public interest.

On the other hand, including public participation in planning decisions does broaden the debate to include views that otherwise might not be expressed and incorporated. This approach could possibly help to diffuse the controlling influence of a few powerful elites – such as property developers – on local public decision-making processes. Attempts to recognize social and environmental considerations in the planning process reflect an awareness of the need for more livable urban environments, and by widening the public debate, it is also possible to develop more innovative ideas about how to best deal with land-use issues. One such innovation is the grassroots *community gardens* phenomenon that is flourishing throughout Canada and elsewhere (see Box 8.2).

In recent years, the concept of space has expanded to include new metaphorical meanings. Some postmodern analyses of urban politics concern themselves with space as an abstraction, such as in the terms *political space, gendered space, discursive space,* or *virtual space*; all of which refer to non-physical spaces. These abstract notions of space extend the ways in which urban politics may be conceptualized and debated. As Yuval-Davis puts it, "both physical and imaginary territories and boundaries construct the spaces in which citizenship practices and struggles are being carried out."[26] The discussion in this chapter, however, focuses on physical territory and how particular social relationships and political influences contribute to the construction of certain kinds of built environments within cities. As Judith Garber suggests, it is not possible "to appreciate the complex linkages between space and politics if they are removed from their material urban contexts, since many of the most important political referents in cities are located literally on the ground."[27]

## 8.2 Community Gardens

Community gardens have a long, well-established history. Their existence in Canadian communities, however, is somewhat tenuous because, as Corey Helm notes, they have "been primarily motivated by various short-term economic crises and the charitable impulses of landowners and civic reformers."[1] Nevertheless, shared neighbourhood gardens are increasingly seen as important contributors to the social and natural fabric of a community.

The large metropolis of Montreal is well-known for its community gardening enterprise, with numerous gardens supported by the municipal government. In this city, community gardens have been located in parkland zones, which offers them protection from eventual development – a problem that plagues many other community gardens.[2] Helm suggests that "increasing numbers of people are beginning to recognize that community gardens are about more than urban food production; they play a critical role in integrating natural spaces into the places which many people call home, and in fostering the development of a sense of community amongst urban dwellers."[3]

In the 1990s, community gardens surged in popularity throughout Canada. In Helm's study of the twin cities of Kitchener-Waterloo, she noted that from 1990 to 1998 alone, the number of gardens rose from three to fifteen. The City of Kitchener adopted a policy to encourage community gardens. The policy included help for community groups to find suitable sites, encouragement to developers to make land available for community gardens, and where possible the provision of information, assistance, and funding.[4]

---

1  Corey Helm, "Sowing the Seeds of Sustainability: Prospects for Community Gardening in Kitchener and Waterloo" (Master of Environmental Studies thesis, University of Waterloo, 1999), 5.
2  Jacinda Fairholm, "Urban Agriculture and Food Security Initiatives in Canada: A Survey of Canadian Non-Governmental Organizations," Report #25, Lifecycles Project Society Partnership with Cities Feeding People Program (IDRC), October 1998, 9.
3  Helm, "Sowing the Seeds," 7.
4  City of Kitchener, "Community Gardens Policies: Council Resolution, September 27, 1999," in *City of Kitchener Council Policy Manual*, policy document.

That said, social-political divisions are worth considering in the context of physical space because they do affect patterns of development. Social-political divisions in cities can account for the spatial organization of cities and residential differentiation.[28] Three ways in which these divisions could be categorized are by economic, gender and family, and linguistic and cultural distinctions.

## Economic Status and Spatial Organization

The era of globalization is characterized by changing conceptions of time, space, and political power. Improvements in transportation and information communications have enabled the increased mobility of people and goods. The era is also distinguished by "freer" trade, internationalization of capital, and growing social and spatial inequalities between the very wealthy and the poor.

The relative level of control individuals have, or perceive they have, in terms of their own ability to influence their living and working physical environment is strongly related to their economic status. This stratification of rich and poor is manifested physically in a variety of ways, one of which would be through the separation of living environments, such as was noted in the earlier example of gated communities. Differentiation between living environments includes such variables as quality of housing stock and infrastructure, safety, healthy physical environments, access to amenities, aesthetics, and so on.

A second way in which economic status influences spatial organization is through the distribution of employment in the city, leading to what Robert A. Murdie and Carlos Teixeira refer to as a spatial mismatch between home and work. They offer the example of Toronto, where "lower-paid jobs are increasingly found in the inner and outer suburbs, while lower-income households are still concentrated in parts of the central city and the inner suburbs."[29]

A third type of spatial inequality relates to the relative level of mobility that citizens possess in the global economy. Brodie observes, "Those iterated into the global economy are, in many ways, detached from local physical space. Their communities are mobile, global, virtual and corporate. The marginalized, in contrast, are tied to local space. The homeless man huddled to a heating grate for warmth, the welfare recipient without sufficient means to pay for bus fare to seek out employment or the single mother unable to leave the home because there is no alternative childcare are obvious examples of the degree to which the economically marginalized are fixed in the physical space of the home, street and city."[30] The ability of individuals to influence political decisions about the issues that affect them most directly – their living and working environment – is obviously strongly correlated to their economic status.

## Gender, Family, and Space

Twentieth-century cities were planned on certain assumptions that do not match current realities – if they ever did. The biases inherent in urban planning around concepts of nuclear families reflected the interests of the male decision-making elites of the first half of the century, and such patterns have continued. Since the Second World War, demographic shifts, an aging population, and the changing composition of families and households have resulted in different housing needs and community configurations. One obvious example of this was the growth of single-parent families led primarily by women (up from 2.3 percent in 1951 to 17.1 percent in 1996).[31] By 2001, Canada contained 1,311,190 single-parent families out of a total of 8,731,020 families.[32]

Contemporary feminist studies of the urban space have challenged traditional planning assumptions. For example, cities have been planned in a way that separates spatially the private sphere of human activity (the residence or home) from the public sphere (where economic production or employment takes place).[33] Planned suburban residential homes (the private sphere) and central city business cores (the public sphere), for example, are based on assumptions about work and family that are out of step with the dual roles generally performed today by women as both caregivers and employees. Had this planned dichotomy between public and private space been designed to address the needs and interests of women, our cities today would look very different. Recognition would have been paid to safety considerations in planning parks and garages, to the need for daycare centres, to the provision of healthy, natural play areas, and to safe, affordable housing close to areas of employment.[34] Yet as Suzanne MacKenzie observes, many, if not most, women today are engaged in both productive activities (producing society's goods and services) and reproductive activities that are spatially separated.[35]

That stated, women have also altered their environments, creating new solutions to deal with challenges caused by the separate spheres of work and home. "Women are re-designing, or redesignating, homes and neighbourhoods: sharing houses with other single parents, turning basements into workshops, or reoccupying and revitalizing inner cities."[36] New information technologies may also prove a useful tool for women when dealing with spatial challenges of the twentieth-century industrial city. Telework (or telecommuting), a term that refers to people working at their place of residence networked through their computers to their employment, may allow women more flexibility to work at home and adjust their work hours to their other needs.

Much like the cottage or piece worker of early industrial England, however, there are disadvantages. Women can find themselves isolated, working without the bargaining strength of a union to provide job security or a sufficient benefit package, and also lacking the social support offered by the workplace. Studies have also revealed that teleworkers often work during the conventional daily hours to be available to clients and employers, as well as on evenings and weekends.[37]

Telecommuting, if planned well, could nevertheless be used to accommodate the changing needs of families and workers and contribute to a more sustainable approach to urban land use. Laura Johnson notes that decentralized, residentially located telework centres could offer a shared space to home-based workers.[38] If potential users participate in the planning process to ensure that the workspace meets their needs, underused spaces located in shopping centres, commercial properties, high rises, or old houses could be converted into shared work spaces. Johnson suggests that changes to restrictive zoning that has been used to segregate residential land from commercial spaces would allow for innovative solutions to support the concept of telecommuting.[39] Such centres could provide a more flexible work environment and a work location closer to home and family, while reducing adverse environment effects caused by the commuter traffic and lifestyle.

## Cultural/Linguistic Communities

European colonization of Canada dominated by two linguistic groups – French and English – led to the development of many Canadian communities being spatially segregated according to language and culture. At the beginning of the twentieth century, rapid developments in transportation and communications led to monopolies and the concentration of power in many urban centres. In the province of Quebec, Montreal rapidly became a leading industrial, financial centre dominating the rural Quebec communities that were left on the economic margins. This dualism was also reflected in the linguistic and cultural divisions of Quebec society that, in turn, led to spatial segregation in communities. Dickinson and Young wrote, "The anglophone bourgeoisie expanded particular institutions that separated it from daily contact with Quebec society; in Montreal, for example, new anglophone municipalities like Westmount and the Town of Mount Royal provided their own municipal services, such as parks and libraries, which allowed women and children to live in enclaves apart from the larger city. At the same time, in company towns across Quebec separate neighbourhoods, Tudor-style houses, and curling clubs testified to the insular existence of local anglophone managers and engineers."[40]

The French-English spatial divide was visibly manifested in the different qualities of life and housing conditions of linguistic neighbourhoods. In many Quebec communities, one can still see streets of working-class neighbourhoods with French-Canadian names, while English names mark the neighbourhoods that once housed managers and business people. Changes in demographics and immigration patterns, the Quebec Quiet Revolution of the 1960s, and the politics of the subsequent years did much to change and blur the sharp demarcation in urban development along French-English lines. Nevertheless, the linguistically based enclaves are still notable in many French-English communities (see Box 8.3). Accompanying this reality, however, is an increase of other linguistically based neighbourhoods that reflect the multicultural composition of Canada.

Until the mid-twentieth century, the vast majority of Canada's population was of European origin. As a result, these citizens have been the dominant local decision makers. Cities are planned with the values of dominant cultures in mind. In 1967, changes to Canadian immigration policy made it possible for people from a greater diversity of countries to enter Canada. The new system also favoured people who could make an economic contribution. As Abu-Laban notes, this gave an advantage to business immigrants who were primarily well-educated, economically privileged men, but it also led to a decline in European-dominated immigration patterns (from 90 percent before the 1960s to 25 percent by the 1990s).[41] By the year 2000, over 80 percent of Canadian immigrants came from outside Britain, Europe, and the United States. Over half of this group immigrated to

THE POLITICS OF SPACE, PLACE, AND ECOSYSTEMS

## 8.3 Bilingualism: Sherbrooke and Lennoxville

Throughout its history, the City of Sherbrooke has seen a shift from English being the predominant language of business and politics to French. The vast majority of Sherbrooke residents now speak French as their first language, although a great many are bilingual. At the time of amalgamation in January 2002, French was the primary language used in city hall, in public communiqués, and on municipal Web pages. The amalgamation of cities throughout Quebec could affect the culture of those formerly independent cities that had been dominated or strongly influenced by English speakers.

Lennoxville, incorporated in 1871, is one such town. Although Lennoxville is a bilingual community, 66 percent of residents speak English as their first language while 34 percent speak French. This situation reflects its English heritage, as it is named after the English Duke of Richmond, Charles Lennox, governor general in 1819. Street names and architecture reflect the British influence. Lennoxville has a population of 4,000, which swells considerably when 3,000 university students arrive to attend classes at Bishop's University (where classes can be attended in English) and at Champlain College.[1]

The new amalgamated municipality of Sherbrooke includes the former incorporated town of Lennoxville. The new two-tier structure of local government in Quebec may help protect the unique political cultures of the previously independent municipalities. Over time, however, that culture may become subsumed by the new governing municipal system or by other dynamics that extend beyond municipal, or even provincial, borders.

---

1 Town of Lennoxville, Quebec, "Welcome" page on Web site (accessed 1 March 2002; page now discontinued).

one of the three large metropolitan centres – Toronto, Montreal, and Vancouver – leading to a significant difference in ethnic composition between large urban centres and other communities.[42] It has been argued that Toronto, for example, is the most multicultural city in the world, with 70,000 immigrants arriving each year. In 1999, they arrived from over 100 countries (see Box 8.4).[43]

Canada may have a reputation for welcoming immigrants from all nations, but this does not mean that it has not had its share of racism throughout its history. Cross-cultural antagonisms influence issues of housing, planning, policing, social equity, and who ultimately is able to take part in "governing." In British Columbia, Asian immigrants began arriving in the mid-nineteenth century and continued to do so throughout the twentieth century. They were subjected to continuing, well-documented discrimination by both governments and white Canadians. Donald Avery observes that in the ethnic ghettos that developed, such as Chinatown in Vancouver, "residents were harassed by civic officials in the form of special business licenses, arbitrary health inspections, and de facto school segregation."[44]

Today, the City of Vancouver has adopted a civic policy on multicultural relations that states that the city's cultural and ethnic diversity is "a source of enrichment, diversity and strength."[45] Despite this acknowledgment, however, problems and stereotypes persist. Abu-Laban offers the Vancouver example of the surge in the building of huge new houses to accommodate a boom in the last two decades of the twentieth century. Some groups saw the new homes as a threat to the WASP architectural heritage of the city. Sometimes referred to as *monster homes*, these houses with cookie-cutter designs characterize many, if not most, new upscale developments or redevelopments throughout Canada. This phenomenon is unrelated to the homeowner's ethnic background. In Vancouver, however, Abu-Laban suggests that long-time residents who disliked these developments often held Asian homebuyers responsible for both the design of the houses and the changes to the city's visual landscape.[46]

Major policy change that encouraged multiculturalism and equality of status for people of all ethnic and cultural origins was first effectively realized with the federal 1971 Multicultural Act. This legislation was followed by the 1976 Immigration Act and the 1982 Canadian Charter of Rights and Freedoms.[47] Canada's policies and general approach to ethnic diversity and immigration compare very favourably with a number of other Western countries. Despite these official measures at the federal level, though, new Canadians continue to encounter many social and physical barriers in cities and neighbourhoods at the municipal level of government.

The way in which land is spatially distributed can lead to social fragmentation if this aspect of planning is not carefully considered. Unfortunately, political decisions about how Canadian cities should be planned and developed have taken place relatively independently of the changing needs of a multicultural society. Moreover, while traditional local government and planning texts often speak of the goals of effectiveness, efficiency, responsiveness, and local democracy, rarely have these discussions taken place with reference to

## 8.4 Toronto: A Multicultural Metropolis

Toronto is one of the most multicultural cities in the world. According to one source,

- Toronto has one-twelfth of Canada's population but one-quarter of the country's recent immigrants.
- One in five Torontonians arrived in Canada after 1981; one in ten arrived after 1991.
- Toronto's citizens come from 169 countries and speak more than 100 languages (the top three foreign languages are Chinese, Italian, and Portuguese).
- Toronto's cultural and religious diversity is unmatched: Mass is now said in 35 languages; 200,000 Muslims observe Ramadan; 80,000 Sikhs march in the annual Khalsa Day celebrations; and the city is home to half of the country's Jews.
- There are more visible minorities in Toronto than there are residents in any of the Atlantic provinces, Saskatchewan, or Manitoba.

*Source:* Steven Fick and Mary Vincent, "Toronto: The World in One City," *Canadian Geographic* (January/February 2001). See also City of Toronto, "Home page," http://www.city.toronto.on.ca/Toronto_facts/diversity/htm.

citizens' social or cultural needs. As one observer succinctly noted, "Describing city government or municipal politics, the building of an urban economy and the evolution of a city as a polity obviously has value. To do so without understanding ethnicity in the city seems a bit like analyzing the captain and crew of an ocean liner but not noticing the passengers, what they expect of the vessel and why they are traveling."[48]

This does not mean that the topic is wholly unconsidered; the point is simply to note that the use of social-spatial analyses in city planning is a comparatively modern phenomenon. Murdie and Teixeira offer one example of this type of analysis in their study of the "geography of ethnicity," which considers the spatial segregation of ethnic groups. They suggest that this segregation is having significant impact on the shape of Canadian cities as many new arrivals settle in suburbs and others move to inner-city cores. The authors point out that cities vary considerably in their settlement patterns: a number are quite homogeneous while others have dispersed populations. Still others have concentrated pockets of ethnic enclaves. Reminiscent of the problems that the Irish encountered arriving in nineteenth-century New York, the most vulnerable immigrant communities are those composed of recently arrived refugees. They are "highly marginalized with respect to the quality of housing and kinds of neighbourhoods within which they live."[49]

While the rapid growth of multicultural societies in Canada has focused on new arrivals, the phenomenon of spatial marginalization of minority groups is by no means a new one in Canada. In fact, indigenous people have experienced this phenomenon for centuries. Throughout Canada, First Nations peoples disproportionately experience poor living conditions concentrated in some of the more dilapidated and neglected sections of cities and towns.

The way in which governments respond to (or ignore) the needs and preferences of Canada's multicultural society will fundamentally affect the social and physical landscapes of cities for many decades to come. If city planners are to "function principally as mediators between social purpose and city form,"[50] as one analysis would have it, then a major responsibility of city planners today is to recognize that the priorities and social purpose of Canadians as a whole will mean recognizing in practice that Canada is a multicultural society. New arrivals to a city need housing, culturally appropriate social programs, and other services. They require the means for the expression of their needs and preferences. Without such considerations in mind, cities can become fragmented, socially divided entities rather than ones that benefit from a rich plurality of cultural traditions expressed in political, social, and physical spaces.

The lack of ethnic diversity among those who hold civic office may mean that yet another safeguard for civic interest is missing. When we ask the question, "Are we governing ourselves?" many Canadians in this multicultural society may reasonably wonder whether their cultural and social traditions and needs are adequately reflected in the composition of their governing councils.

## Conclusion

More than sixty-five years ago, Lewis Mumford articulated his ideal sense of place and community:

> We must create in every region people who will be accustomed, from school on-ward, to humanist attitudes, cooperative methods, rational controls. These people will know in detail where they live and how they live: they will be united by a common feeling for their landscape, their literature and language, their local ways, and out of their own self-respect they will have sympathetic understanding with other regions and different local peculiarities. They will be actively interested in the form and culture of their locality, which means their community and their own personalities. Such people will contribute to our land planning, our industry planning, our community planning, the authority of their own understanding and the pressure of their own desires.[51]

Such goals continue to be elusive. People who wish to pursue these ideals still face many of the same old barriers, as well as some new ones. Those individuals and groups who have influence over the resources and the shaping of the physical spaces of a community will also strongly influence the culture, social relationships, civics, and quality of community life. The decisions taken in the planning and development of cities have reflected and reinforced the interests of the dominant elites. From the initial planning stages to zoning and subdivision decisions, the modern twentieth-century city was spatially organized in ways that reflected the dominant interests of certain private-sector interests. Those in a lesser position of political influence – women, single parents, or minority groups – were further marginalized by spatial inequalities caused by planning decisions that often limited their mobility and their choices. We see examples of this in all Canadian cities, including our case-study cities.

Nevertheless, some members of these groups have found assorted ways of dealing with inhospitable planned environments by creating alternative political spaces, such as shared neighbourhood initiatives, community gardens, and cooperative daycare centres. As was noted in Chapter 1, these self-governing measures often operate beyond the boundaries of formal political organizations and represent an important aspect of local civil society. In addition to these activities, activists, educators, and others will advocate on behalf of politically marginalized interests, pressuring for local change in the way in which cities are structured. The business sector and its interests still prevail in the ongoing patterns of development and the planning of urban and other local spaces. However, it would be a mistake not to recognize the important role that these alternative activities can have in influencing the local politics of territory.

# 9
# Environmental Challenges: Redefining the Public Interest

O ver the past several decades, the concept of *quality of life* has broadened beyond that of safe streets, pleasant housing, and good civic services. Now, increasingly, it encompasses a wide range of environmental concerns. The social, cultural, and political concerns are interrelated with issues of city form and development. Of equal concern is how we make decisions that affect the biophysical health of communities. Canadians are becoming aware of the ecological price now being paid for the decades of rapid growth and careless development. That said, this awareness appears to have little impact on overall consumption patterns, as increasing numbers of people buy cars and consume resources at a much faster rate than even two decades ago.

Governments are being pressured to rethink their mandates in order to recognize these interconnected factors; they are challenged to provide services financed by economic growth while maintaining a healthy environment. The two objectives often can be mutually exclusive. Attempts to develop policies that encourage economic investment while simultaneously maintaining sustainable, livable neighbourhoods pose problems not readily resolved by local decision makers. A significant part of the difficulty lies with environmental imperatives that do not respect political jurisdictional boundaries.

Establishing institutional mechanisms capable of responding to environmental requirements will not be readily accomplished for several reasons:

- Changing the status quo may not be in the immediate self-interests of influential local decision makers.
- The need for property revenues in the face of provincial downloading and increased public demands constrains the ability of local governments to control environmentally unfriendly development.
- Local governments are jurisdictionally limited in what they can control and regulate, given powerful external political and economic forces
- Hierarchical administrative structures were designed for purposes of efficiency, accountability, and control, and these "silos" do not readily lend themselves to structures that recognize the complex interplay of biophysical, social, economic, and political factors.

Underpinning all this is a well-entrenched liberal ideology and societal belief in individual property rights that undermines the pursuit of collective goals.

THE POLITICS OF SPACE, PLACE, AND ECOSYSTEMS

Today, public decision makers are pressured to devise approaches to governing that can somehow be both proactive in plans for the future while responsive to challenges posed by the interrelationships between human and physical environments. Solutions are sometimes sought in *systems approaches*. These systems approaches challenge traditional *decisional approaches* to governance both analytically and, inevitably, prescriptively.

## The Quest for Sustainability

Environmental issues are vital considerations in local politics. Traditionally the biophysical aspects of the environment were viewed as just a smaller part of a number of distinct policy areas requiring some attention. Issues related to the physical environment were generally shunted into departments of parks and recreation and treated as no more distinctive than transportation or education. As such, they received insufficient policy attention from decision makers, and inadequate analytical attention in the social science literature. For the most part, this is still the case, despite the many fundamental environmental challenges that now confront local governments – challenges that will ultimately determine the health, quality of life, and even viability of communities. Dealing with these problems one by one is seldom cost-effective. A more integrated approach to managing human interactions with biophysical systems is required, but it is difficult to achieve.

In the contemporary quest for economic wealth and environmental health, policy makers are facing challenges that are inherently contradictory and possibly irreconcilable. At the root of the conflict is a liberal-democratic system of values that recognizes the rights of individuals to exercise certain freedoms, own property, and participate in the political process. At the same time, the Canadian political system fosters a philosophy of collective interest, common property, and representative decision making. The tension between these principles is particularly striking when we examine the concept of sustainable communities. Cities have been planned around the demands of individuals, their private property rights, and their private automobiles. Environmental politics has been based on a philosophy of collective rights that, in market systems, have usually been subordinated to assertions of private and individual rights. In such systems, democratic politicians must always strive to achieve workable compromises among major interests. The agendas advanced by reformers, environmental or otherwise, seldom lend themselves easily to compromise. The past few decades have witnessed an explosion of activity, with competing interest groups pressing different agendas. Governments are increasingly compelled to undertake a broad consultative process when making environmental or economic decisions.[1]

An examination of the emergence of local environmental politics reveals the existence of an early struggle between liberal-oriented decision making and the comprehensive planning agendas of civic reformers. Today, these conflicts have intensified. Traditional areas of local responsibility, once largely uncontentious land, water, and waste management issues, are now subjects of intense debate.

Attempts to marry the twin concerns of a healthy physical environment and a healthy economy do not lead readily to a harmonious, integrated community of interest. Public confidence in the ability of governments to deal with these problems is declining. Over-burdened with current deficits and accumulated debts, other governments are off-loading responsibilities to the local level just as the public, too, demands more and more. The search for a stable economy and environmental improvements is supposed to progress in the middle of this two-way squeeze.

Over a hundred years ago, with some notable exceptions, such as public health, environmental concerns were not top priorities for any governments, preoccupied as they were with economic development and prosperity.[2] The rich and diverse working, living, and social environment originally envisioned by the few more radical planners such as Thomas Adams and Lewis Mumford resembles contemporary concepts of ecosystem planning.[3] These planners recognized the need to integrate human with biophysical systems in order to stimulate healthy, desired environments. Their perspectives stand out in marked contrast to the outward suburban sprawl that prevailed, which is instead characterized by undistinguished architecture and development patterns that fostered conformity, uniformity, and a heavy dependence on the automobile. Concerns have also broadened to include other environmental aspects, such as the sacrifice of valued natural habitats, inefficient use of water resources, declining air quality, continued reliance on the automobile, and environmental considerations relating to the disposal of massive amounts of solid waste. Community-based movements have called for the decentralization of economic and political decision making in order to foster healthy, sustainable localities.

Echoing the earlier radical planners, today's trends in community planning are recognizing the relationships between homelessness, poverty, cultural enrichment, community participation, healthy environments, and healthy economies.

## The Struggle to Define the Public Interest

Local planning strategies are now expected to be much more inclusive, encapsulating social, health, and environmental considerations. Concerns about the scarcity of certain physical resources fuels the somewhat contradictory public demand that local governments continue to provide a high level of services at low fiscal and environmental cost. Attempts to reconcile these demands have led to new approaches such as integrated resource planning. Local planning exercises now include considerations of both natural and built environments, although they are a long way from ecosystem planning ideals. The philosophy underpinning arguments for sustainable communities stresses the importance of public consultation and participation in the decision-making process.

If the public is included in the process, it is thought to be more likely that residents will take some responsibility for ensuring the realization of community objectives. From an administrative perspective, it might also be argued that the implementation of policies

THE POLITICS OF SPACE, PLACE, AND ECOSYSTEMS

is likely to go more smoothly if the affected members of the community are involved in such designs. In the 2000s, governments may have no choice but to consult extensively. The public expects a much more direct say on a wide array of issues, whether it is a question of debt financing for a large capital project or the wisdom of a proposed development in a wetland area. Environmental assessment legislation and regulations, as well as other pieces of legislation, often require public consultation on major initiatives. Moreover, in the past twenty years in particular, strong, networked environmental associations represented by legal counsel have often taken issues to court if they failed at other levels.

It is very difficult, however, to achieve the goal of a commonly shared holistic vision if too many diverse and often-conflicting interests are represented at the decision-making table. Individuals hold contradictory perspectives on the environment. It has been sagely noted that "while individual citizens like to see others regulated, they prefer freedom of choice for themselves. They will, however, accept rules for which there are good and valid reasons."[4] One observer has suggested that while many members of the public are aware of the need to protect the environment, the majority tends to view land as "private property, commodity, source of income and profit, provider of recreation, means of waste disposal, emblem of social status."[5] Such views are hard to reconcile with a holistic ecosystem approach.

On the other hand, the public tends to view new development in an increasingly negative light. In urban areas, citizens are often quite vocal in resisting projects that may have an adverse impact on their local neighbourhoods. Phenomena such as NIMBY (not in my backyard) and LULU (locally unacceptable land use) reflect a backlash against continuing growth and spreading development. These reactions demonstrate the public's desire to continue to protect existing property rights and land uses on the one hand, while becoming increasingly concerned about the environmental impact of development activities on the other.

It is not difficult to get diverse groups of interests to agree that sustainable development is desirable. Rarely, however, is there a consensus about exactly what constitutes "sustainability." Some see the process of capital accumulation and growth as antithetical to the requirements of the natural environment. In other words, the concept of a frontier economy where resources are unlimited is ill-suited to the limits suggested by the metaphor of spaceship earth.[6] Herman Daly has noted that the current growth economy requires an "increase in matter/energy throughput that sustains the economic activities of production and consumption of commodities."[7] Throughput refers specifically to the use of raw materials or resources that are depleted and are eventually converted into waste. While conventional economic theory was derived at a time when resources might have appeared infinite, intensifying concerns about the impact of growth and about land, water, and air quality have led to alternative theories that call for *steady-state economies* that are ecologically sustainable in the long term.[8] The adoption of these types of proposals, however, faces ideological, economic, and political barriers.

The degeneration of the environment by the late twentieth century fuelled urgent demands for comprehensive, rational land-use planning. Public consultation exercises proliferated. So too, did the numbers of diverse participants – all with their own agendas. The environmental movement itself was fragmented, often between the goals and objectives of the larger national and international groups and the locally based groups.

Pressure for devolution of authority might be expected to go hand in hand with the environmental agenda. It also could be argued, however, that by giving local agencies and interests more control, the broader environmental agenda might be threatened. Politically influential local interest groups may be more preoccupied with defending their employment opportunities or economic interests than, for example, protecting their local wetlands. Yet, it is also local residents and communities that have the most to lose if planning and development are not handled in an environmentally responsible way. One proposed compromise might be found in the principle of *subsidiarity*.

## Subsidiarity

Subsidiarity suggests that authority and responsibility should be handed down to the smallest unit of government that can deal with the task most effectively. In practice, this means that when a local government does not have the capacity to deal with a particular task, a higher level of government would handle the responsibility. In her critique of the principle of subsidiarity, Janine Brodie quotes the United Nations Development Programme (UNDP) in its claim that "a highly centralized system of government is less democratic than one in which there is a network of local and regional authorities ... when units are small enough for ordinary people to feel that they count."[9]

The principle of subsidiarity may seem to be a reasonable one for the purposes of democracy and efficiency, yet in practice it raises questions that are not readily dismissed. Brodie is skeptical about the overall ability of local governments to advance democracy given what she sees as their relatively weak position within the global economy. Others such as Graham, Maslove, and Phillips point out the practical problems of disentangling the responsibilities of provincial and local governments and determining who should be responsible for what.[10] Also, larger cities may be reasonably well equipped for providing a service such as water management within a strong, provincial regulatory framework. Smaller cities, however, may not have the same resources or political will to carry out provincial mandates. The principle of subsidiarity may work very well in one case, but not in another.

Hodge and Robinson contribute to the debate in their examination of regional planning by suggesting that the focus should rest on *governance* rather than *government*, emphasizing "process, inclusiveness and flexibility as much as structure. Such an approach to region-wide governance relies on a network of interrelationships rather than on a constraining institutional mechanism. It depends upon voluntary, cooperative agreements among all private as well as all public 'stakeholders.'"[11] Examples of this are taking place across the country, from the Lake Ontario Waterfront Trail initiative to Vancouver Island's South Island Sustainable Communities network.[12]

Despite such promising cooperative projects, the demand for publicly inclusive approaches and pressures for decentralization are also being accompanied by a need for governments to cope with environmental issues in a proactive, decisive, and timely manner. That imperative runs counter to ideas about governing ourselves through broadened public participation in decision-making processes that are also open and accountable. The inevitable compromise satisfies few.

## Local Environmental Responsibilities

Given all the difficulties, one might think that very little has been done to protect the local environment. In fact, though, local authorities are being compelled to respond to environmental issues. The increasing salience of environmental issues in the local mass media, as well as unprecedented levels of concern about global climate change and contamination of soil, water, and air, have heightened public concern. Well-organized pressure groups lobby to prevent wetlands from being rezoned for industrial development. Local officials, themselves members of the community, share many of the popular concerns and pass bylaws that reflect changing environmental values.

Changes in local official plans are now emphasizing the importance of sustainable development. Special-purpose bodies or committees dealing with natural resources are established in many regions. A proliferation of bylaws relate to a range of environmental concerns – everything from the preservation of heritage trees, to controlling the use of public beaches, implementing pesticide bans, and instituting no-smoking laws. Local governments have had long-standing responsibilities for many areas of decision making that have now grown enormously in importance. Municipal responsibilities for garbage disposal, sewerage, water services, and zoning have now been recast and placed in the much broader environmental context of waste management, watershed management, and ecosystem planning. Most environmental controversies or accidents occur in local communities, intensifying pressures on local governments to take steps to ensure public health and safety. Toxic waste spills, agricultural run-off, air quality problems, or contaminants leaching from industrial sites all require immediate responses from the local government, along with the other orders of government. If citizens have concerns about their water quality or nearby hazardous wastes, they first look to the municipality.

Three areas that have traditionally fallen under the responsibility of local government and now require new responses include land-use planning, water use, and waste management.

## Land-Use Planning

Local governments have extensive responsibilities in the areas of land-use planning, zoning, and subdivision control. They are responsible for drawing up regional and municipal plans consistent with the guidelines established by provincial planning legislation. Land-use planning is essentially concerned with the relationships among several factors:

- the pattern of private land use and development
- the consequent demand for municipal services and the costs of providing them
- the assessment base on which the municipal exchequer is heavily dependent.[13]

At one time, land seen as useless for development was referred to as wasteland or even SLOAP (space left over after planning).[14] However, so-called wastelands often contain wetlands and important watersheds. An economic value is now being attributed to these resources through *full-cost accounting,* which includes the environmental and social costs in the price of goods and services. Land assessment and taxation systems may be revised in order to ensure that those systems do not discourage the protection of ecologically sensitive areas.[15]

A number of "green" planning strategies have been devised to check urban sprawl and take the pressure off open and undeveloped areas. Ecosystem planning recognizes the importance of people-oriented designs, which were first espoused in Adams's early town-planning model. With the intensification and redevelopment of urban and inner-city areas, cities are investigating ways to reduce the dependency on the automobile, such as introducing walking and bicycle paths or encouraging use of public transit.

Municipalities will also need to make changes as a result of Canada's decision to become a signatory to the Kyoto Accord. The Kyoto Accord, a global initiative that attempts to reduce greenhouse gas emissions, will provide impetus for municipalities to take action to reduce emissions through planning and transportation policies.

Simply put, the ecosystem-planning orientation seeks to plan cities around desired ecosystems rather than around automobiles. Ecosystem planning is advanced to lessen the problems engendered by the socially and environmentally unfriendly consequences of modern suburban living. Ecological diversity in urban areas is encouraged with the introduction or preservation of greenways, waterways, and woodlands. Costs are reduced by replacing labour-intensive mowing and pesticide spraying in open areas and roadsides with the lower-maintenance planting of wildflowers, grasses, and trees. Strategies for dealing with the environment vary considerably across the country, and some of them reflect the natural environment and culture. Each of our case-study cities has developed environmental approaches to respond to its own geographical and environmental circumstances. Examples include the establishment of community forests in Prince George, the cleaning up of the Saint John River in Saint John, managing wastes in Waterloo, and the extensive network of cycling and hiking trails in Sherbrooke.

Throughout Canada, growing recognition of the need to develop integrated land-use strategies in the 1980s led to a number of environmental roundtables and royal commissions on natural resources and land-use development. National and provincial roundtables on the environment and economy were one of Canada's responses to the international commission popularly known as the 1987 Brundtland Commission. Other initiatives included the British Columbia Commission on Resources and Environment (CORE), the Commission on Planning and Development Reform in Ontario, and the New Brunswick Commission on Land Use and the Rural Environment, as well as regionally oriented commissions such as the Royal Commission on the Future of the Toronto Waterfront. The examples of the Toronto harbourfront (Box 9.1) and the Vancouver Livable Region Plan (Box 9.2) illustrate the way in which land-use planning is evolving to reflect the demand for public participation and environmentally responsible decision making.

These examples, as well as the other ecosystem-planning examples mentioned, all highlight the importance of compatible land-use planning, an approach that recognizes the needs of the users, cultural and heritage sites, and the natural environment. These initiatives reflected the unique interests of the particular communities involved. New resource management initiatives, such as community forests, for example, are of great interest to Prince George and other municipalities that have been historically involved in forestry or wood-related production. Community forest initiatives are still at the early stages in Canada, but they are growing in popularity. The underlying principle is to give municipalities the opportunity to manage their own woodlots in a sustainable long-term manner and to serve as stewards over the resources.

Philosophical changes in the way resources are viewed and used are essential for a healthy environment. Equally needed are strategies to cope with the practical realities of political jurisdictional conflicts and competing priorities between economic development and land conservation. Although their record varies tremendously across the country, municipalities, to greater or lesser degrees, do attempt to protect natural resources and regulate development. They are, however, "confined by narrow jurisdictional limits, [and] ... too often lack both an ecosystem context and a coherent set of environmental goals and guidelines."[16] In spite of the best-professed philosophies, the implementation of policies has never been rational and comprehensive in the way they are often first envisioned. Policies, particularly those based on intensive consultation, require time and compromise. By the time a policy has been subjected to numerous reviews and amendments to accommodate multiple views and regulations, the final product often represents only incremental change. One observer dryly notes that "keeping the same slow incremental approach in the urban environment, while seeking a rapid change towards sustainable development, is similar to attempting to escape a head-on collision without changing trajectory."[17]

In her study of the Region of York, located in southern Ontario, environmental planner Melissa Jort concludes that the area's forests are seriously threatened despite massive grassroots efforts to protect valued areas such as such as the Oak Ridges Moraine. Urban

## 9.1 The Royal Commission on the Toronto Waterfront

The commission (established 1988) was asked to come up with recommendations on how to deal with the contaminated waterfront and related lands in the face of "jurisdictional gridlock."[1] The environmental problems were the result of historical cumulative effects, as railways and expressways cut the public off from their waterfront and their river valleys. Paved over and hidden away, the importance of the natural areas was subsumed by the imperatives of economic progress.[2] Once established, the commission was led by David Crombie who, along with filling other public roles, once served as mayor of Toronto. The commission initiated an extensive consultation process, which involved teams composed of developers, environmentalists, traffic engineers, landscape architects, scientists, community activists, federal and provincial public servants, and city officials. The commission determined that its mandate would cover the Greater Toronto Bioregion, extending from the Niagara Escarpment on the west, the Oak Ridges Moraine on the north and east side, and Lake Ontario's shoreline.[3] In its quest to develop approaches to the "regeneration" of the city, the Commission felt that this process was successful, fostering consensus, trust, and partnerships.[4]

But following up on recommendations for bioregional planning in the Greater Toronto Bioregion is not readily accomplished. As Hodge and Robinson note, "it was clear that, because the environment does not correspond to political boundaries, actions in one jurisdiction may well affect the environmental health of others ... Existing institutional arrangements in the GTB are often part of the problem, for its bureaucratic systems are generally rigid and its jurisdictions are fragmented."[5] Hodge and Robinson observed that the government did not adopt the concept of the Greater Toronto Bioregion as the basis for regional planning, although the Waterfront Regeneration Trust was established in 1992 after the report's release. The trust itself would carry out certain projects based on the ecosystem approach.[6]

As of 2002, the Trust was an independently run, non-profit organization operating on the basis of nine principles (clean, green, accessible, connected, open, usable, diverse, affordable, and attractive). One of its many goals is to restore the health of the Toronto waterfront, a major component of which is the eventual completion of the Lake Ontario Waterfront Trail stretching from Niagara-on-the-Lake to Gananoque. The trail includes private- and public-sector partners, including twenty-eight municipalities.[7]

---

1 David Crombie, *Regeneration: Toronto's Waterfront and the Sustainable City*, Royal Commission on the Toronto Harbourfront, Final Report (Toronto: Minister of Supply and Services Canada, 1992), *Regeneration*, 1-2.
2 Ibid., 4.
3 Gerald Hodge and Ira M. Robinson, *Planning Canadian Regions* (Vancouver and Toronto: UBC Press, 2001).
4 Crombie, *Regeneration*, 46.
5 Hodge and Robinson, *Planning Canadian Regions*, 330.
6 Ibid., 332.
7 Waterfront Regeneration Trust, "Lake Ontario Waterfront Trail," http://www.waterfronttrail.org (accessed 18 November 2002).

## 9.2  The GVRD and the Livable Region Plan

In the late 1960s, the burgeoning of Vancouver's population led some far-thinking people, such as The Electors' Action Movement (TEAM) to advocate for a made-in-Vancouver plan to ensure that the city would develop in a "livable" manner while protecting its natural environment. In 1975, The Greater Vancouver Regional District (GVRD) decided to undertake a plan that would serve as a companion to the official community plan that covered the entire Lower Mainland. The "Livable Region Plan," as it became known, was founded on a broad-based citizen participation process, something that was unique for the times.[1]

When the provincial Social Credit government came to power in 1983, it relieved all regional districts in British Columbia of their planning and zoning authority. As Hodge and Robinson succinctly put it, "the regional planning system, for all practicalities, was gutted."[2] They suggest that some saw this dramatic move as a result of a battle between the GVRD and the provincial government concerning agricultural land-use reserves (legislated areas to be used only for rural purposes).[3]

Despite this move by the Social Credit government, the GVRD continued to operate with voluntary municipal support. Another initiative to develop a regional strategy emphasized environmental values over urban development and extensive public participation. Known as The Livable Region Strategic Plan, it was completed by January 1996 and was adopted by the GVRD board. It was signed by the provincial government of the day, the New Democratic Party (which had replaced the Social Credit government) as part of the Growth Strategies Statutes Amendment Act. Hodge and Robinson note that the plan was built on ideas conceived in 1975 and was accomplished through partnerships rather than institutional hierarchies.[4] This regional process stands out for its level of foresight, consensus, and awareness of environmental initiatives. The GVRD, however, continues to deal with numerous environmental challenges that will not be easily managed unless it receives the requisite financial resources – an unlikely prospect given the fiscally conservative provincial government in place in the early 2000s.

---

1  Gerald Hodge and Ira M. Robinson, *Planning Canadian Regions* (Vancouver and Toronto: UBC Press, 2001), 337.
2  Ibid.
3  Ibid., 338.
4  Ibid., 339, 57.

forests play a vital role in maintaining ecological integrity. Despite official plans that proclaim goals of environmental protection, local governments have not proven capable of staving off intense development pressures. Asking the question, "who speaks for trees in York Region?" Jort contends that although there are a number of advocates, the institutional and ideological barriers prevent effective planning strategies.

York Region's explosive population and economic growth is being accommodated without a proper understanding of the ability of the ecological systems to withstand human influences. Not only are we unable to measure the cumulative effects of development on forests, any attempt to move in this direction is impeded by the division of authority between and within governments, the administrative structural problems, the need for revenue generation at the local level (which comes from property development), the pieces of legislation that support private property interests, and certain ideological predispositions on the part of decision makers.[18]

Jort asserts that intergovernmental cooperation would be essential to protecting threatened woodlands, but local governments lack the authority to persuade the provincial government of the importance of "green infrastructure." There are, however, very few options: environmental agendas call for coordinated strategies. This is the situation regarding all natural resources, but one of the most compelling cases of this can be made when considering water and the hydrologic cycle.

## Water: The Neglected Resource

Canadian concerns about water quality and supply are comparatively recent. Water, unlike private property, is a commonly shared commodity and has been traditionally viewed as abundant and virtually unlimited. Over the past thirty years, however, domestic and industrial water use has increased at a rate dramatically disproportionate to population growth. Accompanying this trend was a rise in contaminants introduced directly into freshwater supplies or by seepage into aquifers. Sources of contamination include leaking septic tanks, landfill sites, road salt, pesticides, fertilizers, heavy metals, radioactive materials, and hazardous container disposal.

Water policy and management has, for the most part, been reactive; governments respond when there has been an obvious decline in the quantity or quality of water. The hydrologic cycle, however, does not readily lend itself to site-specific clean-up or remedial action. Pollutants may travel a long way, making it very difficult to contain the effects of a particular contaminant. The combination of yesterday's practices, today's ever-growing demands for water, and tomorrow's limited funds to avoid future environmental problems serve to keep governments from accomplishing very much. This is particularly troublesome because not enough is known about the assimilative capacities of the hydrogeologic cycle. Concerns about water quality in specific areas such as the Great Lakes, however, are beginning to receive concerted attention. A remedial action plan for the Toronto waterfront, for example, was called for after it was discovered that fish and other organisms showed an accumulation of contaminants.[19]

Along with questions about fresh-water quality, groundwater, which is one of the integral components of the hydrogeologic cycle, is now attracting public attention. Canadians have been pumping water out of the ground at escalating rates, though there is only limited knowledge about the sustainability or safe yield of many aquifers (underground water supplies).[20] Over one-quarter of the Canadian population relies entirely on groundwater use for domestic supply, and only recently has there been much concerted policy attention directed at this hidden resource, and that attention was in reaction to a number of problems. Several incidents demonstrated that the various levels of governments were not necessarily able or willing to commit the time and resources necessary to ensure a safe water supply. The most serious of these incidents occurred in the year 2000 in Walkerton, Ontario, where 7 people died of E. coli poisoning and more than 2,000 others became ill.

The Ontario environmental commissioner criticized the province's environmental laws, suggesting that "Ontario has a confused patchwork of laws and policies on protecting groundwater. The Ministry of the Environment should develop a comprehensive groundwater strategy ... that would include identifying sources of contamination and their potential effects on health ... It is essential that the public have confidence in how decisions are being made about managing our groundwater. This is not presently the case."[21] The report of a subsequent inquiry into the Walkerton disaster found that the local public utility operators had engaged in a "host of improper operating practices." It also determined that the provincial government's budgeting cutbacks had led to the "discontinuation of government laboratory testing services for municipalities in 1996" and had reduced the ability of the Ministry of the Environment to monitor municipal water operating practices effectively.[22]

Subsequent boil-water advisories and other problems of contamination throughout the summer following the Walkerton tragedy illustrated that this was not a problem confined to Ontario. Ontario introduced a new strategy in an attempt to protect water quality and prevent further disasters, but it was not alone. In North Battleford, Saskatchewan, a public inquiry was also held when hundreds of people become ill after Cryptosporidium got into the water supply in 2001. This inquiry also raised questions about the adequacy of water supply monitoring at both the city and provincial levels of government.[23] A number of governments throughout Canada began investigating ways to improve their water management systems and regulatory frameworks and made efforts to reassure the public that they were now taking the issue seriously.

"End-of-pipe" approaches and emergency actions to deal with water contamination offer only limited short-term benefits and are extremely costly. Preventative planning around community watersheds is an essential part of a strategy to achieve and sustain a safe, potable water supply. Watershed planning is not easy to achieve, though. First there are technical difficulties in determining the particular impact that development activities have on a given watershed, because each area has its own particular geophysical characteristics. Second, municipal and regional political boundaries rarely coincide with natural boundaries. New special-purpose bodies often need to be established in order to coordinate the overlapping areas of responsibilities. Third, pressures for development may very well conflict with watershed-based planning.[24]

These considerations also apply to coastal communities. Community-based coastal water-protection programs are becoming well established. The Atlantic Coastal Action Programs, for example, initiated by Environment Canada in 1991, are multistakeholder initiatives to clean up and restore coastal environments. Fourteen sites throughout Atlantic Canada, including one in Saint John, "chart their own course" and pursue funding from different levels of government, the private sector, and non-governmental organizations (see Box 9.3).[25]

Local governments have always played an important role in water resources. Municipalities are responsible for monitoring water quality and pricing, and for providing the infrastructure. Municipal utilities supply water to households, commercial establishments, and some industries. Some users are charged a flat fee in exchange for unlimited amounts of water, but increasingly metering is employed to encourage more efficient water use, to conserve resources, and to ensure that the users who benefit the most contribute more to the cost of maintaining and supplying the resource. Canadians are prolific users of water. This is partly a reflection of the country's economic dependence on the production of raw resources, where primary industries such as agriculture, oil extraction, and mining rely extensively on water. The amount used could be cut substantially if the resource were managed more efficiently.

Local decision makers must also ensure that development activities do not adversely affect local water resources. Land-use planning and zoning and subdivision practices will have a significant impact on the quality and availability of water, and many development initiatives can have a detrimental effect on local water supply. Proposed quarries, for example, have often been subject to the NIMBY response, as residents worry whether quarrying activities will affect their supply of well water. Efficient and effective water management will ultimately depend on the ability, will, and resources of local governments to coordinate and harmonize their policies with other governments and other resource users.

## Waste Management: From Dumps to Landfills

Canadians are world leaders in producing garbage. In recent years, municipalities have stepped up their efforts to divert waste from landfills into recycling and composting programs. Local governments are confronted with public pressure and legal requirements to deal with waste in an environmentally sensitive manner. Municipalities must not only deal with the present concerns posed by waste disposal, they must also contend with the landfill sites of the past. The leaking, malodorous, open dumps of yesterday do not closely resemble the contemporary, newly engineered landfills that are designed to capture methane gas and prevent the seepage of nasty liquids. Soil and water contamination from those old dumps is becoming a serious problem for local governments. Some municipalities

THE POLITICS OF SPACE, PLACE, AND ECOSYSTEMS

## 9.3 Atlantic Coastal Action Program: Saint John

Marsh Creek, in the east end of Saint John, feeds into the Saint John River. Untreated sewage and contaminants flowing into the creek are a subject of attention for the community-based Atlantic Coastal Action Plan (ACAP). The organization's newsletter quotes a figure of 800,000 tonnes of contaminants a day flowing into the river. This is one area of concern for the volunteer group that is actively promoting efforts to clean up the area's streams, rivers, and the Saint John Harbour. According to ACAP, the City of Saint John does treat some of its wastewater, making a concerted effort and investment in some areas, and is ahead of a number of other Atlantic cities. It does, however, fall behind other cities in the country, where the average treatment of raw sewage is 92 percent. Some coastal cities do not treat any of the raw sewage discharged into the harbour. Community volunteer groups, such as ACAP, play an active role in lobbying all levels of government and keeping the issue on the public agenda.

*Source:* Andi Rierden, "A Decade of Clean Water Action," *The Gulf of Main Times* 5, no. 3 (2001), n.p.

have responded with innovative projects, such as the Waterloo Landfill Gas Power project. It uses gas from the landfill to produce electricity, and it captures greenhouse gases before they are released into the atmosphere. Initiated in 1999, this project was a public-private' partnership between the Region of Waterloo, Toromont Energy, and Ontario Hydro.[26]

The Greater Toronto Area has been confronted with a huge problem of waste disposal, given its size, lack of proactive initiatives, and few immediate options for disposing of waste destined for landfill (1.2 million tonnes a year).[27] The City of Toronto established the Waste Diversion Task Force 2010 in order to try to divert its waste from landfills. The result of the Task Force report led to a "green bin" program, which separates organics from other materials, with a goal of diverting 60 percent of wastes by 2006. The ideal goal is to achieve 100 percent waste diversion.[28]

Meanwhile, hundreds of thousands of tons of Toronto's waste are transported long distances south to Michigan, a problem that is contributing to congested highways, air pollution, and crowded council agendas. It is a problem that requires a quick resolution.

## Toward Sustainable Communities

A spectrum of approaches has been applied to the management of scarce resources, ranging from a liberal, market-led strategy to a collectivist, planning approach. Liberal strategies call for the adoption of user-pay systems, market incentives for encouraging "green" business practices, and the application of new technologies. The major actors in this approach are those who can most effectively influence market processes and have access to the necessary economic levers.

On the other hand, the 1990s politics of building consensus and partnerships emphasized the importance of planning and developing collective approaches to the environment. Planning also suits the complex and interdependent requirements of a natural ecosystem. Any analyst examining environmental policy arrives at the inevitable conclusion that the natural environment is being seriously compromised by the reactive, uncoordinated policies emanating from the fragmented political system. Integrated resource strategies and political processes across the country call for public participation and cooperation. Ironically, the more governments are called on to plan, and the more the public is asked to participate, the more complicated and slower the decision-making process gets. While the need for environmental protection is high, the ready availability of revenues and the political wherewithal for proactive initiatives is low.

Emerging from these tensions have been new strategies that attempt to integrate competing groups into developing a shared vision for their community. For sustainable development to be successful, it is not enough to look at environmental considerations. Jane Jacobs has noted that, as in a natural ecology, economies and societies must have diversity that allows for greater flexibility, automatic self-correction, and cultural and economic dynamism.[29] Sustainable communities must be based on long-range, comprehensive planning, with an underpinning of widespread public support.[30]

The success of such strategies will depend on the desire of diverse participants to buy into the process of compromise. Ultimately, there would have to be a common understanding of a broader public interest, and along with a changing value system, governments would need to adopt new approaches to accounting for natural resources in their cost-benefit calculations. Local councils would have to make decisions based on much more complex agendas – agendas more in tune with the original town-planning concept, which stressed the importance of the social and physical as well as the economic well-being of a community. These are not agendas that can be successfully tackled without the active participation of citizens. But who should participate and how?

The major difficulty that all governments face is not planning effective waste management schemes, efficient recycling programs, or water conservation schemes, although the magnitude of these tasks should not be underestimated. More fundamentally, governments are wrestling with the question of how to reconcile what are basically incompatible principles inherent in liberal democratic societies: how to define and accommodate individual rights while striving for the common good and how to define the common good in the context of sustainable development. It is, indeed, a complicated exercise that local decision makers have yet to master. Recognizing such complexity has led a number of analysts to consider systems-based approaches to environmental decision making.

## Systemic Approaches

Attempts to deal with systemic environmental problems with a traditional *silo approach* have fallen far from the mark. The term *silo approach* was coined to refer to the bureaucratic habit of government departments and decision makers operating within their own mandates and lines of vertical accountability and communications without sufficient consultation and discussion with other related departments. As a result, complex environmental problems cannot be addressed adequately, because institutional responses are uncoordinated, and sometimes are counterproductive.

The changing perceptions about the nature of the environment and the most effective forms of governance are contributing to new forms of decision-making processes. The term *environment* itself cannot be confined to biophysical considerations alone, nor can environmental problems be readily resolved without recognizing the interconnected relationship of human and natural systems. Social, political, and economic variables all affect the relative health of desired ecosystems.

*Systems theories* are attracting attention as one way of mapping out these interactions and seeing how changes in one variable may affect others. A systems approach to community politics sees local government as only one of a number of variables shaping local politics. Multiple interactions between influential variables will lead to positive and negative feedback loops, so the key to understanding local political influence is to identify which combination of variables will lead to what kinds of desirable and undesirable system responses. This analytical perspective has led to a number of prescriptions for governance, including bioregionalism and watershed-based planning.

Local governments now often recognize the political necessity of consulting a wide diversity of groups when it comes to the health of a community. Recognition of the systemic basis of environmental problems has generated some holistic approaches to decision making. In the local context, the best known has been the Healthy Communities project. A local movement initiated in the 1980s, Healthy Communities acknowledged the relationship between social, economic, and biophysical health. While local governments were quick to pick up the "vision" of this movement – one that included public round tables – they have been slow to internalize the implications of this for public administration and local governance. Conventional approaches to administration and policy making attempt to deal with complexity by breaking up problems and reducing them to manageable pieces. Hence line departments with specific portfolios, hierarchical reporting systems, traditional administrative approaches, and the overall inability of local governments to think about and resolve problems that are not readily separable.

Community sustainability requires a new way of looking at *governance* (as distinct from *government*): both actors and influential variables must be understood in terms of their dynamic interactions and effects. Systems approaches stress that influence is wielded by a multiplicity of actors through a complex network of interacting variables. Complex systems approaches suggest that actors operate at different scales in various times and places, and that they do so while engaging in interdependent relationships within a complex environment. Biophysical, socio-economic, and cultural factors all play into the mix.

As the example of Healthy Communities suggests, governments are now conceptualizing community problems in a more systemic fashion. The challenge is to develop institutions that are both responsive to multiple competing demands and capable of dealing with layers of complexity, while at the same time able to maintain clear lines of accountability and transparent decision-making processes. Systems perspectives focus on the dynamic interactions between political actors and diverse forces. Systemic analysis can encompass interactions between just a few or multiple variables.

Some systems theories include Easton's systems analysis, urban regime theory, urban ecology, political ecology, and ecosystems-based approaches.

### Systems Analysis

One of the best-known political science systems perspectives was conceptualized by David Easton in the mid-twentieth century. Easton's description of a political system considered the flow of interactions between the public (made up of a plurality of interests vying for influence) and government. The public provides inputs into the government through a series of demands and supports. Governments take those demands and respond by converting them into laws and policies (outputs). Easton argued that a political system was never in a state of equilibrium but was always dynamic and open to change in response to factors in the political environment. The concept of a political system is now well entrenched in many political analyses, where it is acknowledged that formal and informal actors and institutions influence the decision-making process. Those inputs are converted into policy as they are interpreted and weighed by a variety of decision makers, who are influenced in turn by a number of other forces.[31]

The patterns of influence in a political system are more complex than a simple model portraying inputs and outputs might suggest. Policy communities are a case in point. A policy community consists of actors or groups that share an interest in a particular policy area and influence outcomes. Policy communities include public actors (government decision makers), members of interest groups, and the attentive public.[32] Members of an urban transit policy community, for example, would include elected officials, the relevant government departments and agencies (public works, planning, engineering, and perhaps a transit commission), other governments (provincial and regional), citizens' groups and individuals, users' advisory committees, the local business association, the local media, and maybe an interested academic or two.

## Urban Regime Theory

*Regime theory* considers how policy communities interact to form a decision-making political regime. As discussed in Chapter 1, urban regime theory is predicated on an understanding that although economic interests do not always prevail in local negotiations and in interactions between influential policy actors, they do systemically influence the decision-making process overall.

Urban regimes are said to have been products of two aspects of local political economy that explain business dominance in local politics: (1) local government depends on property taxes to remain viable, leading municipalities to foster property development and investment and (2) in a capitalist society, the population relies on private investment and profit for employment.[33] In urban regimes, coalitions are formed between property development and private-sector-related interests, elected and bureaucratic political actors, and service providers. At times, during periods of social activism (such as the 1960s to early 1970s), business continued to be dominant but social mobilization did force concessions to those elements of a community that were considered to be a "drain" on a local economy, such as low-income residents.[34]

Christopher Leo uses the urban regime theory to examine coalition building and formal and informal arrangements between public- and private-sector interests, but he goes beyond it to examine its position within a national and global context.[35] The difficulty with urban regime theory – particularly that which has emerged from analysis of American local politics – is that, by omission, it assumes that the national state is separable from local politics.[36] This is not an accurate reflection of the political environment. It also does not provide a rich enough understanding of Canadian political processes, where the activities of the national government influence cities in a variety of ways. One of the most visible national government practices relates to the sponsoring of urban redevelopments, including Toronto's Harbourfront (mentioned in Chapter 8) and Vancouver's Granville Island.[37]

## Urban Ecology

Regimes tell us how alliances and coalitions can form to exert political change. Change also happens when conflict occurs between groups. Pioneering urban ecologists Robert Ezra Parks and Roderick McKenzie considered the way in which cities were moulded by the interactive dynamics of their inhabitants. As Leslie Kennedy notes, germane to this discussion is the notion that cities change and develop as a result of competition: "Just as organisms compete in the natural environment, so too, do people compete in the urban environment for resources and space. The geographic distribution of people is shaped into 'natural areas' or neighbourhoods, gathering together people with similar backgrounds based on ethnicity, family status, or income. The forces of competition underlie seven ecological processes bringing about change in cities. These include centralization, de-centralization, concentration, deconcentration, segregation, invasion and succession."[38]

Kennedy notes that these studies in human ecology proved to be very useful ways to map types of human interaction spatially according to demographic characteristics, but they did little to tell us about individual human behaviour. They also did not take into account the physical environment in which these interactions were taking place.[39]

## Political Ecology

*Political ecology* is one systems theory that attempts to make connections between both the physical systems and the dynamics of power relations at work in human systems. Political ecology recognizes the cause and effect relationship between the decisions of those who possess political power and the impact of those decisions on the environment as broadly understood. Political ecology might be seen as an examination of the inter-action between political and economic structures and ecological processes.

From a political perspective then, one might consider how power relations affect human interaction with the environment. A distinction should be made here between political ecology and environmental politics. Bryant and Bailey suggest that "political ecology encompasses a wider understanding of 'politics' than is traditionally found in environmental politics. In effect, the former addresses a diversity of non-state political interests and activities in 'civil society' that tend to be neglected by the latter. A concern with the spatial aspects of human-environmental interaction also tends to set political ecology apart from environmental politics."[40]

A political ecology model for governance would be based on the principle that societal goals for economic sufficiency, distributive justice, and human health within political structures could only be achievable if they supported the overall health of a broader ecosystem. Like the Healthy Communities model, political ecology emphasizes

THE POLITICS OF SPACE, PLACE, AND ECOSYSTEMS

the importance of decentralized political systems, social justice, and local responses to problem-solving.[41]

This model also looks outside of institutional approaches for explanations of political influence. As an explanatory model, political ecology draws on political economy and class analysis to illustrate connections between structures of inequality and their effects on the broader environment. Peoples who have been politically and economically marginalized are those most likely to "bear the brunt of the costs associated with environmental degradation."[42] Examples include the urban poor who are living in neighbourhoods close to industrial sites, areas with poorer air and water quality, or areas with higher levels of crime. In rural and remote areas and First Nations communities, traditional ways of living may be affected by the introduction of new resource developments leading to adverse impacts on hunting and fishing grounds, work-related health problems, and the erosion of cultural traditions that had connected people to the land.

Political ecology would suggest that the ability of citizens to determine the nature and quality of their own environment is related to considerations such as physical location and resources, socio-economic status, and the degree to which the political system is informed by democratic principles. The proposal to ship Toronto's waste to the Adams Mine located in northern Ontario (discussed in Chapter 8) offers an excellent example for a political ecology analysis. Different coalitions of interest mobilized to protest the transport of the waste to the northern region, and in this case, they were successful. It is still unclear, however, whether the proposal was stopped by the political mobilization of a variety of grassroots, environmental, and political groups, or if it had more to do with an unwillingness of the City of Toronto to accept any potential liability costs associated with the initiatives.

## Ecosystems Perspectives and Planning

A comprehensive *ecosystems perspective* is the most inclusive analytical approach one might take to understanding the interrelationship between questions of power, influence, and the physical environment. Ecosystems analyses include a broad spectrum of actors and variables operating at different scales in time and place. Catherine Dowling, for example, suggests that "an ecosystem approach can be characterized by six elements including natural environmental planning units, a holistic interdisciplinary approach, cross-scale considerations, inclusive multidisciplinary decision making, adaptive and flexible management, and an underlying sustainability ethic."[43] Ecosystems perspectives have led many people to new prescriptions in local decision making. One such approach is the watershed-based planning mentioned in Chapter 8.

However, decisions made to serve the needs of a political jurisdiction may run counter to the requirements of a sustainable ecosystem. This problem led to the concept of *bioregionalism,* which suggests that natural regions, rather than artificially constructed political regions, should be the organizing units of human activity. One way of determining natural boundaries is to assess them on the basis of physical characteristics such as drainage patterns, landforms, vegetation, and climate.[44] As Hodge and Robinson point out, ecosystems approaches have been influencing the way in which theorists, planners, and practitioners are carrying out their work throughout the country.[45]

One of the most visible influential applications of ecosystems planning was that of the Royal Commission on the Future of the Toronto Waterfront. Robert Gibson, Donald Alexander, and Ray Tomalty observe that the Crombie Commission introduced decision makers in Canada to the idea of ecosystems planning as an alternative to conventional planning. Conventional planning, Gibson, Alexander, and Tomalty argue, is based on a belief in the need for economic growth. According to this view, environmental impacts of that growth would be managed through adjustments. In contrast, ecosystems planning "rejects business as usual."[46] It recognizes that not all economic growth is good; in fact, it can undermine the biophysical, social, and economic resilience of a community.

Building on the work of the Crombie commission, Gibson and his colleagues offer the following ten alternative principles for ecosystems planning:

- Base planning units on natural boundaries.
- Design with nature.
- Consider global and cumulative effects.
- Encourage interjurisdictional decision making.
- Ensure consultation and facilitate cooperation and partnering.
- Initiate long-term monitoring, feedback, and adaptation of plans.
- Adopt an interdisciplinary approach to information.
- Adopt a precautionary but positive approach to development that aims not just to avoid further damage but also to reduce stresses, and enhance the integrity of ecosystems and communities.
- Ensure that land-use planning integrates (rather than merely balances) environmental, social, and economic objectives.
- Link ecosystem planning with other aspects of democratic change, social learning, community building, and environmental enlightenment.[47]

Local governments do have a number of environmental committees in place, as noted in our various case studies. Usually, however, these committees and their related activities fall under the jurisdiction of a particular department that deals primarily with physical landscapes or biophysical equality, such as Parks or Waste Management, and they are often issue- or location-specific. Applying an ecosystems approach is something altogether different and it is not readily applied to practical situations. Quite apart from needing the political will and initiative, it is a challenge to craft policies that can accommodate numerous variables, including various spatial and time scales and appropriate boundaries of subsystems and larger systems.

Nevertheless, as George Francis suggests, "collective capabilities to act must extend over a much wider range of spatial and time scales than is commonly considered if certain non-sustainable human activities are to be reversed."[48] In this view, the degree to which desired local ecosystems (including human systems) are healthy constitutes the single most crucial factor in determining the long-term future of communities. The ability to plan on an ecosystem basis is a prerequisite of sustainability. Environmental tragedies, such as occurred in Walkerton and elsewhere, and the speed with which political actors were forced to respond after the fact, are striking examples. As Ann Dale notes in her thoughtful analysis, "it would ... be prudent for human activity systems to reconcile methods of production with the rehabilitation and maintenance of ecosystems that provide the essential services for all life. We need a common language and an adequate conceptual framework within which to work, institutional reform based on a convergence of human and natural system cycles."[49]

Increasingly, ecosystems analysis is beginning to penetrate the margins of political decision making. It is showing up in consultative exercises and voluntary initiatives. Where it seems to have the most difficulty breaking ground, however, is in reshaping formal institutions to reflect the holistic vision that so many governments energetically endorse. Government institutions are established in a way that allows them to maintain social control, and institutional structures offer a means to impose that order and organize civil society in a complicated environment. The more intricate the problems, the more risk-averse organizations become. As environmental concerns become more imperative, governments react in crisis mode and are less able and willing to explore innovative models for governance. As Dale noted, "When one is stuck in a spiralling pattern of exploitation and conservation, systemic learning cannot take place, and reactive rather than proactive policy choices become the norm."[50]

Moreover, those who have a vested interest in maintaining the status quo support bureaucratic, hierarchical structures. There are few built-in incentives for changing existing practices and venturing into a much less certain decision-making environment. Holistic approaches to decision making require adaptive management techniques, long-range decision making, the relinquishment of control, the sharing of information, consensus-building exercises, and the abandoning of long-held world views revolving around notions of rationality, efficiency, and effectiveness. The sheer magnitude and complexity of the task provides ample reason for decision makers who yearn for a simpler world to reduce problems to a few simple resolvable objectives. At the local level, one of the primary historic objectives has been to provide the most services in the most economically efficient manner, assessed in today's dollars rather than in tomorrow's ecological costs. This reliance on old methods of assessing costs and benefits through a simple economic indicator fails to recognize that a viable economy rests on the resilience of the natural and human systems on which it depends.

In their analysis, Gibson and his colleagues suggest that ecosystems approaches offer opportunities for us as citizens to govern ourselves: "It promises to help the citizens of a region to build a greater whole by integrating their sense of community and place and by choosing their mutual future, rather than having a future imposed on them ... it is ... an exercise in both individual empowerment and community building that enriches the links between citizens and their environment."[51]

As noted elsewhere, however, attempts to achieve this kind of change beyond the group or neighbourhood encounter some formidable obstacles. One integrated initiative that appears to have made an impression on local governments has been that of the Healthy Communities movement.

## Healthy Communities Movement

Well-known Canadian community planner Trevor Hancock developed a conceptual model that placed health at the conjunction of three overlapping rings containing community conviviality, environmental viability, and economic adequacy.[52] In terms of governance, this model emphasizes a holistic approach that leads to new processes and political structures, including round tables and consensus building.[53] These processes also can lead to alternative avenues of influence that operate both within and outside the formal structures of local governments.

In 1986, one year before the Brundtland Commission released its report called *Our Common Future,* the World Health Organization met in Lisbon to establish the Healthy Cities Project, an idea that had originated in Toronto in 1984. Two years later, over 300 local governments and communities in Canada (and 1,000 worldwide) had adopted the vision expressed by Healthy Communities (see Box 9.4).

The Healthy Communities movement had many different applications. In some cases, the principles were seen as general goals that local governments should keep in mind when making policy. In others, it was often seen as a blueprint for guiding the community into the future. One such initiative, referred to as Compass Kitchener, was undertaken by Kitchener. Using the Healthy Communities approach as a framework, Kitchener launched into an extensive public consultation process in 1999 to develop a community vision for the future. Other cities have also engaged in visioning exercises using established public consultation processes.

Many citizens from different community groups have participated in these exercises. Long-term citizen engagement, however, requires commitment and a sense of progress on the part of both governments and citizen volunteers. Still, these participatory approaches can make worthwhile contributions to community sustainability *if* councils are committed to supporting them. This is a big *if*. Consultative exercises can seem messy, time consuming, and inefficient from an organizational point of view. Moreover, they are not always politically rewarding for the local council. It takes a government with a clear vision, a strong belief in civic engagement, and a willingness to provide adequate support and funding for these initiatives to be maintained over the long term.

Beyond the setting of vision statements are the challenges of translating holistic integrated principles into operating practices. Established lines of decision making and well-entrenched coalitions of interest do not readily give way to nebulous systems

## 9.4 Healthy Communities

Community activist and environmental studies professor Susan Wismer offers an overview of the Healthy Communities movement.

The idea of Healthy Communities is based on three key assumptions about the nature of health: that local government has a critically important role to play in determining the quality of life of communities and the health of the people who live in them; that capacity for individual health is largely dependent on environmental quality; and that the more equitably the benefits of social and economic development are distributed among people, the better the health of the general population will be ...

Sustainability of communities is based on a set of interdependent and mutually self-determining concerns with ethics, identity and place:

- *Ethics:* Communities are defined by a sense of shared destiny among members, which is reflected in shared culture, history and stories. While every community is diverse with respect to values and ethical positions, a sense of co-determined well-being based on a common ethical understanding of mutual respect and responsibility is the primary bond which defines who is "in" a community and who is outside it.
- *Identity:* ... A strong sense of identity based on a belief in one's own capacity to make a productive and valuable contribution to individual, family and community well-being is at the core of what determines the relative strength or weakness of communities. In this regard, sustainable livelihood strategies are of great importance.
- *Place:* An intimate knowledge of geographical location and the social rules which determine access to and control over local resources is the third key set of factors determining sustainability of communities. In order to maintain identity, to hold to the ethical position that generates a sense of community and a strong sense of self-esteem, and to develop sustainable livelihood strategies in a constantly fluctuating world, access to and control over a set of resources associated with a well-known and well-understood geographical location is essential.

Local interests tend to be concentrated at the local and regional level and, within that level, are broadly diverse, taking into account a wide range of social, environmental and economic concerns related to the fundamental concerns associated with ethics, identity and place.

*Sources:* Susan Wismer, "Women and Community-Building in Kitchener-Waterloo" in *The Dynamics of the Dispersed City: Perspectives on the Kitchener Metropolitan Region*, ed. Trudi Bunting, Kevin Curtis, and Pierre Filion (Waterloo, ON: Department of Geography, University of Waterloo, 1996), 355-72; Wismer, "From the Ground Up: Quality of Life Indicators and Sustainable Community Development," *Feminist Economics* 5, no. 2 (July 1999): 109-14.

approaches. First, there is the practical concern of holding accountable the appropriate individuals – a requirement that is necessary in any functioning large-scale organization, let alone a democracy. Second, if too many people with competing agendas are involved in a systems process that has an unclear mandate and undefined boundaries, the results paralyze a decision-making system. Yet, as history has demonstrated, narrowly defined and designed policies that are imposed on a surprised and unwilling public can be very damaging.

Ultimately, a balance must be struck. In both cases, council has final decision-making authority, at least to the extent that knowledge, resources, and legal powers allow. The degree to which diverse members of the public are encouraged to engage in civic discussions, and the extent to which council and staff take public participation seriously, is a measure of the openness and responsiveness of the local government. In addition, the ability of the local government to incorporate biophysical, social, and economic considerations into its political institutions and processes reflects its relative level of adaptability to complex ecosystem requirements. Openness, responsiveness, and adaptability are adjectives that do not mesh readily with bureaucracy, administration, and hierarchy – hallmarks of established organizations. The journey toward healthy, sustainable communities follows a winding, frequently diverging, and always elusive path.

## Conclusion

Ecosystems perspectives are now beginning to inform the way in which some government decision makers, such as planners, view their cities. They sometimes are also introduced into public consultative processes, particularly those involved in developing a vision for their communities. Such perspectives may even be nibbling at the edges of established assumptions about the kinds of values that should drive a city's future. As yet, however, they do not appear to have led to restructured government administrations and policy processes in ways that might reverse the burgeoning pressures on ecological life-support systems. Although the concept of sustainable or healthy communities seems to be well entrenched among activists and a few other parts of society, the means, mechanisms, and political will for realizing those concepts in practice trail far behind.

Challenges of community sustainability require new ways of looking at governance (as distinct from government), based on an understanding of the dynamic interaction and effects of both actors and influential variables. Systems theories are attracting attention as one way of mapping out these interactions and mutual effects. A systems approach to community politics sees local government as only one of a number of variables that shape local politics. Multiple interactions between influential variables will lead to positive and negative feedback loops, so the key to understanding local political influence is to identify which combination of variables will lead to what kinds of desirable and undesirable system responses.

As the next part of the book discusses, however, local administrative machinery has been slow to respond to such complexity. Governments tend to respond to other imperatives that require different structural approaches. What is more, influential decision makers often lack incentives to change structures to reflect ecosystem concerns. Governments are well acquainted with the cost-benefit exercises associated with providing hard services through bureaucratic structures. They have few tools that would allow them to weigh the relative costs of development and economic growth against the very real, but difficult to assess, natural and social costs.

Moreover, systems approaches could further serve to obscure lines of accountability and responsibility. Maintaining accountability and responsibility is important in a representative democracy, as well as for the functioning of any large bureaucratic organization. Despite these constraints, however, some governments are seeking improvements through developing cross-departmental linkages to provide for more horizontal coordination of policies, and for services that will help them address these interrelated complexities.

Part 4    The Business of Local Administration
         and Policy

Public administrators and managers are influential political players. The administrative machinery of government is often portrayed as a vehicle of the public interest staffed by neutral public servants. However, this representation masks the important political role performed by city employees. Members of city staff serve as influential advisors helping to determine community goals and objectives, often by laying out the major alternatives. After the elected representatives decide on the overall policy goals and destinations, the non-elected city administrators go on to map out the best and most efficient way to get there.

The tendency to dismiss local politics and government as not being important decision-making forums is a perspective that suits some of those with market-driven agendas and others who believe local communities are over-governed. According to this view, "too much government" gets in the way of effective competition, innovation, and productivity, and it stifles the generation of new jobs, products, and opportunities. Adherents to this perspective argue that local communities with the correct incentives can become competitive hubs of economic growth and prosperity. Taken to the extreme, the private sector is given the lead role, and the municipal corporation is the supporting actor. Government departments become "core businesses," and senior managers are often recruited with a background in business and accounting rather than in public administration. The citizen becomes the "customer" who makes demands on the system, rather than a participant in governance.

# 10
# Local Public Administration

One of the seemingly unending quests of local decision makers is to find the most appropriate administrative model for managing municipal affairs. This preoccupation is based on a desire to see decisions made and implemented in a more rational, predictable manner – to impose a sense of order on an increasingly unpredictable environment. Critics suggest that this perspective sees government primarily as an "administrative state" in which governing has little to do with democracy. John Dryzek says that government is "about rational management in the service of a clearly defined public interest, informed by the best available expertise. Managers and experts have well-defined roles within the administrative monolith."[1]

The rationality of the behaviour is assessed primarily on the basis of certain assumptions about economy, efficiency, and professional objectivity. Yet this type of objectivity is not possible. Everyone brings to the profession her or his own set of filters with which to view the world: filters formed not only by the accumulation of personal experiences and education but also by various assumptions and prescriptions about how the world does (and should) work. For some individuals, it is highly rational to frame problems using short-term criteria with a goal of stimulating economic growth. That, in turn, will appear highly irrational to others whose goal is to establish processes compatible with long-term visions of a sustainable society. Nevertheless, rational management approaches, which come with their own sets of ideological baggage, continue to be popular with a number of local managers.

The approach can be traced back to the early urban reform movement (discussed in Chapter 2), which promoted the view that partisan politics should not interfere with the efficient and rational functions of the bureaucratic machinery. In this perspective, the administrative arm of government should be able to fulfill its duties unimpeded by political interference, favouritism, or patronage. Appointments and contracts would be assigned according to "objective" criteria, such as merit, efficiency, and economy. As one popular quotation went, "there is only one way to fill a pothole."[2] By this it was meant that the provision of services should be an apolitical exercise because the delivery of services was so straightforward that no value judgments need be involved. Yet whether potholes should be filled first or whether improved streetlight service in a dangerous neighbourhood should take priority is itself a value question and is unavoidably a political decision.

The rational management approach to government presents some obvious difficulties. Councils, particularly those in large cities, cannot keep track of every issue. Nor are pot-holes the only problem for a public works department. On a daily basis, it is the city staff that make decisions about how to maintain services and keep roads in good repair. As a rule, council does not get involved in what many would see as a minor issue, unless that issue achieves public attention through the media, public activism, or from some other pressure. This is the case with our medium-sized case-study cities, all of which possess a chief administrative officer (or the equivalent) who coordinates daily affairs.

That said, in small and even mid-sized cities, citizens have a much greater opportunity to interact with their elected representatives in regularly held community events, open-ings of facilities, or "town hall" breakfasts. As such, they are able to bring some local issues to the attention of councillors in a way that is not logistically possible in big metro-politan areas. Nevertheless, the non-elected parts of government frequently make impor-tant decisions in terms of allocating responsibilities, giving priority to certain tasks over others, and considering how and when a service should be delivered. Dull though these issues may appear on a one-to-one basis, collectively they affect the governing of local communities. At the heart of all these daily administrative activities are essentially politi-cal decisions – who should get what and how. Those in charge of these administrative decisions wield considerable political influence. It is important, therefore, to gain some understanding of the nature of local public administration.

All local governments are structured, at least formally (if not always in practice), to hold the activities of civic employees and departments ultimately accountable to the council. A well-structured working apparatus is needed to make sure that processes are transparent and that one department does not work at cross-purposes with another. Council, as a col-lective, is responsible for representing the public interest. The interpretation of the pub-lic interest, and the crafting and implementation of policies, however, will reflect the biases, intentional or otherwise, of all those who influence local processes, including rep-resentatives of business interests, the professional interests of local administrators, or any number of others vying for political influence.

To understand how influence is wielded within a municipal corporation, it is not suffi-cient to concentrate solely on how things are organized. It is also necessary to consider the policy process. Local policy making deals with the actual choices of governments, in-cluding what services to provide and how to deliver them, what initiatives to encourage or fund, and what issues to pay attention to and when to do so. Governments might also make a deliberate choice not to act. To use Thomas Dye's classical definition, public policy is whatever governments decide to do or not to do.[3] The actions governments take and the issues that they choose to focus on, as well as the processes used to make and imple-ment decisions, tells a lot about what issues are deemed important and who gets to par-ticipate in the policy process.

The volunteer sector, for example, has always performed an important function in the delivery of services in cooperation with, or in place of, governments. As the welfare state

THE BUSINESS OF LOCAL ADMINISTRATION AND POLICY

grew, governments fulfilled functions that had previously been the responsibility of churches and volunteer organizations. Today, governments once again are looking to volunteer organizations to help in the task of governance.

This practice raises a number of questions. To what extent are citizens included in governing processes? What roles are citizens performing in such areas as community policing, alternative justice, and halfway houses? Citizen participation in decision making and the delivery of services raises important political questions about democracy, accountability, and the distribution of services. How much political influence in formal decision-making processes should be given to non-elected citizens who cannot be readily held accountable for their actions? If governments rely on volunteers for delivering local services, the result could be inequitable because much depends on the interests, strengths, and locations of volunteer associations. Volunteers play such an essential role in local governance that these are important questions. A community cannot thrive without volunteers. In local administration, volunteers often work closely with civic employees who help to organize these activities. This is often the case, for example, in the provision of recreational activities or services to seniors.

Governments do not always welcome all types of volunteer work. For instance, some advocates for, and leaders of, marginalized groups who actively challenge council's priorities may find themselves shut out of decision-making processes if their goals or methods of protest run counter to dominant values or rules of conduct established by the local government. Activists also may lose favour if they can manage to make a council or city administration take decisions or actions that go against official inclinations. This issue has important implications for the concept of governance if only certain groups are recognized as legitimate participants in civic decision making.

Although the actual implementation of the policies and goals of the city council is often touted to be an impartial process, in practice the administration of government is heavily influenced by political forces. The unavoidable reliance of local governments on property taxes and their close association with economic interests inevitably means that business interests play a strong role in determining local priorities. Until governments recognize, in a tangible manner, the important contribution of all types of civic voluntarism to community health, certain perspectives, values, and concerns will dominate over those that do not bring with them much-desired revenues.

## Principles of Public Administration

Public bureaucratic organizations are expected to be accountable to the public's elected representatives. Public *administration* is distinct from private *management* because the responsibilities and duties of a public organization differ from those of a profit-making enterprise. The scope and complexity of government activities and the political environment of decision making require a different set of operating principles and practices.[4]

Governments must respond to a vast array of societal demands, and elected representatives are not able to deal with all the issues that occur on a daily basis. City staff must carry out a multiplicity of tasks dictated by laws, regulations, and guidelines, while responding to the demands of council and citizen requests and concerns. Given the influence that public administration wields, it is important to consider both the "machinery of government" and the role of public administrators in local governance.

B. Guy Peters suggests that six basic principles form the core of traditional public administration. These principles have generally been considered in terms of federal and provincial governments. With some minor alterations, the same basic principles of public administration can be applied to local government. Public administration should be:

- *apolitical:* Public administration should be an apolitical administrative arm where employees are not supposed to demonstrate any particular political allegiances and are expected to implement the policies of the elected politicians regardless of their particular political beliefs. This is considered important because authority for important decisions needs to rest with the elected representatives.
- *hierarchical:* Governments are organized on a hierarchical and rule-bound organizational model (referred to as the Weberian model of management) providing clear lines of authority upwards and ultimately to the elected arm of government.
- *stable:* Citizens need to rely on governments that continue to function and provide services through elections and changes in the elected arm of government. Newly elected representatives also need to rely on the expertise and knowledge of the non-elected government employees for advice and assistance. Stability and continuity are difficult to achieve, and the learning curve would be very steep if there were a frequent turnover of administrators at election time.
- *meritocratic:* Institutionalized public service should be governed, as a corporate body, by principles of merit (where each employee is graded and advanced through the ranks according to objective criteria). In such a system, the administration of the organization could not be unduly influenced by political whims or patronage.
- *responsive:* Public employees are expected to respond to the policy directive of the elected arm of government and to implement the decisions of the council.
- *fair:* Equality of outcome is considered important in this traditional model of public administration. All citizens should be viewed and treated equally both in terms of services received and in the outcome of government decisions.[5]

While these principles may seem ideal for achieving efficiency, effectiveness, and equity, they are not readily applied in practice.

First and foremost, public employees use some set of values when implementing policies, and these decisions are inherently political. Striving to achieve the apolitical ideal has always been a challenge. Acceptance of the myth of objectivity encourages administrators to present their recommendations as purely professional opinions when, in fact, they are inevitably informed by a number of personal and professional biases. Those biases should be transparent.

Second, hierarchical departments responsible for one policy area (such as transportation, or parks and recreation) cannot readily accommodate public demands for participation when those public demands are broader and go beyond one department's jurisdiction. The hierarchical approach does not work well with problems that spill over into more than one department. Governments are now recognizing the need for networking between departments, as well as between other communities of interests.

Third, long-time employees holding the same position in an organization can provide the stability essential to its smooth operation. Employees can get so set in their own ways of doing things, however, that it becomes very hard to make changes. Long-time employees who remain in the same position acquire a tremendous amount of influence by virtue of their knowledge and many years of working in that one job. As such, depending on the personalities involved, it can be difficult for newly elected politicians who rely on them for information to assert and maintain control over the way in which policies are implemented.

Fourth, a distinct, institutionalized public service that carries out its duties in a professional manner, unsullied by political interference, is considered an important element of a modern administration. It is, however, becoming recognized that administrative activities cannot be detached from the citizenry and the political issues of the day – particularly with public demands for participation in planning and policy processes.

Fifth, the notion that the role of civic employees is simply to implement the ideas of the elected politicians does not encourage creative problem solving within the bureaucracy or in cooperation with members of the public.

Sixth, the principle of equality does not give administrators and employees room to treat each problem or issue in the most satisfactory manner given differing contexts. Staying with the rule of law or procedures may be "doing it by the book," but that approach does not allow the flexibility or discretion needed for the most cost-efficient, effective, or perhaps even humane solution.[6]

Finally, the application of the principles of public administration are affected by the size, location, and culture of the local environment. In very small governments, for example, it is difficult to apply these principles. A tiny number of municipal employees cannot possibly respond to a huge variety of demands and challenges on a daily basis. Small departments are often responsible for the general administration of a whole town. Northern administrators will attest to the fact that location can also play a role in the nature of public administration. George Paul, city manager of Prince George, suggests that the challenges of administration in a northern community are very different from those in the south, given the different location, political cultures, and environmental contexts (see Box 10.1).

The ideal of a traditional public administration is one where professional, well-educated employees administer the laws and policies of the elected governments in a neutral, apolitical manner. However, a number of competing factors – personal and professional values, the composition of the council and administration, and the influence of interest groups –

## 10.1 The Challenges of Local Government Administration in Northern Areas

George Paul, city manager of Prince George, British Columbia, discusses the issues involved in local government administration in northern regions.

The challenges of administering local governments in northern areas fall into four categories: service delivery, staffing, economic base, and southern attitudes. Each of these variables is influenced by three main issues. The issues are all relative to southern communities and include the smaller size, isolation, and weather conditions of northern communities.

### Service Delivery
The option of pursuing new service delivery concepts such as public-private partnerships is limited, given the scarcity of private partners with which to contract. As well, availability of local suppliers can pose substantial difficulties. Often economies of scale that allow for more financially effective service delivery are not achieved in northern communities because of their relatively smaller size. Service delivery costs are often dramatically increased by both the resources spent on dealing with snow and ice conditions, as well as the deterioration to the infrastructure that results from severe weather.

### Staffing
The size and isolation of northern communities results in fewer training opportunities for both elected and appointed officials, as well as less informal mentoring of incumbent staff. As a result, both recruitment and retention of qualified individuals are problematic.

### Economic Base
Northern communities tend to rely on an economy that is resource based and, because of their small population base, the service sector is not very large. Because resource-based economies tend to be more cyclical in nature, the economic circumstances in northern communities are not as stable as those in southern communities.

### Southern Attitudes
One of the most challenging aspects of administering a northern city is the attitude exhibited by southern professionals and legislators. They carry a general perception that it is less desirous to live in northern communities because of the size and isolation issues. As well, the weather is seen as a negative consideration, rather than for the opportunities it presents. When this lack of understanding is combined with a "one size fits all" mentality, northern public administrators are faced with legislation, regulations, service models, and professional advice that are inadequate to meet the needs of northern residents and their communities.

inevitably lead to decisions based on specific value systems that are anything but neutral (see Box 10.2).

The "ideal" model of public administration faces many challenges when confronted with daily realities. One of the most important is how to hold government accountable for its actions. Given the many decisions that must be made in a large, modern government, it is difficult to hold any individual accountable for mistakes, particularly if a previously elected government made them. It is also hard to hold elected officials accountable when they rely on professional administrators for their advice, knowledge, and expertise when making involved, detailed financial or other policy decisions. In the case of local governments, serving as a member of council is often considered to be a part-time occupation. Administrators, then, necessarily make many important decisions, particularly when politicians do not have the capability to monitor all the activities of a large bureaucratic apparatus.

## Accountability, Efficiency, and Effectiveness

Accountability is an important concept in public administration. The ways in which governments are structured, administered, and run are based to a great extent on ensuring that they can be held accountable for their actions and can be seen to be serving the public interest.

In federal or provincial governments, in particular, the "neutral" civil servant is thought to be shielded from public view; the role is to serve the elected politicians who make government policy decisions and who must answer to the public. Kernaghan and Siegel note that public administrators are directly accountable to a number of political actors, such as political and administrative superiors, to the courts, and to internal government authorities (required by law or administrative hierarchy). They are not directly accountable to external actors, such as pressure groups, news media, or the general public, although some municipal professionals may very well have their competence assessed by their peers in provincial law societies and the like.[7]

In contrast, at the local government level, there is an absence of ministers (or, in this case, councillors) who are individually formally responsible for specific departments, although they may sit on committees that oversee the work of one or more departments. What is more, the public is much more likely to encounter and interact with local members of the civic administration.[8] Donald Higgins notes that "at the local level, only those officials who are elected by the public and are subject to a re-election process can fairly be held accountable. This necessitates that elected officials be not only informed about what is going on in municipal offices but that they be the people who are actually controlling the decision- and policy-making processes. In sum, considerations of accountability, co-ordination, and ensuring that matters of policy are indeed approached broadly when necessary, all imply and necessitate close links between local administrators and local policy-makers."[9]

## 10.2  Setting Agendas: An Illustration of Local Public Decision Making

A new university is built high up on a hill on land donated for educational purposes; council requires a new road to link the university to the centre of the city below. The different city departments must translate the policies of the council into action in a way that is most effective and efficient. Each department, however, will have its own set of priorities.

The Public Works department may determine that the road should be built in a way that facilitates the most efficient flow of traffic and in an area that has a firm geological foundation that will not shift over time.

The Planning department may have different priorities. It might be more concerned about preserving natural or heritage features, the potential for possible disruption of neighbourhoods, and consistency with the community plan.

Down the hall, staff from the Finance department will consider variables related to cost efficiency. For their part, economic development officers might think that the road should be built in a way that generates local business.

Local city council or influential community members may wish to draw attention to the new university by positioning the road in a way that makes the new institution readily accessible and visible from the city centre.

Other actors in the policy community, including governments, the private sector, and interest groups both local and from outside the community may also present additional alternatives that reflect their particular sets of priorities.

All of these goals must be coordinated in a way that results in a soundly designed road that serves the long-term and various needs of the community. Ideally, in local government, a good decision might be one where the local council listens and responds effectively to the requirements of the community in a way that is compatible with provincial and regional concerns, while drawing on the expertise of city staff to efficiently implement its objectives. In practice, however, there are competing demands and priorities within governments and between citizens. The ability or willingness of council to grapple competently with all these conflicting priorities sometimes falls short. As a result, both roads and desired goals can be undermined and slide downhill.

---

*Note:* This example is based, in part, on a true story, but some facts have been altered for purposes of illustration.

The multiple community responsibilities of civic employees, politicians, and citizen volunteers make it difficult to maintain distinct lines of accountability. The structure of governments also influences the ways in which civic employees might be held accountable. In Canada, local governments are organized in diverse ways that affect the lines of accountability – the internal administrative structures reflect some of the priorities of government and the ways in which they see the mandates of different departments. In some communities, for example, departmental reorganization has taken place with the goal of seeing municipal corporations operate in a more business-like fashion.

## Administrative Models

Provincial governments have responded in a number of ways to unique local situations by creating a variety of public institutions including water boards, regions or districts, school boards, Aboriginal bands, and cities, towns, and villages. Some typical internal administrative models have included the council-committee system, the chief administrative officer or city manager system, the board of management system, and the commissioner system. Recently, several local governments also have been experimenting with their own innovations.

Each of these administrative structures is based on a hierarchy (although some pyramids are flatter than others), and all are ultimately accountable to elected representatives. The most popular – the chief administrative officer (CAO) model – has proliferated and can even be found in smaller towns throughout the country.

### Council-Committee Model

The *council-committee model* (also referred to as the *departmental model*) is one of the oldest municipal structures and has been used in small communities. In this model, the elected council meets as a whole and as members of standing committees. Each department is directly accountable through its department head to the standing committee and then to council. Each standing committee is expected to oversee one department's administration. The standing committee then advises council as a whole on policy, after which council makes decisions as a collective.

The advantage of this model is the strong communication lines between administration and the elected council. Accountability for administrative decisions can be traced in a straight line upward to council rather than first being mediated through a city manager or administrator and then to council. The disadvantage is that this system creates competition between department heads and results in overlapping responsibilities.[10] For these reasons and others, a more streamlined administrative model known as the *chief administrative officer model* has become the popular alternative. Even in towns with fewer than 10,000 people, it is common to see a town manager or clerk overseeing administrative matters and then reporting to council.

## City Manager and Chief Administrative Officer Models

The *chief administrative officer (CAO) model* has often been referred to as a weaker system than the *city manager model* (with the CAO possessing somewhat less power than the city manager over the administrative functions). The idea that one individual should act to coordinate the administrative activities of government emerged out of the early urban reform movement, which placed an emphasis on the application of business principles. The notion that the political act of setting policy and the administrative act of implementing policy should be kept distinct continues to inform most modern administrative structures at all levels of government. This approach entrenches the belief that elected council should be responsible for making the policy decisions while the non-elected administrative arm carries out those policies in a neutral and efficient manner.

The *city manager system* was first developed in the United States, with managers reporting to a council elected at large. All major political-administrative interaction takes place between the city manager's office and the council.[11] In Canada, this city manager model became popular with some of the newer western cities, such as Prince George. Prince George has a system in which most council-administration interaction takes place through the city manager.

In the CAO system, standing committees of council are common. In addition to a CAO who is responsible for the coordination of all the city departments, standing committees of council are responsible for overseeing the activities of one or more departments and for reporting back to the committee of the whole (the council) making recommendations. Department heads also interact with members of the council, as well as through the CAO. In this model, the CAO does not have the same level of supervisory control over the whole administrative organization as does a city manager. In both cases, though, it is very clear that the CAO or city manager is expected to be accountable to the mayor and council, who have the authority and the right to hire and fire senior staff members. While it is not uncommon to hear a city manager stating a somewhat different position than the mayor, when it comes to implementing policy, the administrators must always follow the decisions of council. The city manager or CAO is the most visible member of the administrative staff and is expected to be able to account for the operations of the whole department, including one of the most important responsibilities: the preparation and submission of the budget.

This model, which places one primary administrator at the apex of the administrative hierarchy, is widespread throughout Canada in towns as small as 1,000 up to the very large City of Toronto with its 2.5 million people.

## Commissioner or Board of Management Model

Another model of local government is the *commissioner system*. There are two types of commissioner systems that can be easily confused.

One model that has sometimes been used in Prairie cities is a board of commissioners system, where each commissioner is given responsibility for the activities of a number of

THE BUSINESS OF LOCAL ADMINISTRATION AND POLICY

departments. These commissioners, along with the mayor, are in charge of the city's administration.[12] In this model, responsibility for municipal administration is distributed to several people rather than to one individual.

Such was the case in Calgary until 2000, when a new structure was introduced, designed after a private-sector organizational model employing a chief executive officer (CEO) and five executive officers. As is the case with a city manager, Calgary's CEO reports directly to council while the five executive officers report to the CEO. Today, a number of governments are experimenting with combining different structural elements of older governing models.

A second form of commissioner system provides an additional level of administration between the manager and the departments, as in the case of Toronto or Saint John. Responsibility for administering the entire organization does not rest on the shoulders of one individual but is distributed among a number of people (similar to department heads) who, in turn, report to the city manager. Commissioners can also contribute to interdepartmental coordination, which some see as a useful way of tackling problems and issues that do not fit neatly into the mandate of any one department.

## Departmental Organization

The city manager or CAO is generally responsible for overseeing the functions of a department that is designed to serve a specific policy or service function. Sometimes, as discussed in previous sections, these departments are clustered under the authority of a few commissioners. Despite these variations, throughout Canada, departments under the direct supervision of directors or managers are responsible for similar basic services, although the way in which these services are grouped reveals something about how that government conceptualizes the role.

For example, a public works department that hires a number of engineers will be motivated by a different set of priorities and concerns than that of a planning department that employs professional planners. Engineers might be most concerned about how to build infrastructure while accommodating the public's transportation patterns and the physical realities posed by the geological environment. Planners might recognize the importance of those goals as well, but place more emphasis on preserving neighbourhoods or desired landscapes than would the engineers. Traditionally, these two groups of employees have been placed in separate departments, yet they have many overlapping responsibilities that could lead to inefficiencies and counterproductive approaches.

In a number of cities, departments have been restructured to avoid this problem, which is sometimes referred to as the *silo syndrome*. In Prince George, the city decided to reorganize its departments, and the process continued into 2001 with the amalgamation of development services and public works. By combining these two departments, staff who worked in planning, utilities, environmental planning, transit, and geographic information services (GIS) would be able to work more collaboratively to improve communication and coordination (see Figure 10.1).[13] The City of Waterloo also combined its public works and parks services teams to become Parks and Works Services. The restructured department was given a mandate to "plan, manage, rehabilitate and maintain the city's parks, open spaces, wood lots, urban forests, municipal transportation, parking, fleet, water mains and storm/sanitary sewers."[14] Such a system recognizes that a more effective approach to planning could be achieved by fostering work relationships among city staff who have different types of problem-solving abilities (see Figure 10.2). Kitchener also restructured its services, moving from six departments to five, using some business-management principles as it pledges to operate on a "customer-service philosophy."

An examination of how a city's decision makers structure their organization reveals how they choose to portray local government's responsibilities to the wider public. Kitchener's organization model (Figure 10.3) is distinct from those of the four case-study cities, including its neighbour, Waterloo. This, in part, is due to the unfamiliar categories and titles that require further explanation, but it is also interesting to observe Kitchener's choices about what services should receive visual prominence and how they should be clustered.

For example, all the other case-study cities placed planning and environmental responsibilities under one department, commissioner, or the equivalent. In contrast, one must search deep in Kitchener's organizational structure to find reference to environmental issues. This contrasts with all the other case-study cities across the country, where environmental services figure more prominently in the organization structure. Kitchener did choose to emphasize community services, stressing the importance of the cultural and social health of the city by involving citizens in developing a community spirit in particular areas of community life.

In the early 2000s, many other cities throughout the country were engaged in various types of restructuring initiatives. Combining functions and improving communications between departments is becoming a priority in governments as they seek to provide a more integrated approach to service delivery, while reducing costs. After the province-wide amalgamation in Quebec, the City of Sherbrooke's administrative structure was designed to accommodate the needs of the former cities, which were consolidated into one area governed by a two-tier council – an upper-tier municipal council and lower-tier borough councils. A general manager was given responsibility for five sectors of activity for the whole amalgamated municipality (see Figure 10.4):

- The first sector provides planning, support, and administrative performance and includes: finances and the treasury, human resources, and information technology.
- The second sector provides police and fire-protection services, including 911 emergency services.
- The third sector provides land management and public services, planning and urban development, environmental services, waste management, and infrastructure

and includes: recreation, sports, culture, community life, and building and equipment maintenance.

- The fourth and fifth sectors under the general manager are legal and corporate affairs and the communications division.[15]

The boroughs have their own administrative and political structures that are ultimately accountable to the city. The boroughs are assigned an annual budget set by the city, they are responsible for overseeing the delivery of municipal services, and they have their own council meetings. Each borough also has its own manager. The other distinctive feature of Sherbrooke's city organization is that it has responsibility for administering Sherbrooke Hydro and for receiving revenues from the organization. Utilities in the other cities are handled by a separate elected body.

As noted earlier, some cities have adopted a CAO or city manager and commissioner system, combining the benefits of a hierarchical structure of accountability and the coordinating function provided by commissioners. The new City of Sherbrooke has something similar, using the title Directeur général adjoint (general manager). The City of Toronto and the City of Saint John (two very different cities in size, culture, geography, and local political concerns) both use commissioners.

## Administrative Structure of the City of Toronto
On 1 January 1998 the restructured City of Toronto was launched, creating one of the largest municipalities in North America, in which forty-four councillors, including the mayor, became responsible for a population of 2.5 million people. This statistic does not include the surrounding Greater Toronto Area. A significant proportion of the Canadian population is concentrated in the area and makes regular trips into the city for work, business, or recreation.

Governing a city of this size could not be accomplished without a huge administrative apparatus to back up the elected leaders. In fact, as of 2003, the city has 45,000 employees and manages a $6.4 billion operating budget and a $965 million capital budget.[16] With the restructuring, six major departments were given responsibility for administering forty different services with a CAO, and six commissioners overseeing operations. The CAO's role is to act as both the leader of the corporation and advisor to council in its development of policies and services. The commissioners head up the departments of Works and Emergency Services, Finance, Urban Development Services, Community and Neighbourhood Services, Corporate Services, and Economic Development, Culture, and Tourism. The Audit Committee, a standing committee of council, has responsibility for audit services.[17]

## Administrative Structure of the City of Saint John
As of 2003, the organizational structure in the city of Saint John included commissioners and the fire chief reporting to the city manager, who in turn reported to the common council. The positions of common clerk, city solicitor, city manager, and commissioner of

finance were made directly accountable to council (which consists of the mayor and ten councillors). Each commissioner was given responsibility for overseeing the operations and coordination of a cluster of departments organized according to functions and services. Each department was given its own internal hierarchical structures and mandates (see Figure 10.5).

## Implications of Contemporary Structural Reorganizations

These new organizational structures do little to fundamentally change the balance of power or accountability. As is typically the case, each of the organizational models discussed in this chapter was designed to find a balance between accountability to city council and maximum efficiency. The brief review of the different models suggests that cities throughout Canada are experimenting with a number of different designs to achieve that goal. Organizational redesign has often been a popular treatment for whatever might be seen as ailing a political institution. Recent years have seen the proliferation of the city manager or chief administrative officer model, sometimes with adaptations to include citizen participation on council-appointed committees. On the administrative side, hierarchical models prevail, where the departmental staff report to managers or supervisors, who in turn report to directors, who then report to either commissioners or the city manager or CAO, who directly reports to council. A number of cities also have standing committees, where departmental staff and members of council also work together in various policy areas, so departmental heads might sometimes report to council as well as to their CAO.

Some local structural changes are notable, if for differing reasons. A number of governments are moving toward the delivery of services by coordinating activities through lateral communication and work groups. This is an example of a reasonable public administrative response to a problem caused by the functional and administrative separation of various functions provided by the city administration. Historically, it was not uncommon to see different departments working at cross-purposes with each other. For example, a parks department might attempt to protect an ecologically sensitive area, while public works next door might be planning a traffic corridor that would undermine the environmental protection initiative. Bringing diverse types of expertise to bear when it comes to providing services can result in a much more effective, coordinated planning approach.

On the other hand, some developments in organizational design appear to have little to do with problem solving and more to do with notions that efficiency is best achieved through a private-sector management approach to government. Throughout the 1990s, quite a few governments, including the City of Waterloo and the City of Calgary, responded to the call for a business approach to administration and restructured their administrative departments to represent "core businesses," applying business-management techniques. Still others, such as Prince George and Kitchener, use some of the similar terminology, emphasizing their "customer-driven approaches."

FIGURE 10.1

**City of Prince George, 2003**

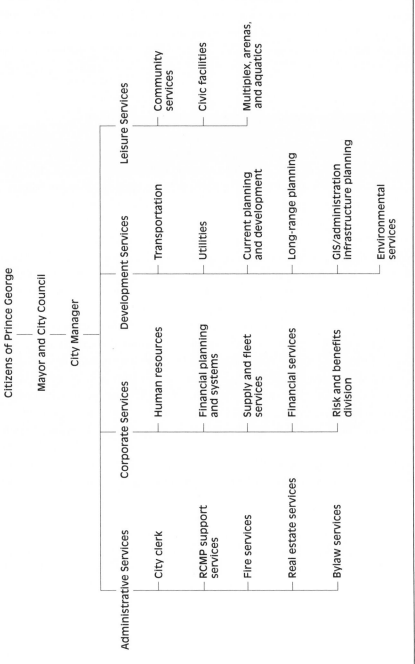

*Source:* City of Prince George, "Organizational Chart," www.city.pg.bc.ca/pages/orgchart.html (last modified 27 October 2003).

FIGURE 10.2

**City of Waterloo, 2003**

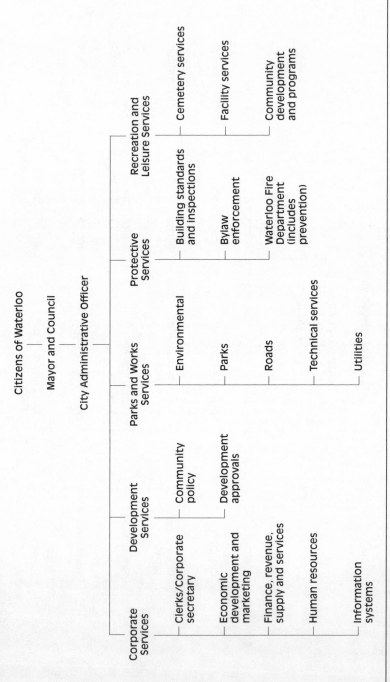

*Source:* City of Waterloo, "Our Organization," www.city.waterloo.on.ca/COUNCIL/index.html (27 June 2003).

FIGURE 10.3

**City of Kitchener, 2003**

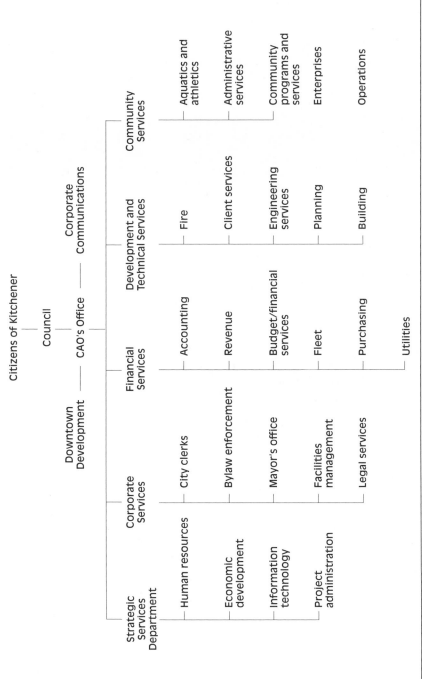

*Source:* City of Kitchener, "Organizational Chart," www.city.kitchener.on.ca/pdf/org_chart.pdf (2003).

FIGURE 10.4

**City of Sherbrooke, 2003**

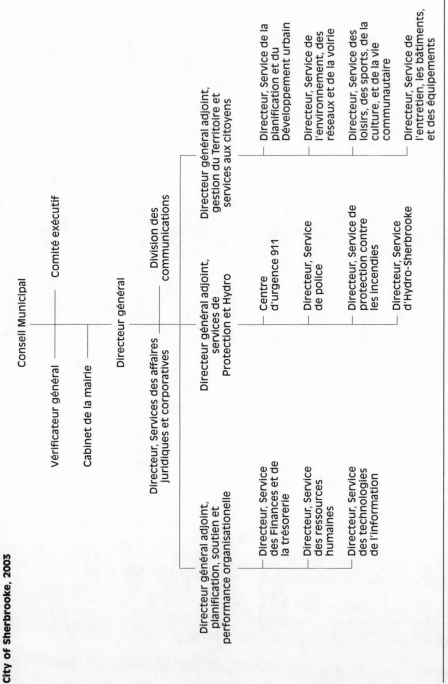

*Note:* This particular organizational chart does not include the second-tier boroughs and their organizational structures.
*Source:* Ville de Sherbrooke, "Organigramme de la structure supérieure de la nouvelle ville de Sherbrooke," http://ville.sherbrooke.qc.ca/fr/images/organigramme2.jpg (June 2003).

FIGURE 10.5

**City of Saint John, 2003**

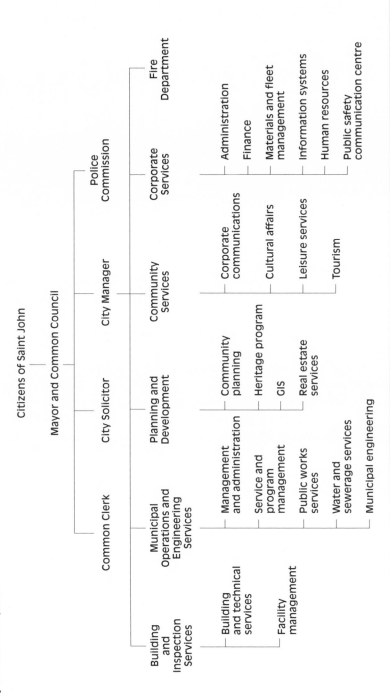

*Note:* Policing services fall under the jurisdiction of a Police Commission.

*Source:* City of Saint John (12 August 2003); updated to reflect 2004 changes, http://www.city.saint-john.nb.ca.

Whether referring to citizens or customers, however, all the case-study cities emphasize the importance of consulting citizens in decision-making processes. In many Canadian municipalities, citizens participate in government decision making in an advisory capacity or in special-purpose bodies.

## The ABCs of Special Purpose Bodies

*Agencies, boards,* and *commissions* have long been part of local government and have also suffered through a long history of criticism. Numerous local bodies have been created, have been given mandates to fill specific functions or purposes, and have been thought to be important enough to have semi-autonomous, permanent status. Police commissions, school boards, transit commissions, housing authorities, and conservation authorities are all examples of special purpose bodies with their own sets of governing actors. Some of these local authorities, such as school boards, are required by provincial statute, while others are established by local council. The history of these special purpose bodies can once again be traced back to the early-twentieth-century reform era in which some services were thought to be too important to be subjected to the whims of elected councils. Possessing their own independent status with a specific budget allocated to them, these bodies were given authority to carry out their mandate without excessive political interference.

These organizations have been criticized for contributing to the fragmentation of political authority, making it difficult for citizens to know who is in charge of local political decisions, while undermining the coordination of services and reducing the ability of elected council to make decisions for the well-being of the whole community. Special purpose bodies can also be seen as a way for city council to avoid dealing with controversial issues and to escape responsibility by creating an arm's length institution to deal with the issue.[18] Over thirty years ago, Stewart Fyfe and Ron Farrow suggested that for government to fulfill its responsibilities – to serve the public effectively – it must have the power to act. They noted that the proliferation of boards and commissions fragmented this power. Although boards and commissions often performed useful work, a "proliferation of special arrangements can only result in the breakup of the whole" and conflict with the work of the council.[19] Fyfe and Farrow also noted that provincial government departments tended to prefer boards and commissions to councils: "their procedures and programs can more readily be brought to conform with those of departments or branches than those of the municipalities. These special purpose bodies have clear implications for local self-government; their proliferation affects the capacity of councils to act."[20]

These are valid concerns, but are special purpose bodies all bad? It could be argued that this type of organization may be just what is needed when a number of issues spill over jurisdictional boundaries. When cities grow, one response of governments has been to amalgamate and create large units (inevitably governed by fewer elected representatives)

THE BUSINESS OF LOCAL ADMINISTRATION AND POLICY

to deal with the expanding population. However, quite apart from the fact that amalgamation does not always tidily encompass all the surrounding suburban communities, leaving inevitable issues of coordination, some problems simply cannot be solved by amalgamation. Moreover, as discussed earlier, diverse citizen interests are not necessarily effectively represented by a formally elected city council in charge of governing a large city. It is difficult for a council to be fully informed and responsive to the demands posed by numerous complex issues that can often stretch across municipal boundaries.

One alternative perspective relates to questions of governance rather than government. Special purpose bodies allow members of civil society to become involved in issues that affect their environment through diverse avenues of influence. Some issues cannot simply be dealt with by expanding municipal boundaries. If, for example, the concern was a biophysical issue, such as a vital watershed area, the most appropriate governing vehicle might very well be an intermunicipal or interjurisdictional body. Ontario's conservation authorities, for example, offer members of civil society an opportunity to participate in sustaining local environmental health. The thirty-six conservation authorities were created by the province through legislation in 1946, with boundaries determined by natural watersheds rather than political jurisdictions. These bodies are described as "community-based environmental organizations dedicated to conserving, restoring, developing and managing natural resources on a watershed basis."[21] The conservation authorities work with local municipalities, provincial agencies, and community organizations. Each governing board cosists of representatives from the municipalities located in the watershed.

These types of special purpose bodies can encourage and allow for diverse participation in local governance and bring different kinds of expertise to bear on a problem. An individual may be more willing to contribute to the local community as a member of a social housing board than as a local councillor. The same is true of boards of policing, planning, health, or myriad other issues. These boards provide citizens with alternative avenues to participate in the governance of their communities. They also allow local governments to deal with a number of issues that reflect their unique heritage and requirements (see Box 10.3). From this perspective, it could be argued that these organizations could serve to strengthen, rather than weaken, the fabric of civil society.

## Public Administration and Policy

While public administration considers the structures for decision-making processes, public policy deals with the decisions and processes themselves. Kenneth Kernaghan and David Siegel suggest that policies are specific courses of action (or non-action) that governments take.[22] Policy analysts have devised a number of public policy models that are either explanatory (that demonstrate how the policy process works) or prescriptive (that demonstrate how it should work). Two of these are the *comprehensive rational approach* and the *incremental approach*.

## 10.3  Boards and Commissions of the City of Saint John, 2003

All cities have boards and commissions tailored to their specific needs, as the following list illustrates.

- Aquatic Centre Commission
- Board of Police Commissioners
- Environment Committee
- Fort Latour Development Authority
- Free Public Library Board
- Greater Saint John Economic Development Commission (Enterprise Saint John)
- Harbour Bridge Authority
- Harbour Station Commission
- Lord Beaverbrook Rink
- Parking Commission
- Planning Advisory Committee
- Power Commission
- Preservation Review Board
- Recreation & Parks Advisory Board
- Rockwood Park Advisory Board
- Saint John Development Corporation
- Saint John Non-Profit Housing
- Trade and Convention Centre Committee

---

*Source:* City of Saint John, "Home page," http://www.city.saint-john.nb.ca.

THE BUSINESS OF LOCAL ADMINISTRATION AND POLICY

The comprehensive rational model emphasizes well-thought-out, proactive strategies, in which all the alternatives are carefully ranked and compared in a rational manner and then implemented. According to Kernaghan and Siegel, this model, in which "policies are subjected to a multi-step analysis" before a decision is made rarely occurs in practice.[23] In addition, comprehensive, top-down approaches based on what are thought to be rational principles may not prove very rational in the long run, when ill-conceived policies run up against political resistance and unanticipated results. The policy world is much more complicated than this approach usually acknowledges.

Conflicting goals, values, and objectives based on competing definitions of rationality are much closer to the norm of public policy development. This was noted by Charles Lindblom, who argued that an incremental policy process not only reflects how policies are actually conceived and implemented but that the application of a less comprehensive, more incremental model of decision making will result in the best policy approach. Through "successive, limited comparisons" against the status quo, desirable changes can be made over time rather than all at once. Incremental, carefully thought-out processes are most likely to be acceptable to all the relevant actors. Lindblom's approach recognizes the reality that public policy is a continuing process.[24]

The incremental model is unsatisfactory for those who believe that governments need a dramatic restructuring in order to deal with important problems. Regardless, changes in public policy are often incremental because the task of governing large modern societies is complex, involving many competing agendas within and outside government administrations. From time to time, governments do introduce massive changes and deep restructuring initiatives without sufficiently considering the interconnections and possible feedback loops throughout the relevant systems and policy communities. When this happens, the adverse results are often unanticipated and the cure can prove to be worse than the original problem. Failure by governments to include those actors who have political influence inside or outside the formal system can result in an overall failure to achieve the original policy goals.

## The Policy Process

In addition to examining the broad models of public policy, studying the policy process itself and the actors who participate in its various stages can tell the observer much about political influence. Michael Howlett and M. Ramesh break the policy cycle into five stages:

1   agenda setting (bringing issues or problems to the attention of government)
2   policy formulation (formulating options within government)
3   decision making (adopting a course of action or inaction)
4   implementation (putting the policy into effect)
5   evaluation (assessing the consequences of the policy).[25]

For an example of how this might work, see Box 10.4.

## 10.4 Local Agenda Setting and the Policy Process: An Illustration

### Agenda Setting
On Friday nights, restless bored youths in a rural, physically isolated town are getting into trouble with the law and are vandalizing many public buildings. The issue becomes a subject of discussion in the local paper and radio station. The Downtown Revitalization Committee, the Chamber of Commerce, local activists, and other community leaders all begin lobbying for a solution through the media, to city staff, and by making representations to council.

### Policy Formulation
The local council requests that some of their city staff examine the problem and suggest alternatives. Various members of city staff are assigned responsibility. The initiative is to be spearheaded by the department of community services in cooperation with city police and the community policing advisory council. Council is presented with some suggestions, including building a new recreation centre to give young people a place to go in their spare time. Meanwhile, other interests, including local organizations, offer their suggestions. The chief of police requests additional funds to patrol the areas where youth gather frequently at night.

### Decision Making
Council considers all the suggestions presented to them and debates each of the following alternatives: setting up a mayor's advisory task force that includes some of the town's youth; building a new recreation centre; or supplying additional funds to community groups so that they can provide activities for young people.

Ultimately, council decides to raise funds to build a recreation centre, noting that they will also be able to charge fees for use of the facility and that regional tournaments held there will also bring in extra revenues to local businesses. A referendum is held on the topic during the next election. Because there is a referendum, more people show up to vote than is customary in local elections (particularly those interested in having a recreational centre). A strong majority of voters favour building the centre.

### Implementation
The recreational centre is built, with the provincial government providing a matching conditional grant. Some of the funds are raised through local organizations. The municipality receives provincial approval to handle the rest of the project costs through debt financing. Unfortunately, the project goes far beyond budget, but new sports teams are organized, youth activities and organizations are created, and the centre is heavily used, particularly by children and young teens.

## Evaluation

Members of city staff conduct an evaluation of the initiative's success. They determine that financially, the cost overruns will lead to unwelcome and unanticipated increases in local property taxes. Moreover, the chief of police reports that it will still be necessary to increase patrolling in areas that continue to be heavily frequented by older teens involved in underage drinking and vandalism. Youth workers, social service agencies, and the police, however, report that there appears to be a decline in destructive behaviour by a number of at-risk youth in the pre-teen category.

The Community Policing Advisory Committee discusses possible strategies for dealing with the continuing problem and, to this end, invite a group of teenagers to meet them. The council decides to subsidize recreational programs for young teens, hoping that the young people will be deflected from illegal activities when they become older. Those programs will receive ongoing monitoring and evaluation.

10.4  Local Agenda Setting and the Policy Process: An Illustration

Actors wishing to influence the policy process are most effective if they understand the importance of each stage. A government's sincerity in wishing to include the public in decision-making processes can be tested by investigating how it has incorporated the public in the policy-making process. It is quite common to hear city staff say that the public is apathetic because so few citizens show up whenever the city holds "open houses" to discuss a new proposed policy or development with the community. The explanation may well be apathy, but the policy analyst might also wonder whether the public had been included throughout the decision-making process. Members of the interested public may have discerned that regardless of their attendance or suggestions at the open houses, the city would proceed as it had originally planned anyway. Perceptions have a way of becoming reality. In order to respond to demands for "meaningful participation," some governments have been moving to engage the public in all stages of the policy cycle, and in some cases, public participation may be provincially mandated.

Today, in some progressive places, citizens can be asked to participate in all five stages of the policy cycle. For example, they might help set agendas by participating in the visioning exercises that set the community's priorities for the future. They may then provide input into the official community plan, recommend courses of action and methods of implementation, and monitor the final results. Diverse forms of public participation in policy making, coupled with expanded responsibilities of local governments, are contributing to pressures for a more holistic, integrated approach to policy making in communities.

## Broadening the Agenda: Policy Making for a Sustainable Community

Many of the policy areas for which local governments have had responsibility include the provision of hard services and infrastructure as well as education, public safety, finance, parks, recreation and leisure, arts, culture and heritage, and so on. In recent years, the responsibilities of local government have expanded and increased in scope. Conventional forms of policing have broadened to include concepts of community policing. Recreation has extended to include diverse services for the rapidly growing population of seniors. Arts, culture, and heritage have diversified to reflect new social dynamics and multiculturalism. Public health has now become the more all-encompassing policy arena of healthy communities (see Chapter 9). Transportation is another case in point (see Box 10.5).

In all of these areas, civic-minded individuals participate in a variety of ways either by questioning or critiquing the policy in question or by actively helping to create and implement various policies.

### Volunteers and Administration
Citizens and interest groups are active players in local governance: they serve an important communications function by helping to articulate the concerns and interests of less

## 10.5 Challenges of Contemporary Transportation Policy

Transportation policies, in many ways, shape the landscapes, form, and culture of cities. Roads define neighbourhood boundaries, dictate pedestrian patterns, determine the location of businesses, and fundamentally affect the quality of life.

As Edmund P. Fowler and Jack Layton point out, with half of all urban land devoted to cars, transportation policy is a complex field, particularly with the emergence of serious environmental considerations: "Awareness of the negative effects of auto use is growing. At the same time, pressures for expanded road systems are also on the rise, as trucking continues to replace rail haul, as offices and factories move to greenfield sites with lower taxes on the urban fringe, and as subdivision after subdivision replaces farmers' fields. More complications are added by changing price structures: gas prices rise and fall, transit fares almost always rise, and now tolls are being introduced."[1]

Beyond the infrastructure itself, public policy determines how people can be transported around their communities and whether governments continue to invest extensively in road building and maintenance or in alternative public transportation. How influential are the actors involved in maintaining and expanding the existing infrastructure versus those who wish to encourage alternatives? Fowler and Layton offer a lengthy list of actors, including those involved in the "movement industries" (such as car manufacturers, transportation companies, car washes, gasoline stations), the land developers and the property industry, the media, planners and experts, the public transit sector, the environmental and community groups, and the municipal, provincial, and federal governments.

---

1   Edmund P. Fowler and Jack Layton, "Transportation Policy in Canadian Cities," in *Urban Policy Issues: Canadian Perspectives,* 2nd ed., ed. Edmund P. Fowler and David Siegel (Don Mills, ON: Oxford University Press, 2001), 110, 116-21.

politically active members of the public; they are influential shapers of the local political culture; and in conjunction with local administrators and city staff, citizens often help inform, design, administer, and implement programs (see Box 10.6).

In a national survey on volunteering, Canadians were reported in 1997 to have contributed $4.5 billion and over one billion hours of volunteer service to charities and non-profit organizations. Almost 92 percent of Canadians made donations (either financially or in kind). It should be noted, however, that only 11 percent of all Canadians were responsible for providing just over half of all financial donations.[26] *Civic participation* includes the active engagement of individuals in activities such as voting, keeping politically aware and informed, and joining neighbourhood associations, non-government bodies, unions, sports, recreation, and leisure clubs, and similar organizations. Many of these activities constitute valuable voluntary contributions to community life. Citizens also serve voluntarily on a number of government-appointed advisory committees (see Chapter 3). Fifty-one percent of the population was engaged in such activities in one form or another.[27] By 2000, the level of volunteering had experienced some decline since 1997. Seven percent of all Canadians provided 73 percent of volunteer hours in 2000.[28]

The Canada-wide study suggests that a minority of people are responsible for steering much of the volunteer community's activities – at least, as volunteers have been conventionally defined. Furthermore, it was noted that volunteers are not representative of the diversity of Canadians. Those most likely to volunteer time or money share one or more of these characteristics: they are middle aged, well educated, possess higher income, or have strong religious affiliations.[29] How then, does this relate to the overarching question about local political influence? To the extent that they listen to volunteers and citizen groups, local governments are most likely be persuaded by the values of those who possess economic and other advantages in society. The demographic group that volunteers often shares similar socio-economic characteristics with those who dominate formal decision-making processes.

The nature of volunteerism has also changed over the years. Forty years ago, for example, much of the volunteer activity was organized on a spatial basis, which meant it was involved in neighbourhood planning. While those activities are present today, volunteers are also organized on a non-geographic basis according to other types of shared interests, such as ethnicity, gender, sexual orientation, or social activism.

The way in which volunteers are conceptualized in local government may mean that the volunteer work of a number of people may be dismissed and not considered an important civic contribution by the members of the governing local institutions. Certain forms of activism and social movements, for example, are often (though not always) directed at improving the overall quality of life. An activist group that decides to sponsor a peaceful rally encouraging people to ride their bicycles for a day rather than using cars is volunteering its members' time, raising awareness, and educating citizens about air quality. Those kinds of initiatives – marches, parades, and rallies relating to a social, political, or environmental cause – are not traditionally included or recognized as important

## 10.6  Volunteer Activities in the City of Toronto

It has been estimated that more than 26 percent of people living in the Toronto census metropolitan area volunteer their time. Areas of city-recognized volunteer work include:

- Children/youth services
- Community development/community centres
- Community and public health services
- Immigrant/newcomer services
- Libraries/information centres
- Seniors services/Housing and homelessness support services

*Sources:* City of Toronto, "Toronto Community Service Volunteer Awards 2003," http://www.city.toronto.on.ca/volunteer_awards/index.htm; Ontario Ministry of Citizenship and Immigration, "Statistics on Volunteering in Ontario," http://www.gov.on.ca/mczcr/English/citdiv/voluntary/stats.htm (updated 30 October 2003).

volunteer work. Another type of volunteer work may include the efforts of those who live on the economic margins of society and who work together sharing some of the daily living responsibilities, helping each other find shelter, or organizing shared childcare. These activities may be differently packaged and presented; nevertheless, they do constitute a voluntary contribution of a person's time and energy directed at improving overall community sustainability. These types of diverse activities are important to the civic spirit and culture of a community.

The role of volunteers, and even the way in which volunteers are defined and viewed, affects local governance. Much as financial capital and natural capital (environmental resources) are essential to the maintenance of a healthy community, so too is what some refer to as *social capital*. Robert Putnam defines social capital as "features of social organization, such as networks, norms, and trust, that facilitate coordination and cooperation for mutual benefit."[30] As Putnam points out, communities quite simply do better, from a practical standpoint, if they have an abundant stock of social capital. In fact, where communities might lack other natural advantages, they can often do well and compensate with an active and dynamic civic spirit. Putnam compares and contrasts different regions of Italy and describes the impact on regions that possess a healthy dose of social capital: "Citizens in these regions are engaged by public issues, not by patronage. They trust one another to act fairly and obey the law. Leaders in these communities are relatively honest and committed to equality. Social and political networks are organized horizontally, not hierarchically. These 'civic communities' value solidarity, civic participation, and integrity. And here democracy works."[31]

Putnam suggests that social capital is a *public good*; it can strengthen not only social networks but economic and political ones as well. Governments rely on the volunteer sector to help deliver the social services, policies, and programs that society expects. Beyond the contribution of social capital in building a civil society, the third sector plays an important role in providing concrete services. The degree to which governments facilitate the work of volunteer networks reveals the degree to which they are willing to share responsibility for the development of the community.

## Conclusion

In any study of political influence, public administration is important. The daily management and public decisions involving cities with multimillion-dollar budgets rests, in large part, in the hands of the administrative staff. Despite the application of the ideal principles of public administration, in practice decisions must often be taken that do not reflect the ideals. The challenges facing administrators will vary with the size of the city, the political culture of the area, the geographical location, and so forth.

The degree to which administrators are influential depends, in part, on the structure of the organization and legal and regulatory strictures. As important, however, is the informal authority that individuals wield by virtue of the personalities involved, leadership ability, professional and personal values, and knowledge. Despite the bureaucratic ideals, public servants do not operate in a vacuum. The information they bring to the decision-making environment is necessarily informed by their own experiences and values.

With the cutbacks in government revenues, a growth in demand for a diversity of services, and pressures for increased consultation, governments are looking to volunteers to meet a number of political goals in most, if not all, of the major areas of government activities. From the vantage point of community health, an active civil society is essential. From the perspective of political influence, however, most volunteers share the same demographic characteristics of those active in other aspects of governance. What of those residents of the city that have been relegated to the margins of civic life because of their lack of social, economic, or political standing? If a city is to thrive as a whole, marginalized people will also need to be actively recognized as part of the civic society and its decision-making processes. Unfortunately, all too often they are treated by administrators as passive recipients of services rather than as important actors in an overall governing process. It is difficult for actively engaged citizens to get that kind of recognition; it is many times more challenging for those with few resources at their disposal.

The chasm between the society-centred civic governing process and institutional local government processes becomes apparent when one considers the subject of the next chapter, the new public management and business approaches to government. These approaches tend to prioritize efficiency over equity and define effectiveness in terms of delivering programs in a cost-effective manner. Those individuals who know best how to operate and profit by such a regime are inevitably the ones who will become most influential.

# 11
# Business, Management, and the Municipal Corporation

One of the crucial roles of local government is to manage relations with the business sector. Local governments have long been viewed as responsible for providing hard services, such as infrastructure and making land-use and development decisions. The ability of government to provide these local services rests a great deal on generating revenues through property taxes, fees, and grants. It is important, therefore, to understand the nature of the relationship between decision making and the private sector, and the implications of that association for local governance.

Regardless of motivation – whether altruistic or self-serving – the ideological orientation of business heavily influences local councils. They, in turn, base their decisions on a set of assumptions that inevitably will advance certain interests at the expense of others. Leaders of the local private sector have often served on city council and promoted public services that also were often useful to their own particular interests. Those efforts would frequently provide the community with necessary services, such as a sewage system, clean water, public transit, and electricity. Other times, however, city officials and business-people have been reluctant to take initiatives that might deal with other important public matters, such as the adverse environmental and social impacts that could accompany industrial activity.

Of interest here is the role that business actors and considerations have played in setting the issue agendas or priorities of local governments. One enduring and pervasive ideological belief is that governments would be run more effectively and efficiently if they adopted business principles. This belief has been reinforced in practice through the close relationship between private interests, local councils, and other decision-making elites. Related to this perspective is an argument that the application of economic principles to government also stimulates local innovation and competitiveness. In the face of declining grants from senior government and rising expectations, local decision makers have recently been increasing the pace of their search for ways to maximize efficiency. This quest has led to a renewed emphasis on business-type principles of decision making and the adoption of such terms as *alternative service delivery, customer service,* and *total quality management.*

## The Municipal Corporation

The belief that local governments should be managed in a business-like fashion has a long

THE BUSINESS OF LOCAL ADMINISTRATION AND POLICY

history, and it continues to be popular today. Guy Peters notes that this belief is now reflected in the *new public management* approach that focuses primarily on the financial accountability of local governments and seeks to confine their activities to narrowly prescribed limits.[1] Similarly, Donald Higgins describes this viewpoint as one that essentially sees local governments operating mainly as public corporations with their primary mandate being to offer goods and services "in strict conformance with only those powers delegated explicitly to local government by a charter of incorporation."[2] Higgins suggests that, in this sense, local government is analogous to a business corporation offering services only where it is economically feasible to do so.[3] Accountability is principally assessed through the corporation's financial performance in offering a limited range of defined services using market mechanisms.

Frank A. Rodgers suggests that the only way to create local governments was to give them corporate status through a charter or statutory enactment because they lacked constitutional status. He cautions, however, that "it is important to remember that coming into existence in this way does not make a municipal corporation a company."[4] Many advocates of a more business-like approach to local government have ignored this distinction. They draw instead on other perceptions to support their misleading claims that the goal of local government is to provide public goods efficiently in much the same manner as the private sector.

## Science, Business, and Early Public Administration

The late 1880s through the 1920s was a period of rapid industrialization and urban development throughout North America. Business was seen as a basic requirement for city growth, which in turn led to "the good life" for all. Before the Wall Street crash in 1929, the endless possibilities offered by new advances in science and business held the public in thrall. Meanwhile, politicians, entrepreneurs, and efficiency experts waxed eloquent about the ways in which scientific management based on business principles could improve the administration of society, industry, government, and the economy. In 1887, Woodrow Wilson (later an American president) set out just this position in a classic piece on public administration: "The field of administration is a field of business. It is removed from the hurry and strife of politics; it at most points stands apart from even the debatable ground of constitutional study. It is a part of political life only as the methods of the counting-house are a part of the life of society, only as machinery is part of the manufactured product ... Administration lies outside the proper sphere of politics. Administrative questions are not political questions. Although politics sets the tasks for administration, it should not be suffered to manipulate its offices."[5]

Wilson's statement also illustrates that the most common analogies for the modern cities, and for society in general, tended to be of a mechanical nature, with comparisons to wheels, machines, and clockworks. Workers, citizens, and leaders all were cogs in that giant wheel, which efficiently powered the engine of prosperity. Henry Ford first set up his automobile company in 1903, and within ten years was cranking out automobiles in a new, efficient system called an assembly line. Years later, social reformers used the term *Fordism* to represent the dark side of the alienating industrial working environment that occupied the lives of so many urban residents of the industrial era. In 1912, industrial efficiency expert Frederick W. Taylor coined the term *scientific management*. He argued that scientific methods could be applied to workers in factories to improve their productivity. The social problems associated with the machine age were effectively captured in Charlie Chaplin's last silent film, the satiric 1936 classic *Modern Times*. Nevertheless, throughout the Western world, mechanization became a metaphor for progress – industrial, social, economic, and political.

In this respect, Canadian urban centres were no different. In the case of Berlin, Ontario, it was noted that "the city was like a watch; wheels within wheels. The factories were the great wheel, industry the mainspring: the Council the balance wheel and the Board of Trade the hair-spring."[6]

Citing the editor of Berlin's first daily newspaper, *The Daily News*, Elizabeth Bloomfield writes, "in scores of competitive urban centres in Ontario between the 1870s and the 1920s, community leaders worked through municipal councils, boards of trade and local newspapers to grant inducements to manufacturers. The widely accepted rationale was the conviction that 'manufacturing establishments' are prime factors in the progress and development of a town because with the investment of capital industry 'every interest will be benefited.'"[7] Bloomfield suggests that the initiatives of the local entrepreneurs were aided by "deliberate municipal policies of encouraging industry in the community."[8]

A primary, if not the primary, goal of the council was to ensure that entrepreneurs had the assistance they needed to prosper. As Bloomfield suggests, "Shortage of capital for the factory and its machinery might be made up by subscription of shares by local investors or by the grant of a cash bonus or loan by the municipal council. Whenever possible, community leaders preferred to use the power of a municipal government. Inducements to manufacturers could include one of or several of the following: the grant of money as gift or cheap sale or rental of a factory-site; the opening or improvement of access roads; free or cheap water, light and power; and a total or partial exemption from local taxation."[9]

Early Kitchener (formerly Berlin) was well known for its business orientation to local politics (see Box 11.1). This orientation persists in many cities today; economic development is seen as a central priority for maintaining the revenues that allow cities to provide a certain level of services. Community leaders would be quick to point out that businesses are the economic engines of cities, and that they make all kinds of other social services possible. For example, the Chamber of Commerce of Kitchener-Waterloo has stated, "the Chamber is committed to being a constructive, steady voice to move our community forward not just economically but on many fronts like health care, education and government effectiveness."[10] That local businesses contribute in many ways to the vitality of a city is widely recognized. That contribution is also matched by their ability to be a very influential lobby group contributing to the formation of local policy.

As discussed in Chapter 2, urban reformers, in their purported attempts to establish apolitical, neutral systems of government and administration, were actually ensuring that governments were responsive to the interests of one very powerful lobby group – the middle and upper-middle classes, which usually included most local business people. This community of interest could hardly be considered neutral in their aspirations for their cities.

## The Welfare State

By the middle years of the twentieth century, the Depression and the Second World War made it abundantly clear that individual enterprise and ingenuity were not going to solve the major social and economic challenges of the times. Governments became very active in building up the national and provincial economies and social and health services. The growth of the *welfare state* shifted public attention to more senior levels of government, and local governments increasingly found themselves with ever-diminished authority. Provincial ministries or departments of municipal affairs were established, special purpose bodies proliferated, and authority for planning and education became increasingly centralized. At the same time, burgeoning urban growth was leading to demands that local governments respond with a variety of services, policies, and plans of actions.

Adding to local governments' troubles, by the end of the century many provincial and federal governments decided that it was time to scale back expenditures and rein in their debt through cost-reductions, diminishing the size of governments and off-loading responsibility for the implementation of many of their policies on local governments. Local governments, no longer able to depend on sizable grants from provincial and federal governments, and having few options, looked to alternative approaches to efficient service delivery. Once again, business management approaches – now referred to as the *new public management* – were looked to for inspiration.

## Alternative Service Delivery

One of the approaches that became influential in the 1990s was that of *alternative service delivery* (ASD). ASD was an approach used at all levels of government to attempt to reduce the size of government by having services and other activities delivered by the private sector or by organizations other than the public sector. The following optimistic view of ASD suggests that the reduction of government would stimulate innovation:

## 11.1 Business and the Public Interest in Berlin (later Kitchener)

Throughout Berlin's early history, many councillors and mayors were also leading business-men in the community. It was thought that favourable tax assessments and exemptions for business helped create employment and contribute to the overall public interest. In many ways, this was true. Unfortunately, neither business nor the local government was as ready to consider or deal with the adverse social or environmental impacts of industry. However, in 1902, a new provincial statute stated that financial incentives to industries would have to be ratified by two-thirds of the eligible voters (those owning property).

John English and Kenneth McLaughlin paint a lively portrait of the times when they discuss the close city-business relationship. They note in one example that the city accepted one company's outright refusal to pay taxes. Another time, the city council agreed to grant money to help the Board of Trade promote a "yes" vote during a plebiscite that would grant $25,000 of the taxpayers' money to assist the development of a sugar beet factory. English and McLaughlin describe how one outraged individual, Allen Huber, repeatedly and vocally pro-tested the illegal manner in which the city continued to support the Board of Trade. In 1907, Huber denounced Berlin's municipal financial mess and ran for local mayor. He chastised the municipality for various irregularities, including its decision to "put through a $83,000 deben-ture for the street railway purchase without citizen approval" and for the special treatment of certain businesses, such as the grant of printing contracts to the *News-Record*. The editor of the newspaper, W.V. Uttley, was also running for mayor and was a member of council. At the final election tally, Uttley was declared the mayor with a win of 890 to Huber's 886. Ultimate-ly, after serious irregularities in the electoral process were revealed, the provincial govern-ment intervened and a new election was held. Huber won the election to become the new mayor.

In his short one-year tenure as mayor, Huber decided to tax all businesses at 100 percent and eliminated any bonusing, causing great consternation in the business community. He opened Victoria Park to all citizens and ended the practice of charging admission, and he in-troduced the concept of conflict of interest to the Light Commission. Despite Huber's short, explosive appearance on the municipal scene, to paraphrase English and McLaughlin, the poli-tics of Berlin continued to be the politics of business. Progress in the city was synonymous with the progress of business development.

---

*Source:* John English and Kenneth McLaughlin, *Kitchener: An Illustrated History* (Waterloo, ON: Wilfrid Laurier University Press, 1983), 94.

Since the 1990s, the public service of Canada has been severely battered by fiscal restraint initiatives, resulting in an unprecedented reduction in human resources. The past management philosophy has been that public servants must adjust to these fiscal realities by *doing more with less,* creating an environment where goals and objectives are not only unrealistic, but unattainable. For the public servant, ASD offers previously unknown opportunities for creating innovative agencies, which, free from centralized controls, will provide better public services, at a lower cost. Another positive spin-off of ASD is that it has the potential to substantially improve morale by employing innovation.[11]

Local governments, faced with the reality that the promised innovation would not be forthcoming quickly enough to forestall the imposition of a sharp increase in local property taxes, did not necessarily share the optimistic interpretation. Still, they had little choice but to pursue alternative avenues of funding and delivering services, including privatizing services where possible, raising fees for licences, permits, and parking, and increasing their reliance on the volunteer sector. In various parts of the country, provincial governments imposed a number of further measures on local governments, including reducing the number of elected representatives and amalgamating local units into larger political jurisdictions (see Chapter 5).

The capacity of local governments to exercise authority has always been constrained by a lack of constitutional and legal authority, a narrow taxation base, and limited resources. As Saul points out, "Central governments everywhere are in a long-term funding crisis, in good part because they get less and less tax revenue from the large corporations who, in a global marketplace, play one country off against another ... our governments are handing essential, but now unfundable, programs down to the regional level in the name of increased democracy. But the regional governments are also in a funding crisis. 'Too bad,' say the central governments. 'You'll just have to raise taxes to pay for the programs. Go on, assume responsibility.'"[12]

Having responsibility without authority does not increase the abilities of local authorities to self-govern. Some argue, however, that a decrease in the scope of government overall, and the privatization of public services, will lead to an increase in choices for individual citizens and control over their own immediate environment. A strengthening of the influence of the private sector, however, does not necessarily increase the level of freedom for members of the public to govern themselves as a community. This is a point that has been argued from both sides of the political spectrum.

As Hugh Segal notes from the perspective of a progressive conservative, individual freedom rests on the strength of community. He sees the importance of supportive institutions to all sectors of society. As he observes, the presence of a permanent and hopeless "underclass" undermines the whole community, including the wealthy. "The importance of community is no luxury or Fabian prayer. It is at the very essence of stability and freedom. It is the true guarantor of the 'order' in law and order."[13] André Carrel adds his voice of concern about local government's preoccupation with the goal of economic efficiency. He suggests that "community values cannot be measured in economic units, but they can be destroyed when manipulated in the pursuit of economic efficiencies. To subject public policy to economic measures, and to sacrifice community values to the anonymity of the global market, is to undermine the very foundation of our communities. The primary duty, responsibility, and obligation of every mayor, councillor, and administrator are to take a sober look at the values on which their community's survival depends, and to act in support of those values, whether that increases or decreases taxes and expenditures."[14]

In sum, despite their history, structures, and reliance on the private sector, local governments still retain goals that are distinct from those of private corporations in a number of ways. Private companies have one primary, clearly definable goal: to produce the best profit possible for their shareholders. The goal of government administrations is more complex, but essentially it is to provide a service to the public and respond to the demands and requirements of the broader community as articulated through those able to exercise influence. Sometimes governments cannot provide essential services in a cost-efficient manner. They must also offer services in areas where the private sector would not find it profitable to do so. Governments also provide public goods that are universally shared for the benefit of the whole community. Examples of this would be public parks, policing, and public health and environmental policies. Without the stabilizing environment provided by governments, the community, including its business enterprises, would not be able to prosper.

Those who take a new public management perspective might observe that governments are inefficient organizations, even if they do serve a worthwhile regulatory and stabilizing function. Part of the difficulty, the argument goes, is that there are not enough individual incentives built into the system to encourage members of the public service to do the job more effectively. As such, they say, some of the mechanisms at work in the private sector might be applied effectively to the administration of public services to increase their efficiency.

## The New Public Management

Peters suggests that at the heart of the *new public management* approach is the belief that markets are the most efficient mechanism for allocating resources within a society.[15] Advocates argue that unlike in the private sector, there is little incentive for public organizations to limit the scope of their activities, their size, and their budget. As a result, such organizations will grow unnecessarily and provide services inefficiently. Adherents of this view often believe that whether you are referring to public or private organizations, the management function is essentially the same. Private-sector organizational techniques can just as readily be applied to the public sector. Hence, it is unnecessary to have a separate practice or school of public administration.[16]

The new public management approach has been widely applied in local administrations across the country. It is now quite common to hear business terminology peppering discussions about how the municipal corporation should be run. The political, balancing, humanizing activities of local government are downplayed. In this environment, citizens are sometimes referred to as customers, government departments as core businesses, and councils as boards of directors. *Total quality management* (TQM) has been embraced as a method of sorting out organizational inefficiencies and saving expenditures. TQM is a team-based participatory approach to management that involves employees in decision making; this is a form of empowerment that Peters suggests involves a "substitution of collective decision-making for some aspects of hierarchy" in order to achieve a product of high quality.[17]

One of the best-known arguments in favour of this approach is articulated by David Osborne and Ted Gaebler in their book *Reinventing Government.* Osborne and Gaebler are in favour of governments and see them as an essential means for people to act collectively. They also state that they believe in equity and equal opportunity. But where their ideas differ from other ideological perspectives, such as those held by social democrats, for example, is that they argue that the only way to achieve the goals is through a competitive, entrepreneurial model applied to government practices.[18] *Decentralized, innovative, flexible, adaptable, customer choice, performance measures, customer service,* and *competition* are all buzzwords of this "reinvented" type of government.[19]

The administration of the City of Waterloo adopted this type of approach in February 1996 in its corporate redesign. Departments were restructured into five "core businesses" comprising several smaller "business units." The consolidation of functions and processes was designed in a way to "deliver specific products and/or services to customers [i.e., citizens]" facilitating the measurement of results. The emphasis on success was also couched in market-based terms: "Business plans and business measurement systems will be developed that link business objectives with the corporate objectives outlined in the City's Strategic Plan. True business costs, revenue potentials and our bottom line or the level of tax support required will be identified. Internal staff business consultants will lead the Units through the business plan preparation stage. Business planning will clearly identify the businesses we should be in, opportunities for cost savings and revenue enhancement and provide a common measurement system to help us make better decisions."[20]

Waterloo is not the only municipality that has taken this approach. Aspects of it have been applied to many cities throughout North America, and there are criticisms of this adoption of business-based principles. Peters noted, "Sceptics question whether TQM is really suitable for the public sector. In the first place, there may not always be the latitude for involvement and job-shaping in the public sector that is found in the private sector. The duties and obligations of public employees are shaped by law, so that they simply cannot decide that doing a job differently is a good idea ... Secondly, definitions of quality may also be more contestable in the public sector, when any clear bottom line is lacking to assess whether a program has been a success."[21]

Adherents of this business-type approach often refer to *measurement* of the fulfillment of objectives. Yet measurement is a scientific term, and measuring is possible only in the context of simple, clearly counted outcomes, such as the number of pencils used in an organization. Counting the number of children using a public skating rink or softball diamond is easy. Measuring the relative physical and social values of these activities is not, regardless of the number of indicators that might be applied. If something cannot be measured under this system – something that requires a qualitative assessment rather than a quantitative accounting – should it be disregarded as unimportant? How does this approach tackle the qualitative concerns that are not easily compartmentalized and reduced to a numerical item? Value judgments inevitably must be used, but the values are those based on private-sector principles, and as Peters noted, those criteria of success are different from the criteria used in the administration of public concerns.

Other important observations should be considered with respect to the application of TQM. Motivating employees to participate in their jobs and recognizing that they play an important role in an organization are two very worthwhile objectives that are often included in TQM approaches. The adoption of TQM also signals recognition of the inherent complexity of governance. Departments operating within their own isolated silos are not structured in a way that would allow them to respond to problems. A more organic or holistic structural model acknowledges interdependent requirements. TQM, as an approach, does recognize that problem solving is complex and adopts a holistic approach that more readily recognizes the interdependent nature of many public issues that governments must consider. On the other hand, there are important limitations to this model when applied to public decision making. One of the most important of these relates to the question of accountability. As noted earlier, TQM encourages participatory management. To what extent should employees be "empowered" when they are supposed to be accountable upwards, ultimately to the elected council and the citizens who elected council to represent them? Consider the case of RIM Park in Waterloo.

### The Case of RIM Park and Waterloo Inc.

RIM Park, named after one of the corporate donors, is situated in the far northeast corner of the City of Waterloo on 500 acres. This Millenium Recreation Project contains twelve outdoor fields and six ball diamonds, an eighteen-hole golf course, a large multi-use recreation facility (including four ice pads and two double gymnasiums), banquet/reception rooms, a pro shop, fifteen kilometres of paved trails, and park lands.[22] This park also cost the City of Waterloo millions of dollars more than anticipated and revealed, among other things, a weakness in the public accountability process. This issue highlights the challenges faced by part-time municipal councils in holding city staff in large municipal corporations accountable for sizable financial expenditures.

RIM Park was not financed through the issuing of debentures or raising taxes. In addition to some other fundraising activities, the City of Waterloo decided to arrange what it thought would be a lease through a financial services company. The lease amounted to

THE BUSINESS OF LOCAL ADMINISTRATION AND POLICY

$48.3 million for an overall payout of $112.0 million over thirty-one years. The city believed that it was entering into an agreement with a company by the name of MFP Financial at a very low rate of interest (less than 5 percent). It was operating on the understanding that the company, in turn, would benefit from the transaction by receiving tax deductions. Some time after the deal was signed, the local newspaper, the *Kitchener-Waterloo Record*, discovered that the City of Waterloo would have to pay twice the amount (and the interest rate) that the council and staff thought was the case. According to a news report, "The actual interest rate proved to be 9.2 percent, for a total cost of $227.7 million. Waterloo sued MFP and the insurance companies that hold the debt, Clarica and Maritime Life. Out-of-court settlement last year reduced the payout to $145.7 million, $32.8 million more than first planned."[23]

What happened? Concerns about how the deal transpired resulted in the city council calling for a judicial inquiry, also an expensive pursuit but one deemed necessary given concerns over public financial accountability. When the council signed the financing agreement on 25 September 2000, they were operating on the information presented to them by senior staff that they were receiving an interest rate of less than 5 percent. For his part, the treasurer said that he did not have time to check the figures, having received them from the financing company minutes before the council meeting when the agreement was to be signed. He was quoted as saying that he was given only a list of payments for the first six years of the thirty-one-year deal and a formula for calculating the rest of the payments. The chief administrative officer admitted that he had never read the financing documents and according to the inquiry's final report, testified that he was directed by council to build relationships with "important partners."[24] Among a number of other findings, the judicial inquiry concluded that the evidence provided by a company representative who played a key part in arranging the deal with the city, Dave Robson, "lacked credibility on all issues."[25] Furthermore, the inquiry found that "Mr. Robson pulled off a scam, properly characterized as a 'bait and switch.'"[26]

The issue of public responsibility is an interesting one. Who in city government was ultimately responsible? Formally, the elected council is expected to be accountable for municipal decisions. The city solicitor, however, stated that it was not reasonable to expect part-time city councillors to "police" staff but that they should be able to count on staff for details. The chief administrative officer noted that he had been encouraged to socialize with members of the private sector in order to develop good corporate relations. He was reported as viewing Dave Robson, the individual at MFP Financial who had arranged the deal, as a friend.[27] The city treasurer shouldered his share of responsibility, but what does this say about the overall structure of accountability within a city?

The inquiry found a number of parties responsible for the financial deal. On the city's side, in addition to determining that the chief administrative officer and the city treasurer had failed in their duty, the report of the inquiry stated that the mayor and council had "failed in their collective obligation to develop a proper understanding as 'laymen' of financial matters."[28] In his report, the commissioner did congratulate the parties involved in the mediated settlement "on bringing to a satisfactory conclusion what would have been a lengthy and expensive process."[29] The subsequent mayor of Waterloo, Lynne Woolstencroft, who had been a councillor at the time of the deal, negotiated the out-of-court settlement on behalf of the city, reducing the city's overall debt associated with the deal by $80 million.

Woolstencroft, in reflecting on the factors that contributed to the financial deal, offered a general critique of what she saw as an underlying systemic problem. She directed attention to a culture that was often referred to as "Waterloo Inc.," a label that referred to an administrative culture that was seen to direct the city as if it were a private corporation. The mayor suggested that while this culture conveyed the impression that the city was open for business, it did not imply that it was "open to the public process." The implication was that this business approach to government contributed to a closed process leading to poor financial decision making.[30] This analysis was confirmed in the report of Justice Ronald C. Sills, commissioner of the RIM Park Financing Inquiry: "The system of governance in Waterloo not only permitted but also encouraged 'schmoozing' with suppliers by senior staff. This led to economically unhealthy relationships between senior staff and suppliers. The system did not contain checks and balances that would head off situations that could have been more transparent."[31]

This type of problem is by no means confined to the City of Waterloo. Other organizations found themselves in a similar position; the City of Toronto had also arranged a leasing deal. Again questions were raised about the extent of golfing and socializing that took place between city officials and company representatives.[32]

This situation highlights the argument advanced by urban regime theorists, who note the embedded relationships that operate within local government. The reliance of government on property taxes leads to levels of interactions between influential city officials and members of the business sector far beyond those with other citizens in the city. The latter must make ongoing, concerted initiatives in their spare time to influence city hall. They too, can make an impact issue by issue, but they generally lack the informal and formal access to decision makers available to those considered "producers" rather than "consumers" of goods and services.

To what extent should non-elected city employees be allowed to exercise discretion? A pragmatist might suggest that these employees, in fact, do interact with the public a fair bit and that attempts to maintain the myth of a neutral bureaucrat operating completely at the behest of the elected representatives do not serve the public interest. The interactions of elected members with many staff or citizens may be minimal given the multiple other tasks that consume their time. The interactions between city staff and members of the private sector (or other members of civic society) need to be properly recognized, understood, and accounted for in institutional structures and processes. This may involve, among other things, drawing up more stringent conflict of interest guidelines and introducing more transparency into decision-making processes.

The RIM Park case highlights the dangers of perpetuating the myth that the business management approach to government is apolitical. Business or "market" approaches reinforce the influence of the private sector while undermining public accountability by limiting the number and diversity of political players or interests that can participate in the decision-making process. More attention needs to be paid to questions of accountability in a modern city administration. If administrative roles and functions are defined through such business tools as TQM, and members of city staff are "empowered" to make decisions, then it is important to recognize that those values will also have an influence on the form, function, and culture of the community. Business principles reduce citizens to customers and councils to boards of directors. Citizens, however, are not just consumers of services – to view them in this light changes them into passive recipients of cost-effective services rather than active participants in a healthy civic society; they are individuals who have responsibilities as well as rights.[33]

The Ontario Progressive Conservative government in the 1990s did not share this perspective; it adopted the market philosophy. Success was primarily judged on the basis of efficient service delivery at the lowest possible cost. Attempts to reduce overlapping responsibilities and costs led to amalgamations, the reduction in any areas of government that were not seen to be revenue generating, and a reduction in the number of politicians. Unconsidered in this process was the possibility of much greater costs arising from the long-term social, economic, or environmental ramifications of a decision made on the basis of short-term financial considerations. In the case of representative government, a reduction in the number of politicians in charge of large budgets can also lead to an inefficient and unaccountable decision-making process.

Peters suggests that the market model of government may be responding to the wrong signals, with success assessed on the basis of the immediate bottom line. In such models, outputs are what count, not the procedures by which governments make decisions, or how they make them, or who is involved.[34] William Kennedy, a former municipal director of finance, has raised similar concerns, arguing that public administration and public management serve distinct functions. To understand this distinction, it is worth considering the functions of one particularly important department in every municipal administration – the department of finance.


## The Case of Finance: Administration and Management

Departments of finance play a crucial role in influencing local politics. Yet, buried as they are in municipal administration, and sometimes being occupied with economic models and complex formulas, their preoccupations may seem better relegated to the apolitical realm of the professional expert. Nevertheless, urban public finance is fundamentally about politics. Choices that are made about how to allocate revenues for the provision of public goods and services tell the observer a great deal about the goals and objectives that the decision makers think are most important. The proportion of resources devoted to such services as economic development, public transit, forests, halfway houses and shelter, recreational complexes, and so on, tells much about a city and its values.

Departments of finance play an important role in informing the council about what they think is financially possible and what the city can afford. Those departments also make recommendations about how programs might be carried out and financed after considering options for delivering those services. Should the service be provided by the government to all members of the community? Could it be offered on a "user pay" basis, or could it be delivered by another, possibly private-sector, organization (alternative service delivery)? These are fundamental political decisions that determine who gets what and how. In other words, who should pay for a service and who should benefit?

## The Municipal Budget

The most important task of a department of finance is to keep the government solvent. The department has a major responsibility for overseeing the preparation of the annual budget in a way that will provide financing for municipal programs and objectives. Bird and Slack suggest that "local budgeting is thus the main institutional mechanism for maintaining financial control over spending and improving financial planning as well as implementing local government policies and programs."[35]

That said, it should be noted that municipalities have many limitations placed on their discretion when crafting the budget, and they are constrained in a number of ways. Municipalities are not generally allowed to run deficits in their operating budgets "although they can incur a debt for capital expenditures subject to certain guidelines"; provinces exercise significant control over service provision, and hence over the spending of revenues.[36] Local governments traditionally relied on the provinces for conditional grants to help fund services, "though that has dramatically declined in recent years."[37] Taxes must also be collected for special purpose bodies, and cities must service their debt charges.

Despite these limitations on spending, each year cities of 80,000 people or more have multimillion-dollar budgets that need to be allocated in a manner that reflects the priorities of the city. Some of the main players in the budgetary process include the finance committee of council, the city manager or CAO (and possibly commissioners), and the director of finance or city treasurer. While the key personnel vary from city to city, the budgetary process itself tends to follow a fairly standard pattern. Council provides guidelines to the CAO or director of finance. The individual departments submit their requests for funds to either the CAO or city manager or to the director of finance, who in turn compiles and evaluates the requests and presents them to the budget committee of council. The committee, in turn, asks questions of department heads and will often seek revisions to the budget. After further changes, the proposed budget goes to council, where it will be debated further.[38]

A comparative consolidated statement of the revenues and expenditures of each municipality's annual budget will tell the reader little about the comparative financial health of a community. Results will vary not only in terms of population size but also with respect to the division of responsibilities (between the provinces, the districts or regions, and the municipalities), provincial constraints on cities in how they can set their tax rates, different environmental and social requirements, and the alternative sources of revenues available to a city. For example, in the City of Waterloo in 2003, the average homeowner paid $2,300 in total property taxes.[39] Of that amount, only 28 percent belonged to the City of Waterloo. Because the City of Waterloo is a lower-tier member of a two-tier system of government, 48 percent of the property tax goes to the regional government, and 24 percent of the total goes to the province, which now controls the education budget.[40] The city, along with the other Ontario cities, was also required in 2001 to lower the tax burden paid by commercial and industrial properties. These business properties had a higher assessed tax ratio than homeowners and, as a result, had been paying two or three times the amount.[41]

In those areas of finance where a municipality does have discretion, the process of allocating those monies can be primarily the domain of city hall, or it could be an inclusive process. As noted in Chapter 2, the idea of a "people's budget," as demonstrated in Porto Alegre, Brazil, and as was lobbied for in Toronto, is one example of local participatory democracy. For its 2003 and 2004 budgets, the City of Saint John decided to initiate a new budgetary process; it was to encourage active public engagement. The city advertised for citizens and business owners to participate in a public consultation document about how funding should be allocated, within the limits placed on them by legislative and operating responsibilities.[42] While this initiative may not be a people's budget, as such, it does signal a recognition on the part of the government that the question of finance is not necessarily the sole purview of city council and staff. Similarly, in June 2003 the City of Prince George distributed a Financial Plan Survey to residents to ask them what their priorities were with respect to city services, to assist the city in future financial planning.[43]

Other important political decisions associated with finance have to do with the way in which revenues are raised to pay for services. Generally, the literature suggests that revenues are raised according to principles of equity, efficiency, and the stability of the source; that is, governments need to be able to count on a stable flow of revenues from the tax base.[44] However, what one group of taxpayers, such as homeowners, may see as an equitable approach to taxation may differ considerably from the views of business owners who pay a different tax rate. Local governments have traditionally relied on property taxes and grants from senior levels of government as their main revenue sources, together with fees for services. Yet as has been noted in this chapter and in Chapter 6, grants are a decreasing source of revenue for the municipalities. Property taxes are based on a mill rate (x dollars of tax for every $1,000 of assessed value), and the assessed value is usually calculated on the basis of what a buyer is willing to pay in the market.[45]

The equity of tax assessments could be determined in a number of ways. Basing taxes on the consumption of resources, for example, might be one way of deciding how much tax individuals should pay. Alternatively, it might be thought that the most equitable solution would be for those who are wealthiest to pay higher taxes. Competing ideas about equity and efficiency make it difficult to translate these principles into reality. The levying of property taxes, for example, is a highly contentious subject with property owners. Boadway and Kitchen recognize that one widely held criticism of property tax is that it is regressive because the tax consumes a larger proportion of the income of a lower-income earner than of that of high-income earners.[46] Boadway and Kitchen suggest, however, that one must be cautious about drawing these kinds of conclusions. For example, lower-income households in Canada are dominated by young adults and the elderly. In the case of young adults, they are beginning their careers and may be living in houses that reflect their future, rather than current, earnings. For their part, the elderly may be income poor but asset rich.[47] If wealth is assessed on the basis of assets or property, rather than income, it could be argued that a property tax is actually progressive.

What then of the situations when governments attempt to impose something called full market value assessment (MVA)? At these times, newspapers run stories about pensioners who have lived in a house in Vancouver or Toronto that they purchased decades earlier for a few thousand dollars. These residents may be living on a property whose market value assessment is many times more than was reflected in their property tax rate. This is not unusual, because the homeowner may have been benefiting from a system that under-assessed residential properties. When new assessments reflecting true market value are introduced by a government, the jump in taxes can be dramatic, making it difficult for some homeowners to pay the rate at the newly assessed market value, particularly for the elderly, who are asset-rich but income-poor. Boadway and Kitchen point out that provincial and municipal programs can alleviate such a burden on low-income households. There is a wide range of them, including provincial grants, exemptions, tax credits, deferrals, and municipal relief schemes.[48]

Municipalities can also impose special charges on a property to cover infrastructural or other costs, including special assessments, municipal bonusing, and development charges. *Special assessments* are often applied to commercial developments to pay for improvements on adjoining properties. *Municipal bonusing* occurs where developers are granted an exemption to a density or height bylaw if, in exchange, they agree to provide some other benefit, such as preserving nearby heritage houses. Development charges are imposed to pay for the capital costs of the development, and they can cover everything from infrastructure to park areas.[49]

Municipalities are squeezed for revenues. Property taxes cover an ever-diminishing share of a municipality's costs, and grants from senior levels of governments have declined dramatically. This is a common story across the country.[50] In all the case-study cities, municipalities found themselves throughout the 1990s facing overall cuts in their unconditional grants. For example, in ten years, the City of Waterloo saw its grants decrease from 17 percent of its overall revenues to 2 percent.[51] Municipalities must now look to other sources of revenue.

Other possible alternatives to property taxes include poll taxes (a head tax where each individual rather than property is taxed), local income taxation, municipal retail sales tax, hotel and motel occupancy taxes, and municipal fuel taxes. Poll taxes are not used in Canada and are generally considered inequitable, as they hit the low-income earner the hardest. Boadway and Kitchen suggest that although there would be complex issues to resolve, the introduction of local income taxation rather than a continuing reliance on increasing property tax "would almost certainly produce a more progressive distribution of the tax burden for funding local services."[52] Of course, the provincial and federal governments would have to go along with the idea, and the initiative does not appear to have been eagerly embraced. Local retail sales taxes are also a possibility, but they would be difficult for a municipality to implement when it is in competition with other communities for the retail dollar and with consumers being quite mobile in their shopping habits. Hotel and motel occupancy costs can be applied, particularly in large cities in downtown areas, where visitors wish to be centrally located. This can, however, also cause a competitive problem. Conventions, for example, might be held outside the municipality where there are no additional charges. Finally, fuel taxes are receiving increasing attention. This idea has merit, particularly, as Boadway and Kitchen note, because funds could be earmarked for other public purposes such as transit.[53]

As noted previously, municipalities have limited alternatives to property taxes. User fees (fees paid by individuals for services they use) are rising to fill the gaps caused by reduced provincial grants and growing local demands. The extent to which individuals should pay for a service, and the extent to which the city should subsidize it, are questions that have implications for social equity, economic development, and quality of life. Should a city, for example, subsidize the building of a golf course when, frequently, only those with a car and the money to pay for the green fees will be able to take advantage of the service? On the other hand, should a city help develop and maintain amenities such as golf courses, recreational centres, and concert halls in order to attract business people and their families and their employees to the city, because such people will bring with them much-needed revenue? Which services should be provided universally, which should be subsidized, and which should be provided on a user-pay basis?

Then there is the question of the use of taxation to promote desirable behaviour. It could be argued that users should pay the actual costs of waste disposal and water consumption in order to encourage conservation. Yet this approach raises other considerations. First, such a system would discriminate against the poor and would not necessarily encourage conservation among the rich, who may be the largest consumers of the environmental good. Second, user-pay systems may not always lead to the desired result if people decide to dump their garbage furtively in parks and alleys in order to avoid paying the waste collection fee.

Other questions about user-pay services reflect very much the current values of our society. In an era dominated by a car culture, it does not seem at all unusual to many drivers that an efficient urban road system should be readily available as a universal service, while use of public transit contains a user fee component. When, and if, the environmental or efficiency costs of maintaining a policy that facilitates heavy urban traffic patterns becomes too high, the political climate may change to an extent where the use of buses will become a free service and urban roads will have tolls. Some cities in other parts of the world already charge motorists for using their roads. The relative convenience of using one mode of transportation or another has a great deal to do with the way in which governments decide to design cities and encourage certain modes of behaviour. Determining what the public wants in the absence of immediate viable alternatives leads to a process of incremental decision making and careful reliance on the cost calculations of the professionals in the local departments of finance. They are, however, as subject as anyone else to popular, class-oriented views about "motorists rights" and other such values.

In sum, it is clear that financial decisions are highly political ones in which professional expertise is used to assist in helping make those choices. Efficient management of those choices is desirable. Unfortunately, efficient management sometimes can become the goal of the exercise itself rather than a means for implementing the actual task of administering the public interest. The danger of combining the two is that, under such a model, non-elected administrators may be making important political decisions while operating under the illusion that they are simply addressing apolitical management issues best left to the experts. In his analysis of local financial administration, William Kennedy suggests that when the crucial distinction between these two functions is ignored, the political policy-making role of local finance goes unrecognized (see Box 11.2). Regarding finance primarily as the purview of the professional manager removes the public from this very political, value-laden activity. This is an ill-advised approach to dealing with public money. It is important that administrators be held accountable for decisions that have significant community consequences.

Local governments can be very large corporations that require people to have sophisticated knowledge of complex financial transactions. Municipalities build recreational centres, arts centres, theatres, and other public facilities, and developments of this kind often involve public-private partnerships. These multimillion-dollar deals are often intricate and are beyond the expertise of city councils, who need to be able to rely on their staff to inform them about whether the negotiated deal is financially sound. Private-sector companies can afford to hire top financial experts to ensure that the company profits from the venture. Yet underfunded municipalities, particularly the smaller ones, often do not have enough staff or in-house expertise to adequately advise council on the many financial or policy decisions that occur on a daily basis. If cities lack the requisite resources to hire enough employees possessing the necessary level of expertise, the result could prove much more costly than what had initially been saved by cutting municipal jobs. This is a particularly important consideration given the current trend in provinces

## 11.2   Local Financial Administration versus Local Financial Management

William Kennedy, former director of finance, City of Prince George, British Columbia, provides a summary of the distinction between fiscal administration and fiscal management in the context of local government.

In day-to-day usage, we tend to use the terms *administration* and *management* more or less interchangeably, overlooking the differences between two major views of local government finance:

- managing the finance function in the most effective, efficient, and economical method possible
- the broader process, whereby financial objectives and values are established.

Local financial management is concerned with questions of practice such as

- determining how the tax billing function can be organized to minimize cost and maximize collections while observing values such as fairness and equity
- identifying techniques that can be used to invest public funds to maximize returns while minimizing risk.

It is also concerned with questions of control and accountability. Local financial management is largely the preserve of the "professional," subject to the values and culture of the organization. Local financial administration goes beyond financial management to include the processes used in setting the organization's financial objectives and values. It addresses issues of public financial policy such as the extent to which "user pay" or "fee for service" approaches should be used in financing services, the allocation of the burden of taxation among the components of the community, and the balance between debt financing and "pay as you go" policies.

It also involves processes such as public information and consultation, and the linkage between community planning and the local government financial plan. While finance professionals are intimately involved in local financial administration, elected officials, employees, and members of the community are also active participants. It is important that the distinction between financial management and financial administration be recognized. Recognizing the distinction helps us avoid policies, administrative structures, or processes that do not allow adequate public debate and consensus building, and which diminish political accountability. A local government's financial objectives and values are, in essence, political choices and should be capable of being influenced by political, and not just managerial, considerations. On the other hand, recognizing the distinction between financial management and financial administration may help us to avoid politicizing issues that should be largely managerial in nature.

across Canada, where provincial governments are encouraging municipalities to engage in public-private-sector ventures. The Waterloo RIM Park case noted previously emphasizes the important role that public employees play in the life of a community. It also demonstrates that the penny-wise, pound-foolish approach of senior governments can generate undesirable, and unanticipated, costly feedback loops. This is the case whether one is speaking about the retroactive costs associated with a contaminated municipal water supply or a poorly understood financial deal.

In short, relying primarily on business principles to achieve the public interest can backfire if policy objectives are forgotten in the pursuit of an "efficiently" run corporation. Finally, it is worth noting that the public management approach to increasing efficiency itself is based on a debatable assumption; that is, that private corporations are necessarily more efficient financial operations than public corporations. As a number of high-profile cases have demonstrated, including the massive Enron securities fraud case in the United States, that assumption is questionable.

## Public Choice and Education Policy

Some observers suggest that trying to apply business approaches to increase the efficiency of public organizations is undemocratic because it serves to undermine the political process, as explained earlier in the chapter. Others argue that the opposite might be true.

One market-based approach to decision making is known as *public choice*. The prescriptive idea behind public choice is that citizens should be given the opportunity to exercise their rights by having an array of public services from which to choose. Encouraging competition in service delivery is one way to achieve this goal. Alternative service delivery and decentralization of political authority and departments are all approaches consistent with this model. Many advocates see this approach as promoting the democratic rights of individuals as well as breaking the inefficient monopolistic practices of governments that have little incentive for providing better services at a lower cost to the taxpayer.

Education policy offers an excellent example of how this particular debate is played out. This policy area has seen many changes over the years, reflecting societal and institutional changes. It has long been seen as an important responsibility of local government, and in many ways it has served to express community ideals and culture. Peter Woolstencroft suggests that "schools embody the central values of a society, and education debates mirror fundamental social values. Along with health care and income maintenance and security, public education is a pillar of the modern welfare state. It also represents the first extension of the state in what had been a private (that is, family or religious) matter. That extension, which occurred more or less without rancorous debate, except in Manitoba and Quebec, was motivated by the need to foster social order and economic growth; only latterly has education been justified as a means for encouraging individual self-development."[54]

In recent years, governments have been scrutinizing public education, not only for the costs associated with its delivery, but also because of its role in the economy. To some governments, a crucial aspect of education policy is to invest in young people in order to build economic growth.[55] The impacts of policy decisions, however, are much wider than such narrowly interpreted mandates would allow. If success in education is only assessed through testing of student abilities to acquire skills that lead to jobs, other important societal values will be discounted. Such tests, for example, will not capture the relative abilities of students to contribute toward a healthy or civil society. The public is not concerned only about global competitiveness. Different societal groups are making a wide variety of demands on the educational systems, calling for responses to perceptions of growing violence in schools and the diverse needs of children ranging from special education to cultural or religious requirements.

Some critics of the current educational system who call for increased public choice have suggested that competition is required to inspire innovation in public education. This could, in part, be achieved by giving parents the right to choose where their children go to school and how the curriculum should be delivered. Not uncommonly, governments favouring competition amongst schools are also predisposed toward breaking up educational monopolies and allowing private-sector competition with the public sector to deliver services. One way of achieving this is to provide parents with vouchers to offer them more choices.[56]

A fundamental principle of the welfare state has been to strive for equality of opportunity no matter where a citizen resides or what her or his socio-economic status. The reasons for this philosophy are based on the recognition not only that all citizens should have the right to a minimum standard of services, but that a well-educated population strengthens the economy and the country as a whole. As Woolstencroft points out, however, equality of opportunity in practice can be interpreted in different ways when one is considering how to distribute resources for the provision of educational services.[57] Equality of opportunity means recognizing that students have differing needs, abilities, and religious and cultural requirements. It also means that all students should have the opportunity to receive the same quality of education as everyone else. Providing a specific type of education while maintaining a universal standard of education with a common curriculum is a difficult balance to strike.

It was announced in the Ontario 2001 provincial budget that the government would offer tax credits to parents who send their children to independent (private or religious-based) schools in a move said to increase parental choice in their children's education.[58] This decision resulted in protests from groups concerned that it would fragment and further weaken the public school system, while using taxpayer dollars to support wealthy taxpayers who sent their children to exclusive private schools.[59] The initiative died with the election of a new provincial government.

Increasing choice is not an easily implemented policy approach. In practice, the socio-economic status and geographical location of individuals in Canada have not led to a system of universal services, where policies have an equitable impact and all individuals have equality of opportunity. Although the Canadian welfare state went a long way toward a more equitable distribution of resources, disillusion in the welfare state and dissatisfaction with the delivery of services, such as education, have led some to call for increasing the public's choices. Public choice approaches, however, may benefit only those who are in a position to make those choices. Individuals who can exercise choice have the opportunity to look elsewhere for employment, housing, and schools more suited to their individual preferences. People with limited social or economic resources and limited education do not have the same level of mobility, nor do they necessarily believe that they are in a position to change their personal circumstances.

## Conclusion

Public administration is not a science. It cannot be exercised in a "rational" manner because there are as many competing definitions of rationality as there are different values, goals, and objectives brought to any decision-making process. In an ideal sense, public administration is also about administering the public interest in ways that go beyond achieving a profit. Efficiency is an important part of the public administration approach. Cost-efficiency, however, is not the only consideration and does not constitute the sole measuring stick for assessing the effectiveness of local government. As many have observed, sometimes the goals of cutting operating costs are incompatible with political priorities.[60]

Moreover, as can be seen in examples of environmental contamination, homelessness, or simply ill-considered administrative or policy decisions, cutting costs as a short-term strategy can prove extremely costly in the long term. The application of public management principles can be very useful in producing favourable patterns of organizational behaviour and for achieving managerial objectives. The warning signs go up, however, when these principles become the goals themselves, rather than the tools that should be serving the public interest. Treating citizens as customers, for example, may be a useful way of reminding the city staff that they are working for the public interest. That said, there is a danger of effectively disenfranchising citizens if they are viewed only as consumers of a service rather than as people who might wish to govern themselves as responsible, decision-making members of the broader community. Conventional models of public administration, despite their flaws, recognize that by being responsive to the general public interest, the field constituted much more than responding to the financial bottom line. In the quest to achieve that bottom line, and by placing priority on that one objective more than other goals, the values of public management may undermine the ability of other members of society, including the elected representatives, to participate in many important local decisions.

The new public management approach is also a reflection of the values held by many public decision makers. City employees are heavily influenced by the value system and the culture in which they find themselves. As Christopher Leo, Mickey Lauria, and others have pointed out in their analysis of regime theory, there is an embedded system of rewards and reinforcements for certain kinds of behaviours within city government.[61] The case of financing Waterloo's RIM Park was a good illustration of how local administrators are encouraged to develop a good working relationship with revenue-generating groups in the local community. Those kinds of contacts not only foster a strong city-business relationship; they also lead to a shared set of values and perspectives about what constitutes the general public interest of the community. Unsurprisingly, significant elements of a community, those that Hugh Segal has referred to as an "underclass," have much more limited access and interactions with influential players at city hall. Political marginalization of a large section of a community threatens a city's political, social, and economic stability. The business model of government, with its quest for economic efficiency, makes little room for a broader, more comprehensive understanding of good governance.

Understanding the structures, policies, and models of public administration and management helps one to recognize how decisions are made and how city administrators and staff influence the process. Studying the formal internal structures, governing machinery, and policy processes, however, tells only part of the story. Formal hierarchies, public releases to the press, and recitations of department mandates do not necessarily reflect the actual flows of political influence. An examination of the informal patterns of decision making can reveal a great deal more about how decisions get made and by whom. One of the ways of garnering an understanding of these informal processes is through a study of political communications, as will be discussed in the next chapter. Here, at the beginning of a new millennium, global and local economies are resting on this so-called new information age. More analysts are now paying attention to the flows and patterns of communications and what they have to say about political influence.

Part 5    Surfing into the Twenty-First Century:
Local Political Communications

Political ideology, legal and constitutional institutions, natural and social environments, economics, and administrative structures all contribute to the patterns of local politics. Largely unconsidered in many analyses, however, are the actual channels that convey the local political messages. This is an unfortunate oversight. Those who control the dominant message or the medium of local communications, or both, also have tremendous political influence.

Although this has always been the case, rapid development in communications and information technology is now leading to an intensification of interest in local political communications. The very concept of *community* itself, as a territorially constrained notion, is coming into question, with the ascendance of the notion of *virtual communities*. Communications then, is another important perspective that needs to be considered when determining *who* influences *what* agendas, and *how*.

# 12
# Local Channels of Information

I deology, history, institutions, and the social and biophysical environment are some of the forces that have a bearing on the politics of local influence. Often overlooked, however, is the role of political communications. Political communications provide the means by which individuals and groups can advance their goals and set political agendas. *Who governs* depends very much on who is *plugged in* – on who has access to the relevant information. Various forms of communication can be used as tools to extend the authority of dominant elites. Occasionally, they can be used to boost the political influence of people who are usually left out, the people rarely heard from in formal decision-making processes.

The definition of political communications can be fairly simple: *political communications* refers to the whole range of information and messages that deal with public governance. Those messages may be spoken, written, sent by electronic media, communicated through symbols, or even acted out in body language. A mayor, for example, will use a gavel or wear a chain of office to communicate her or his official role in council. Local newspapers frequently publish pictures of elected officials in hard hats, with shovels in hand or posed on construction equipment at new development projects. The intended communication to the voter is that an active, "progressive" government is in charge. Whether a picture works that way is, of course, another matter. Political communications also includes more than just messages exchanged between citizens and the elected government. It also includes communications that flow between and among governments, program staff members, pressure groups, party officials, media, citizens, mayors, and councillors. The messages that are sent and received (as well as the choices made about which messages should be communicated and which should not) are value laden, affecting public agendas and the priorities of opinion and political leaders.

Beyond the messages themselves, politics can be influenced by the choice of medium used to communicate. The means chosen will affect not only the content of the messages but also the way in which they are received and acted upon. In Canada, the impact the medium can have on the message first received widespread attention through the work of economic historian Harold Innis, and later, communications theorist Marshall McLuhan. Predicting that information technology would fundamentally restructure human relationships, McLuhan spoke of a phenomenon that is commonly referred to as the *global village*.

Information channels – much like the transportation channels mentioned in earlier chapters – are important variables in understanding the patterns of influence.

Who has control over those channels of information? How are those channels used? What are the ways in which local political actors use information in order to achieve their goals? Members of the media, the private sector, citizens, and governments all act as *gatekeepers* of political information. They decide what the composition of the audience should be, what is important, and what information will be disseminated.

Information, access to information, and the medium by which it is transmitted have always played an important, if largely unconsidered, part in local politics. New information technologies are now beginning to focus the attention of academics, decision makers, and other groups on the way that access to certain types of information can influence local politics. People who are not "in the know" are out in the cold; they cannot be part of who governs. The proliferation and application of different information technologies in a variety of public and private settings is affecting relationships among governments, elites, citizens, the information-rich, and the information-poor. The technologies are also being applied in ways that have fundamental implications for concepts of community, giving rise to new buzzwords such as *smart communities* or *virtual communities*.

One of the most important questions concerns the extent to which new information technologies will change existing structures of political influence. Access to these technologies might make it possible for the less influential citizens and communities to achieve a greater measure of authority and self-governance. Alternatively, it might be argued that while the traditionally less prominent actors may be able to effect some political changes using new technologies, their efforts will be overshadowed by the dominant economic and political elites. Those elites, after all, will have at least as many of the same tools to advance their interests, and they are more likely to have the resources and abilities to exploit these media most effectively.

## Early Communications

Harold Innis once said, "the subject of communication offers possibilities in that it occupies a crucial position in the organization and administration of government and in turn of empires and of Western civilization."[1] One of the most important contributions of this aspect of Innis's work was the recognition that a message communicated on one form of medium, such as a clay tablet, was distinctly different from one communicated in another form, such as a newspaper.[2] Innis's theory of communication divided media into two "biases" – *time-binding media* and *space-binding media*.

Time-binding media, such as manuscripts and oral communication, have limited distribution potential. James Carey notes that time-binding media "favored relatively close communities, metaphysical speculation, and traditional authority."[3] Space-binding media, such as print and electronic media, are concerned with expansion and control. Again, according to Carey, space-binding media "favored the establishment of commercialism, empire and eventually technocracy."[4]

Innis saw that modern Western history began with temporal organization before moving on to spatial organization. Carey writes, "it is the history of the evaporation of an oral and manuscript tradition and the concerns of community, morals, and metaphysics and their replacement by print and electronics supporting a bias towards space."[5] Developing this line of thought, Marshall McLuhan emphasized that the technology or tool used to communicate was as influential in shaping opinion as was the message itself – the "medium is the message." Edwin R. Black noted that throughout history, technology limited and shaped communications. "So long as recording was limited to soft stone and what could be chiselled into it, the contents were brief, very important, and accessible only to people living in that one place. The invention of paper-and-ink systems greatly magnified the range of possible contents and physical locations where it might be read. Without horses and physically light message forms Rome would have been unable to build and defend its huge, ancient empire."[6]

Until the fifteenth-century invention of the Gutenberg press, a relatively few people controlled the spread of knowledge. In Europe, these individuals were generally the only people who could read and write, the men of the Church who disseminated information through oral communication to relatively small groups within society. The invention of the Gutenberg press soon made it possible for information to be widely distributed. The shattering of this monopoly of knowledge held by the few contributed enormously to the development of modern forms of government, to liberalism, and to individualism.

Prior to the spread of twentieth-century forms of communication, local governments were usually remote from the seats of central government power, both in terms of physical distance and access to information. That could be both a blessing and a curse for early local decision makers. In some ways, their isolation gave communities more independence to make local decisions than appears to be the case today. But that very isolation made it more difficult to resist the imposition from above of legislation and taxation regimes. Local decision makers were constrained by their limited legal authority and the lack of financial skills, information, and connections with other communities, which might have allowed them to build much broader support. As such, they were not in a position to mobilize constituents, civic leaders, or other communities in a manner that would allow them to mount an effective counter strategy to the more powerful levels of government. As noted by Harold Innis in his "bias of communication" thesis, access to channels of communication is a tremendous tool for advancing political goals.

In examining Canada's early history, Innis saw channels of communications much the same way as he saw channels of water (in the case of Canada, the St. Lawrence Seaway and Hudson Bay). They were avenues by which central governments could control territories or build empires. In Canada, geopolitical positioning was not the only major influence on development of the various local political cultures. Control, or more often, lack of control, over different types of communications technology was also influential. Local, independently owned newspapers carried large sections of community news reflecting the spatially smaller interests of their advertisers and readers. In the 1830s, for example, when Kitchener's (then Berlin) first newspapers, the *Canada Museum,* and its replacement, *Der Deutsche Canadier,* first began publishing, information such as advertising, news items, and editorials all blended and merged together in an interconnected web of local events. Bill Moyer reports, "there were as many public service notices, and business, political, community service, and religious announcements carried in these newspapers as there was actual news coverage. But these filled a definite and growing need in Berlin and neighbouring communities for knowledge of local activities and events."[7]

Individual citizens knew more about politics locally than those of far-off capitals, whether provincial, national, or otherwise. The twentieth-century advent of mass media, such as television, made the reverse more often the case. Black has argued that beyond personal affairs, "the population's information patterns are generally the same as those dominating the mass media."[8] Mass-oriented television brought reduced competition among local papers, the rapid expansion of newspaper chains, and enormous concentration of ownership of the political media. Both the "chattering" and the governing classes became steadily more concerned for the future of liberal democracy. Recognizing the important political role the media played in shaping public agendas, the federal government intensified its investigation into the implications of corporate media mergers. In 1970, the report of the Special Senate Committee on the Mass Media stated, "what matters is the fact that control of the media is passing into fewer and fewer hands, and that the experts agree that this trend is likely to continue and perhaps accelerate. The logical ... outcome of this process is that one man or corporation could own every media outlet in the country except the CBC."[9]

The committee had reason to be concerned. Throughout the 1970s, a number of city newspapers folded, often leaving only one daily paper. This was only the beginning of a trend that led to increasing consolidation of ownership of newspapers and other forms of mass media while government moved to limit newspaper holdings. A decade later, another investigation, this time a Royal Commission (the Kent Commission), reached similar conclusions: "Too much power is put in too few hands; and it is the power without accountability. Whether the power is in practice well used or ill used or not used at all is beside the point. The point is that how it is used is subject to the indifference or to the whim of a few individuals, whether hidden or not in faceless corporations."[10]

Despite the efforts of the various inquiries, media concentration continued through the remainder of the twentieth century. The concerns raised by these commissions are still very much an issue. Media concentration is difficult to avoid in a world of global commerce and integrated communications systems. Behind the shadow of these preoccupations, political communications and other systems affecting the use of government information were developing and changing.

## Integrated Communications and Political Influence

By the last two decades of the twentieth century, information technology was again undergoing a transformation, and integrated systems and digital networking posed a new set of questions for democratic theorists to ponder. Would the advent first of the Internet and then of the World Wide Web, with its anarchical structure, present an effective counterbalance to the centralizing trends of the mass media? Possibly, but the integration and networking of different forms of communications also could lead to a citizen's diminished control and influence over her or his own environment. Information technology, as a tool, could be used to deepen and extend the control of the existing political and economic elites already dominant in society.

Optimists and advocates of new, readily available forms of information suggest that such things as *teledemocracy* – a form of direct democracy – are just around the corner. This development, some may argue, might lead to a revitalized sense of community and a direct connection between citizens and their government. Easy access to e-mail addresses of councillors, mayors, and administrators gives the politically aware local citizen more information about public services, and with it increased opportunities to influence local decisions. In principle, citizens could also use new technologies to vote from their homes on issues of local importance. Increasingly, news Web sites use this mechanism to informally gauge the general public's opinion. Ease of access and convenience could even broaden the base of citizen participation.

There are pitfalls. As noted in Chapter 3, political elites still control decisions about whether there will be plebiscites and how those questions will be worded. The application of technology will do little to resolve that problem. Can such plebiscites actually enhance the citizen's ability to influence the decision-making process? Does the addition of another avenue of communications really open up access to decision making? The use of the Internet and e-mail does bring about new patterns of local and national political involvement, but it is not yet clear whether or not the new technologies make any substantial difference in the composition, nature, or degree of public participation.

Broadly available information may enhance participation by those who were predisposed in the first case to get involved in local issues but were dissuaded by the inconvenience of having to go to city hall or wade through layers of bureaucracy. The type and comprehensiveness of information provided on the city Web site will demonstrate the government's commitment to facilitate public access.

The Internet makes it possible to consult large groups of people inexpensively through *virtual conferences* and other methods of engagement; whether governments actually do anything with the resulting input is the same problem that arises with any type of consultation. The use of integrated information technologies to alter the nature of participation will also depend on the availability of other avenues that can serve the same purpose. Does information technology such as e-mail actually provide a means of increased interaction between government and citizens? That is debatable. The volume of e-mail may be such that citizen requests and comments get buried every bit as much as do telephone calls and other communications. Spatial considerations will also influence the choice of technologies for government-citizen communications. For northern communities situated in large, sprawling districts, such as Iqaluit, Nunavut, new information technologies could very well alter the avenues of communication between citizens and their governments in quite a distinctive way if enough citizens are able to make effective use of this medium. The politics in a highly populated metropolitan region with many different means and modes of communication and travel may be influenced quite differently.

Finally, it should be noted that general public access to computers, the Internet, and governments should not be taken as a given. As F. Christopher Arterton notes, "any mechanism of communication that costs money to use will necessarily produce inequalities of access among social and economic groups. When these media become conveyors of political participation, differential access, both as to speakers and listeners, can become unduly restrictive from the viewpoint of a democracy. The goal of political equality, or at least something approaching a near equal opportunity to be heard and to listen, is probably not achievable in an absolute sense, but public policies need not reinforce those inequalities."[11]

## Gatekeepers of Information

In all types of political circles, at least four different sets of issue priorities are in play: those of the political and the bureaucratic arms of the public authorities, those of the mass media, and those of the watching public (each of which is generally more politically influential than the inattentive mass public whose responses too often are included in crude surveys claiming to report "political agendas").[12]

How a local decision comes into being depends a great deal on the weight given to certain information at particular times. For example, city council may be debating whether to increase the budget for public safety. A citizen whose house was vandalized might think crime rates were dramatically increasing and might lobby intensively for more resources to be put into law enforcement. The chief of police will press city council for a larger budget in order to do what he or she thinks is essential to ensure public safety. News reporters looking for good copy will sometimes generate alarmist accounts of crime, thereby raising public concern. Administrators, trying to respond to such accounts, might examine crime rate statistics over the years and decide that the public's concerns were not supported by the data. They might then recommend that resources be allocated elsewhere. Yet even the statistics used to support that conclusion cannot be entirely neutral. They, too, are affected by the assumptions and biases of those who decided which bits and pieces would be accumulated and recorded to make up the statistical tables. Each piece of information, once placed within a particular context, carries its own set of internal biases, most of which are not evident to the user.

A communication system is a technology embedded in a set of social arrangements implying power, purpose, and organization. As all social subsystems come complete with political biases and ideologies, every information system, no matter how high tech or scientific it may be, always favours one place over another, one set of values instead of others, and one group of people rather than another. Many, if not most, Canadian municipal governments have installed, are now using, and must continue modifying various data-processing systems on which they rely for both day-to-day work and medium-term planning. Yet they do so without much awareness of the built-in biases of these systems. Regardless of whether they are supplied by senior governments, chambers of commerce, or social activists, the data bits that are fed into local government channels are equally as biased as the communication systems as a whole. Without a social context, there is no such thing as *information* – only data bits. It is only by being organized socially that data acquires meaning.

Information gathered for purposes of provincial assessment and equalization programs, for example, are used locally for tax planning and collection, then for zoning regimes, by-law enforcement, traffic planning, commercial boosterism, school and park allocations, and so on. Information gets changed at every step. Those data, however, usually enjoy the status of being official, computerized, and "scientific." Seldom does one branch of local government or a councillor ask questions about the integrity of the basic data, about the deliberate or unintended transformations to which it has been subjected, or about the violence done to the information – usually unintentionally – through its manipulation for presentation purposes. Given the volume of information that individuals are required to absorb to make daily decisions, little time, energy, or consideration would be given to a systematic investigation of the way the information itself is shaped by political processes. Those wishing to discover who has influence, and how, in local government could learn a great deal by asking the following questions:

- Who specified that that particular bit of data or information was needed?
- Who created it and for what purpose? How did it get to city hall?
- What office got it first? How was it changed, by whom, and why?
- When did it become an item of information?
- Is it equally valid for political decisions as for management?
- How many people used it as different items of information?
- When the decision was finally taken, how recognizable was the original data bit?

In examining the ebb and flow of information in local politics, investigators must think about how both routine and specialized data come into being. Different pieces of information have different provenances: some come directly from their original creators (such as from the downtown business association, the local conservation group, or the police commission). Others have travelled through many hands, and very little information can go very far without being transformed in some way. The varied value frameworks that give birth to these data and their transformations are generally taken for granted and seldom made explicit. Data useful for deploying police constables and cruisers about a community may not have the same reliability when used in deciding a council's budget priorities. If statistics lie at all, incorporating them into pretty graphs for council consumption and decisions turns statistics into quicksand for the unwary.

The formal structures of a local government are important in a communication-focused inquiry. The larger, more complex local governments are going to have different communication patterns than those of a small village. They may have more sophisticated managements and a better sense of how to exploit technological possibilities for their city's betterment. But in either case, it is important not to confuse the formal accountability structure with the effective power structure. They are rarely the same. Determining who controls the information flow into, within, and out of the unit will tell you something – occasionally everything – about who has power. All governmental and political organizations comprise a series of interrelated networks, some dominant, others subordinate, and many of them changing from one policy sector to another.

While every opinion or issue group has its own agenda, not many of them can get their issues on the local decision makers' agenda. That success depends on their access to the various information channels. The power to decide *what* gets on the agenda is at least as important as directing the decisions themselves. Often local councillors find themselves like back-bench members of Parliament: their time is almost entirely consumed in grappling with agenda items virtually dictated by supervising governments and their own senior managers. In other cases, influence over local decision processes flows from the ability to control either external intelligence itself or its publication. Local daily newspapers do seem to exercise inordinate influence in some local issues. Nevertheless, the power of the press, even in local affairs, is a sometime thing rather than commonplace. Even the ability to get city hall talking about preferred issues depends on the alignment of local socio-political forces and the place among those forces that the newspaper has won for itself.[13] This is as much the case today as it was a hundred years ago (see Box 12.1).

Channel controllers are found in every part of the political web: municipal treasurer, public relations agent, city clerk, police desk sergeant, and so on. Just how open those channels are to the different citizens of a community is a key determinant of the forms and amount of public participation. No study of local problems will be complete until it is known, issue area by area, who decides and shapes the questions that get on the civic agenda, and who shapes the supporting data sets. These are input questions of the highest order.

If, for example, a local referendum is held, and a performing arts centre is built as a result, one might assume that the city government was responding to public demand in a democratic manner. Yet did the initiative to build the centre really come from the public? If one were to take a communications approach to analyzing the situation, the first question to be asked would be how the performing arts centre and not some other project

SURFING INTO THE TWENTY-FIRST CENTURY

## 12.1 Kitchener (Berlin) and the *News Record*

By 1912, there were three daily newspapers in Berlin: *The News Record*, the *Daily Telegraph,* and the German-language *Berliner Journal*. When Britain declared war on Germany, a local debate ensued about changing the name of the town from Berlin. The *News Record* took a strong editorial stand against changing the name. A number of people saw this as an unpatriotic stance and began heckling employees, and then began to vandalize the building and surround its offices. Soldiers had to be brought in to subdue the dispute.

When it was decided that there would be a name change, the local press wrote several very supportive editorials and stories about Lord Kitchener, suggesting that his would be a good name for the city.

*Source:* Bill Moyer, *Kitchener Yesterday Revisited: An Illustrated History* (Burlington, ON: Windsor Publications, 1979), 55-56.

ended up on the ballot. Where did the initial idea originate? Who took the issue and made it a community concern: the city's administrators, the chamber of commerce, the mass media, an interest group, or, perhaps, the council? If one were to trace the communications pattern of such an initiative, a fair bit would be revealed about the decision-making process of governments and some fundamental questions of governance might be addressed, such as who benefits and who decides. When one begins to unravel these questions, a much better understanding of the process of public decision making will be gained.

If much can be understood about power by analyzing budgets and financial resources, just as much, and sometimes more, can be understood by analyzing patterns of technology use and communication. Moreover, an understanding of the flow of information reinforces long-standing notions about community power and influence. Nelson Polsby argued that, contrary to much uninformed opinion, there is no "single locus of decision-making."[14] No single group can either control the local agenda completely or guarantee the success of all its proposals. Decisions of a non-routine, unbureaucratized, or innovative variety will sometimes require public voting approval (but more often in the United States than in Canada). That said, at other times, the elites may expect to prevail as usual. The communications patterns discovered through information-oriented research may be expected to mirror that proposition.

No single player controls information channels. Some commentators are much impressed with what they call the "democratization of information," and they see that as the key to social change. That may be, but we must always remember the many purposes (biases) that go into the creation of information. Given the differences among the agendas of individual political actors, those who command communication channels most successfully are the ones who get their business onto the decision makers' calendar. In all of this, we must not neglect to ask what is happening to the traditionally influential pressure groups and whether they still set agendas. To what extent, if at all, are high-tech developments changing the existing structures of influence? Do they continue simply to reinforce the status quo?

## The Channel Controllers

Local political actors, such as the media, government (including the elected politicians and the administrative city staff), citizens, and the private sector, use communications to influence decision-making agendas. It is worthwhile to consider how each of these sets of actors can exercise a degree of political power.

### The Local Media and Agenda Setting
Most people who watch the daily news or read a paper are well attuned to the fact that the media, in their varied forms, have an influence on politics. As yet, however, the precise

effects of that influence are not known with any degree of certainty. Over forty years ago, social scientist V.O. Key Jr. suggested that the media do not actually tell the public what to think, but are very good at telling the public what to think about.[15] That still seems valid today. Whatever the powers of the various media yesterday or today, those powers continue to evolve along with communications technology, content changes, and audience shifts. What is clear is that the local media can affect society in a number of ways, ranging from the routine reporting of governmental activities to acting as a channel of influence among decision-making elites. E.R. Black observes that "daily newspapers have undoubtedly led local politicians to particular policy decisions that the newspapers preferred and that, if left entirely to their own discretion, the politicians would not have taken."[16] Black cautions, however, that the ability of the media to *set* the agendas of city hall depends greatly on the social and political dynamics in the community, and the position within that of the different local media.

One of the important roles of the media is related to the question of civic literacy and public engagement in political issues. Henry Milner suggests that the relationship between media consumption and civic engagement is an important one. He notes that the trend away from reading a daily newspaper to relying on television-generated "infotainment" has serious negative repercussions for civic literacy, and by extension, democracy. He suggests that this problem can happen in at least two ways. The first, as has been noted by Robert Putnam, is that television watching reduces the time citizens spend in civic engagement.[17] Second, Milner observes that the reliance on television leads to "a reduction in direct exposure to more accurate sources of political knowledge through print media."[18] A poorly informed electorate will have a difficult time holding their governments accountable.

At the local level, the media can play a very important political role as watchdog. They can bark quite effectively, but first publishers and station managers must be supportive of that role. Once appropriate resources have been made available, investigative journalism can bring to light important public decisions and the implications that might otherwise have slipped past public attention. One recent example of the watchdog role was that played by *The Kitchener-Waterloo Record,* a newspaper serving the Region of Waterloo in Ontario. It investigated the financial negotiations behind the multimillion-dollar recreational RIM Park in Waterloo and revealed that the city would be paying much more for the park than its officials had thought.[19] (See Chapter 11 for a more complete discussion.) Further investigations revealed that several other public institutions in the province were in similar positions.

Recognition of the media's service to the public in holding governments somewhat accountable should be tempered by an acknowledgment that it may be even harder to hold the media accountable for their own actions. Who is watching the watchdog? Laws, like those dealing with official secrets, libel, and slander may not be enough of a constraint. It is hard to control or regulate irresponsible or sensational journalism without running the risk of suppressing freedom of the press, and by implication undermining the goals of a democratic society. The best defence against this problem is to ensure that a diversity of news sources and opinions is publicly available so that the media are, to a certain extent, self-regulating. That is why governments and the public become concerned about media concentration and its possible threat to the public's ability to obtain the kind of information necessary to hold governments, media, and other opinion-leaders responsible for their activities.

That the media do influence public agendas is a fact exploited by many activists. Stephen Dale noted this in his book, *McLuhan's Children: The Greenpeace Message and the Media.* Greenpeace, in its "quest for coverage" has become very sophisticated in using the media to get maximum attention for its objectives. Dale stated that "the founders of Greenpeace recognized the truth in McLuhan's assertion that these new electronic networks now directed the course of human events and represented one of the few sources of true power still accessible to ordinary people.[20] Different groups exploit different types of media to get maximum attention. One example of this was acted out in northern British Columbia. There, a number of local political actors, citizens, and members of the media teamed up against all the odds to win provincial approval and money for a new university.

### The Campaign to Build a University in Northern British Columbia

By the 1980s, northern British Columbians had become tired of seeing their children go south for their education and stay there for their careers. They were unhappy, too, about economic injustice. Northern resource wealth was draining southward into majority population areas while the north was not getting back its share of public services. Education was the key to more economic development, higher levels of employment, and better opportunities for all. Over 90 percent of northern BC residents favoured the concept of building a university in the north.[21] Tom Steadman, one of the primary individuals who engineered the university campaign, notes, "the story of the concurrent preparation required to bring that need to the centre stage is a fascinating personality-filled story. It involved a grassroots, bottom-up effort by thousands of B.C. northerners that dragged a reluctant provincial government, kicking and delaying, into the future. In the process, the strengths and weaknesses of northerners were exposed to all."[22]

The idea to build a university in northern British Columbia had been discussed at many times and places over many years. Things came together in the late 1980s. Good political timing, energetic local champions, and a coordinated campaign with widespread support won the north the political commitment and resources it needed. The freestanding university they wanted was won despite arguments from the existing universities "down south." The existing institutions were pressed for resources and argued that demands for their services were much greater than demands would be for a university in the north. What was more, the provincial government of the day did not always display very enlightened attitudes toward the north. One account quoted the minister of Advanced Education as having said, "In the Interior, people don't think of education beyond

Grade 12. The questions they ask at the end of the day are 'How many trees did you cut today? or 'How were things down at the mine?'"[23] Perhaps it was that politically ill-advised statement that gave the campaign its final nudge, coming as it did on the heels of a very effective, coordinated media and public relations effort (see Box 12.2). As one university founder and northern resident, Ruth Rushant, stated, "The greatest satisfaction is that UNBC is a living example of the democratic process in action. We have it because a large number of the local population made their wishes known to their political representatives. For once, they listened."[24]

The widespread support of all the opinion leaders in northern British Columbia, including those within the local broadcast and print media, together had a powerful impact on southern agendas. In today's world, any governments, citizens, or groups that cannot get the mass media's attention will have trouble pushing whatever causes they think important. Those that do get the media's attention can be very influential.

## Government Use of Information

An ability to influence political decisions requires access to important information. This is an age-old truth, long recognized by church and state well before the introduction of the Gutenberg press enabled the broad dissemination of the printed word. Governments have always used information to organize and control behaviour. In fact, well-placed administrators who have insider knowledge and can tap the right communications networks are often more influential than their elected political bosses. This aspect of political office is particularly tough for people just elected for the first time. They usually lack both the knowledge of how governments really work and the time to figure it all out. This problem can be intensified when the job is deemed to be part-time, or partially voluntary, as it often is at the local level. That situation forces the elected representatives to rely heavily on administrative staff for both information and political guidance, which places considerable power in the hands of non-elected staff, if councils pay attention to the advice.

Members of the public are at an even greater disadvantage. Whatever chance they have of calling governments to account depends considerably on their knowledge of what goes into government decisions. This concern has led many jurisdictions to adopt information access and privacy laws. Ideally, good access-to-information laws let citizens find out how governments spend their tax dollars, see whether administrators are following through on their own laws and regulations (for example, in ensuring the environmental or human rights laws are upheld), and discover government incompetence or failure to fulfill its mandate. In practice, however, it is not easy to gain ready access to all the information one might want, even assuming one had the time and interest to track it down.

In the past, a great many local governments were small enough that it was easy to maintain personal contact between citizens and elected representatives. Councillors would see their constituents regularly on the street. The volume of public interest could be handled through telephone calls, petitions to council, public meetings, and so on. But just as cities and their governments have grown, so too have the public's expectations that they

## 12.2 Lobbying and the Media

Local media play an important role in community politics. If they do not actually set the public agenda, the media can certainly act as important conveyors of selected information and provide a forum for lobbying. In the following excerpt written on 6 June 2001, Ron East, who was an active member of the committee formed to promote the establishment of a university in the BC interior and owner of a local broadcast station, discusses the role played by the local media in helping to establish the university.

The committee to promote a new university in northern British Columbia sought the assistance of all print and electronic media in the northern half of the province and received widespread support airing and printing news releases. The university committee solicited donations for advertising campaign dollars to place ads in all media at all communities served in northern BC The media themselves also contributed to costs by supplying free space and time. Simultaneously, the committee offered a "membership" at a cost of $5.00 and gained 15,000 members in a show of support. (This route was chosen rather than a simple petition. The thinking was that people who would pay $5.00 for a membership are serious compared to the usual petition that is widely displayed and costs nothing.)

Politically, the three colleges at Prince George, Terrace/Kitimat/Prince Rupert and Dawson Creek/Ft. St. John also supported the degree-granting university concept even though the first- and second-year students of the university would be "competitive" with the college system. The government responded with the offer of establishing "college universities" to add advanced education facilities throughout the province ... but the UNBC promoters and supporters held firm and launched a campaign to "fill the office of the Advanced Education Minister" with mail, faxes, etc. We also sold "Use the 'U' Word" buttons and challenged all political people to use the words "full standing degree-granting university" when they referred to our needs. With all this resultant public support, including local politicians, the political agenda was influenced and the long result was the granting of the UNBC charter. UNBC now thrives and is a much valued education facility serving all residents of northern British Columbia.

So, with all this activity during their reporting, did the media rile the populace into action or did the residents define the university agenda and activity for the media? Which is the chicken and which is the egg?

be kept informed. Some local governments have been taking these concerns seriously – direct contact through councillors, government departments, consultative exercises, and volunteer settings continue to be a part of local politics. Today, with the rapid development of the World Wide Web, local governments are all quickly learning to make use of that medium to disseminate information to their communities.

Most of the larger local governments have a communications branch to keep both the public and the city staff informed. Continuing developments in electronic technology give governments new opportunities to improve citizen information, public services, and overall city management, as well. A federal government initiative, entitled Smart Communities, provided funding to localities that wished to provide an integrated communications service that, it was hoped, would serve to connect citizens and local government, and also function as an economic development tool.

## Public Access to Information and the Protection of Privacy

Canada has had a federal Access to Information Act since 1983. Since then, the provinces have brought in their own access and privacy acts that included the municipalities. By 2001, Prince Edward Island had drafted its own legislation, the last of the provinces to do so.

Ontario's 1988 Freedom of Information and Protection of Privacy Act applies to all of Ontario's provincial ministries and agencies, boards, and most commissions, as well as to other bodies such as community colleges, health councils, and so on. A 1991 Municipal Freedom of Information and Protection of Privacy Act was also passed to cover municipalities, local boards, agencies, and commissions. It ranged from information held by a city clerk to a school board, board of health, public utility, or police commission.[25] The legislation "requires that the government protect the privacy of an individual's personal information existing in government records. It also gives individuals the right to request access to government information, including most general records and records containing their own personal information."[26] In Ontario, an office of the Information and Privacy Commissioner (IPC) operates at arm's length from the government. The IPC investigates such things as refusals of government to release information, or privacy complaints about information held by the government.

Access-to-information acts contain many exemptions, leading critics to suggest that they may be ineffective. Exemptions have been justified on the grounds that they would help protect the general public interest or the individual privacy of third persons. The challenges of ensuring public access to information include finding an acceptable balance between withholding and releasing public information. Implementing the spirit of such legislation brings in a major resource problem – governments need to be willing to invest enough resources to make information publicly available and to let the information or privacy commissioner do her or his job well. That does not always happen, although the principle of "information openness" is in place legally, and that is a start.

Given the place of information technology in today's decision-making areas, this legislation is particularly relevant when considering issues of government accountability. The old saying that "knowledge is power" is still relevant. Now the question is not so much who *has* particular information, but who *has access* to it. Do modern communications give the individual a vastly enlarged and improved array of tools with which to gather information? Is the citizen getting more in touch with governments? Does more accurate and up-to-date information flow freely, and is it readily available on government Web sites? Alternatively, are citizens becoming more and more alienated because their elected representatives cannot look after the voters as well as they once did? After all, our much larger electoral districts means that those elected must rely increasingly on technocrats and computer-generated information to deal with the public as well as to help make important decisions.[27]

There are no ready answers to these questions. Information technology can help in the pursuit of any number of competing goals. It can give government a powerful advantage over the citizens and, in theory, it can be used to give citizens greater control over government.

## Government Communications Departments

Even a casual Web surfer can assess the level of sophistication or commitment of a government to providing information to the public. For example, can citizens go on the Internet and carry out all of their routine transactions, buy their licences, check garbage pickup dates, and find out when *their* street will be plowed? What about council? Can every member of council or city staff member go to the city network and get all the civic information they need to do the job well?

All governments routinely use communications to persuade the public to comply with local bylaws, adopt community goals, promote civic spirit, participate in volunteer activities, and act as local entrepreneurs. Critics might view the funding of communications departments as free advertising for the existing council, allowing it to increase its own legitimacy at taxpayers' expense. Be that as it may, these departments can also serve important functions. They are charged with ensuring that communications are running smoothly within the municipal organization, thereby improving the administration of the public interest. They provide information to citizens about events within a city and developments that affect the health and welfare of the community, and they facilitate community development initiatives. Uninformed citizens cannot hold governments accountable for their activities, and communications departments can provide the public with important civic information. The City of Sherbrooke's Communications Department, for example, has offered its citizens and others coverage of city activities in a variety of media and formats (see Box 12.3).

For citizens to hold governments accountable and to influence the decision processes, they need to be adequately informed about government initiatives. Communications departments, however, have historically operated to disseminate information to the public rather than to engage the public in an interactive process. Thus, the communications process has often been unidirectional. Public consultation exercises have been seen as separate

## 12.3 Sherbrooke's Communications Department (Division des communications)

Information provided by the Sherbrooke Communications Department is disseminated both for internal corporate purposes and for external communication about the city. In Sherbrooke, that department also has been responsible for providing information and communications services to Hydro-Sherbrooke. The department's primary services could be grouped into three areas: provision of information, consultation, and public relations.[1] Its public has included citizens, the media, special purpose bodies, institutions, consultants, the private sector, community organizations, and other governments. It is also responsible for providing services to the council, the municipal corporations, and employees.

The Department has produced a number of free publications that include a wall calendar distributed widely to the citizens. Through this medium, the public has been provided with ready access to the phone numbers of city employees and council, bylaws, community events, information on recycling and waste management, and other useful information about the community. It also released numerous brochures on city activities and services, a newspaper entitled *info Sherbrookois* that offers extensive municipal information, a Web site, and a journal, *Le Tour de Ville,* for municipal employees explaining initiatives and new city developments.

The Communications Department has also kept the public informed about all the important administrative and political issues related to the amalgamation process, including matters ranging from the new electoral and governing structures to the way in which waste would be collected.

---

1  Ville de Sherbrooke, Division des communications, http://Ville.Sherbrooke.QC.CA/fr/mainframe.html (accessed 6 January 2003).

initiatives and are handled through advisory committees or through other vehicles. In the past few years, however, Web sites have made it technologically possible for citizens to interact with their local government on a daily basis.

What are the implications of the increased use of the Web site medium in terms of enhancing the interested public's ability to influence government decision making and effect change? Some would suggest very little. The growth of government Web sites and their online services could be seen as part of a larger trend of the new public management school, where the ultimate goal is to cut costs and increase efficiency. If this were the case, the net result would be to distance governments even further from citizens by reducing personal contact and downsizing city hall personnel whose job descriptions included interaction with the public. It could be argued that the interested public has always been able to make connections at city hall and to exert political pressure without the use of the technology. It is also unlikely that those who are uninterested in local politics are going to become more engaged in the civic process because municipal Web sites are now available. Innovations will do little to change that reality.

Web sites could prove to be a useful tool for extending citizen-government networking, particularly if the Web pages are established and well funded, offering quick responses to individual requests. A number of examples that encourage participation can be found across the country. In Prince George, one can find readily accessible links under the heading "e-business" that allow citizens to make pothole and streetlight reports, seek travel grants, and apply for public special occasion applications (beer gardens). Cities such as Kitchener and Waterloo also include some electronic services on their sites, including a list of employment opportunities and registration for city-offered programs. Saint John has an extensive list of services available online, to which they are adding continuously. They also seek user input into how the Web site might offer improved e-services (see Box 12.4).

The relative quality of the individual municipal Web sites throughout Canada is not just an indication of government size and available resources. In many ways, publicly useful Web sites that are kept up to date often indicate the value that governments place on using these pages to engage citizens, and the abilities and creativity of the technical staff. As mentioned at the beginning of this section, one of the tests of a good Web site is to examine how interactive it is. A second way to evaluate a site is to consider how quickly individuals can navigate their way around to find what is needed. Web sites also reveal something about the commitment of a government to make itself available to public requests through that particular medium.

Local governments also use Web sites for other political purposes. For example, during the amalgamation process, the City of Toronto used its site to proclaim its concerns about the provincially imposed amalgamation.[28] In 2001, the City of Halifax also used this medium to explain its opposition to a provincial proposal to equalize funds.[29] Such Web sites, however, are only tools. In and of themselves, they do not make governments more or less accessible, though they may provide more convenient and readily available

## 12.4  City of Saint John Electronic Services, 2003

The following list shows the types of services that the city offers citizens through the Internet:

- Application forms
- Bylaws
- Council meetings, schedules, and agendas
- Employment opportunities
- E-services
- Facility booking and program registration
- Licences, permits, and application forms
- Meeting schedules, agendas, and minutes
- Parking
- Payments
- Policies and procedures
- Purchasing
- Purchasing strategies
- Reference library

Information about business start-ups or for businesses interested in relocating to Saint John can be found on a separate "Enterprise Saint John" Web site.

*Source:* City of Saint John, "E-Service," http://www.city.saint-john.nb.ca/1.cfm?PageID=1-3-0 (accessed 5 June 2003).

information that could lead to a more informed citizenry if the public chooses to avail itself of the services.

It is up to local governments to determine the extent to which their Web sites will be accessible and interactive. Moreover, these Web sites will need to have adequate resources and be staffed by people knowledgeable about what kind of information and level of services to offer. These "gatekeepers of information" play an important role in shaping citizens' perspectives of their local government. They will also help to determine whether the information provided improves or limits the degree of access citizens have to city hall.

## Smart Communities

The Smart Communities program, part of a global strategy, has been established in this country as part of the "Connecting Canadians" initiative through the federal department of Industry Canada. A *smart community* has been defined in the following manner: "A Smart Community is a community with a vision of the future that involves the use of information and communication technologies in new and innovative ways to empower its residents, institutions and regions as a whole. As such, they make the most of the opportunities that new technologies afford – better health care delivery, better education and training and new business opportunities."[30] In 1999, the federal government launched a three-year program that provided $5 million for each of twelve Smart Community demonstration projects (one in each province, one in the north, and one in an Aboriginal community) with the goal of bringing together private- and public-sector partners to provide extensive online information and services.

A number of communities (129 of them) in partnership with other organizations across the country applied for funding. Each community emphasized different priorities. Those that were in more remote locations chose to emphasize projects that would overcome barriers to community goals posed by distance and more limited provision of services. Goals such as local access to health, education and information services, and community development were considered very important.

Urban centres had their own set of priorities. Ottawa's SmartCapital project was one of the chosen pilot projects. One of its initiatives promoted "one-stop access" to government information and "e-democracy" services in both official languages. Navigation was to be made easier through specific channels targeting different groups, such as the "Seniors" and the "Parents" channels. SmartCapital was also designed to ensure that individuals could gain access to, and interactive services with, local public institutions, including facilities such as schools and libraries. Virtual classrooms, "webcasting initiatives," telehealth, entrepreneurial centres, and investment services were all projects designed to take advantage of the existing high technology enterprises in the region while promoting other economic, social, and political goals.[31]

While only some communities were selected for pilot projects by the federal government, other communities made it to the second stage of the competition and continued to develop their initiatives. This was the case with Prince George and Canada's Technology Triangle (CTT), consisting of the Ontario cities of Cambridge, Guelph, and Kitchener and Waterloo. The Prince George proposal was entitled "The Northern Edge – The Prince George Integrated Community Network," and it was submitted by the Prince George Regional Development Corporation. In 2001, work was underway on phase one of a development to locate a transit exchange in Prince George (see Box 12.5).

Along with various federal government measures, such as Smart Communities, and efforts to encourage the development of advanced communications infrastructure, provinces also began their own interconnectivity initiatives among communities. Alberta, for example, launched what it called the SuperNet, a shared-cost project with the private sector. The goal was to provide high-speed broadband connections for every hospital, school, library, and provincial government facility in 422 communities across the province. Internet service providers also made services widely available, enabling businesses and residents to have access to high-speed Internet connections. Government investment was focused on many rural communities where the private sector did not think that it could make a reasonable return on its investment.[32]

The point of all these initiatives was to help communities to foster economic development and competitiveness in the global economy, govern themselves more effectively, provide access to educational opportunities, facilitate community health, and strengthen citizens' abilities to interact effectively with government. The degree to which this is possible will be constrained by economic, legal, geographic, and institutional considerations. As noted earlier, success will also depend on whether the communicator can deliver the requisite information and resources, and whether the intended audience is prepared to pay attention.

It is important to consider the values driving the Smart Communities program and similar technology applications. Much importance is placed on the need to improve productivity and global competitiveness – driving forces behind Industry Canada's initiative. Smart Communities may make it easier for citizens to become informed and active members of a local polity, and it may also make it possible for local business to gain ready information about government contracts posted on the Web site. Such open access to competition can cut two ways. For local businesses that felt shut out of the bidding process and were concerned about possible local corruption and the exchange of political favours, it might be a welcome change. However, under the new system, contracts posted on the Web could be bid on immediately, and often, from anywhere in the world. As Nathan Newman notes, "any attempt by local government to build up local businesses may be undercut by global businesses scooping up government bids off the Internet and underbidding local contractors based on volume sales."[33] Similarly, access to vast quantities of readily available information may not lead to a more interconnected local community. Rather, it might turn out much like the coming of mass media; Internet users might well turn away from issues preoccupying a local council to follow events in the world at large.

## 12.5 The Prince George Transit Exchange

The Northern Edge, Prince George's Integrated Community Network, like other Smart Community initiatives, is based on partnerships, including private-sector telecommunications companies Telus and Nortel, educational institutions, and a loose-knit community group. Related to this initiative is the Prince George transit exchange.

In 2001, in partnership with the University of Northern British Columbia, the City of Prince George began developing a municipal transit exchange to allow users to obtain service from providers connected to the exchange. The plan envisioned that a dark fibre and wireless network in the area would connect all public-sector organizations through the exchange. A local loop (the transit exchange) would provide low-cost communications for users, becoming the hub for other Internet service providers.[1] A memorandum of understanding was signed between the City of Prince George, the University of Northern British Columbia, and BCNET (a non-profit society for the development of advanced networks within the province). The agreement, signed on 15 November 2002, would bring advanced technology networks to the north.[2]

Historically, northern and remote communities in Canada have paid much higher costs for information technology than the larger urban centres, while the levels of access have been much lower. The local provision of an advanced Internet infrastructure of this kind would make it possible for high-tech companies and other businesses to operate competitively in the area while providing the benefits of high-speed Internet to other end users in the region.

---

1   City of Prince George and the University of Northern BC, *Transit Exchange – Phase 1*, grant request submitted to the Province of British Columbia, 8 March 2001.
2   City of Prince George, UNBC, BCNET, "City of Prince George, UNBC, and BCNET Sign Agreement on Innovation and Technology for the North," news release, 15 November 2002.

## Citizens and the Net

The Internet does give citizens a handy tool for organizing political associations and communities outside of the established institutions. Such citizen-based networks on the Web, or virtual communities, introduce a new politically influential community into local politics. It is also a community that is unconstrained by the rules imposed by jurisdictional boundaries and territorially based governments. The new technologies have implications for how citizens form political identities, as well as how they perceive and interact with existing structures of government.

The rapid adoption of information technology in homes, cars, businesses, public places, and government is leading toward a reconceptualization of community and its boundaries. As Roger Gibbins notes, "We phone individuals rather than, as in the past, a place, hoping that the person we are calling is 'home.' Home is where the cell is, and not the heart. Newsgroups create virtual communities unbounded by territory ... Simply put, ICTs [information and communication technologies] have the potential to erode, and erode rapidly, the territorial foundations of our lives."[34] Gibbins suggests that the movement toward globalization may simultaneously reinforce connections to local communities at the expense of the nation-state. He argues that with a "secure local base" and ready technological access to the global community, individuals have less need for other territorial communities. Rather, citizen loyalties and identifications will shift toward local communities.[35]

Gibbins states that this might be due to a number of factors, including:

- the off-loading of service delivery on local governments
- the urbanization of Canadian society
- the growing assertiveness of "highly stressed" local governments
- the amalgamation of local governments in the largest urban centres, giving rise to notions of the city-state
- the urban phenomena of immigration and cultural changes
- the social activism at the local level by younger Canadians.[36]

All these developments have been discussed in previous chapters, and the arguments do have a certain resonance with students of community politics. It is possible that citizen identification with local communities may increase at the expense of provinces, as Gibbins suggests. Whether that happens will probably depend on the size, location, and character of the home town. Mohammad Qadeer, however, offers an alternative perspective: "In a society where individuals continually change jobs, homes, places of residence and, even friendships, where the family is no more an enduring group and is often configured and reconfigured, it is unlikely that strong, persistent and resourceful communities will be formed."[37]

In any event, a shift in citizen identification toward the local community would not necessarily be accompanied by reallocations of governmental power. Constitutional and legal authority remains with the higher orders of government, as does control over much-needed sources of revenue. The imperatives of a global economy and domestic structural constraints leave local governments little room to exert any wider influence. This remains the case even though the senior governments negotiate international agreements with economic, social, and environmental fallouts that land on the doorsteps of local governments, which are left to respond as best they can.

Local governments may continue to struggle with their limited political or economic options, but the choices for citizens are certainly changing and, in some cases, expanding. Communities appear to be much more open and fluid than in the past – *open* to both the influences of a barrage of messages from the interconnected world, and *fluid* as people move more rapidly in and out of occupations and become more mobile. In his observations of what he calls *cyber communities,* Anderson suggests that "both human mobility and the growth of communications networks have the effect of reducing the predominance of geography as a force in shaping community. It is still an important factor, but many communities are much more fluid and some are placeless."[38] Citizen-based networks sprang up very quickly at the end of the 1990s and presented the public with a new oppositional forum in politics. Citizens have used the Internet to achieve many political goals. In recent years, the Internet has been used to muster support and organize grassroots environmental campaigns, to fight government decisions or development initiatives that would adversely affect their neighbourhoods and communities, to fight amalgamation, and to lobby for more self-government.

In Canada, a number of active "CitizenNets" have allowed communities of interests to rally around issues. For example, a group of prominent citizens (a number of them based in Toronto) began a local self-government Web site devoted to "the need to increase local self government in Canada and to help local communities achieve more autonomy."[39] One of the animating topics of this group is the concern that the country's largest cities lack authority and financial resources to deal with many of the challenges associated with urban centres. Chronic under-funding and centralized authority have led local government leaders to advocate for more authority. The purpose of this lobby was to pressure provincial and federal governments to give local governments the means to govern themselves in an efficient, effective, and democratic manner. Not all citizen-based networks have this focus. CitizensontheWeb.com, an Ontario-focused group, was set up to champion a number of social justice and environmental issues in opposition to the dominant public- and private-sector elites.[40]

What are the implications of these new networks for local political identity? Political identity is shaped by more than information technology; it is also a reflection of shared territory, history, culture, and economic circumstances. We may not see a shift of political loyalties from one jurisdiction to another. Information technology and increased societal mobility have changed and broadened the type and nature of communities to which any individual might belong. It is possible to be a Winnipegger as well as a Manitoban and a Canadian. The availability of multiple communities – some territorially based and others potentially reaching around the globe via the mass media and the Internet – may inspire political identities that are transient and fluid, readily shifting as circumstances change. Citizens may well gravitate to those governments perceived to have the most power to fulfill an individual's needs or able to attract loyalty by effectively exploiting the power of the mass media. Business people and other professionals who travel regularly, for example, may look to the federal government to ensure a good investment climate and standardization of services. Senior citizens, on the other hand, may be more concerned with the recreational and supplemented social services and convenient forms of public transportation delivered by local governments. Activists may be distrustful of any established government and identify politically with a social movement.

It is not easy to predict the implications of information technology for questions of political identity and community. It is well known that communities of interest can exist outside of a physical territory – Internet-based communities or virtual communities have been formed in cyberspace (see Box 12.6). Yet before the advent of mass media and information technology, many of these communities could be understood and analyzed only within the context of a physical territory. Physical territory could be readily defined and governed by political, social, and economic institutions. Information technology has introduced a new dynamic into the mix. It may well provide citizens – at least those who have access to the technology – with more political choices, access to public information, and influence in shaping political agendas. But others might see the new technologies as little more than tools of the private sector.

## The Private Sector

Mass media ownership is becoming more concentrated, technologies are converging, software giants such as Microsoft are directing the way in which the vast majority of individuals connect and communicate through their Internet browsers, and governments are eagerly seeking partnerships with telecommunications providers and other businesses. None of this is new. The medium might vary, but communications has always been a powerful tool of the marketplace. That said, the scope, pace, intensity, and level at which all this is now happening make it very difficult to regulate and to assess the implications for governance.

Users are unwittingly steered and tracked as they surf the Web. Unwary customers are technologically assisted to make particular consumer choices. Individuals are encouraged to sacrifice privacy for convenience and economy. People's consumer, political, or social preferences are readily tracked, often through the voluntary release of personal information. All these developments suggest a level of private-sector control that was not previously possible and that is very difficult to regulate – assuming governments even wish to do so. Governments often look to the private sector to help provide a number of services to the public. The desire to regulate the activities of the private sector will inevitably be tempered by the recognition that business requires a profit. Increasingly, governments

## 12.6  The Virtual Community of Cassiar

Cassiar, an asbestos mining town, with a population of 2,000 at its peak, was situated in an alpine valley in the far northern reaches of British Columbia. In the early 1950s, Cassiar was founded, and it expanded over the years to become a centre of exploration for the area.[1] In 1992, the company running the mining operation went into bankruptcy, forcing the closure of the town. The infrastructure of the town, mill, and mine was auctioned off.

Former residents Simone Rowlinson and Herb Daub recognized that the community was more than just its physical infrastructure. As a result, Rowlinson began a Web site that Daub took over and expanded, encouraging former Cassiarites to sign in, take a trip down memory lane, contribute their own memories and videos, maintain contact, and keep informed about upcoming reunions. At the July 2001 reunion, 800 people showed up. By this time, the Web site proved to be a lively forum with dozens of hits, messages, and interactions every day.

1  Bill Plumb, "The Making of a Mine – The Early Days of Cassiar," *Mining Magazine*, 1989, reprinted on the Cassiar Web site, http://www.cassiar.ca (accessed 15 November 2003).

are contracting out services that were once considered too important to be left with the private sector. These services include the gathering of public information, which raises obvious important questions about the access to government information (who now owns it?) and the protection of privacy (how secure is it?).

Information technology, then, is a powerful tool in the hands of those who have the economic resources to invest in it. As a result, Vincent Mosco argues that the applications of information technology have served to deepen and extend existing inequalities in society. In particular, he observes that the growing use of information technology by the private sector enhances the power of markets at the expense of those who lack political or economic power.[41]

Mosco and others have expressed concern about the growth of privatization of government activities and services. This trend will serve to restrict even further citizens' access to information vital for informed democratic participation. Without such access, it will be difficult to hold governments and powerful private-sector actors accountable for their activities.

Businesses use communications in a variety of ways that inadvertently or deliberately help to shape local political agendas. Critics such as Mosco argue that new developments in communications are enabling the private sector to extend its influence at the expense of other actors. Others might argue that the reverse could also be the case; that is, private-sector initiative and competition encourage the development of a plurality of new technologies available at low costs, enabling a broad cross-section of the population to engage in civic activities that would have been impossible a generation ago.

Either way, in this era of preoccupation with productivity in the global marketplace, access to information and information technologies is seen essential to local economic development. As noted previously, the Smart Communities initiative heavily emphasized the importance of this force in the survival of local communities. Members of the private sector are influential players in bringing communications technologies, infrastructure, and the mass media (and often the message as well) to communities. With cross-media ownership and integrated communications systems, private-sector interests can find themselves in a powerful position – a position that is difficult for governments to regulate.

Manuel Castells notes that it is important to recognize that the quest for productivity cannot be decoupled from social development if it is to be successful in the long run. "Without social development, without institutional stability, there may still be a diffusion of economic development around the world, but it will be based upon a cost-lowering formula, rather than a productivity-enhancing model. Furthermore, both spirals (the high road to informational productivity, and the low road to economic competitiveness through cost cutting) are cumulative and contagious."[42] The requisite social development will not take place, however, without some regulatory framework. In the era of globalization, this may be difficult to achieve.

## Conclusion

Different actors influence the public agenda in a variety of ways: members of the media act as watchdogs or advocates, governments act as social controllers or service providers, citizens act as decision makers or critics, and businesses act as investors. An examination of how these gatekeepers collect, use, and control the dissemination of public information will tell much about who has influence in local politics.

Information has always played an important role in political interactions. Now that we are well launched into the twenty-first century, though, an examination of communication flows seems to be more salient than ever before. Governments are pressed to respond to demands for greater public consultation and to agendas and forces that are not confined to municipal boundaries. Citizens are expected to grapple with the imperatives of integrated systems, digital networks, interconnected policy communities, complex ecosystems, multifaceted global-local interactions, and conflicting notions about paradoxical trends leading to such peculiar nomenclature as "virtual communities." To devise policy solutions to these challenges, it is important first to understand the actors and variables that affect political processes. A communications analysis that traces the ebb and flow of political information will provide the observer with an additional means to decipher these interactions. On a broader level of analysis, political communications will, no doubt, reflect the same overall distribution of influence noted in other chapters with respect to economic, social, and institutional factors. Access to new forms of communication will do little to change that situation.

Citizen Web-based networks, the media, and other forms of communication, however, do offer alternative sources of information about government actions. As Milner notes, civic literacy is an important prerequisite of a democratic state. Without such knowledge, it is impossible to hold governments accountable. Moreover, these networks will allow individuals and groups to mobilize and express their political interests in a variety of ways through activism, lobbying, or participating in community forums. The possibilities are there. As Vincent Mosco warns, however, one must also keep in mind that much of societal communications reflects the priorities of those who have the means, time, and resources to articulate their preferences.

# Notes

## Part 1

1 Harold Lasswell, *Politics: Who Gets What, When, How* (New York: Meridian Books, 1958).
2 George Francis, "Exploring Selected Issues of Governance in the Grand River Watershed," *Canadian Water Resources Journal* 21, no. 3 (1996): 303.

## Chapter 1: Local Self-Government

1 Henry Milner, "Civic Literacy in Comparative Context: Why Canadians Should Be Concerned," *Policy Matters* 2, no. 2 (2001): 7.
2 Jack Masson, *Alberta's Local Governments and Their Politics* (Edmonton: Pica Pica Press, 1985), 8.
3 James Manor, Mark Robinson, and Gordon White, *Civil Society and Governance: A Concept Paper* (Civil Society and Governance Program Office, University of Sussex, 1999), http://www.ids.ac.uk/ids/civsoc/public.doc (accessed 20 January 2003).
4 Ibid.
5 Mohammad Qadeer, "Communities and Public Welfare," *Policy Options* 16, no. 8 (October 1995): 46.
6 Timothy D. Sisk, ed., *Democracy at the Local Level: International IDEA's Handbook on Participation, Representation, Conflict Management and Governance* (Stockholm, Sweden: The International Institute for Democracy and Electoral Assistance [IDEA], 2001), overview.
7 Ibid.
8 Dilys M. Hill, *Democratic Theory and Local Government* (London: George Allan and Unwin, 1974), 21.
9 George Langrod, "Local Government and Democracy," *Public Administration* 31 (Spring 1953): 25-33, reprinted in *Politics and Government in Urban Canada*, 4th ed., ed. Lionel D. Feldman (Toronto: Methuen, 1981), 3-14; Leo Moulin, "Local Self-Government As a Basis for Democracy: A Further Comment," *Public Administration* 32 (Winter 1954): 433-37, reprinted in *Politics and Government in Urban Canada*, ed. Feldman, 19-24.
10 Keith Panter-Brick, "Local Government and Democracy – A Rejoinder," *Public Administration* 31 (Spring 1953): 344-8, reprinted in *Politics and Government in Urban Canada*, ed. Feldman, 14-19; Moulin, "Local Self-Government As a Basis for Democracy: A Rejoinder," *Public Administration* 32 (Winter 1954): 438-40, reprinted in *Politics and Government in Urban Canada*, ed. Feldman, 24-7.
11 Robert A. Dahl, "The City in the Future of Democracy," *The American Political Science Review* (December 1967): 953-70, reprinted in *Politics and Government in Urban Canada*, ed. Feldman, 39-60.
12 Ibid., 57.
13 Willis D. Hawley and Frederick M. Wirt, eds., *The Search for Community Power*, 2nd ed. (Englewood Cliffs, NJ: Prentice-Hall, 1974).
14 Ibid., 4, 6.
15 Nelson W. Polsby, *Community Power and Political Theory* (New Haven: Yale University Press, 1963), 5.
16 Ibid., 29.
17 Clarence N. Stone, "Systemic Power in Community Decision Making: A Restatement of Stratification Theory," *The American Political Science Review* 74, 4 (1980): 980.

18  Ibid., 982-83.
19  Ibid., 985.
20  Ibid., 988.
21  Ibid., 989.
22  Mickey Lauria, "Reconstructing Urban Regime Theory," in *Reconstructing Urban Regime Theory: Regulating Urban Politics in a Global Economy,* ed. Mickey Lauria (Thousand Oaks, CA: Sage, 1996), 1-2.
23  Ibid., 3-4.
24  Ibid., 8.
25  See, for example, Janine Brodie, "Imagining Democratic Urban Citizenship," in *Democracy, Citizenship and the Global City,* ed. Engin F. Isin (London and New York: Routledge, 2000).
26  See, for example, Warren Magnusson's book, *The Search for Political Space* (Toronto: University of Toronto Press, 1996).
27  Ibid., 68.
28  Neil R. Thomlinson, "Gay Concerns and Local Governments," in *The Politics of the City: A Canadian Perspective,* ed. Timothy L. Thomas (Scarborough, ON: ITP Nelson Canada, 1997), 115.
29  Ibid.
30  Evans, "New Spaces in a Decentralizing Welfare State," 173-89.
31  Ibid, 184.
32  Magnusson, *The Search for Political Space,* 21.

## Chapter 2: Local Democracy and Self-Government

1  See Frank Cassidy and Robert L. Bish, *Indian Government: Its Meaning in Practice* (Lantzville, BC: Oolichan Books, and Halifax, NS: Institute for Research on Public Policy, 1989); and Patricia Marshak et al., eds., *Common Property: The Fishing and Fish-Processing Industries in British Columbia* (Toronto: Methuen, 1987).
2  Paul Tennant, "Delgamuukw and Diplomacy: First Nations and Municipalities in British Columbia," http://www.marh.gov.bc.ca/ABORIGINAL/
3  Ibid.
4  Cassidy and Bish, *Indian Government*, 79.
5  Donald J.H. Higgins, *Local and Urban Politics in Canada* (Toronto: Gage Publishing, 1986), 33-39.
6  Kenneth Grant Crawford, *Canadian Municipal Government* (Toronto: University of Toronto Press, 1954), 21.
7  Adam Shortt, "The Beginning of Municipal Government in Ontario," *Queen's Gazette* 7 (1902): 420.
8  Higgins, *Local and Urban Politics in Canada,* 41.
9  H.W. McCready, ed., *Lord Durham's Mission to Canada, an Abridgement of Lord Durham: A Biography of John George Lambton, First Earl of Durham, by Chester New.* 1929; reprint, Toronto: McClelland and Stewart, 1963), 168.
10  Engin F. Isin, *Cities without Citizens* (Montreal: Black Rose Books, 1992), 156.
11  Ibid., 174.
12  Ibid.
13  Crawford, *Canadian Municipal Government,* 84-85.
14  Ibid., 85.
15  Ibid.
16  James D. Anderson, "The Municipal Government Reform Movement in Western Canada 1880-1920," in *The Usable Urban Past: Planning and Politics in the Modern Canadian City,* ed. Alan F.J. Artibise and Gilbert A. Stelter (Toronto: MacMillan of Canada, 1979), 83.
17  Ibid., 84.
18  John C. Weaver, "The Modern City Realized: Toronto Civic Affairs, 1880-1915," in *The Usable Urban Past,* ed. Artibise and Stelter, 35-72.
19  Ibid.
20  Ibid., 47, 49.

21  Ibid., 51.
22  Susan Wismer, "Sustaining Communities: An Historic Perspective on Women's Involvement in Kitchener-Waterloo," in *The Dynamics of the Dispersed City: Geographic and Planning Perspectives on Waterloo Region*, ed. Pierre Filion, Trudi E. Bunting, and Kevin Curtis (Waterloo, ON: Department of Geography, University of Waterloo, 1996), 358.
23  Linda Trimble, "Politics Where We Live," in *Canadian Metropolitics: Governing Our Cities*, ed. James Lightbody (Toronto: Copp Clark, 1995), 103.
24  Susan Wismer, "Sustaining Communities," 355.
25  Doug Smith, "A Strike with an Elusive Meaning," in *Compass Points: Navigating the 20th Century*, ed. Robert Chodos (Toronto: Between the Lines, Compass Foundation, 1999): 70-72.
26  Robert Chodos, "A Generation That Said NO to Plastics," in *Compass Points: Navigating the 20th Century*, ed. Robert Chodos (Toronto: Between the Lines, Compass Foundation, 1999), 258-60.
27  Higgins, *Local and Urban Politics in Canada*, 250.
28  Donald Gutstein, "Vancouver," in *City Politics in Canada*, ed. Warren Magnusson and Andrew Sancton (Toronto: University of Toronto Press, 1983), 202.
29  Christopher Leo, "City Politics in an Era of Globalization," in *Reconstructing Urban Regime Theory: Regulating Urban Politics in a Global Economy*, ed. Mickey Lauria (Thousand Oaks, CA: Sage, 1996), 90.
30  Ibid.
31  More effective were the special purpose committees on which citizens were invited to sit to advise on local policies governing different aspects of community affairs.
32  Christopher Leo, *The Subordination of the Local State: Development Politics in Edmonton*, Urban Resources 5 (Winnipeg: University of Winnipeg, Institute of Urban Studies, 1995), 23.
33  West Edmonton Mall, home page, http://www.westedmall.com (accessed 27 August 2002).
34  B. Guy Peters, *The Future of Governing: Four Emerging Models* (Lawrence, KS: University Press of Kansas, 1996), 47.
35  John Ralston Saul, *The Unconscious Civilization* (Concord, ON: House of Anansi Press, 1995), 172-73.
36  Michael Hall, Larry McKeown, and Karen Roberts, *Caring Canadians: Highlights from the 2000 National Survey of Giving, Volunteering and Participating* (Ottawa: Statistics Canada, 2001), 33.
37  "Address to the Monday night meeting, January 27, 1992," recorded in Toronto by Protest Boy Records, 1997, cited in Julie-Anne Boudreau, *The Megacity Saga: Democracy and Citizenship in This Global Age* (Montreal: Black Rose Books, 2000), 11.
38  Boudreau, *The Megacity Saga*.
39  Ibid., 2-4.
40  Ibid., 10-12.
41  Ibid., 15.
42  Ibid., 16.
43  Ibid., 164.
44  Ibid., 170.
45  Joe Mavrinac, "Kirkland Lake," in *At the End of the Shift: Mines and Single-Industry Towns in Northern Ontario*, ed. Matt Bray and Ashley Thomson (Toronto: Dundurn Press, 1992), 149-54.
46  "Toronto's Garbage Is Going North," *The Record* (Kitchener-Waterloo), 12 October 2000, A3.
47  "City Kills Adams Mine Deal," *Globe and Mail*, 21 October 2000, A1.
48  John Barber, "Recycled Numbers Still Add Up to a Rubbish Deal," *Globe and Mail*, 21 October 2000, A30.
49  For a more complete discussion of this issue, see Mary Louise McAllister, "Grounding Environmental Policy: Rural and Remote Communities in Canada," in *Canadian Environmental Policy: Context and Cases for a New Century*, ed. Robert Boardman and Debora Van Nijnatten (Toronto: Oxford University Press, 2002).
50  Centre Wellington Citizens Coalition, "Chronology: Centre Wellington Citizens Coalition Attempts to Have Community Input in Decision Making," 18 July 2002, http://plg.uwaterloo.ca/~holt/cwcc/content/chronology.htm (accessed 12 September 2002).

51 Centre Wellington Citizens Coalition, "CWCC: Quotations," 18 July 2002, http://plg.uwaterloo.ca/~holt/cwcc/content/quotes.htm (accessed 12 September 2002).

52 Janine Brodie, "Imagining Democratic Urban Citizenship," in *Democracy, Citizenship and the Global City,* ed. Engin F. Isin (London and New York: Routledge, 2000), 118.

53 Ibid., 119. Robertson's original use of the term *glocal* was in R. Robertson, "Glocalization: Time-Space and Homogeneity-Heterogeneity," in *Global Modernities,* ed. M. Featherstone, S. Lash, and R. Robertson (London: Sage, 1995), 24-44.

54 Naomi Klein, "Will the Social Fabric Tear?" *Globe and Mail,* 18 February 2002, A15.

55 St. Laurence Centre Forum, "Doing Politics Differently: Participatory Budgeting in Toronto," Catalyst Centre 2002 Program Report, www.catalystcentre.ca/orginfo/annrep.htm (accessed 1 February 2004).

56 Brodie, "Imagining Democratic Urban Citizenship," 121-22.

57 Caroline Andrew, "Globalization and Local Action," in *The Politics of the City: A Canadian Perspective,* ed. Timothy L. Thomas (Scarborough, ON: ITP Nelson, 1997), 147-48.

58 Ibid.

59 Isin, *Cities without Citizens,* vii.

## Chapter 3: Avenues of Participation in Local Governance

1 Darin Barney, *Prometheus Wired: The Hope for Democracy in the Age of Network Technology* (Vancouver and Toronto: UBC Press, 2000), 14.

2 "Citizens on the Web News – Toronto," http://www.citizensontheweb.ca/ (accessed 4 June 2003).

3 Paul André Linteau, René Durocher, and Jean-Claude Robert, *Quebec: A History 1867-1929,* trans. Robert Chodos (Toronto: James Lorimer, 1983), 188.

4 A referendum is seen as binding in law, whereas a plebiscite is viewed as non-binding, although this distinction is frequently overlooked.

5 Louise Quesnel, *Public Consultation: A Tool for Democracy* (Toronto: Intergovernmental Committee on Urban and Regional Research, 2000), 49.

6 Ibid., 2.

7 André Carrel, *Citizens' Hall: Making Local Democracy Work* (Toronto: Between the Lines, 2001), 44.

8 Quesnel, *Public Consultation,* 70.

9 Jack Masson, *Alberta's Local Governments and Their Politics* (Edmonton: Pica Pica Press, 1985), 325.

10 Ibid., 343.

11 James Lightbody, "Cities: The Dilemmas on Our Doorsteps," in *Corruption, Character and Conduct: Essays on Canadian Government Ethics,* ed. John W. Langford and Allan Tupper (Toronto: Oxford University Press, 1993), 202, 203.

12 City of Vancouver, "General Voting Information" (20 November 1999 election), http://www.city.vancouver.bc.ca/ctyclerk/election99/votegeninfo.htm (accessed 5 July 2001).

13 Donald J.H. Higgins, *Local and Urban Politics in Canada* (Toronto: Gage Publishing, 1986), 316.

14 Kenneth Grant Crawford, *Canadian Municipal Government* (Toronto: University of Toronto Press, 1954), 57.

15 Masson, *Alberta's Local Governments and Their Politics,* 295.

16 Donald Gutstein, "Vancouver," in *City Politics in Canada,* ed. Warren Magnusson and Andrew Sancton (Toronto: University of Toronto Press, 1983), 196.

17 Ibid.

18 Canadian Broadcasting Corporation, "Real-Life Da Vinci Leads Sweep in Vancouver Elections," 18 November 2002, http://www.cbc.ca/stories/2002/11/17/vcr_elxn021117 (accessed 18 November 2002).

19 Katherine A. Graham, Susan D. Phillips, with Alan M. Maslove, *Urban Governance in Canada: Representation, Resources and Restructuring* (Toronto: Harcourt Brace, 1998), 109.

20 Masson, *Alberta's Local Governments and Their Politics,* 296. See also James Lightbody, "Edmonton," in *City Politics in Canada,* ed. Warren Magnusson and Andrew Sancton (Toronto: University of Toronto Press, 1985), 260.

21  Masson, *Alberta's Local Governments and Their Politics,* 298.

22  Lightbody, "Edmonton," 267-68.

23  Higgins, *Local and Urban Politics in Canada,* 338.

24  Ibid.

25  Timothy Lloyd Thomas, *A City with a Difference: The Rise and Fall of the Montreal Citizens' Movement* (Montreal: Véhicule Press, 1997), 24.

26  Karen Herland, *People, Potholes and City Politics* (Montreal and New York: Black Rose Books, 1992), 35-39.

27  See, for example, British Columbia's Municipal Act, RSBC 1979, Chapter 290, Consolidated 5 December 1994 (Victoria: Queen's Printer for British Columbia, 1995), which lays out the legislative requirements.

28  David Siegel, "Small Town Canada," in *Corruption, Character and Conduct: Essays on Canadian Government Ethics,* ed. John W. Langford and Allan Tupper (Toronto: Oxford University Press, 1993), 220-21.

29  Graham, Phillips, and Maslove, *Urban Governance in Canada,* 156.

30  Chantal Maillé, "Gender Concerns of City Life," in *The Politics of the City: A Canadian Perspective,* ed. Timothy L. Thomas (Scarborough, ON: ITP Nelson, 1997), 109.

31  Linda Trimble, "Politics Where We Live," in *Canadian Metropolitics,* ed. James Lightbody (Toronto: Copp Clark, 1995), 110.

32  See Yasmeen Abu-Laban, "Ethnic Politics in a Globalizing Metropolis: The Case of Vancouver," in *The Politics of the City,* ed. Thomas.

33  City of Sherbrooke Transition Committee, 2002, pamphlet #440.

34  Ben Meisner, "The Issue That Won't Go Away," *Prince George Citizen,* 13 November 2002, 4; Dave Parlson, "Money Matters," *Prince George Citizen,* 16 November 2002, 5; Gordon Hoekstra, "Four New Faces on Council," *Prince George Citizen,* 18 November 2002, 1.

35  Gordon Hoekstra, "Major Defends Political Spending," *Prince George Citizen,* 13 November 2002, 1.

36  Lightbody, "Cities: The Dilemmas on Our Doorsteps," 199.

37  Clarence N. Stone, "Systemic Power in Community Decision Making: A Restatement of Stratification Theory," *The American Political Science Review* 74, no. 4 (1980): 988.

38  Frances Bula, "Vancouver Shifts Business Taxes to Homeowners," *Vancouver Sun,* 25 April 2003.

39  Anthony Reinhart, "City Councillors', Mayor's Salaries Create Only Wee Ripple of Interest," *The Record* (Kitchener-Waterloo), 7 November 2002.

40  Federation of Canadian Municipalities, *Quality of Life in Canadian Communities,* second report of *The FCM Quality of Life Reporting System* (March 2001), http://www.fcm.ca/english/communications/qol2001.pdf (accessed 4 June 2003), Table 8.1, 100.

41  Timothy D. Sisk, ed., *Democracy at the Local Level: International IDEA's Handbook on Participation, Representation, Conflict Management and Governance* (Stockholm, Sweden: The International Institute for Democracy and Electoral Assistance [IDEA], 2001), 146.

42  Eudora Pendergrast and John Farrow, *Community Councils and Neighbourhood Committees: Lessons for Our Communities from around the World* (Toronto: Canadian Urban Institute, 1997), 1.

43  Ibid., 29.

44  Townshippers' Association, *Townships Crossroads,* 23, no. 3 (2002); Townshippers' Association, *Annual Report 2001-2002: The Strategic Plan in Action* (Lennoxville, PQ, 2002).

45  Division des communications Ville de Sherbrooke, *Info Sherbrookois: Municipal Information Bulletin* 15, no. 4 (September 2002).

46  Metropolitan Action Committee on Violence Against Women and Children (METRAC), "Welcome to METRAC," http://www.metrac.org/ (accessed 27 September 2002).

47  City of Toronto, "Breaking the Cycle of Violence," www.breakingthecycle.ca (9 February 2004).

48  Government of Quebec, "A egalité pour décider – le gouvernement du Québec soutient 42 organismes pour inciter les femmes à investir les lieux de pouvoir," http://communiques.gouv.qc.ca/gouvqc/communiques/GPQF/Juillet2002/03/c2295.html (accessed 28 September 2002).

49 Susan McFarlane and Robert Roach, "Strings Attached: Non-Profits and Their Relationship with Government," *Canada West Foundation: Alternative Service Delivery Project* 4 (September 1999): 4.
50 Ibid., 10.
51 Sisk, *Democracy at the Local Level,* 140.
52 B. Guy Peters, *The Future of Governing: Four Emerging Models* (Lawrence, KS: University Press of Kansas, 1996), 69.
53 Ibid., 69.
54 Ibid., 69.
55 Ibid., 57.
56 Stephen Owen, "Land Use Planning in the Nineties: CORE Lessons," *Environments* 25, nos. 2, 3 (1998): 23.

## Chapter 4: The Evolution of Provincial-Local Relations and Municipal Government

1 New Brunswick became a province separate from Nova Scotia in 1784.
2 H.J. Whalan, *The Development of Local Government in New Brunswick* (Fredericton, NB: University of New Brunswick, 1963), 12-13.
3 Ibid., 22.
4 Ibid., 23.
5 J.H. Donald Higgins, *Local and Urban Politics in Canada* (Toronto: Gage, 1986), 40.
6 Ibid., 43.
7 Ibid., 35.
8 Ibid.
9 Valerie A. Summers, "Newfoundland and Labrador: Resource Politics and Regime Change in the Federal Era, 1949-1991," in *The Provincial State,* ed. Keith Brownsey and Michael Howlett (Toronto: Copp Clark Pitman, 1992), 11.
10 Peter G. Boswell, "Municipal Renewal in Newfoundland: A Tradition of Cautious Evolution" (paper presented at the annual meeting of the Canadian Political Science Association, Laval University, Laval, PQ, 28 May 2001), 1.
11 Townshippers' Association, *Townships Crossroads* 23, no. 4 (2002): 12.
12 John A. Dickinson and Brian Young, *A Short History of Quebec,* 2nd ed. (1993; reprint Montreal and Kingston: McGill-Queen's University Press, 2000), 110-11, 124.
13 Ibid.
14 Andrew Sancton, "Montreal," in *City Politics in Canada,* ed. Warren Magnusson and Andrew Sancton (Toronto: University of Toronto Press, 1983), 61.
15 Ibid.
16 Dickinson and Young, *A Short History of Quebec,* 195, 197.
17 Sancton, "Montreal," 65.
18 Ibid., 63.
19 Karen Herland, *People, Potholes and City Politics* (Montreal and New York: Black Rose Books, 1992), 7-9.
20 Sherbrooke Historical Society in Cooperation with the University of Sherbrooke, *Sherbrooke 1802-2002: Two Centuries of History,* CD-ROM (Sherbrooke: Sherbrooke Historical Society, 2002).
21 Higgins, *Local and Urban Politics in Canada,* 46-47.
22 John Mitchell, *The Settlement of York County* (Toronto: Municipal Corporation of the County of York, 1952), n.p.
23 Kenneth Grant Crawford, *Canadian Municipal Government* (Toronto: University of Toronto Press, 1954), 32.
24 Alan F.J. Artibise, "Continuity and Change: Elites and Prairie Urban Development, 1914-1950," in *The Usable Urban Past,* ed. Alan F.J. Artibise and Gilbert A. Stelter (Toronto: Macmillan, 1979), 130.
25 Ibid., 131.
26 Ibid., 136.

27  James D. Anderson, "The Municipal Government Reform Movement in Western Canada 1880-1920," in *The Usable Urban Past*, ed. Artibise and Stelter, 84.
28  Higgins, *Local and Urban Politics in Canada*, 49-51.
29  City of Winnipeg, "Historical Profile of Winnipeg," http://www.winnipeg.ca/interhom/about_winnipeg/profile/historical_profile.stm (9 February 2004).
30  Higgins, *Local and Urban Politics in Canada*, 52-3.
31  Ibid., 213.
32  Christopher Dunn and David Laycock, "Saskatchewan: Innovation and Competition in the Agricultural Heartland," in *The Provincial State*, ed. Brownsey and Howlett, 311.
33  S.M. Lipset, *Agrarian Socialism*, 3rd ed. (Berkeley, CA: University of California Press, 1971), 250-51.
34  Ibid., 251-52.
35  Ibid., 11.
36  Jack Masson with Edward C. LeSage Jr., *Alberta's Local Governments: Politics and Democracy* (Edmonton: University of Alberta Press, 1994), 101.
37  Higgins, *Local and Urban Politics in Canada*, 54-56.
38  Jack Masson, *Alberta's Local Governments and Their Politics* (Edmonton: Pica Pica Press, 1985), 85; Masson and LeSage, *Alberta's Local Governments*, 103.
39  Masson, *Alberta's Local Governments and Their Politics*, 65.
40  Ibid., 65, 93, 94.
41  Barry M. Gough, "The Character of the British Columbia Frontier," in *A History of British Columbia: Selected Readings*, ed. Patricia E. Roy (Toronto: Copp Clark Pitman, 1989), 12.
42  Robin A. Fisher, "Gold Miners and Settlers," in *A History of British Columbia*, ed. Roy, 25.
43  Assertion by Sir Edward Bulwer Lytton, then Secretary of State for the Colonies, in Fisher, "Gold Miners and Settlers," 17.
44  Higgins, *Local and Urban Politics in Canada*, 59.
45  Ibid.
46  City of Dawson, "Dawson City," Yukon Web home page, http://www.yukonweb.com/community/dawson/ (accessed 26 July 2001).

### Chapter 5: Municipal Restructuring

1  See s. 92A of the Constitution Act, 1867. See also Part VI, s. 50 amendment to the Constitution Act, 1867 in the Constitution Act, 1982. In the case of the northern territories, the federal government was assigned jurisdiction over local affairs.
2  Terry Christensen, *Local Politics: Governing at the Grassroots* (Belmont, CA: Wadsworth Publishing, 1994), 69.
3  Ibid., 86.
4  States may also pre-empt or overrule local government actions.
5  John Sewell and Advisory Committee, *Local Self Government Bulletin*, 20 (October 2001), www.localgovernment.ca.
6  Caroline Andrew, "Globalization and Local Action," in *The Politics of the City: A Canadian Perspective*, ed. Timothy L. Thomas (Scarborough, ON: ITP Nelson, 1997), 139.
7  Peter Woolstencroft, "Education Policies: Challenges and Controversies," in *Urban Policy Issues*, ed. Edmund P. Fowler and David Siegel, 276-94 (Don Mills, ON: Oxford University Press, 2001).
8  J.H. Donald Higgins, *Local and Urban Politics in Canada* (Toronto: Gage, 1986), 213.
9  Ibid., 193.
10  Ibid.
11  Ibid., 178.
12  Woolstencroft, "Education Policies," 279.

13  Newfoundland and Labrador, "Premier Tobin Announces Referendum on Education Reform," news release, 31 July 1997; Newfoundland and Labrador, "September 2, 1997 Plebiscite Official Results," news release, 9 September 1997.

14  Higgins, *Local and Urban Politics in Canada,* 186-87; Woolstencroft, "Education Policies," 279.

15  Woolstencroft, "Education Policies," 279.

16  Higgins, *Local and Urban Politics in Canada,* 178.

17  C. Richard Tindal and Susan Nobes Tindal, *Local Government in Canada,* 4th ed. (Toronto: McGraw-Hill Ryerson, 1995), 142.

18  Ibid., 16.

19  Peter G. Boswell, "Municipal Renewal in Newfoundland: A Tradition of Cautious Evolution" (paper presented at the annual meeting of the Canadian Political Science Association, Laval University, Laval, PQ, 28 May 2001), 4.

20  Government of Newfoundland and Labrador, Executive Council, "Strategic Social Plan Funding to Be Continued," Newfoundland and Labrador Information Service news release 24 (22 March 2001).

21  Government of Newfoundland and Labrador, "Stronger Communities: A Stronger Province," *Final Report on the Renewal Strategy for Jobs and Growth: Securing Our Future Together* (March 2001), Section 8.

22  Government of Newfoundland and Labrador, Department of Provincial and Municipal Affairs, http://www.gov.nf.ca/mpa; Government of Newfoundland and Labrador, news releases issued by Communications and Consultation Branch, Executive Council, http://www.gov.nf.ca/releases/default.htm. See also Government of Newfoundland and Labrador, Chapter U-8, An Act To Consolidate and Revise the Law with Respect to Urban and Rural Planning in the Province (assented to 12 May 2000) (St. John's, NF: Queen's Printer, 2003).

23  Boswell, "Municipal Renewal in Newfoundland," 17-18.

24  Ibid., 19.

25  Higgins, *Local and Urban Politics in Canada,* 184.

26  Ibid., 184-85.

27  Government of New Brunswick, "A Vision for Local Governance in New Brunswick: Report of the Minister's Round Table on Local Governance," June 2001, http://www.gnb.ca/0009/0361/0005/index.html.

28  New Brunswick Department of Environment and Local Government, "Government Responds to Report of Round Table on Local Governance (01/10/11)," news release, 11 October 2001.

29  Government of New Brunswick, Department of Environment and Local Government, "Response to Local Governance and Regional Collaboration report (03/04/08)," news release (8 April 2003).

30  Higgins, *Local and Urban Politics in Canada,* 181-83.

31  Government of Nova Scotia, Service Nova Scotia and Municipal Relations, *Local Government Resource Handbook,* 20 October 2000, section 1.3, p. 1, http://www.gov.ns.ca/snsmr/muns/manuals/PDF/LGRH/LocalGovernmentResourceHandbook_1.3.pdf (accessed 10 February 2004).

32  Government of Nova Scotia, Service Nova Scotia and Municipal Relations, "Municipal Government in Nova Scotia," http://www.gov.ns.ca/snsmr/muns/info/history/MUNSTRUC.stm#E66E2, updated 27 September 2000 (accessed 10 February 2004).

33  Andrew Sancton, "Metropolitan and Regional Governance," in *Urban Policy Issues: Canadian Perspectives,* ed. Edmund P. Fowler and David Siegel (Don Mills, ON: Oxford University Press, 2001), 64.

34  Government of Nova Scotia, Service Nova Scotia and Municipal Relations, "Municipal Government Act: Progressive Powers for Municipal Governments, Introductory Guide," February 1999, http://www.gov.ns.ca/snsmr/muns/legal/mga/infobltn/ntrogide.stm (accessed 4 October 2002).

35  The Union of Nova Scotia Municipalities and Nova Scotia Housing and Municipal Affairs, *Municipal-Provincial Review of Roles and Responsibilities,* 16 June 1999.

36  Ibid.

37  Service Nova Scotia and Municipal Relations, "Proposal to Address Municipal Inequities," news release, 27 February 2001.

38  David A. Milne, "Politics in a Beleaguered Garden," in *The Provincial State,* ed. Keith Brownsey and Michael Howlett (Toronto: Copp Clark Pitman, 1992), 32-34, 39.

39  David A. Milne, "Politics in a Beleaguered Garden," 48.

40  Statistics Canada, "2001 Community Profiles," http://www.statcan/English/ (accessed 30 December 2003).

41  Louise Quesnel, "Municipal Reorganisation in Quebec," *Canadian Journal of Regional Science* (Spring 2000): 117.

42  Ibid., 119.

43  Andrew Sancton, "Montreal," in *City Politics in Canada,* ed. Warren Magnusson and Andrew Sancton (Toronto: University of Toronto Press, 1983), 80.

44  Higgins, *Local and Urban Politics in Canada,* 189.

45  Ibid., 191.

46  Government of Quebec, "Political Institutions," 2 November 2001, http://www/gouv.qc.ca/Vision/Institutions/InstitutionsPolitiques_en.html#Kativik%20Regional%20Government (accessed 10 February 2004).

47  Quesnel, "Municipal Reorganisation in Quebec," 120.

48  Ibid., 127.

49  Ibid., 117.

50  Elizabeth Thompson, "In Merger's Rough Wake," *Montreal Gazette,* 14 February 2001, A1.

51  Quebec Liberal Party, home page, http://www.plq.org/english/index.html (accessed 25 June 2003).

52  Higgins, *Local and Urban Politics in Canada,* 200.

53  Robert J. Williams and Terrence J. Downey, "Reforming Rural Ontario," *Canadian Public Administration* 42, no. 2 (Summer 1999): 66-67.

54  Ibid., 68.

55  Stewart Fyfe and Ron M. Farrow, *Waterloo Area Local Government Review: Report of Findings and Recommendations* (Toronto: Ontario Department of Municipal Affairs, 1970), 185.

56  Ontario Ministry of Municipal Affairs and Housing, "Restructuring Newsflash," news release, 9 August 2001.

57  Tindal and Tindal, *Local Government in Canada,* 91.

58  Higgins, *Local and Urban Politics in Canada,* 195.

59  Warren Magnusson, "Toronto," in *City Politics in Canada,* ed. Magnusson and Sancton, 111.

60  Meyer Brownstone and T.J. Plunkett, *Metropolitan Winnipeg: Politics and Reform of Local Government* (Berkeley: University of California Press, 1983), 174.

61  See, for example, Julie-Anne Boudreau, *The Megacity Saga: Democracy and Citizenship in This Global Age* (Montreal: Black Rose Books, 2000).

62  Government of Ontario, Ministry of Municipal Affairs, *New Directions: A New Municipal Act for Ontario, August 2001* (Toronto: Queen's Printer, 2001), http://www.mah.gov.on.ca/userfiles/page_attachments/3074204_municipalact0801.pdf, p. 11.

63  Sewell and Committee, *Local Self Government Bulletin* 20.

64  Ibid.

65  James Lightbody, *The Actors in Metropolitan Reform: The Winnipeg Experience,* Occasional Paper 7 (Edmonton: University of Alberta, 1979), 4.

66  Brownstone and Plunkett, *Metropolitan Winnipeg,* 174.

67  Paul G. Thomas, "Diagnosing the Health of Civic Democracy: 25 Years of Citizen Involvement with City Hall," in *The State of Unicity – 25 Years Later: Conference Proceedings (October 3-4 1997),* ed. Nancy Klos (Winnipeg: Institute of Urban Studies, 1998), 47.

68  Matthew J. Kiernan and David C. Walker, "Winnipeg," in *City Politics in Canada,* ed. Magnusson and Sancton, 232-33.

69  Higgins, *Local and Urban Politics in Canada,* 208-10.

70  Lightbody, "The Actors in Metropolitan Reform," 4.

71 Andrew Sancton, "Why Unicity Matters: An Outsider's View," in *The State of Unicity – 25 Years Later,* ed. Klos, 4.

72 Higgins, *Local and Urban Politics in Canada,* 210-11.

73 City of Winnipeg, "History of City Government," http://www.winnipeg.ca/interhom/about_winnipeg/ profile/city_government.stm (accessed 19 December 2003).

74 Tindal and Tindal, *Local Government in Canada,* 111; see also pages 105-11.

75 Sancton, "Why Unicity Matters: An Outsider's View," 5.

76 Ibid., 9.

77 City of Winnipeg, "Plan Winnipeg 2020 Vision," www.winnipeg.ca/interhom/about_winnipeg/inside/ plan_winnipeg/default.stm (accessed 19 December 2003).

78 Association of Manitoba Municipalities (AMM), "Submission to the Capital Region Review," January 1999.

79 Government of Manitoba, "Regional Planning Advisory Committee Terms of Reference," http://www.gov. mb.ca/ia/capreg/rpac (accessed 30 December 2003).

80 Government of Manitoba, "A Partnership for the Future: Putting the Pieces Together in the Manitoba Capital Region, October 2003," http://www.gov.mb.ca/ia/capreg/reports_doc/reports/recent/2003finalrpt/ index.html (accessed 30 December 2003).

81 Association of Manitoba Municipalities (AMM), "Submission to the Capital Region Review," January 1999.

82 Manitoba Department of Intergovernmental Affairs, "Programs and Services: Community Choices," http:// www.gov.mb.ca/ia/programs/community_choices.html (accessed 19 July 2001).

83 Richard C. Rounds, "Rural Consolidation of Municipal Governments in Canada," in *The State of Unicity – 25 Years Later,* ed. Klos, 73.

84 Peter Diamant, "Unicity: Bureaucratic Success, Political Nightmare," in *The State of Unicity – 25 Years Later,* ed. Klos, 23.

85 Government of Manitoba, "City of Winnipeg Charter Introduced in Legislature," news release, 20 June 2002.

86 Rounds, "Rural Consolidation of Municipal Governments in Canada," 75.

87 Saskatchewan Urban Municipalities Association (SUMA), *Urban Voice: The Monthly Newsletter of the Saskatchewan Urban Municipalities Association* (July/August 2000): n.p.

88 Government of Saskatchewan, "Saskatchewan Facts and Figures," http://www.gov.sk.ca/aboutsask/facts/ (accessed 19 July 2001).

89 Government of Saskatchewan, Municipal Affairs and Housing, "Municipalities Today," December 2001, http://www.municipal.gov.sk.ca/PDFs/Municipalities_Today_December_2001.pdf (accessed 2 March 2002; page now discontinued).

90 Government Relations and Aboriginal Affairs Municipal Relations Division Saskatchewan, "The Cities Act – Key Features – Principles and Purposes of the Act," 20 May 2003, http://www.municipal.gov.sk.ca/mrd/ ctyprincpurps.shtml (accessed 2 July 2003).

91 Jack Masson, *Alberta's Local Governments and Their Politics* (Edmonton: Pica Pica Press, 1985), 89.

92 Katherine A. Graham, Susan D. Phillips, with Alan M. Maslove, *Urban Governance in Canada: Representation, Resources and Restructuring* (Toronto: Harcourt Brace, 1998), 176.

93 Ibid., 177.

94 Alberta Urban Municipalities Association, "Discussion Paper: Municipal Government Act Amendments," http://www.munilink.net/policy/default.asp (accessed June 2001).

95 Alberta Urban Municipalities Association, "Bigger Property Tax Cut Needed," news release, 24 April 2001.

96 Alberta Urban Municipalities Association, "Municipal Fiscal Capacity, Autonomy, and Accountability: Presentation to the Standing Policy Committee on Agriculture and Municipal Affairs," http://www.munilink. net/policy/default.asp#discussion (accessed 6 January 2004). Quotation from Alberta Urban Municipalities Association, media release, 24 November 2003.

97 Alberta Urban Municipalities Association, "Municipal Fiscal Capacity, Autonomy, and Accountability: Presentation to the Standing Policy Committee on Agriculture and Municipal Affairs," http://www.munilink.net/policy/default.asp#discussion (accessed 6 January 2004).

98 Higgins, *Local and Urban Politics in Canada,* 219.

99 Gerald Hodge and Ira M. Robinson, *Planning Canadian Regions* (Vancouver and Toronto: UBC Press, 2001), 335.

100 British Columbia Home Page, "BC STATs: 2001 Census Profiles of BC Regional Districts," http://www.bcstats.gov.bc.ca/data/cen01/profiles/csd_txt.htm (accessed 10 February 2004).

101 British Columbia Ministry of Municipal Affairs, "Managing Changes to Local Government Structure in British Columbia: A Review and Program Guide," October 2000, http://www.mcaws.gov.bc.ca/gov_structure/structure/CHANGES/changes.pdf (accessed 6 January 2004), p. 11.

102 Government of British Columbia, Bill 31-1998, Local Government Statutes Amendment Act, 1998, 3rd session, 36th Parliament, third reading, http://www.legis.gov.bc.ca/1998-99/3rd_read/gov31-3.htm.

103 Community Charter Council Act, SBC 2001, ch. 5, http://www.qp.gov.bc.ca/statreg/stat/C/01035_01.htm.

104 Ibid.

105 Government of Yukon, "New Municipal Act Provides for More Local Control," news release 252, 17 November 1998.

106 Government of Yukon, "Yukon Facts," March 2001, http://www.gov.yk.ca/facts (accessed 26 July 2001).

107 Government of Yukon, "Yukon Facts," http://www.gov.yk.ca/facts/#POPULATION, updated 30 September 2003 (accessed 6 January 2004).

108 Yukon Department of Community Services, "Message from the Hon. Pam Buckway," public letter on Web page, 27 March 2002, http://www.gov.yk.ca/depts/community/general/minister.html (accessed 14 October 2002; letter has since been replaced).

109 Ibid.

110 Government of Northwest Territories, "Facts about the NWT," July 2000, http://www.gov.nt.ca/research/facts/index.html (accessed 6 July 2001).

111 Tindal and Tindal, *Local Government in Canada,* 39.

112 Government of Northwest Territories, Municipal and Community Affairs and the Canadian Rural Partnership pilot project, "More Than Dogs, Ditches and Dumps, http://www.maca.gov.nt.ca/dogs-ditches-dumps/index.html (accessed 26 July 2001).

113 Government of Northwest Territories, NWT Association of Municipalities and Ministry of Community and Municipal Affairs, *Empowerment through Community Government Legislation: Report of the Review Committee on Phase 2 of the Municipal Legislation Review Western NWT* (1998).

114 Ibid., 2.

115 Northwest Territories Municipal and Community Affairs, "Building Communities," October 2002, www.maca.gov.nt.ca/inits/building_communities.html (accessed 6 January 2004).

116 "Nunavut" means "Our Land" in Inuktitut.

117 Government of Nunavut, "Nunavut Communities," 2000, http://www.gov.nu.ca/communities.htm (accessed 6 January 2004).

118 Government of Nunavut "The Road to Nunavut: A Chronological History," 2000, http://www.gov.nu.ca/road.htm (accessed 6 January 2004).

119 Government of Nunavut, "Nunavut: A New Government, a New Vision," 2000, http://www.gov.nu.ca/flag.htm (6 January 2004).

120 Government of Nunavut, "Department of Community Government and Transportation," 2000, http://www.gov.nu.ca/Nunavut/English/departments/CGT/ (accessed 6 January 2004).

121 Stéphane Dion (Hon.) President of the Privy Council and Minister of Intergovernmental Affairs, "Municipalities and the Federal Government: Notes from an Address" (paper presented at the annual general meeting of the Federation of Canadian Municipalities, Banff, AB, 26 May 2001).

22 André Carrel, *Citizens' Hall: Making Local Democracy Work* (Toronto: Between the Lines, 2001), appendix D.

## Chapter 6: Contemporary Intergovernmental Relations

1  J.H. Donald Higgins, *Local and Urban Politics in Canada* (Toronto: Gage, 1986), 77.

2  Kenneth Grant Crawford, *Canadian Municipal Government* (Toronto: University of Toronto Press, 1954), 358.

3  Enid Slack, "Intergovernmental Fiscal Relations and Canadian Municipalities: Current Situation and Prospects Report to the Federation of Canadian Municipalities" (report to the Federation of Canadian Municipalities, 8 May 2002), http://www.fcm.ca/english/ (accessed 28 October 2002).

4  City of Prince George, "Softwood Lumber," media release, 22 January 2003, www.city.pg.bc.ca/pages/media2003 (accessed 6 January 2004).

5  Higgins, *Local and Urban Politics in Canada*, 106-8.

6  Christopher Leo, "The State in the City," in *Canadian Metropolitics: Governing Our Cities*, ed. James Lightbody (Toronto: Copp Clark, 1995), 31.

7  See, for example, Barbara Wake Carroll, "Housing Policy in the New Millennium," in *Urban Policy Issues: Canadian Perspectives*, ed. Edmond P. Fowler and David Siegel (Don Mills, ON: Oxford University Press, 2001).

8  Stéphane Dion (Hon.), President of the Privy Council and Minister of Intergovernmental Affairs, "Municipalities and the Federal Government: Notes for an Address" (paper presented at the annual general meeting of the Federation of Canadian Municipalities, Banff, AB, 26 May 2001).

9  Higgins, *Local and Urban Politics in Canada*, 112.

10  Dion, "Municipalities and the Federal Government."

11  Thomas Axworthy, "We Must Shore up Our Cities," *Globe and Mail*, 4 October 2001, A19.

12  Casey G. Vander Ploeg, *Big City Revenue Sources: A Canada-U.S. Comparison of Municipal Tax Tools and Revenue Levers* (Canada West Foundation, 2002), http://www.cwf.ca (accessed 27 October 2002).

13  Axworthy, "We Must Shore up Our Cities."

14  Slack, "Intergovernmental Fiscal Relations and Canadian Municipalities."

15  Christopher Leo, "Regional Growth Management Regime: The Case of Portland Oregon," *Journal of Urban Affairs* 20 (1998): 389.

16  Canada, Office of the Prime Minister, Speech from the Throne to Open the Third Session of the Thirty-Seventh Parliament of Canada, 2 February 2004, http://pm.gc.ca/eng/sft-ddt.asp (accessed 13 February 2004), 11-12.

17  Canadian Environmental Law Association, "Anti-Pesticide By-Law Challenged at Supreme Court," news release, 6 December 2000.

18  Supreme Court of Canada, *114957 Canada Ltée (Spraytech, Société d'arrosage) v. Hudson (Town)* [2001], SCC 40, cited in Jerry DeMarco, "Overview of the Hudson Decision" (paper presented at the FCM Big City Mayors' Caucus, 21 October 2001).

19  Government of Saskatchewan, Government Relations and Aboriginal Affairs, "Understanding Municipal Government in Saskatchewan 2003," http://www.municipal.gov.sk.ca/mrd/tocundrmungov.shtml (accessed 8 January 2004).

20  Federation of Canadian Municipalities, "About FCM, Milestones," http://www.fcm.ca/english (accessed 28 October 2002).

21  Federation of Canadian Municipalities, "Municipal Questions Respecting Trade Agreements," 5 November 2001, http://www.fcm.ca/english/index.html (accessed 21 November 2001).

22  Higgins, *Local and Urban Politics in Canada*, 105.

23  Ibid.

24  Federation of Canadian Municipalities, "Milestones: Commanding National Influence: Annual Report 2000-2001," http://www.fcm.ca/english/ (accessed 27 October 2002).

25  Ontario, Minister of Municipal Affairs and Housing, "Guide to Social Housing Reform," 12 October 2000, http://www.mah.gov.on.ca/business/SHT/report_ext-e.pdf (accessed 27 October 2002; page now discontinued).

26  Enid Slack, "The Road to Financial Self Sufficiency for Toronto," in *Toronto: Considering Self Government*, ed. Mary W. Rowe (Owen Sound, ON: Ginger Press, 2000), 58.

27 Ibid., 58-59.
28 Association of Manitoba Municipalities (AMM), "2001 Presentation to Provincial Cabinet," http://www. amm.mb.ca/issues.html (accessed 20 July 2001; page now discontinued).
29 Katherine A. Graham, Susan D. Phillips, with Alan M. Maslove, *Urban Governance in Canada: Representation, Resources and Restructuring* (Toronto: Harcourt Brace, 1998), 271.
30 Ibid.
31 Slack, "Intergovernmental Fiscal Relations and Canadian Municipalities."
32 Saskatchewan Urban Municipalities Association (SUMA), *Urban Voice: The Monthly Newsletter of the Saskatchewan Urban Municipalities Association* 6, no. 9 (November 2001): 1. See also Government of Saskatchewan, "Urban Revenue Sharing Grants," http://www.municipal.gov.sk.ca/municipalities/index.shtml (accessed 19 July 2001; page now discontinued).
33 Saskatchewan Urban Municipalities Association (SUMA), *Urban Voice: The Monthly Newsletter of the Saskatchewan Urban Municipalities Association* (April 2001) and (February 2002) issues.
34 Saskatchewan Urban Municipalities Association (SUMA), "Refueling the Oars Debate," *Urban Voice: The Monthly Newsletter of the Saskatchewan Urban Municipalities Association* 8, no. 4 (2003): 1.
35 Slack, "Intergovernmental Fiscal Relations and Canadian Municipalities."
36 Ibid.
37 James Lightbody, "A New Perspective on Clothing the Emperor: Canadian Metropolitan Form, Function and Frontiers," *Canadian Public Administration,* 40, no. 3 (1997): 438.
38 Ibid., 439.
39 Statistics Canada, "2001 Community Profiles," http://www.statcan.ca (accessed 6 January 2004).
40 Jean Perrault, "The 2003 Budget," *Info Sherbrookois* 15, no. 7 (2002): 2.
41 Lightbody, "A New Perspective on Clothing the Emperor," 446.
42 Ibid., 447-48.
43 Ibid., 450.
44 Terrence J. Downey and Robert J. Williams, "Provincial Agendas, Local Responses: The 'Common Sense' Restructuring of Ontario's Municipal Government," *Canadian Public Administration* 41, no. 2 (1998): 235.
45 Ibid., 231.
46 Andrew Sancton, "Metropolitan and Regional Governance," in *Urban Policy Issues: Canadian Perspectives,* ed. Edmund P. Fowler and David Siegel (Don Mills, ON: Oxford University Press, 2001), 66-67.
47 James Lightbody, "Canada's Seraglio Cities: Political Barriers to Regional Governance," *Canadian Journal of Sociology* 24 (1999): 175-91.
48 Lynne Woolstencroft, Mayor, City of Waterloo, personal communication to author, 16 November 2001.
49 Dion, "Municipalities and the Federal Government."
50 John Sewell, "The City Status of Toronto," in *Toronto: Considering Self Government,* ed. Rowe, 71-72.
51 Canada, House of Commons, *Think Rural: Report of the Standing Committee on Natural Resources* (Ottawa: Canada Communication Group, 1997), 2.
52 David Baxter and Andrew Ramolo, "Resource Dependency: The Spatial Origins of British Columbia's Economic Base," *Urban Futures Institute Report* 55 (2002): 21.
53 Ibid.
54 Canada, House of Commons, *Think Rural,* 3, citing the Federation of Canadian Municipalities.
55 Lightbody, "Canada's Seraglio Cities," 189.
56 Ibid.

### Chapter 7: Core and Peripheries to Networked Societies

1 Attributed to Arthur Lower, historian (1959); Robert M. Hamilton and Dorothy Shields, *The Dictionary of Canadian Quotations and Phrases* (Toronto: McClelland and Stewart, 1979).
2 Lewis Mumford, *The Culture of Cities* (1938; reprint New York: Harcourt Brace Jovanovich, 1970), 367.

3 George N. Hood, *Against the Flow: Rafferty-Alameda and the Politics of the Environment* (Saskatoon, SK: Fifth House Publisher, 1994), 4-5.

4 Hugh Mellon, "New Brunswick: The Politics of Reform," in *The Provincial State: Politics in Canada's Provinces and Territories,* ed. Keith Brownsey and Michael Howlett (Toronto: Copp Clark Pitman, 1992), 84.

5 John A. Dickinson and Brian Young, *A Short History of Quebec,* 2nd ed. (1993; reprint Montreal and Kingston: McGill-Queen's University Press, 2000), 117.

6 W.A. Mackintosh, "Economic Factors in Canadian History," in *Approaches to Canadian Economic History,* ed. W.T. Easterbrook and M.H. Watkins (Ottawa: Carleton University Press, 1984), 12, 15.

7 H.A. Innis, "The Importance of Staple Products," in *Approaches to Canadian Economic History*, ed. Easterbrook and Watkins, 18, originally published in H.A. Innis, *The Fur Trade in Canada: An Introduction to Canadian Economic History,* rev. ed. (1930; reprint Toronto: University of Toronto Press, 1956), 383-86.

8 Paul André Linteau, René Durocher, and Jean-Claude Robert, *Quebec: A History, 1867-1929,* trans. Robert Chodos (Toronto: James Lorimer, 1983), 67-70.

9 Jane Jacobs, *Cities and the Wealth of Nations: Principles of Economic Life* (New York: Vintage Books, 1985), 224.

10 Donald J.H. Higgins, *Local and Urban Politics in Canada* (Toronto: Gage, 1986), 13.

11 Warren Magnusson, "Toronto," in *City Politics in Canada,* ed. Warren Magnusson and Andrew Sancton (Toronto: University of Toronto Press, 1983), 96.

12 Larry D. McCann and Jim Simmons, "The Core-Periphery Structure of Canada's Urban System," in *Canadian Cities in Transition: The Twenty-First Century,* ed. Trudi Bunting and Pierre Filion (Don Mills, ON: Oxford University Press, 2000), 77.

13 Ibid., 87.

14 Ibid., 93.

15 Gordon Laird, "Closing Kemano," *Canadian Geographic* 20, no. 7 (2000): 82-96.

16 District of Tumbler Ridge, "Welcome to the District of Tumbler Ridge," http://www.district.tumbler-ridge.bc.ca/ (accessed 11 June 2001).

17 Regional Municipality of Waterloo, "Waterloo Region in the 21st Century ... Planning Our Future," 18 October 2002, http://www.region.waterloo.on.ca/web/region.nsf/form?OpenForm (accessed 12 January 2003).

18 Joe Berridge, "There's No Need to Sit and Wait for a Handout," in *Toronto: Considering Self Government,* ed. Mary W. Rowe (Owen Sound, ON: Ginger Press, 2000), 15.

19 City of Toronto, "Toronto Key Facts," http://www.city.toronto.on.ca/ourcity/keyfacts.htm (accessed 30 August 2003).

20 Higgins, *Local and Urban Politics in Canada, 76.*

21 Rowe, ed., *Toronto: Considering Self Government,* ix.

22 Ibid.

23 Wallace Immen, "Cities Want Bigger Slice of National Funding Pie," *Globe and Mail,* 21 May 2001, A3.

24 Karen Herland, *People, Potholes and City Politics* (Montreal and New York: Black Rose Books, 1992), 7.

25 James Lightbody, "Canada's Seraglio Cities: Political Barriers to Regional Governance," *Canadian Journal of Sociology* 24 (1999): 175-91.

26 Alan Broadbent, "The Autonomy of Cities in Canada," in *Toronto: Considering Self Government,* ed. Rowe, 3.

27 Roger Gibbins, "Federalism in a Digital World," *Canadian Journal of Political Science* 33, no. 4 (2000): 685.

28 City of Grande Prairie, "Executive Summary for the Cybercity Initiative," http://www.city.grande-prairie.ab.ca/ccy_xsum.htm (accessed 5 August 2001; page now discontinued).

29 Andrew Gillespie and Mark Hepworth, "Telecommunications and Regional Development in the Network Economy," *Telecommunications: A Strategic Perspective on Regional, Economic, and Business Development,* ed. Maurice F. Estabrooke and Rodolphe H. Lamarche (Moncton, NB: Canadian Institute for Research on Regional Development, 1987), 114.

## Chapter 8: The Politics of Urban Planning

1  This chapter is drawn in part from an article written earlier by the author, "Local Environmental Politics: Principles in Conflict" in *Canadian Metropolitics*, ed. James Lightbody (Toronto: Copp Clark, 1995).

2  James Lorimer, *A Citizen's Guide to City Politics* (Toronto: James, Lewis and Samuel, 1970), 4. See James Lightbody, "Cities: The Dilemmas on Our Doorsteps," in *Corruption, Character and Conduct: Essays on Canadian Government Ethics,* ed. John W. Langford and Allan Tupper (Toronto: Oxford University Press, 1993), 212.

3  *Zoning* is a planning tool used to partition land in order to separate incompatible land uses.

4  *Boosterism* generally refers to the initiative of local community leaders to boost or promote their cities as a place to live and do business. This boosterism tends to pit neighbouring cities against each other as they compete for potential revenues from new business enterprises.

5  Paul Tiessen, ed., *Berlin, Canada: A Self-Portrait of Kitchener, Ontario before World War One* (St. Jacobs, ON: Sand Hills Books, 1979), introduction.

6  Gerald Hodge, *Planning Canadian Communities: An Introduction to the Principles, Practice, and Participants,* 3rd ed. (Scarborough, ON: ITP Nelson, 1998).

7  Ibid., 108.

8  Alan F.J. Artibise and Gilbert A. Stelter, "Conservation Planning and Urban Planning: The Canadian Commission of Conservation in Historical Perspective," in *Consuming Canada: Readings in Environmental History,* ed. C. Gaffield and P. Gaffield (Toronto: Copp Clark, 1995), 152-69.

9  Kent Gerecke, "The History of Canadian City Planning," in *The Second City Book: Studies of Urban and Suburban Canada,* ed. James Lorimer and Evelyn Ross with the editors of *City Magazine* (Toronto: James Lorimer, 1977), 151.

10  Ibid., 159-60.

11  Ibid.

12  Lewis Mumford, *The Culture of Cities* (1938; reprint New York: Harcourt Brace Jovanovich, 1970), 205.

13  Ibid., 150.

14  John Sewell, *Up against City Hall* (Toronto: James Lewis and Samuel, 1972); James Lorimer, *A Citizen's Guide to City Politics* (Toronto: James Lewis and Samuel, 1972); James Lorimer and Evelyn Ross, eds., *The City Book: The Politics and Planning in Canadian Cities* (Toronto: James Lorimer, 1976); James Lorimer and Evelyn Ross, with the editors of *City Magazine,* eds., *The Second City Book: Studies of Urban and Suburban Canada* (Toronto: James Lorimer, 1977).

15  The Ghermezian family were well-known large-project developers in Edmonton. Lightbody, "Cities: The Dilemmas on Our Doorsteps," 206.

16  While it is certainly possible to find many examples where council might be seen as "in the pocket" of developers, Lightbody notes that it is also important to recognize that many, if not most, local politicians are hard-working, well-meaning individuals who are provided with limited remuneration for their long hours of community service. Lightbody, "Cities: The Dilemmas on Our Doorsteps," 212.

17  Christopher Leo, "Urban Development," in *Urban Policy Issues: Canadian Perspectives,* ed. Edmund P. Fowler and David Siegel (Don Mills, ON: Oxford University Press, 2001), 217.

18  Ibid., 218-19.

19  Eben Fodor, *Better Not Bigger: How to Take Control of Urban Growth and Improve Your Community* (Gabriola Island, BC: New Society Publishers, 1999), 30.

20  Ibid.

21  Ibid., 31.

22  Christopher Leo, *The Subordination of the Local State: Development Politics in Edmonton,* Urban Resources 5 (Winnipeg: University of Winnipeg, Institute of Urban Studies, 1995), 3.

23  Fodor, *Better Not Bigger,* 30.

24  Federation of Canadian Municipalities, *The FCM Quality of Life Reporting System: Quality of Life in Canadian Communities* (May 1999), http://www.fcm.ca/English/communications/qualitylife.htm (accessed 8 January 2004).

25  Walter Jamieson, Adela Cosijn, and Susan Friesen, "Contemporary Planning: Issues and Innovations," in *Canadian Cities in Transition: The Twenty-First Century,* ed. Trudi Bunting and Pierre Filion (Don Mills, ON: Oxford University Press, 2000), 463.

26  Nira Yuval-Davis, "Citizenship, Territoriality and Gender," in *Democracy, Citizenship and the Global City,* ed. Engin F. Isin (London and New York: Routledge, 2000), 185.

27  Judith A. Garber, "The City As a Heroic Public Sphere," in *Democracy, Citizenship and the Global City,* ed. Isin, 258.

28  Robert A. Murdie and Carlos Teixeira, "The City As Social Space," in *Canadian Cities in Transition,* ed. Bunting and Filion, 198-223.

29  Ibid., 199.

30  Janine Brodie, "Imagining Democratic Urban Citizenship," in *Democratic Citizenship and the Global City,* ed. Isin, 124.

31  Murdie and Teixira, "The City As Social Space," 200.

32  Statistics Canada, "Census Families in Private Households by Family Structure and Presence of Children, Provinces and Territories 2001," http://www.statcan.ca/English/pgdb/famil54a.htm (accessed 6 January 2004).

33  Brian Ray and Damaris Rose, "Cities of the Everyday: Socio-Spatial Perspectives on Gender, Difference, and Diversity," in *Canadian Cities in Transition,* ed. Bunting and Filion, 503.

34  For further discussion of this issue, see Chantal Maillé, "Gender Concerns in City Life," in *The Politics of the City: A Canadian Perspective,* ed. Timothy L. Thomas (Scarborough, ON: ITP Nelson, 1997), 112.

35  Ibid., 26.

36  Ibid., 23.

37  Laura C. Johnson, "Bringing Work Home: Developing a Model Residentially Based Telework Facility," *Canadian Journal of Urban Research* 8, no. 2 (1999): 119-42.

38  Ibid., 137.

39  Ibid.

40  John A. Dickinson and Brian Young, *A Short History of Quebec,* 2nd ed. (1993; reprint Montreal and Kingston: McGill-Queen's University Press, 2000), 197.

41  Yasmeen Abu-Laban, "Ethnic Politics in a Globalizing Metropolis: The Case of Vancouver," in *The Politics of the City: A Canadian Perspective,* ed. Timothy L. Thomas (Scarborough, ON: ITP Nelson, 1997), 79.

42  Donald Avery, "Peopling Canada," *The Beaver* (February-March 2000): 29.

43  Steven Fick and Mary Vincent, "Toronto: A Global Village," *Canadian Geographic* (January 2001): 54.

44  Donald Avery, "Peopling Canada," 33.

45  City of Vancouver, Department of Social Planning, "Multiculturalism and Diversity," http://www.city.vancouver.bc.ca/commsvcs/socialplanning/initiatives/multicult/civicpolicy.htm (accessed 8 January 2004).

46  Yasmeen Abu-Laban, "Ethnic Politics in a Globalizing Metropolis," 89.

47  Avery, "Peopling Canada," 32.

48  Ibid., 81, citing Robert F. Harney, "Ethnicity and Neighbourhoods," *Cities and Urbanization: Canadian Historical Perspectives,* ed. Gilbert A. Stelter (Toronto: Copp Clark Pitman, 1990), 223.

49  Murdie and Teixeira, "The City As Social Space," 218.

50  Walter Jamieson, Adela Cosijn, and Susan Friesen, "Contemporary Planning: Issues and Innovations," in *Canadian Cities in Transition,* ed. Bunting and Filion, 462.

51  Lewis Mumford, *The Culture of Cities* (1938; reprint New York: Harcourt Brace Jovanovich, 1970).

## Chapter 9: Environmental Challenges

1  Mary Louise McAllister, "Local Environmental Politics: Principles in Conflict," in *Canadian Metropolitics,* ed. James Lightbody (Toronto: Copp Clark, 1995), 269-70.

2  Kenneth Grant Crawford, *Canadian Municipal Government* (Toronto: University of Toronto Press, 1954), 338.

3  Lewis Mumford, *The Culture of Cities* (1938; reprint New York: Harcourt Brace Jovanovich, 1970), 205.

4  Prince Edward Island, *Everything before Us.* Vol. 1 of the *Report of the Royal Commission on the Land* (Charlottetown, PEI: Queen's Printer, 1990), 17.
5  Nigel Richardson, *Land Use Planning and Sustainable Development in Canada* (Ottawa: Canadian Environmental Advisory Council, 1989), 39.
6  See, for example, Herman E. Daly, *Beyond Growth* (Boston: Beacon Press, 1996), 58.
7  Ibid., 31.
8  Ibid., 32.
9  United Nations Development Programme (UNDP), cited in Janine Brodie, "Imagining Democratic Urban Citizenship," in *Democracy, Citizenship and the Global City,* ed. Engin F. Isin (London and New York: Routledge, 2000), 121.
10  Ibid.; Katherine A. Graham, Susan D. Phillips, with Alan M. Maslove, *Urban Governance in Canada: Representation, Resources and Restructuring* (Toronto: Harcourt Brace, 1998), 174.
11  Gerald Hodge and Ira M. Robinson, *Planning Canadian Regions* (Vancouver: UBC Press, 2001), 365.
12  Ibid.
13  Richardson, *Land Use Planning,* 12.
14  David Crombie, *Regeneration: Toronto's Waterfront and the Sustainable City,* Royal Commission on the Toronto Harbourfront, Final Report (Toronto: Minister of Supply and Services Canada, 1992), 78.
15  National Round Table on the Environment and the Economy, "You Can't Give It Away: Tax Aspects of Ecologically Sensitive Lands," Issues Paper no. 1992-4 (1992): 22-25.
16  Richardson, *Land Use Planning,* 42.
17  Gerard Divay, "Cities and Sustainable Development: Can Cities Be Remodelled?" in *The Future of Cities in Britain and Canada,* ed. Ian Jackson (Ottawa: Institute for Research on Public Policy, 1991), 103.
18  Melissa Jort, "Who Speaks for Trees in York Region: The Decline of Urban Forests and the Limits of Local Government," in *Written Submission to the Woodlands E-Symposium* (Southern Ontario: Federation of Ontario Naturalists, 2001), 4.
19  Crombie, *Regeneration,* 25.
20  See examples discussed in William O. Karvinen and Mary Louise McAllister, *Rising to the Surface: Emerging Groundwater Policy Trends in Canada* (Kingston, ON: Centre for Resource Studies, Queen's University, 1994).
21  Environmental Commissioner of Ontario, "Urgent Need to Protect Groundwater, Environmental Commission Says," news release, 27 July 2000.
22  Dennis R. O'Connor, *Report of the Walkerton Inquiry: The Events of May 2000 and Related Issues, Part 1: A Summary* (Toronto: Ontario Ministry of the Attorney General, Queen's Printer, 2002), 6-7.
23  Canadian Broadcasting Corporation, "Harsh Words in North Battleford Water Report," 5 April 2002, http://sask.cbc.ca/template/servlet/View?filename=harsh020405 (accessed 18 November 2002).
24  Karvinen and McAllister, *Rising to the Surface.*
25  Andi Rierden, "A Decade of Clean Water Action," *The Gulf of Main Times* 5, no. 3 (2001).
26  Region of Waterloo, "Region of Waterloo Wins a Renewable Energy FCM-CH2M Hill Sustainable Community Award," news release, 18 May 2001.
27  James Rusk, "Toronto to Send All Waste to U.S.," *Globe and Mail,* 5 December 2001, A20.
28  City of Toronto, "Green Bin Program," http://www.city.toronto.on.ca/greenbin/background.htm (accessed 8 January 2004).
29  Jane Jacobs, *Cities and the Wealth of Nations: Principles of Economic Life* (New York: Vintage Books, 1985), 224. See also Ray Spaxman, "City Planning," in *Future of Cities in Britain and Canada,* ed. Jackson, 101.
30  Christopher R. Bryant, "Sustainable Community Development: Partnerships and Winning Proposals," The Good Idea Series in Sustainable Community Development, No. 1 (Sackville, NB: Rural and Small Towns Research and Studies Programme, Mount Allison University, 1991), 21.
31  David Easton, *The Political System: An Inquiry into the State of Political Science,* 2nd ed. (New York: Alfred A. Knopf, 1971).
32  Paul Pross, *Group Politics and Public Policy* (Toronto: Oxford University Press, 1986), 98.

33  Mickey Lauria, "Reconstructing Urban Regime Theory," in *Reconstructing Urban Regime Theory: Regulating Urban Politics in a Global Economy,* ed. Mickey Lauria (Thousand Oaks, CA: Sage, 1996), 2.

34  Ibid., 2-3.

35  Christopher Leo, "City Politics in an Era of Globalization," in *Reconstructing Urban Regime Theory,* ed. Lauria, 78.

36  Ibid., 96.

37  Ibid., 92.

38  Leslie W. Kennedy, *The Urban Kaleidoscope: Canadian Perspectives* (Toronto: McGraw-Hill Ryerson, 1983), 78-9.

39  Ibid.

40  Raymond L. Bryant and Sinéad Bailey, *Third World Political Ecology* (London: Routledge, 1997), 17.

41  Ibid., 19.

42  Ibid., 23.

43  Institute for Research on Environment and Economy, University of Ottawa, *Ecosystem Management: Meeting the Challenges of Community Initiatives* (Proceedings of a workshop, Cornwall, ON, 10 May 1995), 13.

44  Crombie, *Regeneration,* 41.

45  Hodge and Robinson, *Planning Canadian Regions,* 222.

46  Robert B. Gibson, Donald H.M. Alexander, and Ray Tomalty, "Putting Cities in Their Place: Ecosystem-Based Planning for Canadian Urban Regions," in *Eco-City Dimensions: Healthy Communities, Healthy Planet,* ed. Mark Roseland (Gabriola Island, BC: New Society Publishers, 1997), 38.

47  Ibid., 30-35.

48  George Francis, "Exploring Selected Issues of Governance in the Grand River Watershed," *Canadian Water Resources Journal* 21, no. 3 (1996): 306.

49  Ann Dale, *At the Edge: Sustainable Development in the 21st Century* (Vancouver: UBC Press, 2001), 58.

50  Ibid., 108.

51  Gibson, Alexander, and Tomalty, "Putting Cities in Their Place," 39.

52  Trevor Hancock, "Healthy Sustainable Communities: Concept, Fledgling Practice, and Implications for Governance," in *Eco-City Dimensions: Healthy Communities, Healthy Planet,* ed. Mark Roseland (Gabriola Island, BC: New Society Publishers, 1997), 43

53  Ibid., 47.

### Chapter 10: Local Public Administration

1  John S. Dryzek, *The Politics of the Earth: Environmental Discourses* (Oxford: Oxford University Press, 1997), 74.

2  Donald J.H. Higgins, *Local and Urban Politics in Canada* (Toronto: Gage, 1986), 125.

3  For a definition and a broader discussion of public policy, see Thomas R. Dye, *Understanding Public Policy,* 5th ed. (Englewood Cliffs, NJ: Prentice Hall, 1984), 1.

4  See also Kenneth Kernaghan and David Siegel, *Public Administration in Canada,* 3rd ed. (Scarborough, ON: Nelson, 1995), 8-10.

5  Adapted from B. Guy Peters, *The Future of Governing: Four Emerging Models* (Lawrence, KS: University Press of Kansas, 1996), 4-15.

6  Ibid.

7  Kernaghan and Siegel, *Public Administration in Canada,* 323.

8  Higgins, *Local and Urban Politics in Canada,* 126.

9  Ibid.

10  Higgins, *Local and Urban Politics in Canada,* 150; Katherine A. Graham, Susan D. Phillips, with Alan M. Maslove, *Urban Governance in Canada: Representation, Resources and Restructuring* (Toronto: Harcourt Brace, 1998), 152-53.

11  C. Richard Tindal and Susan Nobes Tindal, *Local Government in Canada,* 4th ed. (Toronto: McGraw-Hill Ryerson, 1995), 171.

12  Ibid., 172-73.

13  George Paul, personal communication to author, June 2001.

14  City of Waterloo, "Parks and Works Services Core Business," 3 February 2003, http://www.city.waterloo. on.ca/PWS/index.html (accessed 8 January 2004).

15  City of Sherbrooke Transition Committee, "Towards a New City," *First Column La Nouvelle Newspaper,* 10 October 2001.

16  City of Toronto, "Toronto City Council Approves 2003 Budget," http://www.city.toronto.on.ca/city_budget/ index.htm (accessed 4 July 2003).

17  City of Toronto, "City Departments," http://www.city.toronto.on.ca/departments/index.htm (accessed 30 August 2001).

18  Higgins, *Local and Urban Politics in Canada,* 142-47.

19  Stewart Fyfe and Ron M. Farrow, *Waterloo Area Local Government Review: Report of Findings and Recommendations* (Toronto: Ontario Department of Municipal Affairs, 1970), 163.

20  Ibid.

21  Conservation Ontario, "Conservation Ontario Corporate Profile," http://www.conservation-ontario.on.ca/ profile/profile.htm (accessed 6 December 2002).

22  Kernaghan and Siegel, *Public Administration in Canada,* 115.

23  Ibid., 116-17.

24  Ibid., 117.

25  Michael Howlett and M. Ramesh, *Studying Public Policy: Policy Cycles and Policy Subsystems* (Toronto: Oxford University Press, 1996), 11.

26  Michael Hall, Larry McKeown, and Karen Roberts, *Caring Canadians: Highlights from the 2000 National Survey of Giving, Volunteering and Participating* (Ottawa: Statistics Canada, 2001), 9, 12, 13.

27  Ibid., 13.

28  Ibid., 32.

29  Ibid., 53.

30  Robert D. Putnam, "The Prosperous Community," *The American Prospect* 4, no. 13 (1993), http://www. prospect.org/print/V4/13/putnam-r.html (accessed 1 February 2004).

31  Ibid.

## Chapter 11: Business, Management, and the Municipal Corporation

1  B. Guy Peters, *The Future of Governing: Four Emerging Models* (Lawrence, KS: University Press of Kansas, 1996).

2  Donald J.H. Higgins, *Local and Urban Politics in Canada* (Toronto: Gage, 1986), 71.

3  Ibid.

4  Frank A. Rodgers, "Democracy in the Municipality" (paper presented at the Common Council in Committee-of-the-Whole, Saint John, NB, 13 January 1992), 4.

5  Woodrow Wilson, "The Study of Administration," in *Classics of Public Administration,* 3rd ed., ed. Jay M. Shafritz and Albert C. Hyde (Belmont, CA: Wadsworth Publishing, 1992), 18.

6  W.V. Uttley, *A History of Kitchener* (Waterloo, ON: The Chronicle Press, 1937), as quoted by Elizabeth Bloomfield, "Building Industrial Communities: Berlin and Waterloo to 1915," in *Manufacturing in Kitchener-Waterloo,* ed. David F. Walker (Waterloo: Department of Geography, University of Waterloo, 1987), 24.

7  Bloomfield, "Building Industrial Communities, 22.

8  Ibid., 19.

9  Ibid., 24.

10  The Chamber of Commerce of Kitchener and Waterloo, *The Record* (Kitchener-Waterloo), 12 September 1998 (advertising feature), 6.

11  Robin Ford and David Zussman, "Alternative Service Delivery: Transcending Boundaries," in *Alternative Service Delivery: Sharing Governance in Canada* (Toronto: Institute of Public Administration of Canada/KPMG: April 1997), 10.

12  John Ralston Saul, *The Unconscious Civilization* (Concord, ON: House of Anansi Press, 1995), 111.
13  Hugh Segal, *Beyond Greed* (Toronto: Stoddart, 1997), 126.
14  André Carrel, *Citizens' Hall: Making Local Democracy Work* (Toronto: Between the Lines, 2001), 104.
15  Peters, *The Future of Governing*, 23.
16  Ibid., 28.
17  Ibid., 49.
18  David Osborne and Ted Gaebler, *Reinventing Government: How the Entrepreneurial Spirit Is Transforming the Public Sector* (Reading, MA: Addison-Wesley, 1992), xviii, xix.
19  Ibid.
20  City of Waterloo, *We're Here for You, Waterloo! A Citizen's Guide to City of Waterloo Services* (Waterloo, ON: City of Waterloo, 1996), 4.
21  Peters, *The Future of Governing*, 51-52.
22  City of Waterloo, *Facility Services: Rim Park*, 9 May 2002, http://www.city.waterloo.on.ca/RL/FacilityServices/RimPark/ParkFacilities (cited 18 January 2003).
23  Terry Pender, "Waterloo's Lack of Understanding Puzzled Mfp Staffer," *Kitchener-Waterloo Record*, 24 January 2003.
24  The Honourable Mr. Justice Ronald C. Sills, Commissioner, *RIM Park Financing Inquiry*, Final Report, City of Waterloo, 20 October 2003, section 4.2.3, 6.
25  Sills, *RIM Park Financing Inquiry*, Executive Summary, City of Waterloo, 20 October 2003: 32.
26  Ibid., 10.
27  "Stockie Hoped to Stay Friends," *Kitchener-Waterloo Record*, 10 October 2002.
28  Sills, *RIM Park Financing Inquiry*, Executive Summary, 10.
29  Ibid.
30  Christian AAgaard, "Mayor Wants Inquiry," *Kitchener-Waterloo Record*, 4 March 2002.
31  Sills, *RIM Park Financing Inquiry*, Executive Summary, 13.
32  James Rusk, "Bureaucrat's Heavy Golf Habit 'Shocked' Lastman," *Globe and Mail*, 5 December 2002.
33  See also Peters, *The Future of Governing*, 42.
34  Ibid., 43.
35  Richard M. Bird and N. Enid Slack, *Urban Public Finance in Canada* (Toronto: John Wiley & Sons, 1993), 45.
36  Ibid., 46.
37  Ibid.
38  Ibid.
39  City of Waterloo, Revenue Services, *2003 Property Taxes*, brochure (Waterloo, ON: City of Waterloo, 2003).
40  City of Waterloo, Revenue Services and Region of Waterloo, *Important Information about Your 2001 Property Taxes*, brochure (Waterloo, ON: City of Waterloo, 2001).
41  Ibid.
42  Shirley A. McAlary, "Mayor's Message: Participate in the 2003-2004 Budget Process Consultation," http://www.city.saint-john.nb.ca (accessed 19 January 2003; page has since been changed).
43  City of Prince George, "Year 2003 Financial Plan Survey," 2 June 2003.
44  Katherine A. Graham, Susan D. Phillips, with Alan M. Maslove, *Urban Governance in Canada: Representation, Resources and Restructuring* (Toronto: Harcourt Brace, 1998), 211.
45  Bird and Slack, *Urban Public Finance in Canada*, 79-102.
46  Robin W. Boadway and Harry M. Kitchen, *Canadian Tax Policy*, Canadian Tax Paper No. 103 (Toronto: Canadian Tax Foundation, 1999), 353.
47  Ibid., 363.
48  Ibid., 367.
49  Ibid., 378-80.
50  See also ibid., 343.
51  Lynne Woolstencroft (mayor of the City of Waterloo), telephone communication, October 2001.

52  Boadway and Kitchen, *Canadian Tax Policy,* 392.

53  Ibid., 394-95.

54  Peter Woolstencroft, "Education Policies: Challenges and Controversies," in *Urban Policy Issues: Canadian Perspectives,* ed. Edmund P. Fowler and David Siegel (Don Mills, ON: Oxford University Press, 2001), 277.

55  James M. Flaherty, "Responsible Choices: 2001 Ontario Budget Speech," (paper presented to the members of the Legislative Assembly of Ontario by the Honourable James M. Flaherty, Minister of Finance, Toronto, ON, 9 May 2001), 25.

56  Peters, *The Future of Governing,* 31.

57  Woolstencroft, "Education Policies," 282-86.

58  Flaherty, "Responsible Choices," 26.

59  John Barber, "School Disaster Forced on Our Heads," *Globe and Mail,* 24 May 2001, A21; Richard Mackie, "Parent Coalition Rallies to Defend Public Schools," *Globe and Mail,* 25 May 2001, A17.

60  See, for example, Kernaghan and Siegel, *Public Administration in Canada,* 8.

61  Mickey Lauria, "Reconstructing Urban Regime Theory," in *Reconstructing Urban Regime Theory: Regulating Urban Politics in a Global Economy,* ed. Mickey Lauria (Thousand Oaks, CA: Sage, 1996); Christopher Leo, "City Politics in an Era of Globalization," in *Reconstructing Urban Regime Theory,* ed. Lauria.

### Chapter 12: Local Channels of Information

1  Harold A. Innis, *Empire and Communications,* 2nd ed., revised by Mary Q. Innis (Toronto: University of Toronto Press, 1972), 5.

2  Graeme Patterson, *History and Communications: Harold Innis, Marshall McLuhan, the Interpretation of History* (Toronto: University of Toronto Press, 1990), 35.

3  J. Carey, *Communication As Culture: Essays on Media and Society* (New York: Routledge, 1992), 134.

4  Ibid.

5  Ibid., 160.

6  Edwin R. Black, *Politics and the News* (Toronto: Butterworths, 1982), 20.

7  Bill Moyer, *Kitchener Yesterday Revisited: An Illustrated History* (Burlington, ON: Windsor Publications, 1979), 22.

8  Black, *Politics and the News,* 50.

9  Canada, The Special Senate Committee on the Mass Media, *Report, The Uncertain Mirror* (Ottawa: Queen's Printer, 1970), 6, cited in Andrew M. Osler, "From Vincent Massey to Thomas Kent: The Evolution of a National Press Policy in Canada," in *Communications in Canadian Society,* ed. Benjamin D. Singer (Don Mills, ON: Addison-Wesley, 1983), 104.

10  D. Keith Davey, "Newspapers Jolted into Hysteria," *Globe and Mail,* 16 September 1981, cited in Osler, "From Vincent Massey to Thomas Kent," 106.

11  F. Christopher Arterton, *Teledemocracy: Can Technology Protect Democracy?* (Newbury Park, CA: Sage Library of Social Research, 1987), 203.

12  Information for this section of the chapter was drawn from a paper written by Edwin R. Black and Mary Louise McAllister, "Channels of Influence: Information Politics in Local Government" (paper presented at the annual meeting of the Canadian Political Science Association, University of Calgary, June 1994).

13  See Black, *Politics and the News,* 201-3; Edwin R. Black and Peter Snow, "The Political Agendas of Three Newspapers and City Governments," *Canadian Journal of Communication,* 8, no. 2 (January 1982): 11-25.

14  Nelson W. Polsby, *Community Power and Political Theory* (New Haven: Yale University Press, 1963).

15  V.O. Key Jr., *Public Opinion and American Democracy* (New York: Knopf, 1964).

16  Black, *Politics and the News,* 203.

17  Henry Milner, "Civic Literacy in Comparative Context: Why Canadians Should Be Concerned," *Policy Matters* 2, no. 2 (2001): 19.

18  Ibid., 98.

19  Kevin Crowley, "Ontario Taxpayers on the Hook," *The Record* (Kitchener-Waterloo), 15 December 2001.

20  Stephen Dale, *McLuhan's Children: The Greenpeace Message and the Media* (Toronto: Between the Lines, 1996), 17.

21  Ron East, e-mail to the author, 6 June 2001.

22  Charles J. McCaffray, *UNBC – A Northern Crusade: The How and Who of B.C.'s Northern U* (Duncan, BC: Charles J. McCaffray, 1995), 284.

23  Ibid., 161.

24  Ibid., 278.

25  Office of Information and Privacy Commissioner, Ontario, "A Mini Guide to Ontario's Municipal Freedom of Information and Protection of Privacy Act," http://www.ipc.on.ca/ (cited 2 August 2001).

26  Ibid.

27  Mary Louise McAllister, "Access to Government Information in an Electronic Age" (MA thesis, Queen's University, 1983), 1-2.

28  Judy Curry, "Finding Local Government Information on the Web," *Government Information in Canada/ Information gouvernementale au Canada* 4, no. 1 (1997), http://www.usask.ca/library/gic/v4n1/curry/curry. html (accessed 8 January 2004).

29  Halifax Regional Council, "An Open Letter from the Halifax Regional Council to Honourable Angus MacIssac Minister, Service Nova Scotia and Municipal Relations, 27 March 2001, http://www.region.halifax. ca/equalizationoptions.html (accessed 8 January 2004).

30  Industry Canada, "What Is a Smart Community," http://smartcommunities.ic.gc.ca/def_e.asp (accessed 5 August 2001).

31  Industry Canada, "Demonstration Projects," http://smartcommunities.ic.gc.ca/demoprojects/demoprojects_e.asp (accessed 5 August 2001).

32  Government of Alberta, "Supernet Approach Set to Take Alberta to New Heights," news release (24 July 2001).

33  Nathan Newman, "Virtual Sunshine May Rain on Local Economic Development," *Enode* 1, no. 1 (1996).

34  Roger Gibbins, "Federalism in a Digital World," *Canadian Journal of Political Science* 33, no. 4 (2000): 667.

35  Ibid., 681.

36  Ibid.

37  Mohammad Qadeer, "Communities and Public Welfare," *Options Politiques* (October 1995): 46.

38  Walter Truett Anderson, "Communities in a World of Open Systems," *Futures* 31 (1999): 460.

39  John Sewell and Advisory Committee, *Local Self Government Bulletin* no. 15 (April 2001), http://www. localselfgovt.ca (accessed May 2001; page now discontinued).

40  CitizensontheWeb.ca, home page, http://photosc.msspro.com/citizen/start.htm (accessed 9 August 2001).

41  Vincent Mosco, *The Pay-Per Society: Computers and Communications in the Information Age* (Toronto: Garamond Press, 1989), 29-33.

42  Manuel Castells, "Information Technology, Globalization and Social Development" (paper presented at the UNRISD Conference on Information Technologies and Social Development, Palais des Nations, Geneva, 22-24 June 1998).

# Selected Bibliography

AAgaard, Christian. "Mayor Wants Inquiry." *The Record* (Kitchener-Waterloo), 4 March 2002, 1-2.

Abu-Laban, Yasmeen. "Ethnic Politics in a Globalizing Metropolis: The Case of Vancouver." In *The Politics of the City: A Canadian Perspective*, edited by Timothy L. Thomas. Scarborough, ON: ITP Nelson, 1997.

Anderson, James D. "The Municipal Government Reform Movement in Western Canada 1880-1920." In *The Usable Urban Past*, edited by Alan F.J. Artibise and Gilbert A. Stelter, 73-111. Toronto: MacMillan of Canada, 1979.

Anderson, Walter Truett. "Communities in a World of Open Systems." *Futures* 31 (1999): 457-63.

Arterton, F. Christopher. *Teledemocracy: Can Technology Protect Democracy?* Newbury Park, CA: Sage Library of Social Research, 1987.

Artibise, Alan F.J., and Gilbert A. Stelter. *The Usable Urban Past: Planning and Politics in the Modern Canadian City*. Toronto: MacMillan of Canada, 1979.

Axworthy, Thomas. "We Must Shore up Our Cities." *Globe and Mail,* 4 October 2001.

Barney, Darin. *Prometheus Wired: The Hope for Democracy in the Age of Network Technology.* Vancouver: UBC Press, 2000.

Baxter, David, and Andrew Ramolo. "Resource Dependency: The Spatial Origins of British Columbia's Economic Base." *Urban Futures Institute Report* 55 (2002).

Bird, Richard M., and N. Enid Slack. *Urban Public Finance in Canada.* Toronto: John Wiley, 1993.

Black, Edwin R. *Politics and the News.* Toronto: Butterworths, 1982.

Boadway, Robin W., and Harry M. Kitchen. *Canadian Tax Policy.* Canadian Tax Paper no. 103. Toronto: Canadian Tax Foundation, 1999.

Boardman, Robert, and Debora Van Nijnatten. *Canadian Environmental Policy: Context and Cases for a New Century.* Toronto: Oxford University Press, 2002.

Boswell, Peter G. "Municipal Renewal in Newfoundland: A Tradition of Cautious Evolution." Paper presented at the annual meeting of the Canadian Political Science Association, Laval University, Laval, PQ, 28 May 2001.

Boudreau, Julie-Anne. *The Megacity Saga: Democracy and Citizenship in This Global Age.* Montreal: Black Rose Books, 2000.

Bray, Matt, and Ashley Thomson. *At the End of the Shift: Mines and Single-Industry Towns in Northern Ontario.* Toronto: Dundurn Press, 1992.

British Columbia. Community Charter Council Act. SBC 2001, ch. 35.

Brodie, Janine. "Imagining Democratic Urban Citizenship." In *Democracy, Citizenship and the Global City,* edited by Engin F. Isin, 110-28. London and New York: Routledge, 2000.

Brownsey, Keith, and Michael Howlett, eds. *The Provincial State: Politics in Canada's Provinces and Territories.* Toronto: Copp Clark Pitman, 1992.

Brownstone, Meyer, and T.J. Plunkett. *Metropolitan Winnipeg: Politics and Reform of Local Government.* Berkeley: University of California Press, 1983.

Bryant, Raymond L., and Sinéad Bailey. *Third World Political Ecology.* London: Routledge, 1997.

Bunting, Trudi, and Pierre Filion, eds. *Canadian Cities in Transition: The Twenty-First Century.* Don Mills, ON: Oxford University Press, 2000.

Carey, J. *Communication As Culture: Essays on Media and Society.* New York: Routledge, 1992.

Carrel, André. *Citizens' Hall: Making Local Democracy Work.* Toronto: Between the Lines, 2001.

Carroll, Barbara Wake. "Housing Policy in the New Millennium." In *Urban Policy Issues: Canadian Perspectives,* edited by Edmund P. Fowler and David Siegel, 69-89. Don Mills, ON: Oxford University Press, 2001.

Cassidy, Frank, and Robert L. Bish. *Indian Government: Its Meaning in Practice.* Lantzville, BC: Oolichan Books, and Halifax, NS: The Institute for Research on Public Policy, 1989.

Castells, Manuel. "Information Technology, Globalization and Social Development." Paper presented at the UNRISD Conference on Information Technologies and Social Development, Palais des Nations, Geneva, 22-24 June 1998.

Christensen, Bev. *Prince George: Rivers, Railways, and Timber.* Burlington, ON: Windsor Publications, 1989.

Christensen, Terry. *Local Politics: Governing at the Grassroots.* Belmont, CA: Wadsworth Publishing, 1994.

Crawford, Kenneth Grant. *Canadian Municipal Government.* Toronto: University of Toronto Press, 1954.

Crombie, David, Commissioner. *Royal Commission on the Toronto Harbourfront, Regeneration: Toronto's Waterfront and the Sustainable City: Final Report.* Toronto: Minister of Supply and Services Canada, 1992.

Dahl, Robert A. "The City in the Future of Democracy." *The American Political Science Review* (December 1967): 953-70. Reprinted in *Politics and Government in Urban Canada,* edited by Lionel D. Feldman, 39-60. Toronto: Methuen, 1981.

Dale, Ann. *At the Edge: Sustainable Development in the 21st Century.* Vancouver: UBC Press, 2001.

Dale, Stephen. *McLuhan's Children: The Greenpeace Message and the Media.* Toronto: Between the Lines, 1996.

Daly, Herman E. *Beyond Growth.* Boston: Beacon Press, 1996.

DeMarco, Jerry. "Overview of the Hudson Decision." Paper presented at the FCM Big City Mayors' Caucus, 21 October 2001.

Diamant, Peter. "Unicity: Bureaucratic Success, Political Nightmare." In *The State of Unicity – 25 Years Later: Conference Proceedings (October 3-4 1997),* edited by Nancy Klos, 17-23. Winnipeg: Institute of Urban Studies, 1998.

Dickinson, John A., and Brian Young. *A Short History of Quebec,* 2nd ed. 1993. Reprint, Montreal and Kingston: McGill-Queen's University Press, 2000.

Downey, Terrence J., and Robert J. Williams. "Provincial Agendas, Local Responses: The 'Common Sense' Restructuring of Ontario's Municipal Government." *Canadian Public Administration* 41, no. 2 (Summer, 1998): 210-38.

Dryzek, John S. *The Politics of the Earth: Environmental Discourses.* Oxford: Oxford University Press, 1997.

Dunn, Christopher, and David Laycock. "Saskatchewan: Innovation and Competition in the Agricultural Heartland." In *The Provincial State: Politics in Canada's Provinces and Territories,* edited by Keith Brownsey and Michael Howlett. Toronto: Copp Clark Pitman, 1992.

Dye, Thomas R. *Understanding Public Policy,* 5th ed. Englewood Cliffs, NJ: Prentice Hall, 1984.

Easterbrook, W.T., and M.H. Watkins, eds. *Approaches to Canadian Economic History.* Ottawa: Carleton University Press, 1984.

Easton, David. *The Political System: An Inquiry into the State of Political Science,* 2nd ed. New York: Alfred A. Knopf, 1971.

English, John, and Kenneth McLaughlin. *Kitchener: An Illustrated History.* Waterloo, ON: Wilfrid Laurier University Press, 1983.

Filion, Pierre, Trudi E. Buntings, and Kevin Curtis, eds. *The Dynamics of the Dispersed City: Geographic and Planning Perspectives on Waterloo Region.* Waterloo, ON: Department of Geography, University of Waterloo, 1996.

Fisher, Robin A. "Gold Miners and Settlers." In *A History of British Columbia: Selected Readings,* edited by Patricia E. Roy, 24-48. Toronto: Copp Clark Pitman, 1989.

Fodor, Eben. *Better Not Bigger: How to Take Control of Urban Growth and Improve Your Community.* Gabriola Island, BC: New Society Publishers, 1999.

Francis, George. "Exploring Selected Issues of Governance in the Grand River Watershed." *Canadian Water Resources Journal* 21, no. 3 (1996): 303-9.

Fyfe, Stewart, and Ron M. Farrow. *Waterloo Area Local Government Review: Report of Findings and Recommendations.* Toronto: Ontario Department of Municipal Affairs, 1970.

Gaffield, C., and P. Gaffield, eds. *Consuming Canada: Readings in Environmental History.* Toronto: Copp Clark, 1995.

Gibbins, Roger. "Federalism in a Digital World." *Canadian Journal of Political Science* 33, no. 4 (2000): 667-89.

Gibson, Robert B., Donald H.M. Alexander, and Ray Tomalty. "Putting Cities in Their Place: Ecosystem-Based Planning for Canadian Urban Regions." In *Eco-City Dimensions: Healthy Communities, Healthy Planet,* edited by Mark Roseland, 25-40. Gabriola Island, BC: New Society Publishers, 1997.

Gillespie, Andrew, and Mark Hepworth. "Telecommunications and Regional Development in the Network Economy," In *Telecommunications: A Strategic Perspective on Regional, Economic and Business Development*, edited by Maurice F. Estabrooke and Rodolphe H. Lamarche, 107-28. Moncton: Canadian Institute for Research on Regional Development, 1987.

Gough, Barry M. "The Character of the British Columbia Frontier." In *A History of British Columbia: Selected Readings,* edited by Patricia E. Roy, 12-23. Toronto: Copp Clark Pitman, 1989.

Graham, Katherine A., Susan D. Phillips, with Alan M. Maslove. *Urban Governance in Canada: Representation, Resources and Restructuring.* Toronto: Harcourt Brace, 1998.

Gutstein, Donald. "Vancouver." In *City Politics in Canada,* edited by Warren Magnusson and Andrew Sancton, 189-221. Toronto: University of Toronto Press, 1983.

Hall, Michael, Larry McKeown, and Karen Roberts. *Caring Canadians: Highlights from the 2000 National Survey of Giving, Volunteering and Participating.* Ottawa: Statistics Canada, 2001.

Hancock, Trevor. "Healthy Sustainable Communities: Concept, Fledgling Practice, and Implications for Governance." In *Eco-City Dimensions: Healthy Communities, Healthy Planet*, edited by Mark Roseland, 42-50. Gabriola Island, BC: New Society Publishers, 1997.

Hawley, Willis D., and Frederick M. Wirt, eds. *The Search for Community Power,* 2nd ed. Englewood Cliffs, NJ: Prentice-Hall, 1974.

Herland, Karen. *People, Potholes and City Politics.* Montreal and New York: Black Rose Books, 1992.

Higgins, Donald J.H. *Local and Urban Politics in Canada.* Toronto: Gage, 1986.

Hill, Dilys M. *Democratic Theory and Local Government.* London: George Allan and Unwin, 1974.

Hodge, Gerald. *Planning Canadian Communities: An Introduction to the Principles, Practice, and Participants.* Toronto: ITP Nelson, 1998.

Hodge, Gerald, and Ira M. Robinson. *Planning Canadian Regions.* Vancouver: UBC Press, 2001.

Hood, George N. *Against the Flow: Rafferty-Alameda and the Politics of the Environment.* Saskatoon, SK: Fifth House Publisher, 1994.

Howlett, Michael, and M. Ramesh. *Studying Public Policy: Policy Cycles and Policy Subsystems.* Toronto: Oxford University Press, 1996.

Innis, Harold A. *Empire and Communications,* 2nd ed. Revised by Mary Q. Innis. Toronto: University of Toronto Press, 1972.

Isin, Engin F. *Cities without Citizens.* Montreal: Black Rose Books, 1992.

–, ed. *Democracy, Citizenship and the Global City.* London and New York: Routledge, 2000.

Jackson, Ian, ed. *The Future of Cities in Britain and Canada.* Ottawa: Institute for Research on Public Policy, 1991.

Jacobs, Jane. *Cities and the Wealth of Nations: Principles of Economic Life.* New York: Vintage Books, 1985.

Johnson, Laura C. "Bringing Work Home: Developing a Model Residentially Based Telework Facility." *Canadian Journal of Urban Research* 8, no. 2 (1999): 119-42.

Jort, Melissa. "Who Speaks for Trees in York Region: The Decline of Urban Forests and the Limits of Local Government." In *Written Submission to the Woodlands E-Symposium.* Southern Ontario: Federation of Ontario Naturalists, 2001.

Karvinen, William, and Mary Louise McAllister. *Rising to the Surface: Emerging Groundwater Policy Trends in Canada.* Kingston, ON: Centre for Resource Studies, Queen's University, 1994.

Kennedy, Leslie W. *The Urban Kaleidoscope: Canadian Perspectives.* Toronto: McGraw-Hill Ryerson, 1983.

Kernaghan, Kenneth, and David Siegel. *Public Administration in Canada.* 3rd ed. Scarborough, ON: Nelson, 1995.

Key Jr., V.O. *Public Opinion and American Democracy.* New York: Knopf, 1964.

Kiernan, Matthew J., and David C. Walker. "Winnipeg." In *City Politics in Canada,* edited by Warren Magnusson and Andrew Sancton, 222-54. Toronto: University of Toronto Press, 1983.

Langford, John W., and Allan Tupper, eds. *Corruption, Character and Conduct: Essays on Canadian Government Ethics.* Toronto: Oxford University Press, 1993.

Langrod, George. "Local Government and Democracy." *Public Administration* 31 (Spring 1953): 25-33. Reprinted in *Politics and Government in Urban Canada,* 4th ed., edited by Lionel D. Feldman, 3-14. Toronto: Methuen, 1981.

Lasswell, Harold. *Politics: Who Gets What, When, How.* New York: Meridian Books, 1958.

Lauria, Mickey. "Reconstructing Urban Regime Theory." In *Reconstructing Urban Regime Theory: Regulating Urban Politics in a Global Economy,* edited by Mickey Lauria, 1-9. Thousand Oaks, CA: Sage, 1996.

Leo, Christopher. "The State in the City." In *Canadian Metropolitics: Governing Our Cities,* edited by James Lightbody, 27-50. Toronto: Copp Clark, 1995.

–. *The Subordination of the Local State: Development Politics in Edmonton, Urban Resources 5.* Winnipeg: University of Winnipeg, Institute of Urban Studies, 1995.

–. "City Politics in an Era of Globalization." In *Reconstructing Urban Regime Theory: Regulating Urban Politics in a Global Economy,* edited by Mickey Lauria, 77-98. Thousand Oaks, CA: Sage, 1996.

–. "Regional Growth Management Regime: The Case of Portland Oregon." *Journal of Urban Affairs* 20 (1998): 363-94.

–. "Urban Development." In *Urban Policy Issues: Canadian Perspectives,* edited by Edmund P. Fowler and David Siegel, 215-36. Don Mills, ON: Oxford University Press, 2001.

Lightbody, James. *The Actors in Metropolitan Reform: The Winnipeg Experience.* Occasional Paper no. 7. Edmonton: University of Alberta, 1979.

–. "Edmonton." In *City Politics in Canada,* edited by Warren Magnusson and Andrew Sancton. Toronto: University of Toronto Press, 1985.

–. "Cities: The Dilemmas on Our Doorsteps." In *Corruption, Character and Conduct: Essays on Canadian Government Ethics,* edited by John W. Langford and Allan Tupper. Toronto: Oxford University Press, 1993.

–. "Canada's Seraglio Cities: Political Barriers to Regional Governance." *Canadian Journal of Sociology* 24 (1999): 175-91.

Linteau, Paul André, René Durocher, and Jean-Claude Robert. *Quebec: A History 1867-1929.* Translated by Robert Chodos. Toronto: James Lorimer, 1983.

Lipset, S.M. *Agrarian Socialism.* 3rd ed. Berkeley, CA: University of California Press, 1971.

Lorimer, James. *A Citizen's Guide to City Politics.* Toronto: James, Lewis and Samuel, 1970.

McAllister, Mary Louise. "Access to Government Information in an Electronic Age." MA thesis, Queen's University, 1983.

–. "Local Environmental Politics: Principles in Conflict." In *Canadian Metropolitics,* edited by James Lightbody, 269-89. Toronto: Copp Clark, 1995.

McCaffray, Charles J. *UNBC – A Northern Crusade: The How and Who of B.C.'s Northern U.* Duncan, BC: Charles J. McCaffray, 1995.

McCready, H.W., ed. *Lord Durham's Mission to Canada, an Abridgement of Lord Durham: A Biography of John George Lambton, First Earl of Durham, by Chester New.* 1929. Reprint, Toronto: McClelland and Stewart, 1963.

McFarlane, Susan, and Robert Roach. *Strings Attached: Non-Profits and Their Relationship with Government.* Canada West Foundation, Alternative Service Delivery Project 4, September 1999.

MacKenzie, Suzanne. "Building Women, Building Cities." In *Life Spaces: Gender, Household, Employment,* edited by Caroline Andrew and Beth Moore Milroy, 13-30. Vancouver: UBC Press, 1988.

Mackie, Richard. "Parent Coalition Rallies to Defend Public Schools." *Globe and Mail,* 25 May 2001.

Magnusson, Warren. "Toronto." In *City Politics in Canada,* edited by Warren Magnusson and Andrew Sancton, 94-139. Toronto: University of Toronto Press, 1983.

–. *The Search for Political Space.* Toronto: University of Toronto Press, 1996.

Maillé, Chantal. "Gender Concerns of City Life." In *The Politics of the City: A Canadian Perspective,* edited by Timothy L. Thomas. Scarborough, ON: ITP Nelson, 1997.

Manor, James, Mark Robinson, and Gordon White. *Civil Society and Governance: A Concept Paper.* Civil Society and Governance Program Office, University of Sussex, 1999. http://www.ids.ac.uk/ids/civsoc.

Masson, Jack. *Alberta's Local Governments and Their Politics.* Edmonton: Pica Pica Press, 1985.

Masson, Jack, with Edward C. LeSage Jr. *Alberta's Local Governments: Politics and Democracy.* Edmonton: University of Alberta Press, 1994.

Metropolitan Action Committee on Violence Against Women and Children (METRAC). Home page. http://www.metrac.org/.

Milner, Henry. *Civic Literacy in Comparative Context: Why Canadians Should Be Concerned. Policy Matters* 2, no. 2 (2001).

Mitchell, John. *The Settlement of York County.* Toronto: Municipal Corporation of the County of York, 1952.

Moulin, Leo. "Local Self-Government As a Basis for Democracy: A Further Comment." *Public Administration* 32 (Winter 1954): 433-37. Reprinted in *Politics and Government in Urban Canada,* 4th ed., edited by Lionel D. Feldman, 19-24. Toronto: Methuen, 1981.

Moyer, Bill. *Kitchener Yesterday Revisited: An Illustrated History.* Burlington, ON: Windsor Publications, 1979.

Mumford, Lewis. *The Culture of Cities.* 1938. Reprint, New York: Harcourt Brace Jovanovich, 1970.

Newman, Nathan. "Virtual Sunshine May Rain on Local Economic Development." *Enode* 1, no. 1 (1996). http://www.nathannewman.org/other/ENODEvirtualsunshine.html.

Osborne, David, and Ted Gaebler. *Reinventing Government: How the Entrepreneurial Spirit Is Transforming the Public Sector.* Reading, MA: Addison-Wesley, 1992.

Osler, Andrew M. "From Vincent Massey to Thomas Kent: The Evolution of a National Press Policy in Canada." In *Communications in Canadian Society,* edited by Benjamin D. Singer, 101-14. Don Mills, ON: Addison-Wesley, 1983.

Owen, Stephen. "Land Use Planning in the Nineties: CORE Lessons." *Environments* 25, nos. 2, 3 (1998): 14-26.

Patterson, Graeme. *History and Communications: Harold Innis, Marshall McLuhan, the Interpretation of History.* Toronto: University of Toronto Press, 1990.

Pendergrast, Eudora, and John Farrow. *Community Councils and Neighbourhood Committees: Lessons for Our Communities from around the World.* Toronto: Canadian Urban Institute, 1997.

Peters, B. Guy. *The Future of Governing: Four Emerging Models.* Lawrence, KS: University Press of Kansas, 1996.

Polsby, Nelson W. *Community Power and Political Theory.* New Haven: Yale University Press, 1963.

Pross, Paul. *Group Politics and Public Policy.* Toronto: Oxford University Press, 1986.

Putnam, Robert D. "The Prosperous Community." *The American Prospect* 4, no. 13 (1993): http://www.prospect.org.print/V4/13/putnam-r.html.

Qadeer, Mohammad. "Communities and Public Welfare." *Public Options* 16, 8 (October 1995): 46.

Quebec. "A egalité pour décider: Le gouvernement du Québec soutient 42 organismes pour inciter les femmes à investir les lieux de pouvoir." July 2002. http://communiques.gouv.qc.ca/gouvqc/communiques/GPQF/Juillet2002/03/c2295.html.

Quesnel, Louise. "Municipal Reorganisation in Quebec." *Canadian Journal of Regional Science* 23, no. 1 (Spring 2000): 115-34.

—. *Public Consultation: A Tool for Democracy.* Toronto: Intergovernmental Committee on Urban and Regional Research, 2000.

Reinhart, Anthony. "City Councillors', Mayor's Salaries Create Only Wee Ripple of Interest." *The Record* (Kitchener-Waterloo), 7 November 2002.

Rodgers, Frank A. "Democracy in the Municipality." Paper presented at the Common Council in Committee-of-the-Whole, Saint John, NB, 13 January 1992.

Rounds, Richard C. "Rural Consolidation of Municipal Governments in Canada." In *The State of Unicity – 25 Years Later: Conference Proceedings (October 3-4 1997),* edited by Nancy Klos, 72-80. Winnipeg: Institute of Urban Studies, 1998.

Rowe, Mary W., ed. *Toronto: Considering Self Government.* Owen Sound, ON: Ginger Press, 2000.

Sancton, Andrew. "Montreal." In *City Politics in Canada,* edited by Warren Magnusson and Andrew Sancton. Toronto: University of Toronto Press, 1983.

—. "Why Unicity Matters: An Outsider's View." In *The State of Unicity – 25 Years Later: Conference Proceedings (October 3-4 1997),* edited by Nancy Klos, 3-16. Winnipeg: Institute of Urban Studies, 1998.

—. "Metropolitan and Regional Governance." In *Urban Policy Issues Canadian Perspectives,* edited by Edmund P. Fowler and David Siegel, 54-68. Don Mills, ON: Oxford University Press, 2001.

Saul, John Ralston. *The Unconscious Civilization.* Concord, ON: House of Anansi Press, 1995.

Sewell, John, and Advisory Committee. *Local Self-Government Bulletin.* www.localgovernment.ca. February 2004.

Shafritz, Jay M., and Albert C. Hyde, eds. *Classics of Public Administration.* 3rd ed. Belmont, CA: Wadsworth Publishing, 1992.

Sherbrooke Historical Society in Cooperation with the University of Sherbrooke. *Sherbrooke 1802-2002: Two Centuries of History.* CD-ROM. Sherbrooke: Sherbrooke Historical Society, 2002.

Shortt, Adam. "The Beginning of Municipal Government in Ontario." *Queen's Gazette* 7 (1902): 409-24.

Sisk, Timothy D., ed. *Democracy at the Local Level: International IDEA's Handbook on Participation, Representation, Conflict Management and Governance.* Stockholm, Sweden: The International Institute for Democracy and Electoral Assistance (IDEA), 2001.

Slack, Enid. "Intergovernmental Fiscal Relations and Canadian Municipalities: Current Situation and Prospects, Report to the Federation of Canadian Municipalities." 8 May 2002. http://www.fcm.ca/english/.

Smith, Doug. "A Strike with an Elusive Meaning." In *Compass Points: Navigating the 20th Century,* ed. Robert Chodos, 70-2. Toronto: Between the Lines, Compass Foundation, 1999.

Somerville, Malcolm M. "Introduction." In *Saint John: A City of Achievements,* 2nd ed. Saint John, NB: ImPresses, 2000.

Soucoup, Dan. *Historic New Brunswick.* Lawrencetown Beach, NS: Pottersfield Press, 1997.

Stone, Clarence N. "Systemic Power in Community Decision Making: A Restatement of Stratification Theory." *The American Political Science Review* 74, no. 4 (1980): 978-90.

Summers, Valerie A. "Newfoundland and Labrador: Resource Political and Regime Change in the Federal Era, 1949-1991." In *The Provincial State,* edited by Keith Brownsey and Michael Howlett. Toronto: Copp Clark Pitman, 1992.

Thomas, Paul G. "Diagnosing the Health of Civic Democracy: 25 Years of Citizen Involvement with City Hall." In *The State of Unicity – 25 Years Later: Conference Proceedings (October 3-4 1997),* edited by Nancy Klos, 47-62. Winnipeg: Institute of Urban Studies, 1998.

Thomas, Timothy L., ed. *The Politics of the City: A Canadian Perspective.* Scarborough, ON: ITP Nelson, 1997.

Thomlinson, Neil R. "Gay Concerns and Local Governments." In *The Politics of the City: A Canadian Perspective,* edited by Timothy L. Thomas. Toronto: ITP Nelson, 1997.

Thompson, Elizabeth. "In Merger's Rough Wake." *Montreal Gazette,* 14 February 2001, A1.

Tiessen, Paul, ed. *Berlin, Canada: A Self-Portrait of Kitchener, Ontario before World War One.* St. Jacobs, ON: Sand Hills Books, 1979.

Tindal, C. Richard, and Susan Nobes Tindal. *Local Government in Canada.* 4th ed. Toronto: McGraw-Hill Ryerson, 1995.

Trimble, Linda. "Politics Where We Live." In *Canadian Metropolitics: Governing Our Cities,* edited by James Lightbody. Toronto: Copp Clark, 1995.

Université de Sherbrooke. La Société d'histoire de Sherbrooke/Sherbrooke Historic Society in collaboration with Le Département Histoire et Sciences politiques. *Sherbrooke: Deux siècles d'histoire/Two Centuries of History (1802-2002).* CD-ROM. Sherbrooke, 2002.

Vancouver. "General Voting Information." November 1999. http://www.city.vancouver.bc.ca/ctyclerk/election99/votegeninfo.htm.

Vander Ploeg, Casey G. *Big City Revenue Sources: A Canada-U.S. Comparison of Municipal Tax Tools and Revenue Levers.* Calgary: Canada West Foundation, 2002.

Whalan, H.J. *The Development of Local Government in New Brunswick.* Fredericton: University of New Brunswick, 1963.

Williams, Robert J., and Terrence J. Downey. "Reforming Rural Ontario." *Canadian Public Administration* 42, no. 2 (Summer 1999): 160-92.

Wilson, Woodrow. "The Study of Administration." *Political Science Quarterly* 2 (1887).

Wismer, Susan. "From the Ground Up: Quality of Life Indicators and Sustainable Community Development." *Feminist Economics* 5, no. 2 (July 1999): 109-14.

—. "Women and Community-Building in Kitchener-Waterloo." In *The Dynamics of the Dispersed City: Perspectives on the Kitchener Metropolitan Region,* ed. Trudi Bunting, Kevin Curtis, and Pierre Filion, 355-72. Waterloo, ON: Department of Geography, University of Waterloo, 1996.

Woolstencroft, Peter. "Education Policies: Challenges and Controversies." In *Urban Policy Issues: Canadian Perspectives,* edited by Edmund P. Fowler and David Siegel, 276-94. Don Mills, ON: Oxford University Press, 2001.

# Photography Credits

# Index

assembly lines, 234
Association communautaire de Centre-Sud (ACCENTS), 35
Association cooperative d'économie familiale, 35
Association of Municipalities of Ontario, 102
associations: community, 34, 46, 66, 67; municipal, 123-25, 136; professional, 46; women's, 30. *See also* groups; organizations
Atlantic Coastal Action Programs (ACAP), 184, 185
automobile use, 120, 172, 173, 174, 178, 248
autonomy, 21; of cities, 133, 150; of larger cities, 150, 153; of local governments, 15, 123, 131, 132, 136, 137; and Loyalists, 4; of northern communities, 134; of organizations, 70
Avery, Donald, 168
Axworthy, Thomas, 121

**B**affin. *See* Qikiqtaaluk
Baie d'Urfé (QC), 80, 97
Bailey, Sinéad, 190
Baldwin, Robert, 25, 82
Baxter, David, 133
BC Rail Limited, 146
BCNET, 278
Beaconsfield (QC), 80
Berlin (ON), 8, 31, 155, 156, 234-35, 236, 260, 265. *See also* Kitchener
Berridge, Joe, 147, 149
biases, in information, 262, 263
bilingualism, 6, 167
bioregionalism, 188, 191-92
Bird, Richard M., 244
Bish, Robert L., 24
Bishop's University, 167
Black, Edwin R., 259, 260, 267
Bloomfield, Elizabeth, 234
Boadway, Robin W., 246, 247
board of commissioners system, 210-11
board of management model, 210-11
boards, 58, 220-21
Boise (Idaho), 121
boosterism, 83, 155, 156
Boswell, Peter, 91-92
Boudreau, Julie-Anne, 39-40
Brandon (MB), 3
"Breaking the Circle of Violence" (program), 68, 70
British Columbia, 47, 60-61, 85-86, 111, 112, 145, 168, 180, 181, 270; Commission on Resources

and Environment (CORE), 179; municipal re-structuring, 109-12; regional districts, 109-11, 116, 181. *See also* Prince George and names of other places; University of Northern British Columbia
British North America Act, 86, 90. *See also* Constitution
Broadbent, Alan, 151
Brodie, Janine, 43, 164, 176
Brownstone, Meyer, 101, 104
Brundtland Commission, 123, 179, 194
Bryant, Raymond L., 190
budgets, 244-48, 250; cutbacks (*see* fiscal constraints); people's, 43, 245
Building Communities strategy, 114
business interests: in coalitions, 20; community development and, 30; and elections, 52; influence of, 19, 242; and urban reform movement, 44
business sector, 4, 8; development and, 170, 171; in elected office, 60; ideological orientation, 232; and issue agendas/priorities, 232; local governments and, 232, 242; planning and, 170, 171; property taxes, 245; as volunteers, 30. *See also* private sector
businesses: high-tech, 152; location of, 152. *See also* corporations
Byrne Commission, 92

**C**airns, Alan, 42
Calgary, 53, 55, 66, 67, 83, 85, 108, 130, 131, 150, 214
Cambridge (ON), 7, 100, 147, 277
campaign finance, 60-61, 72
Camrose (AB), 134
Canada Mortgage and Housing Corporation (CMHC), 120, 121
Canada West Foundation, 70, 121
Canada's Technology Triangle (CTT), 147, 277
Canada-US softwood lumber dispute, 9, 120, 140, 146
Canadian Charter of Rights and Freedoms. *See* Charter of Rights and Freedoms
Canadian Environmental Law Association, 122
Canadian Federation of Mayors and Municipalities (CFMM), 117, 120, 124-25
Canadian Pacific Railway, 27, 82-83
Cape Breton Municipality Act, 94
capitalism, 20, 157, 189

Carey, James, 258-59
Carrel, André, 48, 49, 117, 237-38
Carrier First Nations, 9
Cassiar (BC), 282
Cassidy, Frank, 24
Castells, Manuel, 283
Caucus Task Force on Urban Issues, 121
census metropolitan areas, 129
central government. *See* federal government
Centre Wellington, 42, 45
Champlain College, 167
channels of communication, control over, 264, 266
channels of information, 258
Chaplin, Charlie, 234
Charlottetown, 78, 96
charter cities, 5, 133, 147, 149, 151, 153
Charter of Rights and Freedoms, 39, 168
chief administrative officer (CAO) model, 209, 210, 213, 214
chief administrative officers (CAOs), 244
chief executive officers (CEOs), 211
child poverty, 37
Chrétien, Jean, 121
Christensen, Bev, 146
cities: autonomy, 133, 150; beautiful, 155, 157; the C5, 150; capital, 5; charter, 5, 133, 147, 151, 153; and competition, 190; as cores/hubs, 141, 144, 150, 152; dependence on property taxes, 121; First Nations peoples in, 170; growth of, 220-21, 233; healthy, 157, 194; hub, 141, 144, 150, 152; ideal size for democracy, 18; inner, 34, 36, 105, 154, 158; larger, 52, 72, 73, 150, 151, 153; location, 140; mechanical analogies, 233-34; mega- (*see* mega-cities); mid-sized, 4t; neighbourhoods within, 36, 154; peripheral, 141, 152; physical divisions, 154; population boom, 34; redevelopment of centres (see urban revitalization); senior government involvement in, 121; size, 131; social-economic divisions, 154-55, 164; spatial organization, 154-55, 164; wards within, 28. *See also* municipalities
citizen advisory committees. *See* advisory committees
citizen participation. *See* participation
CitizenNets, 280
citizens: as consumers, 243, 252; as customers, 214, 220, 252; effectiveness, 12; and Internet, 279-81; needs, 22; participation in decision

making, 203; right of appeal, 42; roles in governing processes, 203; self-determination, 15; self-government (*see* self-government); sued by councils, 42
Citizens for Local Democracy (C4LD), 38-40
citizensontheWeb.com, 280
city councillors. *See* councillors
city councils. *See* councils
city employees, 204; exercise of discretion by, 242; influence of, 205; political role, 200; values of, 204-5. *See also* public employees
city manager model, 210, 213, 214
city managers, 211, 214, 244
City of Sherbrooke. *See* Sherbrooke
city-state, Greek, 17
civic culture, 8
civic literacy, 15; and media, 267
civic participation. *See* participation
civil society, 13, 15, 44, 193, 231
Coalition for Alternatives to Pesticides, 68
Coalition of Progressive Electors (COPE), 53, 54, 72
coalitions, 20, 189, 191
collaboration, defined, 70
collective good, 21
collective vs individual rights, 173
colonialism, 25, 44
Comité de citoyens du Saint-François, 35, 36
commissioner model, 210-11, 213
commissioners, 214
Commission of Conservation, 157
commissions, 58, 220-21
committees: citizen participation on, 214; standing, 209, 210, 214
common good, 187
common interest, and referendums, 48
communication(s), 142; bias of, 259; channels of, 259, 264, 266; citizen-based networks, 280; and city size, 18; defined, 257; elites and, 257; globalization and, 140; government departments of, 272-76; groups and, 257; and influence, 256, 266; information technologies and, 266; and marginalized citizens, 257; medium of, 257-58; patterns of, 266; political agendas and, 257; and power, 266; in Saint John, 5; systems, 263
community/-ies: associations, 34, 46, 66, 67; biophysical health, 172, 174; capacity building in, 16; coastal, 184; concept of, 256; development, 30, 106-7; devolution upon, 16; differences in

and elections, 12; elites' attitudes toward, 27; governing institutions and, 15, 21; and government vs governance, 12-13; and grassroots organizations, 15-16, 20; ideal-sized city for, 18; and inequality, 73; influence and, 21-22; and informed citizenry, 17; and lawsuits against citizens, 42; liberal, 15; local governments and, 17, 21, 45; and Loyalists, 26; process, 38; and public debate, 40; public participation and, 12, 15, 18; representative, 41, 48; self-determination and, 15; society-centred, 45; tension within, 14; theory, 17

denominational schools, 90

departmental model, 209

departments, 209, 211-14, 243-44

Depression. *See* Great Depression

developers, 61, 154, 158

development, 36; and business sector, 170, 171; effect on watersheds, 183; and elections, 52; and elites, 171; and environment, 161, 175; and neighbourhoods, 158; public views on, 175; regulation of, 179; sector, 160 (*see also* developers); social costs, 161; sustainable (*see* sustainability)

Devine, Patrick, 158

Diamant, Peter, 107

Dickinson, John A., 79, 166

Dion, Stéphane, 131

direct democracy, 25, 48, 261

disadvantaged groups, 16, 28

discursive space, 162

disentangling, of intergovernmental responsibilities, 176

Disero, Betty, 158

division of powers, 88

Dowling, Catherine, 191

Downey, Terrence J., 99, 129

downtown. *See* inner cities

Drapeau, Jean, 34, 53, 56, 96

Dryzek, John, 201

Dunn, Christopher, 84

Durham, Lord, Report of, 25, 82

Durocher, René, 144

Dye, Thomas, 201

**E**ast, Ron, 270

Eastern Townships, 6, 66, 79

Easton, David, 188

ecology, 144, 190-91

economy/-ies: and ecology, 144; environment and, 174; global (*see* global economy); steady-state, 175

ecosystem planning, 174, 177, 178-79, 182, 191-94, 196

Edmonton, 53, 55, 61, 83, 85, 108, 130, 158

Edmonton-Calgary corridor, 145

education: control over funding, 89; funding for, 125; policy, 89, 250-52; province-wide standards, 89; tax credits for, 90, 251; and values, 89. *See also* schools

effectiveness: accountability and, 207, 209; citizen, 12; and colonialism, 44; of special-purpose bodies, 59

efficiency: accountability and, 207, 209, 214; amalgamations and, 130; colonialism and, 44; and environment, 172; and local governments, 238; and private-sector approach, 214; and public administration, 252; and public service, 238; and rational management, 201; and representation, 130-31; and services, 243; and urban reform movement, 29. *See also* inefficiency

egalitarian uniformity, 17

"Egalité pour décider" (program), 70

elected office: barriers to participation, 60, 72; campaign expenses, 60-61; lack of ethnic diversity in, 170; as public service, 61-62; requirements for, 60. *See also* representation

elections, 12, 45; at-large, 28, 29, 50, 51; business interests and, 52; development and, 52; organizations' activity and, 52; platforms, 52; political parties, 28; in Quebec, 24; universal, 17; voter turnout, 63; ward-based, 28

electoral systems, 46-47, 50-51, 63

elites, 18, 19, 27, 72, 78, 83, 171, 257, 261, 266

Elora (ON), 42

e-mail, 261-62

England, party system in, 52

Englehart (ON), 40

English, John, 236

English-speaking population, 4, 6, 35

Enron securities fraud, 250

Enterprise Saint John, 93

Environment Canada, 184

environmental movement, 176

environment(s), 158, 159; accountability and, 172; alterations to, 142; assessment and regulation, 175; committees, 192; costs, 178; and devolution of authority, 176; and economy, 174; efficiency

and local governance, 43-44; and neo-liberalism, 147; productivity vs social development, 283; social development vs productivity, 283
glocal, defined, 43
gold rush, 85, 86
Golden Horseshoe, 147, 149
good life, 27, 233
Goods and Services Tax, 122
Gough, Barry M., 85
governance: community differences in, 3; government vs, 12-13, 176, 188, 196, 221; over-, 102
government(s): absolutist, 24; apolitical nature, 204; business principles in, 210, 232, 250; centralist, 24; centralized, 17; choices, and policymaking, 202; communications departments, 272-76; community responsibility and, 16; complementary roles served by all levels, 136; cost reductions, 235; debt reduction, 126, 235; equality and, 204, 205; fairness, 204, 205; federal (*see* federal government); funding for groups, 68, 70; goal, 238; governance vs, 12-13, 176, 188, 196, 221; hierarchical organization, 172, 193, 204, 205, 214; information availability in, 16; information use to control behaviour, 269; larger than local, 14; larger vs smaller units of, 18; legitimacy of, 71; local (*see* local government[s]); minimal, 16; objectivity in, 201; offloading of responsibilities, 43, 118, 172, 174, 235; over-government, 200; and private sector, 20, 281, 283; private-sector management approach, 214; provincial (*see* provincial governments); rational management approach to, 201, 202; regional forms of, 128; relations with non-profit organizations, 70; representative, 17; responsiveness, 204, 205; size of, 14, 18, 102, 129, 235; stability, 204, 205; and taxes, 77, 78; transparency in, 16; two-tier, 128; Web sites, 274
Graham, Katherine A., 53, 66, 126, 176
grain producer cooperatives, 84
grain trade, 142
Grand Trunk Railway, 142
Grande Prairie (AB), 152
Granville (BC), 86
grassroots, 13; anti-globalization, 43; control by, 38; organizations, and democracy, 15-16, 20
Great Depression, 78, 80, 83, 85, 124, 157, 235
Greater Sherbrooke Economic Development Corporation (SDÉRS), 148

Greater Toronto Area (GTA), 102, 147, 149, 186, 213
Greater Toronto Bioregion, 180
Greater Vancouver Regional District (GVRD), 111, 135, 181
Green Party Political Association of BC, 54
Greenfield (SK), 107
Greenpeace, 268
groundwater, 183
groups: and access to information, 264; anglophone (*see* English-speaking population); communications and, 257; conflict between, 190; disadvantaged, 16; environmental, 122; francophone (*see* French-speaking population); government funding for, 68, 70; lobbying by, 37; of mayors, 124; minority (*see* minority groups); political agendas of, 264; pressure (*see* pressure groups); in Prince Edward Island, 95; protest, 52; single-issue, 37. *See also* associations; community/-ies; organizations
growth, 9; amalgamation and, 116; of cities, 220-21, 233; and conventional vs ecosystem planning, 192; impact on resources, 175; population, 6, 80; of Prince George, 9; rational approaches to, 201; of Sherbrooke, 80; smart, 159; suburban, 34, 36; urban, 83, 140, 160, 233. *See also* urban sprawl
Guelph (ON), 147, 277
Gutenburg press, 259, 269
Gutstein, Donald, 34, 53
Gwyn, Richard, 149

**H**alifax, 78, 94, 127, 131, 149, 274
Hamilton (ON), 80
Hammond, George, 146
Hancock, Trevor, 194
Hanson, Eric, 85
hard services, 125, 126, 154, 226, 232
Harris, Mike, 99, 129
health: care systems, 37; conditions of poor, 30; impact of business interests, 30
Healthy Cities, 194
Healthy Communities, 188, 194-96, 226
Helm, Corey, 163
Higgins, Donald J.H., 50, 55, 90, 94, 99, 117, 120, 124, 144, 149, 207, 233
hinterland-metropolis relationship, 142, 144-45
Hodge, Gerald, 110, 176, 180, 181, 191-92
Hodgetts, Charles, 157

Web site, 274. *See also* Regional Municipality of Waterloo; Waterloo
Kitchener, Lord, 265
The Kitchener-Waterloo Record, 241, 267
Kitikmeot, 115
Kitimat (BC), 145
Kivalliq, 115
Klein, Naomi, 43
knowledge, control of, 259
Kyoto Accord, 140, 177

labour movement, 32, 33, 53
Labour Welfare Party, 54
La Fontaine, Louis-Hippolyte, 82
Lake Ontario, 177, 180
land: scarcity of, 37; use, 36, 119, 154, 159, 160, 175, 178-79, 182, 184; value, 155
Langrod, George, 17
language rights, 6
Laurentian thesis, 144
Lauria, Mickey, 253
Laurier, Wilfrid, 157
Laval (QC), 97
Laycock, David, 84
Layton, Jack, 227
League for Social Reconstruction, 157
Leduc oil discovery, 108
Lennox, Charles, Duke of Richmond, 167
Lennoxville, bilingualism in, 167
Leo, Christopher, 20, 34, 36, 120, 122, 160, 161, 189, 253
Lethbridge (AB), 85
letters to the editor, 46
Lévis (QC), 97
liberal colonialism, 25
liberal democracy, 15, 30, 173
Light Commission, 236
Lightbody, James, 50, 53, 55, 61, 104, 128, 130, 136, 158
Lindblom, Charles, 223
Linteau, Paul André, 144
Lipset, Seymour Martin, 84-85
lobbying, 37, 123, 124, 270
local governance, and globalization, 43-44
local government(s): autonomy, 15, 136, 137; and business sector, 232, 242; business terminology in, 239; central government vs, 17; and citizens' needs, 22; communication patterns, 264; communication with citizens, 269, 271; constitutional powers, 151; in constitutions, 117; constraints upon, 76, 237; as corporations, 238; decline in authority, 89; deficits and, 244; and democracy, 17, 21, 45; devaluing of, 32; developers and, 158; in early society, 259; economic efficiency of, 238; and education policy, 89; embedded relationships, 242; and environment, 172, 174, 177, 192; farmers' attitudes toward, 27, 84-85, 87; federal transfer funds, 119-20; financial accountability, 233; functions, 89; funding grants, 118, 125, 127, 244, 246-47; grant reduction to, 116; importance as decision-making forums, 200; influence in intergovernmental affairs, 123; innovations in, 209; jurisdictional authority, 76; and land development profits, 160-61; land-use policy, 119; as large corporations, 248, 250; legislation regarding, 89, 118-19; lobbying by, 123; in northern areas, 206; parties in, 52-55; and party system, 52; planning responsibilities, 119, 178; powers of, 18, 102-3, 119; and private sector, 20, 116; and private vs public spheres, 21; as public corporations, 233; responsibilities of, 226; responsible parliamentary government and, 104; responsiveness to constituencies, 20-1; restructuring, 115-17; safety and, 27; and self-government, 14; self-sufficiency, 131; social order and, 27; and social problems, 16; and social services, 125-26; staff expertise, 248, 250; structure, 202; taxation regime, 108; taxes and, 27, 85, 127, 247; tensions with other governmental levels, 118; as vehicles of state, 44; volunteers and, 230; and water resources, 184; Web sites, 274, 276; women in, 30, 44, 59; and World Wide Web, 271
local improvement districts, 78, 85
local self-government, defined, 117
locally unacceptable land use (LULU), 37, 175
Longeuil (QC), 97
Lower Canada, 25, 80
Loyalists, 4, 25, 26, 27, 77, 80, 87, 143
lumber industry, 146. *See also* Canada-US softwood lumber dispute
Lynch, Charles, 5

machine politics, 27-28, 29
McBride, Richard, 146
McCann, Larry D., 145
McGill University, 34
MacKenzie District, 86

McKenzie, Roderick, 190
MacKenzie, Suzanne, 165
Mackenzie, William Lyon, 80, 82
McLaughlin, Kenneth, 236
McLuhan, Marshall, 257-58, 259
McLuhan's Children, 268
Magnusson, Warren, 20, 144
majority rule, 17
Manitoba, 55, 83-84, 103-6, 106-7, 126
marginalized groups, 8, 73, 191, 203, 230, 231, 257. *See also* minority groups; women
Martin, Paul, 122
Maslove, Alan M., 53, 66, 126, 176
mass media. *See* media
Masson, Jack, 48, 52, 53, 55, 85, 108
mayors, 55-56, 131; and access to information, 56; in board of commissioners system, 210-11; campaign expenses, 60; in CAO model of governance, 210; of Centre Wellington, 42; functions, 55-56; groups, 124; networking by, 56; part- vs full-time, 62; political agendas and, 56; in political communications, 257; of Prince George, 61, 120; in Quebec, 79; salaries, 62t; in Saskatchewan, 107; of Toronto, 80, 82; voting for, 46; of Waterloo, 56, 57, 62; of Winnipeg, 83, 105; women, 59; of Yellowknife, 86
media, 71, 207, 260, 262, 266-68, 270, 281; Special Senate Committee on the Mass Media, 260
medicare system, 84
mega-cities, 131, 136; Toronto, 38-40, 45, 102, 147
Meliseet people, 5
Mellon, Hugh, 142
Mennonites, 8, 156
Mervin (SK), 107
Metro Network for Social Justice, 39
metropolis-hinterland relationship, 142, 144-45
Metropolitan Action Committee on Violence Against Women and Children (METRAC), 68
metropolitan areas, as city-states, 133. *See also* cities; mega-cities
MFP Financial, 241
Michigan, Toronto waste trucked to, 41, 186
Micmac people, 5
middle classes, 28, 30, 44, 60
Mill, John Stuart, 17
Milne, David, 95
Milner, Henry, 15, 267, 284
Ministry of State for Urban Affairs (MSUA), 121

minority groups, 20-21, 28, 37, 44, 46, 59, 60, 73, 89, 169. *See also* marginalized groups
Mitchell, John, 80, 81, 82
Modern Times (film), 234
Moncton (NB), 92
monster homes, 168
Montreal: amalgamation of, 38, 80, 127-28; in C5, 150; Citizens' Movement, 53; city charter, 79, 149; Civic Party, 53, 56; community gardens, 163; development, 52; economic rise, 142; Expo '67, 56; immigrants in, 168; incorporation, 80; manufacturing, 142; Metropolitan Corporation, 96; Mount Royal, Town of, 166; Olympic Games in, 56; population, 97, 131; suburbs, 80, 96; Westmount, 166
Montreal Urban Community (MUC), 96-97
Mosco, Vincent, 283, 284
Mount Royal (QC), 80
Moyer, Bill, 260
Multicultural Act (1971), 168
multiculturalism, 44
Mumford, Lewis, 141, 157, 171, 174
municipal associations, 123-25, 136
municipal bonusing, 246
municipal corporations, 25, 44, 200, 232-33
municipalities: formation, 25; incorporation, 25, 77-78. *See also* cities; local government(s)
municipal-provincial relations, 88, 102-3, 115-16, 118-19, 150, 161, 182, 237, 244
Murdie, Robert A., 164, 170
Muskoka, 99

National Crime Prevention Program, 120
national government. *See* federal government
National Housing Act, 120
National Planning Commission, 157
nation-states, 18, 279
natural persons' powers vs creature of the state approach, 102
natural resources. *See* resources
neighbourhood associations, 34, 36, 46, 64, 66
neighbourhood government, in Winnipeg, 104
neighbourhoods, 36, 37, 150, 154, 158, 159, 166, 228. *See also* community/-ies; inner cities
neo-liberalism, 150; and environment, 172
New Brunswick, 47, 60-61, 77, 78, 92, 94, 179
New Democratic Party (NDP), 52, 55, 103-4, 157, 181

new public management approach, 233, 235, 238-40, 250, 253
New Westminster (BC), 86
Newfoundland and Labrador, 78-9, 90, 91-92
Newman, Nathan, 277
newspapers, 260, 265, 267
Niagara Escarpment, 180
Niagara Falls, 156
Niagara-on-the-Lake, 180
Non-Partisan Association (NPA), 34, 53, 54
non-profit organizations, grants for, 70
Nortel, 278
North American Free Trade Agreement (NAFTA), 124, 147
North Battleford (SK), 183
North Dumfries (ON), 7-8, 100, 147
northern areas/communities, 132-34; Aboriginal peoples in, 86; autonomy, 134; centre-periphery differences and, 134; devolution of authority in, 112-15; gold rush, 86; House of Commons report on, 133, 134; information technologies and, 262; local governments in, 205, 206; provincial governments and, 134; southern attitudes toward, 206; wealth of, 133. *See also* territories
North-West Territorial Council, Municipal Ordinance, 84
Northwest Territories, 86, 113-14
not-in-my-backyard (NIMBY), 37, 40-42, 175, 184
Nova Scotia, 78, 94-95
Nunavut, 3, 86, 114-15

Oak Ridges Moraine, 179, 180
official plan, 160-61
Ontario: amalgamations in, 97, 102, 129; Baldwin Act, 82, 102; Bill 103, 38, 102; Commission on Planning and Development Reform, 179; conservation authorities, 221; Court of Appeal, 42; District Councils Act, 82; environmental commissioner, 183; environmental laws, 183; Freedom of Information and Protection of Privacy Act, 271; Information and Privacy Commissioner (IPC), 271; "less government" in, 129; Liberal government in, 90; Loyalists in, 77, 80; Ministry of the Environment, 183; Municipal Act, 102-3; Municipal Corporations Act, 25, 82; Municipal Freedom of Information and Protection of Privacy Act, 271; municipal restructuring in, 99-102,

129; Planning and Development Act (1917), 156; population, 149; private schools in, 90; Progressive Conservative government, 90, 99, 243; regional government in, 99, 101, 116; responsibility for services in, 125-26; Roman Catholic school system, 90; school boards, 90; Superior Court, 42; tax credits for education, 90, 251; two-tier government in, 82; urbanization in, 96; water quality in, 183
Ontario Coalition Against Poverty, 39
Ontario Hydro, 186
Ontario Hydro Electric Power Commission, 156
Ontario Municipal Board (OMB), 42
Opportunities for Alternative Revenue Sources, 127
organizations, 13; accountability to representatives, 203-4; activity during elections, 52; autonomy of, 70; grants for non-profit, 70; grassroots, 15-16, 20; profit-making enterprises vs, 203-4; volunteer, 13. *See also* associations
Osborne, David, 239
Ottawa, 70, 276
Ottawa-Carleton, 99
Our Common Future (Brundtland Commission), 194
Outaouais Regional Community (ORC), 97
Owen, Stephen, 72

Pacific Great Eastern Railway, 146
Panter-Brick, Keith, 17
Parks, Robert Ezra, 190
participation, 72; avenues of, 46; as central theme, 37; civic, 228; and civic literacy, 15; on committees, 214; constraints on, 36; in decision making, 24, 63, 72, 226; and democracy, 12, 15, 18; in elected office, barriers to, 60; and government Web sites, 274; in healthy communities movement, 194; and information technologies, 261-62; and interests, 34, 41; parties and, 52; in planning, 162, 174-75; in policy process, 226; in representative democracy, 41; and special-purpose bodies, 221; traditional methods of, 34, 63, 71; voting and, 18
partnerships, 106-7, 116, 120, 161, 186. *See also* cooperative enterprises
party system, 52
patronage, 27, 28, 29
Paul, George, 205, 206

66; trails network, 178; urbanization, 80; working group on pesticides, 66, 68; world wars and, 80. *See also* Greater Sherbrooke Economic Development Corporation

Siegel, David, 58, 207, 221, 223

Sills, Ronald C., 242

silos, 172, 187, 211, 240

Simcoe, John Graves, 24

Simmons, Jim, 145

Slack, Enid, 121-22, 125, 127, 244

slavery, 26

SLOAP (space left over after planning), 177

Smart Communities, 258, 271, 276-77, 278, 283

smart growth strategy, 159

Smith, Doug, 32, 33

Smithers (BC), 134

social: agencies, 36; assistance, 30; capital, 230; costs, 161, 178; justice, 39, 190, 191; movements, 16, 46, 158, 228; order, 27, 44, 193; problems, 16; services, 8, 28, 37 (*see also* services)

Social Credit government, 181

La Société d'histoire de Sherbrooke, 35

soft services, 125, 154

softwood lumber dispute, 9, 120, 140

South Island Sustainable Communities, 177

sovereignty, 14

spaces, non-physical, 162

spatial organization: economic status, 164; and family life, 164-66; French-English, 166; and gender, 165; of housing, 166; by language, 166; of minority groups, 170; and private sector, 171; and social fragmentation, 168, 170

special-purpose bodies, 58-59, 220-21

speculators, 154. *See also* developers

spillovers, 128

Steadman, Tom, 268

Stone, Clarence N., 19, 61

student radicals, 32, 34

subdivision(s), 154, 161, 178

subsidiarity, 123, 176-77

suburbs, 154; and assumptions about work and family, 165; CMHC and, 120; cost to city, 128, 130, 150; and ecosystem planning, 174, 178; growth of, 34, 36, 159-60; Kitchener, 8; Montreal, 96; Waterloo, 8; Winnipeg, 105. *See also* urban sprawl

Sudden Acute Respiratory Syndrome (SARS), 140

Summerside (PE), 78, 96

Supreme Court of Canada, 23, 122, 123

sustainability, 159-60, 172, 173-74, 175, 188, 195, 201

Sydenham, Lord, 25

systems: analysis, 188-9; theories, 187-88

taxes, 244; assessments, 246; credits for education, 90, 251; government and, 77, 78; on hotel/motel occupancy, 247; income, 247; local government and, 27, 85; and promotion of behaviour, 247; property (*see* property taxes); retail, 247

Taylor, Frederick W., 234

TEAM (The Electors Action Movement), 53, 181

Technology Partnerships Program, 120

Teixeira, Carlos, 164, 170

telecommunications, 141

teledemocracy, 261

television, 260, 267

telework, 165-66

Telus, 278

Tennant, Paul, 23-24

territorial governments, 76

territories: municipal-style government in, 27. *See also* northern areas; Northwest Territories; Yukon

Thomas, Paul, 104, 106

Thomas, Timothy, 56

Thomlinson, Neil, 20-21

throughput, defined, 175

Timiskaming First Nation, 41

Tindal, C. Richard, 105

Tindal, Susan Nobes, 105

Tocqueville, Alexis de, 17

Tomalty, Ray, 192, 193-94

Toromont Energy, 186

Toronto: administrative structure, 213; aldermen in, 29; amalgamation, 38-40, 45, 127; Board of Control, 29; CAO model of governance, 210, 213; City of Toronto Act, 149; commissioners, 213; corruption in, 29; council, 41, 134; Crombie commission, 179, 188, 192; early advantage, 144; expressway protests, 34; harbourfront, 179, 180, 190; Healthy Cities Project, 194; immigrants, 168, 169; incorporation, 80, 82; Keele St. Waste Management site, 40; leasing deal, 242; manager and departments level of administration in, 211; mayors, 80, 82; as mega-city, 38-40, 45, 102,

administrative officer (CAO), 241; citizen delegations in, 65; city solicitor, 241; community gardens in, 163; and CTT, 147, 277; departmental reorganization, 212, 216; electoral system in, 51; grants to, 246-47; Inc., 242; industries, 153; Landfill Gas Power Project, 186; mayors, 56, 57, 62; organizational chart, 216; petitions in, 65; population, 9; property taxes in, 245; RIM Park, 240-42, 243, 253, 267; size of council, 134; total quality management in, 239; university, 8; waste management, 178; Web site, 274. *See also* Kitchener; Regional Municipality of Waterloo
watersheds, 183-84, 188
waterways, 141
Watson Lake, 113
Weaver, John C., 29
Web sites, 46, 274, 276
Weberian model of management, 204
welfare, 27, 39; state, 80, 126, 150, 202-3, 235, 251, 252
Wellesley (ON), 8, 100, 147
West Edmonton Mall, 36
West Nile Virus, 140
western provinces, 144; boosterism in, 83; development, 142; elites, 83; municipal-style government in, 27; plebiscites, 50; school boards, 90; self-reliance, 87; settlement patterns, 82-83; urban growth, 83
Whalen, H.J., 77
Whitehorse, 86, 113
Wilfrid Laurier University, 8
Williams, Robert J., 99, 129

Wilmot (ON), 8, 100, 147
Wilson, Woodrow, 233
Windsor-Quebec City corridor, 145
Winnipeg, 32, 33, 53, 55, 83-84, 103-7, 131, 149, 150. *See also* Unicity Winnipeg
Wismer, Susan, 30, 32, 195
women: associations, 30; in Berlin (ON), 31; on councils, 59, 60, 73; dual roles, 165; information technologies and, 165; in local politics, 30, 44, 59; mayors, 59; middle-class, 30; and private vs public spheres, 30, 32, 165; violence toward, 68, 70; voting eligibility, 46
woodlands. *See* forests
Woolstencroft, Lynne, 56, 57, 130, 242, 251
Woolwich (ON), 8, 100, 147
World Economic Forum, 43
World Social Forum (2002), 43
world wars, 80, 157, 235
Worldwide Declaration of Local Self-Government, 117
World Wide Web, 261, 271. *See also* Internet

Yellowknife, 86, 114
York: incorporation, 81. *See also* Toronto
York Region, 179, 182
Young, Brian, 79, 166
Young Women's Christian Association (YWCA), 31
Yukon, 86; peoples in, 113
Yuval-Davis, Nira, 162

Zoning, 154, 157, 159, 160, 165-66, 177, 178, 184